# The State of the Field

The study of association football has recently emerged as a vibrant field of inquiry, attracting scholars worldwide from a variety of disciplinary backgrounds. 'Soccer As the Beautiful Game: Football's Artistry, Identity and Politics', held at Hofstra University in April 2014, gathered together scholars, media, management, and fans in the largest ever conference dedicated to the game in North America.

This collection of essays provides a comprehensive view of the academic perspectives on offer at the conference, itself a snapshot of the state of this increasingly rich scholarly terrain. The diversity of approaches range from theory to pedagogy to historical and sociological engagements with the game at all levels, from the grassroots to the grand spectacle of the World Cup, while the international roster of authors is testimony to the game's global reach.

The chapters in this book were originally published as a special issue of *Soccer & Society*.

**David Kilpatrick** is Associate Professor in the School of Liberal Arts at Mercy College, USA, and Club Historian at the New York Cosmos. He earned his PhD in Comparative Literature and MA in Philosophy at Binghamton University, USA.

# Sport in the Global Society: Contemporary Perspectives

Series Editor: Boria Majumdar, *University of Central Lancashire, UK*

The social, cultural (including media) and political study of sport is an expanding area of scholarship and related research. While this area has been well served by the *Sport in the Global Society* series, the surge in quality scholarship over the last few years has necessitated the creation of *Sport in the Global Society: Contemporary Perspectives*. The series will publish the work of leading scholars in fields as diverse as sociology, cultural studies, media studies, gender studies, cultural geography and history, political science and political economy. If the social and cultural study of sport is to receive the scholarly attention and readership it warrants, a cross-disciplinary series dedicated to taking sport beyond the narrow confines of physical education and sport science academic domains is necessary. *Sport in the Global Society: Contemporary Perspectives* will answer this need.

For a complete list of titles in this series, please visit:
https://www.routledge.com/series/SGSC

**Recent titles in the series include:**

**Junior and Youth Grassroots Football Culture**
The Forgotten Game
*Edited by Jimmy O'Gorman*

**Gender in Physical Culture**
Crossing Boundaries – Reconstituting Cultures
*Edited by Natalie Barker-Ruchti, Karin Grahn and Eva-Carin Lindgren*

**DIY Football**
The Cultural Politics of Community Based Football Clubs
*Edited by David Kennedy and Peter Kennedy*

**A Social and Political History of Everton and Liverpool Football Clubs**
The Split, 1878–1914
*David Kennedy*

**Football Fandom in Italy and Beyond**
Community through Media and Performance
*Matthew Guschwan*

**Numbers and Narratives**
Sport, History and Economics
*Wray Vamplew*

**Healthy Stadia**
An Insight from Policy to Practice
*Edited by Daniel Parnell, Kathryn Curran and Matthew Philpott*

**Young People and Sport**
From Participation to the Olympics
*Edited by Berit Skirstad, Milena M. Parent and Barrie Houlihan*

**Reviewing the AFL's Vilification Laws**
Rule 35, reconciliation and racial harmony in Australian Football
*Sean Gorman, Dean Lusher and Keir Reeves*

**The State of the Field**
Ideologies, Identities and Initiatives
*Edited by David Kilpatrick*

# The State of the Field

Ideologies, Identities and Initiatives

*Edited by*
**David Kilpatrick**

LONDON AND NEW YORK

First published 2018 by Routledge

2 Park Square, Milton Park, Abingdon, Oxfordshire OX14 4RN
52 Vanderbilt Avenue, New York, NY 10017

*Routledge is an imprint of the Taylor & Francis Group, an informa business*

First issued in paperback 2019

*British Library Cataloguing in Publication Data*
A catalogue record for this book is available from the British Library

ISBN 13: 978-1-138-56973-7 (hbk)
ISBN 13: 978-0-367-89243-2 (pbk)

Typeset in Times New Roman
by RefineCatch Limited, Bungay, Suffolk

**Publisher's Note**
The publisher accepts responsibility for any inconsistencies that may have
arisen during the conversion of this book from journal articles to book chapters,
namely the possible inclusion of journal terminology.

**Disclaimer**
Every effort has been made to contact copyright holders for their permission to
reprint material in this book. The publishers would be grateful to hear from any
copyright holder who is not here acknowledged and will undertake to rectify
any errors or omissions in future editions of this book.

# Contents

*Citation Information*                                                                vii
*Notes on Contributors*                                                              xi

Introduction – Ideologies, identities and initiatives: 'The State of the Field'        1
*David Kilpatrick*

## Ideologies

1. Does soccer explain the world or does the world explain soccer?
   Soccer and globalization                                                           4
   *Scott Waalkes*

2. The aesthetic and ecstatic dimensions of soccer: towards a philosophy
   of soccer                                                                         19
   *Yunus Tuncel*

3. Three soccer discourses                                                          26
   *Tamir Bar-On*

## Identities

4. Civic integration or ethnic segregation? Models of ethnic and civic
   nationalism in club football/soccer                                              42
   *Glen M.E. Duerr*

5. The 1883 F.A. Cup Final: working class representation, professionalism
   and the development of modern football in England                                56
   *James R. Holzmeister*

6. The British isolation from world football in the middle decades of the
   twentieth century – a myth?                                                      68
   *Paul Wheeler*

7. 'To Cross the Skager Rack'. Discourses, images, and tourism in early
   'European' football: Scotland, the United Kingdom, Denmark, and
   Scandinavia, 1898–1914                                                           83
   *Matthew L. McDowell*

CONTENTS

8. Soccer clubs and civic associations in the political world of Buenos Aires
   prior to 1943                                                          108
   *Joel Horowitz*

9. The history of the Zenit Soccer Club as a case study in Soviet Football Teams   124
   *Karina Ovsepyan*

10. Can Hong Kong Chinese football players represent their 'Fatherland'?
    The Cold War, FIFA and the 1966 Asian Games                          134
    *Chun Wing Lee*

11. Devolution of *Les Bleus* as a symbol of a multicultural French future   149
    *Lindsay Sarah Krasnoff*

12. Cooper's Block: America's first soccer neighbourhood                  158
    *Thomas A. McCabe*

13. Rethinking 'ethnic' soccer: the National Junior Challenge Cup and the
    transformation of American soccer's identity (1935–1976)             168
    *Kevin Tallec Marston*

14. Soccer, politics and the American public: still 'exceptional'?        186
    *Christian Collet*

## Initiatives

15. Transforming soccer to achieve solidarity: 'Golombiao' in Colombia    206
    *Ricardo Duarte Bajaña*

16. Innovation in soccer clubs – the case of Sweden                       212
    *Magnus Forslund*

17. Sustainability initiatives in professional soccer                     234
    *Taiyo Francis, Joanne Norris and Robert Brinkmann*

18. Teaching history and political economy through soccer                 245
    *Nigel Boyle*

19. Soccer changes lives: from learned helplessness to self-directed learners   256
    *Judith Gates and Brian Suskiewicz*

    *Index*                                                               269

# Citation Information

The chapters in this book were originally published in *Soccer & Society*, volume 18, issue 2–3 (March–May 2017). When citing this material, please use the original page numbering for each article, as follows:

**Introduction**
*Ideologies, identities and initiatives: 'The State of the Field' – an introduction*
David Kilpatrick
*Soccer & Society*, volume 18, issue 2–3 (March–May 2017), pp. 163–165

**Chapter 1**
*Does soccer explain the world or does the world explain soccer? Soccer and globalization*
Scott Waalkes
*Soccer & Society*, volume 18, issue 2–3 (March–May 2017), pp. 166–180

**Chapter 2**
*The aesthetic and ecstatic dimensions of soccer: towards a philosophy of soccer*
Yunus Tuncel
*Soccer & Society*, volume 18, issue 2–3 (March–May 2017), pp. 181–187

**Chapter 3**
*Three soccer discourses*
Tamir Bar-On
*Soccer & Society*, volume 18, issue 2–3 (March–May 2017), pp. 188–203

**Chapter 4**
*Civic integration or ethnic segregation? Models of ethnic and civic nationalism in club football/soccer*
Glen M.E. Duerr
*Soccer & Society*, volume 18, issue 2–3 (March–May 2017), pp. 204–217

**Chapter 5**
*The 1883 F.A. Cup Final: working class representation, professionalism and the development of modern football in England*
James R. Holzmeister
*Soccer & Society*, volume 18, issue 2–3 (March–May 2017), pp. 218–229

## Chapter 6

*The British isolation from world football in the middle decades of the twentieth century – a myth?*
Paul Wheeler
*Soccer & Society*, volume 18, issue 2–3 (March–May 2017), pp. 230–244

## Chapter 7

*'To Cross the Skager Rack'. Discourses, images, and tourism in early 'European' football: Scotland, the United Kingdom, Denmark, and Scandinavia, 1898–1914*
Matthew L. McDowell
*Soccer & Society*, volume 18, issue 2–3 (March–May 2017), pp. 245–269

## Chapter 8

*Soccer clubs and civic associations in the political world of Buenos Aires prior to 1943*
Joel Horowitz
*Soccer & Society*, volume 18, issue 2–3 (March–May 2017), pp. 270–285

## Chapter 9

*The history of the Zenit Soccer Club as a case study in Soviet Football Teams*
Karina Ovsepyan
*Soccer & Society*, volume 18, issue 2–3 (March–May 2017), pp. 286–295

## Chapter 10

*Can Hong Kong Chinese football players represent their 'Fatherland'? The Cold War, FIFA and the 1966 Asian Games*
Chun Wing Lee
*Soccer & Society*, volume 18, issue 2–3 (March–May 2017), pp. 296–310

## Chapter 11

*Devolution of* Les Bleus *as a symbol of a multicultural French future*
Lindsay Sarah Krasnoff
*Soccer & Society*, volume 18, issue 2–3 (March–May 2017), pp. 311–319

## Chapter 12

*Cooper's Block: America's first soccer neighbourhood*
Thomas A. McCabe
*Soccer & Society*, volume 18, issue 2–3 (March–May 2017), pp. 320–329

## Chapter 13

*Rethinking 'ethnic' soccer: the National Junior Challenge Cup and the transformation of American soccer's identity (1935–1976)*
Kevin Tallec Marston
*Soccer & Society*, volume 18, issue 2–3 (March–May 2017), pp. 330–347

## Chapter 14

*Soccer, politics and the American public: still 'exceptional'?*
Christian Collet
*Soccer & Society*, volume 18, issue 2–3 (March–May 2017), pp. 348–367

**Chapter 15**

*Transforming soccer to achieve solidarity: 'Golombiao' in Colombia*
Ricardo Duarte Bajaña
*Soccer & Society*, volume 18, issue 2–3 (March–May 2017), pp. 368–373

**Chapter 16**

*Innovation in soccer clubs – the case of Sweden*
Magnus Forslund
*Soccer & Society*, volume 18, issue 2–3 (March–May 2017), pp. 374–395

**Chapter 17**

*Sustainability initiatives in professional soccer*
Taiyo Francis, Joanne Norris and Robert Brinkmann
*Soccer & Society*, volume 18, issue 2–3 (March–May 2017), pp. 396–406

**Chapter 18**

*Teaching history and political economy through soccer*
Nigel Boyle
*Soccer & Society*, volume 18, issue 2–3 (March–May 2017), pp. 407–417

**Chapter 19**

*Soccer changes lives: from learned helplessness to self-directed learners*
Judith Gates and Brian Suskiewicz
*Soccer & Society*, volume 18, issue 2–3 (March–May 2017), pp. 418–430

For any permission-related enquiries please visit:
http://www.tandfonline.com/page/help/permissions

# Notes on Contributors

**Tamir Bar-On** is Professor-Researcher at Tec de Monterrey, Campus Querétaro, Mexico.

**Nigel Boyle** is Professor of Political Studies at Pitzer College, USA. His research focuses on the political determinants of social inequality, most recently regarding welfare-to-work policy.

**Robert Brinkmann** is Vice-Provost for Research and Engagement and Associate Dean of the Graduate School, Hofstra University, USA. He is the founder of Hofstra's Sustainability program and is passionate about the environment and research.

**Christian Collet** is Senior Associate Professor at the International Christian University, Japan. His research and teaching interests concentrate on American and comparative politics of the Asian Pacific, including Japan, with a substantive focus on public opinion and race, ethnicity and nationalism.

**Ricardo Duarte Bajaña** has completed his Doctorate in Social Anthropology at the Universidad Iberoamericana Mexico City, Mexico.

**Glen M.E. Duerr** is Associate Professor of International Studies at Cedarville University, USA. His research interests include nationalism and secession, comparative politics, international relations theory, sports and politics, and Christianity and politics.

**Magnus Forslund** is Senior Lecturer at the Department of Organisation and Entrepreneurship at Linnæus University, Sweden. His research focuses on leadership of change and renewal processes in different contexts. One area of focus is sport organizations.

**Taiyo Francis** is a Manager at Herndon Optimist Youth Baseball. He was a Student Research Associate at the National Center for Suburban Studies at Hofstra University, USA.

**Judith Gates** is a board member at Coaches Across Continents.

**James R. Holzmeister** is a Grants Manager at Maryland New Directions, USA. He earned his PhD at Auburn University, USA.

**Joel Horowitz** was Professor of History at St. Bonaventure University, USA.

**David Kilpatrick** is Associate Professor in the School of Liberal Arts at Mercy College, USA, and Club Historian at the New York Cosmos. He earned his PhD in Comparative Literature and MA in Philosophy at Binghamton University, USA.

**Lindsay Sarah Krasnoff** is a sports writer, historian, and consultant. She is a leading expert on French sport, particularly the youth development programs that produce top-tier talent for global markets.

**Chun Wing Lee** is Lecturer of Social Sciences at The Hong Kong Polytechnic University. His research interests lie in class analysis, social stratification, and social movement studies. As a sports fan, he is also interested in the political/sociological aspects of sport.

**Kevin Tallec Marston** is Honorary Visiting Research Fellow at the School of Humanities, De Montfort University, UK. His research interests include sport history, history of youth and childhood, and governance.

**Thomas A. McCabe** teaches History in the Faculty of Arts and Sciences at Rutgers University, Newark, USA. His expertise covers two diverse subjects: Newark history and the world history of soccer.

**Matthew L. McDowell** is Lecturer in Sport Policy, Management and International Development at ISPEHS, University of Edinburgh, Scotland. His research interests are primarily in the history of Scottish, British, and 'North Atlantic' sport.

**Joanne Norris** graduated from Hofstra University, USA, with a Bachelor of Science in Sustainability Studies.

**Karina Ovsepyan** is an Administrator at The State Museum of Political History, Russia. She previously earned a Master's degree in Russian History at the European University at St. Petersburg, Russia.

**Brian Suskiewicz** is Chief Executive Strategist at Coaches Across Continents.

**Yunus Tuncel** teaches at the New School for Public Engagement, The New School, USA. His research interests include agonism (the culture of competition), eroticism, the culture of the troubadours, and other areas of culture where art, literature, and philosophy intersect.

**Scott Waalkes** is Professor of International Politics at Malone University, USA. His research includes the global economy, comparative politics, and U.S. Foreign Policy.

**Paul Wheeler** is Programme Leader for Sport Business and Management, University of Chichester, UK. His research interests include social history of golf, history of golf tourism, and assessing the impact of learning and teaching and pedagogical support on student retention in Higher Education.

# Ideologies, identities and initiatives: 'The State of the Field'

## Selected essays from 'Soccer as the Beautiful Game: Football's Artistry, Identity and Politics', Hofstra University, Hempstead, New York, USA, April 2014

David Kilpatrick

The study of association football continues its emergence as a vibrant field of inquiry, attracting scholars worldwide from a variety of disciplinary backgrounds. 'Soccer as the Beautiful Game: Football's Artistry, Identity and Politics', held at Hofstra University in April 2014, gathered together scholars, media, management and fans in the largest ever conference dedicated to the global game in North America. With one eye glancing back to the sesquicentennial of association football's formation and another eye forward to the upcoming FIFA World Cup in Brazil, it was a fitting time for such an ambitious assemblage. This collection of essays provides a comprehensive view of the academic perspectives on offer at the conference, itself a snapshot of the state of this increasingly rich scholarly terrain. The diversity of approaches range from theory to pedagogy to historical and sociological engagements with the game at all levels, from the grassroots to the grand spectacle of the World Cup.

The essays are structured sequentially in a manner perhaps analogous to tactical formations, with the first section on ideologies providing a theoretical basis or framework like a defensive back line. The second section on identities is, like the midfield, where the bulk of the possession battle is waged; various ethnic, civic and national self-conceptions are teased out historically, from nineteenth-century foundational efforts to establish the game to contemporary reconstitutions of various self-hoods formed in and through the game. The third section on initiatives is akin to a forward attack, examining contemporary efforts to transform the way the game is played or perhaps transform the world through playing the game.

Conference directors and Hofstra University faculty Stanislao Pugliese and Brenda Elsey assembled over 125 speakers from 20 countries or more, a diverse gathering representing diverse engagements with the game ranging from academics and journalists to fans, coaches and players, including arguably the greatest player of all time, Pelé, present to receive an honorary doctorate from Hofstra University and attending the season opening match as Honorary President of the club he made famous, the New York Cosmos.

This collection of essays, of course, cannot pretend to represent the breadth or totality of what ensued when so many different worlds collided – like so many different types of players squeezed on a tiny playing space in a frenzied pickup game of *pelada*, learning to play with and against one another – contesting habits, styles and visions of the game. A fitting capstone to the conference was precisely that, the playing of the game, with two extremes of informality and formality. When panels and presentations were concluded, a pickup game of soccer was played among conference participants who had brought the game from the pitch to the podium, finishing days of play with the game back on the pitch, and this game of amateurs was paired off with a professional match between the Cosmos and the Atlanta Silverbacks in a North American Soccer League match at Hofstra's Shuart Stadium, which brought the conference to its formal closure.

The essays gathered for this special issue of *Soccer & Society* nonetheless provide a fair sampling of the various academic approaches to soccer on display throughout the conference. Historical methodologies perhaps predominate, with theoretical, philosophical, sociological or political studies becoming more prevalent as scholars in those related areas in the humanities and social sciences expand the exploration of that fresh terrain. Soccer is all about space and time, and these essays cover eras and geography comprehensively. The 22 authors of these 19 essays represent institutions from eight nations (England, China, Japan, Mexico, Russia, Scotland, Sweden and the United States), another indicator of the cosmopolitan nature of both the unique conference and this special issue.

The Ideologies section begins with Scott Waalkes offering an ambivalent perspective on soccer's role in processes of globalization. Yunus Tuncel attempts to blend Kantian and Nietzschean aesthetic approaches to the game, and Tamir Bar-On identifies three dominant discourses on soccer's geopolitical significance.

Identities kicks off with Glen M.E. Duerr's evaluation of how various ethnic and civic nationalisms manifest in and through club football. James R. Holzmeister, Paul Wheeler and Matthew L. McDowell look at English, British and Scottish discourses of national identity, each separately examining hotly contested contemporary issues through historiographical lenses. Joel Horowitz explores how soccer clubs and other civic associations were sites of identity formation in Argentina during the first half of the twentieth century. Karina Ovseypyan and Chun Wing Lee investigate the lives of footballers negotiating their identities in relation to the communist states of the Soviet Union and the Republic of China. Lindsay Sarah Krasnoff focuses on the French National Team as symbolic of an emerging or evolving sense of nationhood. Thomas A. McCabe, Kevin Marston and Christian Collet close off the Identities section with three treatments of soccer's contentious, often marginalized status in American culture wars.

The issue concludes with five essays that discuss transformative pedagogies in the Initiatives section. Ricardo Duarte Bajaña describes the Colombian government's efforts to promote *golombiao*, a recreational form of soccer aimed at social change. Magnus Forslund looks at innovative efforts of Swedish football clubs to remain culturally relevant and financially viable. Taiyo Francis, Joanne Norris and Robert Brinkmann show how professional soccer can help promote environmental awareness with initiatives towards a sustainable future. Nigel Boyle describes the experimental pedagogies he has employed teaching soccer courses in universities in

California and Germany and prisons in California and Uganda. The last essay of the collection, by Judith Gates and Brian Suskiewicz of Coaches Across Continents, features their unique approach to utilizing soccer as a transformational pedagogy in developing communities.

Together, these essays serve to extend the time and place of the 'Soccer as the Beautiful Game: Football's Artistry, Identity and Politics' conference, keeping the ball rolling well beyond the gathering at Hofstra University in Hempstead, New York during April 2014. While the international roster of authors and range of topics are testimony to soccer's global reach, this special issue offers a state of the field for soccer studies and a road map for further exploration.

## Acknowledgements

Stanislao Pugliese and Brenda Elsey not only served as conference organizers, they suggested I assume chief editorial responsibility for this collection and helped greatly in the initial selection of contributions as assistant editors. Erik Stover, Chief Operating Officer of the New York Cosmos, offered vital support for the conference in countless ways. His support for quality writing and rigorous thought on soccer is of inestimable value. Lastly, the guidance and patience of Kausik Bandyopadhyay and Boria Majumdar ensured the challenge of bringing this collection together always had ample support.

# Does soccer explain the world or does the world explain soccer? Soccer and globalization

Scott Waalkes

Does soccer explain the world? Or does the world explain soccer? Is soccer a cause of global integration? Or does it result from global integration? These questions animate much recent writing on the beautiful game. Analysing this writing from the perspectives of the globalization of politics, economics and culture, this essay concludes that the game follows globalization trends more than it causes them in the realms of politics and economics. However, it shapes the cultural realm significantly by forming a hybrid, cosmopolitan 'glocal' culture. Soccer may not bring world peace or move global markets, but it does bring cultures together under the 'sign of play'. It is a triumph of the global imaginary, if not yet a driving force in global politics or economics.

Those who play and watch the global game of soccer can appreciate a soft touch on the ball, a well-timed tackle, a stingy back line, a wide-open counter-attack, a crisp give-and-go in the midfield, a perfect cross, a dashing run into the box, a brilliant save or a swerving volley from distance sailing into the upper corner. They love each stage of the World Cup, the spectacle of cup tournaments or the drama of following a club through wins and losses, season after season. They find beauty and meaning within the game. Soccer is a form of meaningful play.

Many critics contend that all this playing of games is merely a way to divert the attentions of the working class, akin to Roman 'bread and circuses'.[1] Others see the game as a theatre-like spectacle. However, this essay aligns with Nick Hornby, who writes in *Fever Pitch* that football is 'not an escape, or a form of entertainment, but a different version of the world'.[2] We can learn a great deal about the world from this global game. As Markovits and Rensmann note, the game itself constitutes a language 'that is understood on a global scale', making it arguably '*the* single most prominent and ubiquitous sports language in the world'.[3] But how significant is this global language? Does it affect the rest of the world? Or does it merely reflect prevailing patterns of economics, politics, or culture? Is soccer truly the most apt expression of a 'global imaginary' or a global identity?[4]

A host of journalists and social scientists has come forward in recent years to publish books or articles exploring such questions. In laying out his 'unlikely theory of globalization', for example, Franklin Foer famously argued that soccer could explain the world.[5] Similarly, Simon Kuper once wrote a book about how 'soccer affects politics, and … it always has'.[6] But he later retracted that view and said 'soccer is ceasing to explain the world'.[7] Richard Giulianotti and Roland Robertson state that the game 'has been a significant component of globalization processes' and even accelerated the formation of a global society.[8] They suggest that

> if our fellow social scientists are serious about understanding globalization in the twenty-first century, then all of us need to look far more closely at *the* global cultural form that transfixes and fascinates so many diverse societies and so many millions of the world's citizens.[9]

They are, of course, talking about global football.

But are we witnessing the 'footballization'[10] of the world or merely the globalization of football? Does soccer explain the world? Or does the world explain soccer?[11] To be more precise, is soccer a cause or a consequence of global integration? Thankfully, these questions animate much recent English-language writing about the global game, and we can answer them here. David Goldblatt, for example, in his magisterial global history of soccer, captures the dialectic between soccer and politics, economics and culture. As he puts it, global football alone

> has not altered the course of history … did not kick-start the industrial revolution or build the world's cities … does not start, end or replace wars … [and] does not make the peace or redraw the borders of the world.[12]

At the same time, however, he argues, 'No history of the modern world is complete without an account of football'.[13] A truly global game, soccer both shapes and reflects politics, economics and culture.

Taking the globalization of politics, economics and culture in turn, this essay looks at both sides of the equation: How soccer affects globalization and how globalization affects soccer. The evidence suggests that soccer competition affects the world on a global scale primarily in the realm of culture, where the game influences how we imagine ourselves as globalized humanity. But in the realms of politics and economics, it is easier to see how soccer reflects political and economic globalizations more than it contributes to them. The global state system and global economy have shaped the game more than the game has moved world markets or created cooperation between nation states. Although soccer will not lead to world peace or dominate the world economy, it still carries great significance for the expansion of a hybridized and cosmopolitan 'glocal' culture of play.

## 1. The globalization of politics

### 1.1. Soccer as a cause of cooperation

It is commonplace to hear that global sports competitions like the Olympics and the FIFA World Cup advance international understanding. Proponents of sports diplomacy have long argued that athletic competitions can advance 'global integration and cooperation'.[14] Soccer is a truly global game.[15] Expressed most simply, the notion is, 'If you play football with [someone], then you won't want to kill [them]'.[16] Kofi Annan, then-Secretary-General of the United Nations, said that he couldn't think of anything that could bring people together like soccer. 'For 90 minutes at a time, [he said] people become one nation'.[17] FIFA head Sepp Blatter talked recently about his belief 'in the extraordinary power of football to unite people in peace and friendship, and to teach basic social and educational values as a school of life'.[18] But is it possible to argue credibly that the World Cup or league competitions lead to global cooperation? Is there a 'global football family'?[19]

At one level, there is no doubt that World Cup competition, for example, plays a role in fostering relationships between players, between spectators and host countries, or between delegates from national federations who interact at FIFA meetings. The games themselves are a form of international cooperation. Continued testimonies to the power of sport suggest that many of us see how soccer can shape political cooperation at local levels. But it is not clear that this is enough to foster wider transnational cooperation. The power of the nation state remains. In fact, the World Cup only deepens the entrenchment of national identities through the competition of national teams. The competition is transnational, but the rallying of identity occurs within nation states.

Nonetheless, three examples in recent soccer writing illustrate the significant power of the game to foster local cooperation and community. First, the history of the game in England and elsewhere suggests that it emerged within industrial cities to provide a sense of cohesion to workers and their towns.[20] In just those places where community was lacking, the game found some of its earliest and most fervent adopters.

Second, in the book *Outcasts United*, Warren St. John describes how Luma Mufleh, a young Jordanian graduate of Smith College, gradually discovers a passion to coach a club soccer team that unites refugee boys and helps them adjust to the difficulties of living in Clarkston, Georgia. The central storyline – that love of the game drove Luma to intervene in the lives of her young players with tutoring and social support – captures the way that sports can rally groups and unite divided communities around the pursuit of the game.

Third, Gwendolyn Oxenham's film *Pelada* and her subsequent memoir, *Finding the Game*, tell the previously untold story of casual pickup soccer games around the world – a 'global phenomenon spanning race, religion, and class'.[21] These informal games unite groups in places as diverse as Trinidad, Brazil, Uruguay, Bolivia, Peru, France, Italy, Germany, England, Israel, Egypt, Kenya, South Africa, Ghana, Togo, Japan and Iran. Oxenham and her friends travel to these places, join the games and discover what they mean to participants. Along the way, she learns about herself, about the world and about the game itself. Like *Outcasts United*, this is a story of how the game itself creates communities. Oxenham and her friends discover how pickup games unite local communities among slum-dwellers in Nairobi, among jailed prisoners in Bolivia, among women in Iran and among ageing men in Brazil. Communities emerge around the global game, but mostly at local levels.

Thus, rhetoric of soccer bringing world peace is hyperbole. Cooperation at local levels does not automatically spill over to the global level. World Cups alone cannot bring world peace. In 1936, athletes from Great Britain and Germany competed against each other at the Berlin Olympics. Three years later, their countries were at war. Certainly, FIFA as a non-governmental sports federation could well have some modest influences on world politics. But it is hard to imagine that an organization with 400 staff people that is really just a federation of national associations will cause governments of the world to stop launching wars. Clearly, contact between peoples is hardly enough to guarantee cooperation between governments.

### 1.2. *Soccer as a cause of political conflict*

Furthermore, other writers suggest that soccer can even contribute to conflict. The 1969 Soccer War between Honduras and El Salvador is the most famous case, in which fan violence at World Cup qualifiers helped trigger a brief border war.[22] Similarly, an October 2014 qualifying match for Euro 2016 between Serbia and Albania was abandoned when fighting broke out on the field after a drone carried a provocative pro-Albanian flag into Serbia's home stadium in Belgrade. Soccer journalists Franklin Foer, Simon Kuper and James Montague all remind us that soccer can also cause conflict – or at least enflame existing political conflicts – even at the local level. Three famous cases in point are Barcelona vs. Real Madrid, the Old Firm rivalry in the Scottish city of Glasgow between Celtic and Rangers, and recent events in Egypt.

In the case of Barcelona, both Kuper and Foer trace how Barcelona embodies leftist Catalan 'cosmopolitan nationalism' (to quote Foer) over against the royalist, statist, conservative and Castilian identity of Madrid.[23] This entrenchment of identities dates back at least to the 1920s.[24] While Foer stresses the peaceful nature of Barça fans, he does confess that they have a 'pathological hatred toward Real Madrid'.[25] Furthermore, Barcelona fans look down at their intra-city rival, Espanyol, whose name is a reminder of their attempt to curry favour with the Castilian centre.[26] Club soccer, it seems, can deepen political divides rather than ameliorate them.

Similarly, the Glasgow divide between Protestant Rangers fans and Catholic Celtic fans seems to have taken on a life of its own. Foer explains that the sectarian rivalry dates back to an influx of poorer Irish Catholics following the Irish potato famine in the 1840s. Staunchly Presbyterian at the time, Glasgow was hardly receptive to these immigrants. As a result, the newcomers formed their own Catholic associations, including the Celtic football club, which was founded in 1888. After Celtic won four of the first six league championships, Protestant Scots quickly rallied behind the Rangers as a 'Scottish' (Protestant) team.[27] Since the 1920s, violence between supporters in the annual rivalry games has been a steady threat. Instead of merely reflecting political and religious or sectarian rivalries, Kuper writes, 'the Old Firm rivalry has survived as a phenomenon because the fans enjoy it so much. They are not about to give up their ancient traditions just because they no longer believe in God'.[28] The claim is that the club rivalry deepens and prolongs conflicts that might have otherwise eased. In this case, too, it seems that soccer deepens conflict – or at least mirrors it.

Given its conflict-ridden history, the Middle East region forms an ideal case to challenge the proposition that soccer promotes cooperation. As James Montague contends, we often hear 'how the "Beautiful Game" can bring nations and peoples together. And sometimes, in rare cases, that's true. But soccer … can also be a destructive force that entrenches prejudice'.[29] Montague cites the violent clashes that broke out between Egyptian and Algerian national team supporters during World Cup qualifying in late 2009, which led to a diplomatic rupture between the Algerian and Egyptian governments. Similarly, in February 2012, nearly a year after the ouster of the Mubarak regime in Egypt, a deadly riot broke out after a match between the Cairo-based Al Ahly club and the home side Al Masry in the city of Port Said, in which 79 people were killed and more than 1000 injured. Most of the dead appear to have been so-called Ultra supporters of Al Ahly who supported the ouster of

Mubarak. Whether the Ultras were targeted for their political beliefs or for their club loyalties – or both – there is no denying that the game contributed to conflict.[30] Far from being a pacifying force, the game helped deepen Egypt's political divisions.

### 1.3. Soccer as a consequence of political globalization

Historians and social scientists would be more comfortable affirming that soccer follows politics than affirming that it causes political outcomes. Consider two prominent cases of soccer following the globalization of politics.

First, David Goldblatt shows that the game's spread worldwide was closely tied to the rise of the British Empire and its industrial economy in the second wave of globalization (subsequent to the first wave of European expansionism in the early modern period). After the game originated in nineteenth-century England, it spread fairly quickly. As Goldblatt puts it, 'The immensity of Britain's formal and informal empire, its enormous merchant and royal navies, its engineers, bankers, teachers and travellers, had helped spread the game all over the world'.[31] While some have argued that this is primarily a 'testimony to Britain's economic might ... [and] not its political power',[32] a political science 'regime theory' perspective would suggest that the two were inseparable.[33] As with American dominance after the Second World War, British military and economic power reinforced each other throughout the long nineteenth century, as the British navy backed up British economic hegemony. The post-war American imperium was similar. As Thomas Friedman once put it, 'The hidden hand of the market will never work without a hidden fist ... Indeed, McDonald's cannot flourish without McDonnell Douglas, the designer of the U.S. Air Force F-15'.[34] Football became a global game because of the British and American Empires. Political and military power contributed to the game's rise in the post-war global economy.

The formation and ongoing work of FIFA illustrates a second case of a global political actor influencing the spread of soccer. In 2006 *FIFA Magazine* made the case for FIFA's role:

> They [Christians] took centuries to accomplish their mission whereas FIFA has achieved a similar goal with football in only decades. It has 'colonised' the earth by planting football in foreign soil and watching it grow. Seen from this vantage point, the FIFA President commands respect over a realm in which the sun never sets but rather is much greater than the largest kingdom ever conquered by a military leader.[35]

In a less dramatic fashion, sociologists in the 'world polity' school have also described FIFA as an example of the global spread of institutional practices.[36] The diffusion of the game worldwide would never have occurred, on this view, without an agency to promote standardization and the convergence of practices – an agency like FIFA. Instead of focusing on 'the pressure of political power or the deals of profit-seeking businesses', this explanation focuses on 'the mutual modeling of voluntary organizations with global aspirations' or 'script enactment'.[37] By standardizing and rationalizing rules and practices that govern games, leagues, national soccer associations, tournaments and calendars, FIFA facilitates the spread of the global game.[38] The game itself required FIFA's institutional framework to facilitate its spread. The World Cup did not happen spontaneously; it was the result of concerted institutional networking and standard setting.

Given the power of nation states and national identities, the spread of the game is hardly going to create world peace. The transnational realm of organizations like FIFA is not about to trump the power of entrenched political interests. The nation state remains dominant, even in soccer; indeed, the spread of the nation state to the globe is itself part of globalization, and national federations' membership in FIFA reinforces state sovereignty.[39] However, the spread of the game is due partly to political factors. It also reflects global economic trends.

## 2. Soccer and the globalization of economic activity

The globalization of soccer quite obviously moved in tandem with the third great wave of globalization of the world economy in the post-cold war era (the first era being the early modern age of exploration and the second era being the long nine-teenth century from 1815 to 1914). This third wave crested in the 1990s, and professional football felt its effects. Thus, Giulianotti and Robertson pointed to the '"footballization" of national and global economies'.[40] But has soccer truly helped to drive economic globalization? Are the economic elements of soccer globalization causing further economic globalization or merely reflecting trends in the global economy? Most evidence suggests that soccer has a modest effect on the global economy and instead mainly reflects its larger patterns.

### 2.1. Soccer as a cause of economic integration

In at least four ways, however, professional club soccer has led global economic trends. First, thanks to the 1995 European Court of Justice ruling in the *Bosman* case, foreign players flooded into European leagues, especially the English Premier League.[41] 'From less than 5 per cent of the Premiership playing force in 1992, foreign players comprised nearly 60 per cent of Premiership squads in 2004, hailing from sixty-one different countries'.[42] As a result, economist Branko Milanovic asserts that 'the market for professional soccer players is, by far, the most globalized labor market'.[43] Thus, he argues, the richest clubs continue to attract the best global talent, leaving others the leftovers. Those who resent Chelsea, Manchester City or Bayern Munich, will not be surprised to find that the teams that spend the most on players from around the world tend to win more often.[44] They can afford the best global talent, so they keep on winning.[45] But as they pluck up players from Africa, Asia, Latin America, (and occasionally North America), they are advancing the globalization of labour markets. They are a leading sector of the world economy when it comes to scouring the world for the very best players.

Second, a global market for coaches and managers has also emerged, both for club and national teams.[46] As the top European clubs compete for players and revenues, there is some evidence for the emergence of a network of managers, agents and players that make up a global or 'transnational capitalist class'.[47] Club or country teams can hire from a global pool of manager talent.

Third, the influx of foreign owners buying up top European teams – American citizens owning Arsenal, Aston Villa, Fulham, Liverpool, Manchester United and Sunderland; a Russian citizen owning Chelsea; Arab princes owning Manchester City and Paris St. Germain; a Malaysian citizen owning Cardiff – captures the integration of soccer with a global business elite. Elite club soccer is a globalizing industry in terms of ownership.

Likewise, the global branding of top teams plays a large role in helping them pay their high-salary bills.[48] With millions of fans around the world tuning in via satellite to every game, the possibilities for merchandizing are suddenly endless. Tony Karon illustrates:

> Where once, Manchester United may have hoped to sell around 30,000 replicas of its uniform a year to its fans in the city and elsewhere in Britain; today it can expect to move millions of shirts and other paraphernalia to a global fan base, with the Asian market representing a huge new growth market.[49]

Thus, pre-season tours take top clubs like Barcelona to exhibitions around the world. Millions of supporters outside of Europe watch closely and wear the kits and scarves of clubs like Manchester United, Liverpool, Chelsea, Arsenal, Barcelona, Real Madrid, Bayern Munich, Roma, Inter Milan, or AC Milan.[50] These top clubs are clearly global brands, with fans ranging from North America to South America to Africa to Asia.

However, they hardly begin to rival truly globally saturated brands like Nike or Starbucks – both of whom are in the Fortune Global 500, whereas no soccer clubs even come close to joining that group. Thus, we should not exaggerate the scope of soccer clubs' influence on the global economy. The revenues of even the largest global clubs make them equivalent to medium-sized corporations, putting them well below the size of the smallest of the Fortune Global 500 companies.[51] The most valuable club in 2012, for example, Real Madrid, pulled in revenues that were equivalent to less than 3% of the revenue of the five hundredth company on the Fortune Global 500.[52] Likewise, the combined revenues of the top 10 clubs in the Deloitte Football Money League only added up to 22% of the revenues of the five hundredth company.[53] In short, soccer and sports in general are only small parts of total measurable global economic activity, so we would expect them to have only a modest impact on the global economy. Furthermore, soccer clubs are rarely profitable businesses and typically lose money.[54] Nonetheless, as we will see, their symbolic, non-quantifiable role is significant.

## 2.2. Soccer success or failure as a consequence of economic integration or isolation

Kuper and Szymanski's *Soccernomics* book (titled *Why England Loses* in the United Kingdom market) famously drew on national-level economics to explain the success and failure of national teams. Kuper and Szymanski use a regression model with three variables to predict the number of goals a national team will score per game: population size, size of the country's economy and years of experience in international competition.[55] Applying this model, they argue that England's regular results in the World Cup look typical for a country with a population of 51 million.[56] Their point is well taken. We should expect national team success from countries with large populations, well-developed economies and extensive World Cup experience. A country's size and place in the global economy clearly help to explain its national team's success. Soccer results flow from economic success.

By contrast, the failures of talented national teams from poorer countries also start to make more sense when we think about the place of their countries in the global economy. African states, for instance, have rarely gone far in the World Cup. As David Goldblatt notes,

> Africa has continued to produce players of exceptional quality [but] its domestic football economy has become less and less able to hold on to them; and as the stars have departed so the interest and quality of club football appears to decline, locking African football into a familiar downward spiral of underdevelopment.[57]

Without strong professional leagues or national federations in Africa, much local talent fails to develop. The problem has everything to do with African states' struggles with governance and economic development in a globalizing world, and little to do with the quality of African players. Kuper and Szymanski state the problem in its most acute form:

> Isolation – a distance from the networks of the world's best soccer – is the fate of most poor countries. Their citizens can't easily travel to Italy or Germany and see how soccer is played there, let alone talk to the best coaches. Some can't even see foreign soccer on television, because they don't have a television. And only a handful of the very best players in these countries ever make it to the best leagues in the world. One reason poor countries do badly in sports – and one reason they are poor – is that they tend to be less 'networked,' less connected to other countries, than rich ones. It is hard for them just to find out the latest best practice on how to play a sport.[58]

In short, globalization creates hierarchies that are played out on the field all too often. The game doesn't usually drive economic trends; it more often reflects them.

## 3. The globalization of culture

Nonetheless, economics can only take us so far in understanding the game itself. As Goldblatt says, 'In the realms of pleasure and pain, meaning and vacuity, identity and idolatry, the economist is mute'.[59] To these realms of symbolism and meaning – the realms of culture – we now turn.

### 3.1. Soccer as a transnational cultural activity

In the club realm, global branding can bring together audiences of soccer supporters who become a global class of consumers. Thanks to the Internet and satellite television, supporters around the world can follow the fortunes of their favourite clubs and players, wearing their kits and scarves. A globalized media culture follows global celebrities like David Beckham or Cristiano Ronaldo. But this seems like a shallow kind of culture based on consumption of the ephemeral.

However, the World Cup is the epitome of a globalized media event that evokes deeper meaning than mere consumption. As David Goldblatt writes, television viewing of the World Cup finals is now 'the single greatest *simultaneous* and human collective experience'.[60] Live broadcasts also make it an *instantaneous* experience.[61] If we take Jan Aart Scholte's definition of globalization, the World Cup is an apt example of globalization, since Scholte suggests that what is new about contemporary globalization is that transnational events happen *instantaneously* and *simultaneously* across the globe.[62] Although FIFA likely exaggerates when it claims that a billion people watch the final match, it is likely that up to 400 million tune in every 4 years.[63] FIFA's 'geographical spread', according to Goldblatt, 'was far in excess of the reach of global Catholicism', and its 'devotees, measured by the viewing figures for the 1998 World Cup Final, were far greater in number than Rome's flock'.[64] To put it mildly, the game has a truly global reach. It crosses territorial boundaries, but is it just a global spectacle or does it actually form a culture?[65]

Here we need to return to the beginning of this paper, to the notion of soccer as play. In short, soccer *is* a global culture, a global language and a global community of play. The estimated hundreds of millions who actively play the game are participants in local levels of play that connect them to players at higher levels. It is something more than just a mass media spectacle. It creates participation in a transnational community. And this community of play makes room for both diversity and uniformity.

### 3.2. *McDonaldization, glocalized hybridity or rooted cosmopolitanism in soccer culture?*

Many commentators worry about the increasing uniformity of the game. Evoking the aesthetic appeal of the beautiful game, for example, the Uruguayan writer Eduardo Galeano famously wrote,

> I play therefore I am: a style of play is a way of being that reveals the unique profile of each community and affirms its right to be different. Tell me how you play and I'll tell you who you are. For many years soccer has been played in different styles, expressions of the personality of each people, and the preservation of that diversity is more necessary today than ever before.[66]

This is the canonical view among soccer connoisseurs and many journalists, whose broad generalizations about national styles are familiar to soccer fans: Brazilians play the beautiful game, and *futebol* even expresses their 'way of life'[67]; the Dutch organize space on the pitch, work the angles, and play Total Football[68]; the Spanish play beautiful tiki-taka possession soccer; the English kick and run after long balls, play with heart and always lose penalty shoot-outs; the Italians play a defensive, counter-attacking, mental game; the Germans play in a well-organized and relentless manner, with precision on set pieces; African teams emphasize creativity and individual possession; and the Americans just try hard.

But many fear that stylistic variety within the game is under threat. Thus, Galeano says that preserving a diversity of styles is, to repeat, 'more necessary today than ever before'.[69] A passionate critic of globalization, Galeano contends that globalization equals Americanization, which equals marketization, which equals homogenization. In his anti-globalization book, *Upside-Down*, Galeano shares a similar worry in the area of cuisine, contending that ancient culinary traditions 'are being steamrolled by the globalization of hamburgers, the dictatorship of fast food'.[70] The 'flat world' that Thomas Friedman mostly celebrates, on this view, is a world of bland sameness, the McDonaldization of the world bemoaned by sociologist George Ritzer.[71] (For the record, even Friedman laments the appearance of a Taco Bell restaurant along the waterfront cornice in Doha, Qatar.[72]) This worry about the loss of diversity is a valid worry, in part, about how competition drives cultural convergence. As soccer competition gets fiercer, we may see an increasingly globalized and homogenous style of play – a race to the bottom, to the styles of play that generate results, without attention to quality or style. Chris Anderson and David Sally, in their book *The Numbers Game*, argue that the nature of the game itself – the scarcity of goals – makes the game in the elite professional leagues fundamentally similar. As they put it,

> It does not matter whether your league has more foreign players or is reliant on home-grown talent; it does not matter if your tactical blueprint was originally inspired by

Rinus Michels and Johan Cruyff or by Nerero Rocco and Helenio Herrera, the grand-masters of the *catenaccio*; it does not matter a jot if your league is infused with imports from northern Europe and France, like the Premier League, or Brazil and Argentina, like Spain and Italy, or Eastern Europe, like Germany. It may or may not be true that English players are fair, energetic, and robust, that Argentines are wily and erratic, that Brazilians are rhythmic and inventive, and that South Koreans and Japanese players are hardworking and well organized. None of it is important when we look solely at goals in soccer's top leagues.[73]

They conclude, 'The nature of the game is incredibly uniform at the top level'.[74] Instead of distinct national or club cultures, the game may start to look the same everywhere, as successful tactics and practices spread around the world.

Are we condemned to a world of bland soccer uniformity or will there be a backlash of anti-globalizers? Roland Robertson's concept of *glocalization* is especially helpful here.[75] As he and Giulianotti see it, the soccer world has elements of both global convergence and local divergence.[76] On the one hand, they also see the convergence of playing styles feared by Galeano and celebrated by Anderson and Sally. As they write,

> The world's best teams are increasingly prepared and organized according to identical principles, while individual performances are measured according to performative criteria, such as pass completion or tackle rates, shots on- or off-target, and distances run during matches. Unpredictable clashes of playing style rarely occur at international tournaments since the world's elite players now play in the same leagues, compete regularly against each other, and are drilled in similar tactical thinking.[77]

On the other hand, critics of stifling uniformity like Galeano rise up to protest this uniformity, to colourfully describe national styles and to innovate tactically within the constraints of actual games. The threat of homogenization breeds its own resistance. For every tactic there is a counter tactic.

Thus, the McDondaldization – or universal standardization – of soccer could well be fostering a desire to find authentic local versions of the game – or least localized hybrids – driven by the desire to play the game well and win. We may be seeing the beginnings of a kind of slow food movement towards authentic local play. In fact, Franklin Foer argues that loyalty to localized national and club cultures may actually be increasing because of globalization – 'and', as he puts it, 'not always in such a good way'.[78] Globalization may well be breeding localization. Galeano may not have to worry. Glocalization will always emerge.

This ongoing contest between the globally uniform and the locally unique may therefore cause us to overlook the inherent culture of play in the game itself, which may actually be creating a kind of transnational, glocalized hybridity.[79] Some scholars suggest that close students of the game may in fact be developing a 'rooted cosmopolitanism'[80] that combines love of one's own team with love of the game. As Giulianotti and Robertson put it,

> Most supporters are socialized into a cosmopolitan appreciation of the aesthetic possibilities of the game itself, even if these qualities are manifested by opponents during fixtures. In playing football, technical development and improvement are only possible through watching and learning from other cultures.[81]

A soccer fan who wishes to 'watch and follow the best of the best' may end up accepting 'an otherwise possibly disliked "other"' when that 'other' excels at the game.[82]

The great Pelé, for example, describes how fans in Sweden, the host nation for the 1958 World Cup, applauded the Brazilian team's moves, even though their own team lost 5–2.[83] Recently, Barcelona fans applauded Atlético Madrid for winning the Spanish Leauge title by defeating the home side in the final game of the season. Shared appreciation for the game thus creates a culture that connects previously disparate cultures. True fans can embrace the excellent play of an opposing team player, even if he or she defeats their favoured side.[84] And it is precisely the *play element* of this culture that allows those who would otherwise be enemies or rivals to appreciate excellence in the other side. When the better team wins through individual brilliance or tactical ingenuity, their opponents can only appreciate the result. Although the fans may blame the referees or storm the pitch in protest, they also see that winning result. And, to win fairly, even these fans realize that you have to play the game better than your opponent. That's what playing the game means.

## 4. Conclusion: the sign of play

We have seen that soccer may not bring world peace or move world markets. Instead, the game tends to reflect and reinforce the political power of the nation state. And soccer clubs just aren't large enough or profitable enough to move the world economy like corporations in the Fortune Global 500. We can conclude that the game of soccer follows globalization trends more than it causes them in the areas of politics and economics. However, in the cultural realm, the global game forms a language that facilitates communication between fans of the game. It brings people together in play, forming a global culture of the game itself.

David Goldblatt concludes that the appeal of the game is 'rooted … in humanity's need and desire to play' and that the global game continues on 'under the sign of play'.[85] What does the playing of football mean for the globe? The beauty of individual plays, the drama of seasonal competitions or the spectacle of global tournaments between national teams – all of these hint at something beautiful, something good and something true. They all promise the possibility of excellence (what the ancient Greeks called *arête* or virtue) at play. To live 'under the sign of play' is to hope for what 'play' promises: to hope for excellence, to hope for victory and to hope for a better world, where play puts rich and poor on a level pitch, where play trumps war and where play unites cultures.[86] Global soccer is a triumph of the global imaginary, if not yet a driving force in global economics or global politics.

## Disclosure statement

No potential conflict of interest was reported by the author.

## Notes

1. Goldblatt, *The Ball is Round: A Global History of Soccer*, 902.
2. Hornby, *Fever Pitch*, 156.
3. Markovits and Rensmann, *Gaming the World*, 15, 43.
4. Steger, *Globalization: A Very Short Introduction*, 8.
5. Foer, *How Soccer Explains the World: An Unlikely Theory of Globalization.*
6. Kuper, *Soccer Against the Enemy*, 272.
7. Kuper, 'Soccer Explains Nothing'.
8. Richard Giulianotti and Roland Robertson, *Globalization and Football*, 29.

9. Ibid., 172.
10. Giulianotti and Robertson, *Globalization and Football*, 63, first wrote of the 'footbal-lization of the world economy'.
11. The phrasing of these questions comes from Karon, 'What Soccer Means to the World'.
12. Goldblatt, *The Ball is Round*, xvi.
13. Ibid., xviii.
14. Goldberg, 'Sporting Diplomacy: Boosting the Size of the Diplomatic Corps', 63.
15. Bar-On, *The World Through Soccer: The Cultural Impact of a Global Sport*, 126–7.
16. Goldblatt, *Ball is Round*, 227, quoting Lord Decies, vice president of the British Olympic Association.
17. Giulianotti and Robertson, *Globalization and Football*, 157.
18. Early, 'Pingpong Balls, Security Guards, and Groups of Death'.
19. Giulianotti and Robertson, *Globalization and Football*, 161.
20. Goldblatt, *Ball is Round*, 51–82, 195 (on Vienna); and Kuper and Szymanski, *Soccernomics*, 137–44.
21. Oxenham, *Finding the Game: Three Years, Twenty-Five Countries, and the Search for Pickup Soccer*, 14.
22. For a helpful overview by Duke University students, see 'The Soccer War'. This is a blog created by and for a Duke class on 'World Cup and World Politics', taught by Laurent Dubois.
23. Foer, *How Soccer Explains the World*, 199.
24. Goldblatt, *Ball is Round*, 212.
25. Ibid., 212.
26. Kuper, *Soccer Against the Enemy*, 105.
27. Foer, *How Soccer Explains the World*, 44–5.
28. Kuper, *Soccer Against the Enemy*, 264.
29. Montague, 'Unity Through Soccer? Not in the Middle East'.
30. BBC News, 'Football Violence Leaves Many Dead in Port Said'.
31. Goldblatt, *Ball is Round*, 76; also see 901.
32. Markovits and Rensmann, *Gaming the World*, 68.
33. See Krasner, ed., *International Regimes*.
34. Friedman, *TheLexus and the Olive Tree: Understanding Globalization*, 464.
35. Giulianotti and Robertson, *Globalization and Football*, 114, citing *FIFA Magazine*'s March 2006 issue.
36. Giulianotti and Robertson, *Globalization and Football*, 41; and Boli and Thomas, 'World Culture in the World Polity: A Century of International Non-Governmental Organization'.
37. Lechner, *Globalization: The Making of World Society*, 43, 45, 154–9.
38. Giulianotti and Robertson, *Globalization and Football*, 41.
39. Ibid., 99–100, 102, 110.
40. Ibid., 63.
41. Dodson and Goddard, *The Economics of Football*, 182–5, 216–36; Kuper and Szymanski, *Soccernomics*, 147; and Giulianotti and Robertson, *Globalization and Football*, 64.
42. Goldblatt, *Ball Is Round*, 733. In 2014, the proportion of foreign players in the Barclays Premier League was just over 60%. Van Wijk, 'Premier League Has the Second Highest Number of Foreign Players in Europe'.
43. Milanovic, 'The World at Play: Soccer Takes on Globalization'. In 2007, 55% of Eng-lish league players were foreign, 45% in Germany, 34% in Spain, 32% in France and 29% in Italy. Roughly 33% of MLS players in the United States are foreign. Source: Sage, *Globalizing Sport: How Organizations, Corporations, Media, and Politics are Changing Sports*, 73, 75.
44. Anderson and Sally, *Numbers Game*, 161–76. They argue that data and analytics are levelling the playing field (as in Michael Lewis' *Moneyball*), yet their own data about Premier League salary spending suggest that money buys success on the field. Conver-gence may only occur between the rich clubs.
45. As Milanovic, 'World at Play', points out, 'During the last 15 years, all English soccer championships but one were won by the so-called "Big Four": Manchester United, Chelsea, Arsenal and Liverpool. The concentration is greater in Italy: Only once during

the last 20 years has a non-top four club won the Italian Serie A. It's no surprise that the top four Italian clubs, like the top four English clubs, are on the list of the 20 richest clubs in the world. In Spain, Real Madrid and Barcelona shared 17 out of the last 20 championships. In Germany, 13 out of the last 16 championships were won by two clubs'.

46. Kuper and Szymanski, *Soccernomics*, 291–306.
47. Giulianotti and Robertson, *Globalization and Football*, 89.
48. Sue Bridgewater, *Football Brands* (New York: Palgrave Macmillan, 2010).
49. Karon, 'What Soccer Means to the World'.
50. Kuper and Szymanski, *Soccernomics*, 177.
51. Kuper and Szymanski, *Soccernomics*, 76; Markovits and Rensmann, *Gaming the World*, 8, 321; and Bridgewater, *Football Brands*, 139.
52. $650 million (revenues of Real Madrid) divided by $23 billion (revenues of Ricoh, Inc., number 500 on the Fortune Global 500 list). Sources: CNN Money, 'Fortune Global 500'; Ozanian, 'Soccer's Most Valuable Teams: At $3.3 Billion, Real Madrid Knocks Manchester United From Top Spot'.
53. Deloitte, 'Football Money League 2014'.
54. Kuper and Szymanski, *Soccernomics*, 78–80.
55. Kuper and Szymanski, *Soccernomics*, 33–8, 280–1.
56. Ibid., 38, 44.
57. Goldblatt, *Ball is Round*, 881–2.
58. Kuper and Szymanski, *Soccernomics*, 269.
59. Goldblatt, *Ball is Round*, 686.
60. Goldblatt, *Ball is Round*, 527. Emphasis added.
61. Ibid., 528.
62. Scholte, *Globalization: A Critical Introduction*, 61.
63. Giuliannoti and Robertson, *Globalization and Football*, 133, n. 102.
64. Goldblatt, *Ball is Round*, 514.
65. On 'media sports spectacles' like Olympic ceremonies, see Tomlinson, *Sport and Leisure Cultures*, 25–7.
66. Galeano, *Soccer in Sun and Shadow*, 209.
67. Bellos, *Futebol: The Brazilian Way of Life*; and Pelé, *Why Soccer Matters*, 92, on 'how the Brazilian style of play also reflects our national character: full of joy, improvisation, and our willingness, for better and for worse, to ignore established rules and conventions'.
68. Winner, *Brilliant Orange: The Neurotic Genius of Dutch Soccer*; and Lechner, 'Imagined Communities in the Global Game: Soccer and the Development of Dutch National Identity'.
69. Galeano, *Soccer in Sun and Shadow*, 209.
70. Galeano, *Upside-Down: A Primer for the Looking-Glass World*, 253.
71. Friedman, *The World is Flat: A Brief History of the Twenty-first Century*; and Ritzer, *The McDonaldization of Society*.
72. Friedman, *Lexus and the Olive Tree*, 278.
73. Anderson and Sally, *The Numbers Game*, 87–8.
74. Ibid., 89.
75. Robertson, 'Glocalization: Time-Space and Homogeneity-Heterogeneity'.
76. Giulianotti and Robertson, *Globalization and Football*, 47–59.
77. Ibid., 49.
78. Foer, *How Soccer Explains*, 5.
79. On hybridity, see Pieterse, *Globalization and Culture: Global Mélange*; and Pieterse and Kraidy, *Hybridity, or the Cultural Logic of Globalization*.
80. Appiah, 'Cosmopolitan Patriots'.
81. Giulianotti and Robertson, *Globalization and Football*, 58–9.
82. Markovits and Rensmann, *Gaming the World*, 2; see also 14 and 326.
83. Pelé, *Why Soccer Matters*, 112.

84. Pelé, *Why Soccer Matters*, 198, notes that opposing teams sold record numbers of tickets for his finals games for Santos. 'It reminded me of how, while our biggest opponents loved their teams, they *loved* the game of soccer above all. That love was something that united fans and players, no matter what team or country they played for'.
85. Goldblatt, *Ball is Round*, 905.
86. On a similar note, see Goldblatt, 'Another Kind of History: Globalization, Global History, and the World Cup'. Thanks to Bruce Berglund of Calvin College for alerting me to this new text.

## References

Anderson, Chris, and David Sally. *The Numbers Game: Why Everything You Know about Soccer is Wrong*. New York: Penguin, 2013.

Appiah, Kwame Anthony. 'Cosmopolitan Patriots'. *Critical Inquiry* 23 (Spring 1997): 617–39.

Bar-On, Tamir. *The World Through Soccer: The Cultural Impact of a Global Sport*. Lanham, MD: Rowman and Littlefield, 2014.

BBC News. 'Football Violence Leaves Many Dead in Port Said'. *BBC News*, February 2, 2012. http://www.bbc.co.uk/news/world-middle-east-16845841.

Bellos, Alex. *Futebol: The Brazilian Way of Life*. New York: Bloomsbury, 2002.

Boli, John, and George M. Thomas. 'World Culture in the World Polity: A Century of International Non-Governmental Organization'. *American Sociological Review* 62 (April 1997): 144–81.

CNN Money. 'Fortune Global 500'. *CNN*, 2013. http://money.cnn.com/magazines/fortune/global500/2013/full_list/?iid=G500_sp_full.

Deloitte. 'Football Money League 2014'. *Deloitte*, January 2014. https://www.deloitte.com/assets/Dcom-UnitedKingdom/Local%20Assets/Documents/Industries/Sports%20Business%20Group/uk-deloitte-sbg-dfml-2014.pdf.

Dodson, Stephen, and John Goddard. *The Economics of Football*. 2nd ed. New York: Cambridge University Press, 2011.

Early, Ken. 'Pingpong Balls, Security Guards, and Groups of Death'. *Slate*, December 6, 2013. http://www.slate.com/articles/sports/sports_nut/2013/12/world_cup_draw_fifa_dreams_of_a_peaceful_united_tournament_at_the_draw_ceremony.html.

Foer, Franklin. *How Soccer Explains the World: An Unlikely Theory of Globalization*. New York: Harper, 2004.

Friedman, Thomas L. *The Lexus and the Olive Tree: Understanding Globalization*. New York: Anchor Books, 2000.

Friedman, Thomas L. *The World is Flat: A Brief History of the Twenty-first Century*. New York: Farrar, Straus and Giroux, 2005.

Galeano, Eduardo. *Soccer in Sun and Shadow*. Trans. Mark Fried. London: Verso, 2003.

Galeano, Eduardo. *Upside-Down: A Primer for the Looking-Glass World*. Trans. Mark Fried. New York: Picador, 2000.

Giulianotti, Richard, and Roland Robertson. *Globalization and Football*. Los Angeles, CA: Sage, 2009.

Goldberg, Jeffrey. 'Sporting Diplomacy: Boosting the Size of the Diplomatic Corps'. *Washington Quarterly* 23 (Autumn 2000): 63–70.

Goldblatt, David. 'Another Kind of History: Globalization, Global History, and the World Cup'. In *The FIFA World Cup 1930–2010: Politics, Commerce, Spectacle and Identities*, ed. Stefan Rinke and Kay Schiller. Göttingen: WallsteinVerlag, 2014.

Goldblatt, David. *The Ball is Round: A Global History of Soccer*. New York: Riverhead Books, 2008.

Hornby, Nick. *Fever Pitch*. New York: Riverhead Books, 1992.

Karon, Tony. 'What Soccer Means to the World'. *Time*, July 21, 2004. http://content.time.com/time/arts/article/0,8599,671302-1,00.html.

Krasner, Stephen D., ed. *International Regimes*. Ithaca, NY: Cornell University Press, 1983.

Kuper, Simon. *Soccer Against the Enemy*. New York: Nation Books, 2006.

Kuper, Simon. 'Soccer Explains Nothing'. *Foreign Policy*, July 21, 2010. http://www.foreign policy.com/articles/2010/07/21/soccer_explains_nothing.

Kuper, Simon, and Stefan Szymanski. *Soccernomics*. New York: Perseus Books, 2009.

Lechner, Frank J. *Globalization: The Making of World Society*. Malden, MA: Wiley, 2009. 215–29.

Lechner, Frank J. 'Imagined Communities in the Global Game: Soccer and the Development of Dutch National Identity'. In *Globalization and Sport*, ed. Richard Giulianotti and Roland Robertson. Malden, MA: Blackwell, 2007.

Markovits, Andrei, and Lars Rensmann. *Gaming the World: How Sports Are Reshaping Global Politics and Culture*. Princeton: Princeton University Press, 2010.

Milanovic, Branko. 'The World at Play: Soccer Takes on Globalization'. *YaleGlobal Online*, June 15, 2010. http://yaleglobal.yale.edu/content/world-play-soccer-takes-globalization.

Montague, James. 'Unity Through Soccer? Not in the Middle East'. *Foreign Policy*, June 11, 2010. http://mideastafrica.foreignpolicy.com/posts/2010/06/11/unity_through_soccer_not_in_the_middle_east.

Nederveen, Pieterse Jan, and Marwan Kraidy. *Hybridity, or the Cultural Logic of Globalization*. Philadelphia, PA: Temple University Press, 2005.

Oxenham, Gwendolyn. *Finding the Game: Three Years, Twenty-Five Countries, and the Search for Pickup Soccer*. New York: St. Martin's Press, 2012.

Ozanian, Mike. 'Soccer's Most Valuable Teams: At $3.3 Billion, Real Madrid Knocks Manchester United From Top Spot'. *Forbes*, April 17, 2013. http://www.forbes.com/sites/mikeozanian/2013/04/17/soccers-most-valuable-teams-real-madrid-dethrones-manchester-united-from-top-spot-at-3-3-billion/.

Pelé. *Why Soccer Matters*. New York: Celebra, 2014.

Pieterse, Jan Nederveen. *Globalization and Culture: Global Mélange*. Lanham, MD: Rowman and Littlefield, 2005.

Ritzer, George. *The McDonaldization of Society*. 2nd ed. Los Angeles, CA: Pine Forge Press, 2007.

Robertson, Roland. 'Glocalization: Time-Space and Homogeneity–Heterogeneity'. In *Global Modernities*, ed. Mike Featherstone, Scott Lash, and Roland Robertson. Thousand Oaks, CA: Sage, 1995. 25–44.

Sage, George H. *Globalizing Sport: How Organizations, Corporations, Media, and Politics are Changing Sports*. Boulder, CO: Paradigm, 2010.

Scholte, Jan Aart. *Globalization: A Critical Introduction*. New York: Palgrave, 2005.

'The Soccer War'. *Soccer Politics/The Politics of Football*. http://sites.duke.edu/wcwp/research-projects/the-soccer-war/.

Steger, Manfred. *Globalization: A Very Short Introduction*. 2nd ed. New York: Oxford University Press, 2009.

Tomlinson, Alan. *Sport and Leisure Cultures*. Minneapolis: University of Minnesota Press, 2005.

Van Wijk, Jim. 'Premier League Has the Second Highest Number of Foreign Players in Europe'. *Independent*, January 21, 2014. http://www.independent.ie/sport/premier-league-has-the-second-highest-number-of-foreign-players-in-europe-29937662.html (accessed March 21, 2014).

Winner, David. *Brilliant Orange: The Neurotic Genius of Dutch Soccer*. New York: Bloomsbury, 2001.

# The aesthetic and ecstatic dimensions of soccer: towards a philosophy of soccer

Yunus Tuncel

Soccer remains to be the most played and watched form of sport at the international level, and soccer games bring together millions of people. The beauty and the playfulness of the game and its appeal to the many from different social strata are both the source of greatness of this sport and yet also related to its social problems. None of these problems, in my view, are inherent to soccer itself, but soccer, just like any other sport, is a microcosm of the world in which it lives and reflects its problems. In this essay, I would like to explore the aesthetic and the ecstatic dimensions of soccer and show how the spirit of soccer is antithetical to the social phenomena listed above. Under the aesthetic dimension, I will approach soccer insofar as it is the field of playfulness, game-making, imagination and beauty. Under the ecstatic dimension, I will attempt to understand how soccer creates a community, an ecstatic communion, around a sporting event.

## Introduction

Soccer has become the most experienced sport on an international scale in the last few decades; in its size and scope, it has exceeded the mass appeal of religions and political ideologies. As Kilpatrick observes 'Today the cathedral has been replaced by the stadium'.[1] Its universality can be explained by its appeal to beauty, intense emotions and the spirit of community. It brings both aesthetic and ecstatic functions together in a higher degree than any other sport. Despite such appeal, soccer remains entrenched in the problems of our world today, which may have to do with problems in our dominant aesthetic and ecstatic experiences. This forms a paradox to me, a paradox that must be addressed. Soccer is as repugnant to many due to its problems as much as it is attractive to many others. Clearly, there are many variations among teams and players. Great players such as Pelé, Beckenbauer and Messi can make spectators forget these problems with their beautiful styles, but the problems persist. In this essay, I will explore the ecstatic and aesthetic dimensions of soccer, while reflecting on some of its endemic problems through these same dimensions.

## Aesthetics of soccer

Why do we call something beautiful? Does it lie in the object itself so that one can say that which is beautiful is universally beautiful? Or is it entirely subjective, that it resides entirely with the subject and subjective conditions? Kant solves, or he claims to solve, the problem of the aesthetic by locating the aesthetic experience in the function of imagination, a faculty of the human mind that is indispensable to our experiences. Imagination is the faculty of presentation, and Kant claims that in aesthetic experience, the imagination is sustained in a playful mode as it no longer serves cognition, in either its scientific or moral mode. He associates the former suspension with the aesthetic of the beautiful and the latter with the sublime. I would like to first examine how soccer can be construed as a beautiful game under the conditions that Kant sets for the aesthetic of the beautiful in four moments of judgement of taste: quality, quantity, relation and modality.

First moment: 'Taste is the ability to judge an object, or a way of presenting it, by means of a liking or disliking *devoid of any interest*. The object of such a liking is called *beautiful*'.[2] This position raised much controversy in the post-Kantian age, but Kant's position regarding the qualitative moment has to do with the relative independence of aesthetic experience. The idea of disinterestedness simply indicates that in the experience of the beautiful, there is no scientific or moral interest. He has simply demarcated an aesthetic domain apart from other two domains. This can be applied to the experience of soccer and other sports as much as works of art. Imagination no longer serves the cognitive faculties for the production of scientific or moral judgements but rather sustains itself in a playful mode. The emphasis in the 'disinterestedness' is placed on this relative independence of imagination vis-à-vis understanding, the most cognitive faculty of the mind.

In the second moment, Kant shows how, while being subjective, aesthetic experiences can be construed as universal or what is universal in them. How do we call the same object beautiful, let's say, the same soccer game? Where does the universality reside? This becomes a paradox especially when we consider that all aesthetic judgements are singular; here lies the issue of quantity. Kant then locates the universality in the communicability of the mental state in which imagination and understanding enter into a free play. Based on this idea of universality, Kant concludes 'beautiful is what, without a concept, is liked universally'.[3] Clearly, the beauty of a soccer game, or of some parts of the game, is universally liked in the soccer community, more often than not, even among opponents.

Kant demonstrates in the third moment, which has to do with relation, how the aesthetic of the beautiful lies at the intersection of purpose and no-purpose. 'Beauty is an object's form of purposiveness insofar as it is perceived in the object without the presentation of a purpose'.[4] This moment has to do with the relation to the object of aesthetics, which cannot be construed to have a specific purpose or use or a direct use. We may not call an ordinary object that we use in everyday life beautiful, because it serves a specific function for self-preservation, but those fields, like sports and arts, which do not fall within the useful everyday functions, provide aesthetic objects. Soccer, like any other sports, has no direct utility for self-preservation; therefore, we do not subject the experience of soccer to a utilitarian assessment. A soccer game is experienced as a sport event, in itself and not for any purpose.

Finally, the fourth moment which has to do with modality. Here, Kant explains how we can have shared acceptance of what beautiful is without relying on our strictly cognitive understanding. To show that 'a judgment of taste requires everyone to assent', he discusses 'common sense', distinct from 'common understanding', and comes to the conclusion that this common sense underlies the attunement among the faculties of the human mind, an attunement that is needed for the cognitive functioning of the mind, which rests on a feeling and its communicability.[5] This feeling is not a private one, but rather a common one. It serves cognition, but is not cognitive itself, since there is no concept that is attached to it. Hence, Kant defines this moment as follows: 'Beautiful is what without a concept is cognized as the object of a *necessary* liking'.[6] In soccer, we may speak of universal feelings of euphoria and excitement as those feelings that are communicated throughout the soccer community.

Many objections can be raised against considering soccer (or any other sports) as beautiful and the application of Kant's four moments to soccer. One may further object that Kant or any philosopher before him limited their conception of beauty to nature and art, and by art, they understood only those arts established and considered to be art (the so-called seven sisters). This objection, however, no longer holds in the post-Kantian age. Why would we call a tree beautiful, a Van Gogh painting beautiful, a scene in a drama beautiful, though in different senses in each case, but not a performance by a solo performer or a work of digital or installation art, or a performance by an athlete in any sport field? If the central criterion of aesthetic experience is the playful sustenance of imagination and its universal communicability, then all these other fields (beyond the seven sisters) also fulfil this criterion.

Kantian aesthetics, however, does not end with the beautiful–the beautiful is that which can be presented – it also presents the aesthetics of the sublime, which has to do with the formless and which the imagination cannot present. Here, the so-called object is too grand to be presented. In this case, it sustains itself in a playful mode with reason, the faculty in charge of morals. In the case of the experience of the sublime, the imagination is no longer serving the faculty of reason. This has to do with issues of greatness whether they be in nature or human life. In the after-math of the death of God and the rise of the over-human, as Nietzsche announced, we need to find examples of greatness in human life and struggle. In soccer, they are the exceptional moments when talent meets chance through competition and the ball; the ball as a sacred object already invokes greatness. The fact that it is bounceable object, perfected by ancient Americans, creates many possibilities for game-making in a field of twenty-two contesting players. Just like much that we have, these are all human inventions, but now they become vessels or media for over-humanly achievements and manifestations of human struggle. The idea of the sublime should now take us to Nietzsche who expanded and radicalized the idea under the notion of the Dionysian.

## Ecstatics of soccer

Nietzsche broadened the notion of aesthetics as he considered existence to be justifiable only as an aesthetic phenomenon. With this paradigm shift, Nietzsche not only broke down the classical paradigm that limited the creative deed to the creation of works of art understood categorically, a static paradigm, but moved towards inclusion of ecstatic disposition in arts. We can say two things at the outset regarding Nietzsche's aesthetics: (1) aesthetics has to do with creation in a broader sense, which includes creation of works of art, cultural formations like sports, institutions and most importantly and primarily one's own self. Under this view, we can consider soccer to be a field of aesthetics, since soccer in its entirety is a field of culture that is created by human beings. It is fictional just like anything else that is human. (2) Nietzsche's aesthetics includes both the Apollonian and the Dionysian forces, as he applied these two terms to understand the ancient Greek drama.[7] The Apollonian is the principle of individuation and has more to do with image, the tangible, whereas the Dionysian is the end of the individuated state. The Dionysian, therefore, is the loss of the self, ecstasy, etc. In arts, Nietzsche associated visual arts more with the Apollonian and musical arts more with the Dionysian. All that exists, whether in nature or human-made, can be explained in terms of the agonistic union of these two types of forces. Since ecstasy is the coming out of the body, the Dionysian has much to do with bodily regimes, an area that is missing in Kant's conception of the sublime.

Now, how do we apply these two aspects of Nietzsche's aesthetics to soccer? First, soccer is aesthetic insofar as the players re-create the game, both individually and collectively. The images and the figures they draw, which are driven by the ball, are pleasurable and the more sophisticated they are the more pleasures they produce. Spontaneity of action intensifies its pleasure. Many ball games produce imagery driven by the ball according to the rules of the game within its own specific field; soccer, due to the size of its field and the number of players, is one of those few sports that can produce a plethora of such imagery. Soccer, just like any other sport, is a human-made projection of human struggle and suffering, and as such, produces pleasurable illusions, just like Greek tragedy.

As for the second aspect of Nietzsche's aesthetics, the visual devices, the field, the field design, individual players – some of them could be heroic, the team, the story or the script, the goal, time frame, scores and the ball are Apollonian artifices. On the other hand, communal spirit of the players, the team as one or even competing teams as creating one game, the losing oneself unto death of the players, the ecstatic communion of spectators and their excitement and euphoria can be counted as Dionysian. Yes, there is no chorus here, there are no direct elements of the cult of Dionysus like satyrs, all of which sustain the Dionysian locus of the event, but the Dionysian forces are present in soccer. What remains is the framing of the event. Whether it was the cult or the theatre, Dionysian forces were channelled into an aesthetic communion. This is one aspect of ancient Greek culture, which had appealed to the young Nietzsche. It was this 'enframed' freedom, or cultic freedom if you will, that made ancient freedom sacred and desirable. It was not a denial of human freedom but it was not its arbitrary or nihilistic expression. The Dionysian community had its own bounds of free act. Soccer could be construed in this way. However, soccer is not experienced in this way in today's world; the problem lies not in the spirit of sporting or soccer itself, but in the broader problems of the world that is out of joint.

In my view, Nietzsche would consider soccer or any team sport in a positive light as long as they are life-affirming and uplifting and insofar as they produce great examples. In 'Nietzsche's Arsenal', Kilpatrick discusses the objection made to such a position that Nietzsche would be for individual sports rather than team sports.[8] He then likens soccer to a Greek tragedy and explains how soccer too can be seen as a union of Apollonian and Dionysian forces. Apollonian elements are the individual and visual elements: the stadium itself, the field, the appearances of players, etc. Dionysian elements are the team spirit, the euphoric and ecstatic dispositions of players and spectators. There is nothing in soccer that correspondence to chorus in Greek drama and the field of soccer is neither a field of music nor of language, although both may not be entirely absent.

Agreeing with Kilpatrick, I must also add the simple fact that tragedy was a group performance, although one tragedian carried the burden as the signatory of the whole dramatic performance. He would be like the coach and the technical director in soccer, whereas the producer the club owner. Another problem emerges in the area of tragic heroism; tragedies were about the rise and fall of a hero known to the community through its shared myths. One may argue that there are heroes in soccer and their rise and fall are associated with their victories and defeats, respectively. Or, their exit from soccer may be taken as their fall.

## Some problems for a philosophy of soccer

The problems that afflict the culture of soccer today are not necessarily endemic to soccer, but they are problems that are embedded in soccer culture. Based on the ideas presented above on aesthetics and ecstasy in soccer, I present the following four problems:

Problem 1: *Active vs. Passive.* One does not see oneself as an aesthetic being, which means a creative, active being. Aesthetic making of the self is not part of the soccer culture, because masses and mass culture weigh heavily on this culture. It ends up running with mere following. Soccer clubs want masses; this is their source of income and fame. Here, we fall into a vicious circle. The problems do not reside simply in some part of the soccer culture but in its totality, from top to bottom. We may then entertain the question as to whether the sporting culture, including the culture of soccer, is taken captive by the society of spectacle understood by Debord or by the Panopticon understood by Foucault. In the first case, human beings are produced by mass media, as they lose their authentic selves. They are mere passive spectators before spectacles that are produced for them. Active spectacle vs. passive spectators dualism is simply grounded in the old metaphysical order, as Debord argues. In the second case, human beings have become docile bodies subject to bio-power regimes of institutions.

Problem 2: *Quality vs. Quantity.* Any mass gathering is not necessarily a Dionysian communion as understood by Nietzsche. In ecstasy, one comes out of oneself to be one with all through a great spectacle, great 'actors' and grand deeds; one becomes godly, or over-humanly to use Nietzsche's phrase. In our dominant moralities, on the contrary, one becomes smaller, mass-like in the face of great players. Great examples do not create grand *affects* on the masses, because masses are not susceptible to such affects. Masses think, if they do, with politics of identity, small camp mentality. They see competition as a permanent animosity. They do not see that the communion of a game weighs more than their club loyalty. They do not understand that their association with a *great* player does not make them great. To a large extent, soccer serves millions of spectators who are lost, who do not have much in their lives; in this nihilistic void, they hang onto soccer. For millions, soccer has replaced religion as a form of mass delusion. This is a problem of the culture of soccer, not of soccer itself.

Problem 3: *Affects: Active vs. Reactive.* In every spectacular event, affects are reproduced at small or great scales. The question to examine here is what those affects are and how, in what context, are they produced? For the sake of simplicity, I would like to split affects into two: internal affects and external affects. By internal affects, I mean those affects that are produced according to the rules of the game. A beautiful shot into the goalie or the way a goalkeeper jumps and kicks the ball away, which could easily have been a goal. Those sport actions that are unique, unusual, spontaneous and over-human invoke awe and inspiration on the part of the spectators. By external affects, I mean those affects that are produced at a game but are not according to the rules of the game. For instance, the incident at the 2014 World Cup when Uruguay's Luiz Suarez bit into the shoulder of Italy's defender Giorgio Chiellini; or, the head butt of France's Zidane against Italy's Marco Materazzi at 2006 World Cup. They clearly belong to the event[9] of the game, but they produce different kinds of affects. I would argue that these types of external affects often produce reactive affects. It opens up more divisiveness among players and among opposing fans of the teams and do not cultivate feelings that are appropriate to the spirit of sport.

Problem 4: *The Problem of Nihilism*. We live in a nihilistic age, which is the consequence of the death of God, as diagnosed by Nietzsche in the nineteenth century. Nihilism signifies several phenomena for Nietzsche: (1) negation of this worldly life; (2) acceptance of *decadent*, reactive values in the absence of great values; and (3) the laissez-faire mentality which operates with an 'anything goes' attitude. Although sport is an *active* field in itself, *reactive* forces, which are nihilistic, have penetrated soccer culture. Some forms of nihilism in soccer culture are as follows: winning at all costs, fraud and match-fixing, bribery, material gains held over the spirit of sporting, favouritism, etc. All of them go against the spirit of sport, but they are rampant in our times. Many players, referees, coaches are implicated in these schemes without realizing the negative impact their actions bring upon the ethos of soccer.

## Epilogue

Soccer as a sporting field presents many beautiful games, but our sociocultural problems exceed its field and penetrate it despite its 'original' aesthetic and ecstatic dimensions. Soccer is a beautiful game, but its beauty is seen today as an external phenomenon. The typical soccer fan does not see the world *aesthetically*, but rather observes it *passively*. By *passive*, I refer to that divide between an active spectacle and a passive spectatorship, as diagnosed by Nietzsche and Debord. Commodification of sport turns sport events into fixed objects that are exchangeable. This stasis betrays sport's fluid dimension. Such problems as hooliganism and fan culture will persist unless there is a paradigm shift, and mass culture is overthrown towards an over-humanly culture, as Nietzsche predicted. Soccer or any other sporting field cannot be expected to solve the problems of the world. However, the sporting community, insofar as it understands the spirit of sport, can resist these problems whether they are the *unaesthetic* attitude of the masses, the problem of *passive spectator* or the problem of *reactive affects*. Sport, like art, is an *active* field of culture; members of the soccer community, at all levels, must live up to it.

## Disclosure statement

No potential conflict of interest was reported by the author.

## Notes

1.  Kilpatrick, 'Nietzsche's Arsenal', 84.

2.   Kant, *Critique of Judgment*, 53.
3.   Ibid., 64.
4.   Ibid., 84.
5.   Ibid., 86.
6.   Ibid., 90.
7.   Cf., Nietzsche, *The Birth of Tragedy*, sections 1–4.
8.   Kilpatrick, 'Nietzsche's Arsenal', 86).
9.   Cf. Farred's *In Motion, At Rest* for a discussion of the event concept.

## References

Debord, Guy. *The Society of Spectacle*. Trans. Donald Nicholson-Smith. New York: Zone Books, 1995.

Farred, Grant. *In Motion, At Rest: The Event of the Athletic Body*. Minneapolis: University of Minnesota Press, 2014.

Foucault, Michel. *Discipline & Punish*. Trans. Alan Sheridan. New York: Vintage Books, 1977.

Kant, Immaneul. *Critique of Judgment*. Trans. J.C. Meredith. Oxford: Oxford University Press, 2009.

Kilpatrick, David. 'Nietzsche's Arsenal'. In *Soccer and Philosophy*, ed. Tom Richards, 37–46. Chicago: Open Court, 2010.

Morrisette, J.-F. 'The Theatricality of Sport and the Issue of Ideology'. *Journal of the Philosophy of Sport* 41, no. 3 (2014): 381–95.

Nietzsche, Friedrich. *The Birth of Tragedy*. Trans. Walter Kaufmann. New York: Vintage Press, 1967.

Nietzsche, Friedrich. *On the Genealogy of Morals*. Trans. Walter Kaufmann. New York: Vintage Press, 1989.

Tuncel, Yunus. *Agon in Nietzsche*. Milwaukee, WI: Marquette University Press, 2013.

# Three soccer discourses

Tamir Bar-On

In this paper, I examine the dominant discourses surrounding the role of soccer in human societies and the international arena. Following Gearóid Ó Tuathail, I argue that there are three types of geopolitical discourses related to soccer: those diffused by intellectuals, states and popular manifestations of geopolitics in civil society. I highlight three prevalent discourses in relation to soccer propagated by intellectuals, states and within civil society, which I call the Soccer War discourse, the Nobel Prize discourse and the Gramscian discourse. I trace the importance of soccer by highlighting how it triggered a Soccer War between two poor central American nations; how it was nominated for the Nobel Peace Prize; and demonstrate how it can both support dictators and the status quo, yet also engender movements for popular social transformation (the Gramscian discourse).

## Introduction

There is no sport rivalling soccer in terms of its global, cultural and political impact. Soccer is the world's most popular sport. The 2006 World Cup final attracted an estimated audience of 715.1 million people.[1] According to FIFA, the group stages of the 2014 World Cup in Brazil reached 'a record numbers of viewers across the world'.[2] Today, it is almost ritualistic to see presidents, prime ministers or monarchs at important international soccer matches. In most of Latin America, soccer is the king of all sports: 'People live for it. They kill for it. It is a source of hope and a reason for suicide. It is a way out of poverty and misery for a very few and an intangible escape for millions more'.[3]

Even the United States, which is supposedly 'exceptional' in opting for American football, baseball, or basketball as its dominant sports,[4] has since the 1994 World Cup in the USA jumped on the global soccer bandwagon. As more North American kids play soccer, the phrase 'soccer mom' is now part of popular culture. Alex Castellanos, a former senior media advisor to Bob Dole, suggested in 1996 that Bill Clinton was targeting a voting demographic called the 'soccer mom'.[5]

Yet, is soccer ultimately a force for good or ill? Does soccer exacerbate existing nationalistic tensions or engender cosmopolitanism? Does soccer support or subvert existing power relations? In this paper, I examine the dominant discourses[6] surrounding the role of soccer in human societies and the international arena. These discourses are circulated through states, the academic world and the mass media, but also among soccer officials and fans and non-fans in civil society. Gearóid Ó

Tuathail argues that there are three types of geopolitical discourses related to intellectuals, practical aspects of statecraft and popular manifestations of geopolitics in civil society.[7] I highlight three prevalent discourses in relation to soccer propagated by intellectuals, states and within civil society, which I call the Soccer War discourse, the Nobel Prize discourse and the Gramscian discourse.[8] I trace the importance of soccer by highlighting how it triggered a Soccer War between two poor central American nations; how it was nominated for the Nobel Peace Prize; and demonstrate how it can both support dictators and the status quo, yet also engender movements for popular social transformation (the Gramscian discourse).

## The Soccer War discourse

In his *Dios es redondo* (*God is round*), the Mexican intellectual Juan Villoro stressed the tribal nature of soccer and argued it was akin to a pagan religion.[9] Soccer stadiums and their ritual are like 'sacred sites' in the eyes of many fans, players and coaches. These 'sacred sites', as Desmond Morris points out, are really 'temples' that fulfil key human functions such as the need for belonging and the power of the group.[10] This tribalism can reproduce extreme nationalism, sexism, racism and anti-Semitism within and outside soccer stadiums. Bill Shankly, the legendary Scottish manager of Liverpool FC between 1959 and 1974, stated the following in a 1981 television interview: 'Some people believe football is a matter of life and death. I am very disappointed with that attitude. I can assure you it is much, much more important than that'.[11]

Villoro, Morris and Shankly are correct. Soccer is tribal, venerated in a quasi-religious manner,[12] and is 'a matter of life and death', but also 'much, much more important than that'. Called 'The Soccer War', or 'The War of 100 Hours', it was fought between Honduras and El Salvador. It was precipitated by tense qualification matches for the 1970 World Cup in Mexico. When the guns of war were silenced after less than one week, 6000 people tragically lost their lives, 12,000 more people were wounded, and 50,000 individuals lost their homes, fields or villages.[13]

As Ryszard Kapuściński and William Durham correctly maintain,[14] the real reasons for the Soccer War in 1969 had little to do with soccer. Why then do we continue to call it the Soccer War? International qualification matches for the 1970 World Cup in Mexico between El Salvador and Honduras were merely an instrument used to heighten existing nationalistic tensions.

At the matches in San Salvador and Tegucigalpa, the respective capital cities of El Salvador and Honduras, opposing national team players and officials were faced with hostile crowds and even feared for their lives. Concentrating on the soccer matches became nearly impossible as rival fans camped outside the hotel rooms of the opposing national team, ensuring that they would have a terrible sleep and not be fully alert for the key match. The El Salvadoran team was not allowed to sleep the night before their key match in Honduras because of the noise of Honduran fans outside their hotel and the local food that had made some players ill with diarrhoea.[15] The discourses of mass media outlets in the respective countries, or the 'ideological state apparatus',[16] contributed to the tense atmosphere between the two countries with crude, jingoistic nationalism – the stock and trade of Latin American military regimes. Both El Salvador and Honduras were ruled by right-wing military juntas, which were not shy about using the 'repressive state apparatus'.[17]

The most significant events of the Soccer War took place off of the soccer field. It is often acknowledged that countries with bigger territories, larger populations and better demographic growth rates outperform smaller countries in terms of Gross Domestic Product.[18] Yet, this was not completely true for El Salvador and Honduras. El Salvador is much smaller than Honduras in terms of territory, but in 1969 at the outbreak of the Soccer War, El Salvador had a population that doubled that of Honduras. By 1969, more than 300,000 Salvadorans were living in Honduras, looking for a better life in a country that had lots of land and very few people. The Salvadorans made up a sizeable percentage of the peasant population of Honduras.

A land reform law was passed in Honduras in 1962 that was more forcefully enforced by 1967. It set the stage for class conflict and tensions between Honduras and El Salvador. The effect of the land reform law was that the Honduran government turned over land occupied legally or illegally by Salvadoran immigrants and redistributed this land to native-born Hondurans. Thousands of Salvadorans were left homeless.

The roots of the Soccer War lie in a deadly cocktail of authoritarian, military governments, nationalism, geopolitics, issues over land reform (including extreme poverty and class conflict), expulsion edits, fears of communist revolt, and immigration and demographic problems. The Soccer War is a classic example of what David Sobek calls a 'diversionary war': a war instigated by a leader or leaders of country in order to distract the population from domestic problems at home.[19] In a 'diversionary war', national unity is engendered through extreme nationalism and a shared enemy, which focuses problems on the external conflict and the war rather than domestic problems. According to this 'diversionary war' theory, wars are manipulated in order to keep leaders in power that have a tenuous grip. Authoritarian regimes, which often have little support in civil society, can more easily engage in a 'diversionary war' because they do not face the scrutiny of the people in regular and democratic elections.

George Orwell noted the Soccer War discourse and saw soccer's international role in largely negative terms. Writing a piece called 'The Sporting Spirit' in the *Tribune* in 1945, Orwell wrote: 'Football has nothing to do with fair play. It is bound up with hatred, jealousy, boastfulness, disregard of all rules and sadistic pleasure in witnessing violence: in other words it is war minus the shooting'.[20]

Hooliganism, racism, anti-Semitism, neo-Nazism and neo-fascism in stadiums are problems throughout Europe. Before a 2012 'friendly' played in Budapest between Hungary and Israel, the Israeli newspaper *Haaretz* (19 August 2012) reported that Hungarian fans chanted 'stinking Jews', 'Heil Benito Mussolini' and 'Palestine, Palestine' during the singing of *Hatikvah*, Israel's national anthem while displaying Hezbollah and Islamic Republic of Iran flags. Hezbollah and the Islamic Republic of Iran are united by a genocidal anti-Semitism and have both called for the elimination of the state of Israel. These racist Hungarian soccer fans were providing intellectuals, states and civil society with a Soccer War discourse (i.e., violent, ultra-nationalistic and racist) that could be used to de-legitimize international soccer at large.

For Terry Eagleton, soccer is a useful tool for conserving the class privileges of rich soccer clubs, their owners and maintaining the gross inequalities of the capitalist system. During the 2010 World Cup, Eagleton went so far as to suggest that the mass following associated with soccer is a real impediment to political change. Writing in *The Guardian* (15 June 2010), Eagleton called soccer 'a dear friend to capitalism', insisting in a slavishly Marxist tone that soccer today 'is the opium of the people, not to speak of their crack cocaine'. He had especially harsh words for the recently retired English soccer star David Beckham, whom he called 'impeccably Tory' (referring to the ruling right-wing Conservative Party of Prime Minister David Cameron) and 'slavishly conformist'. Eagleton's positions on 'the beautiful game' are rather pessimistic and lead him to call for the game's abolition:

> Nobody serious about political change can shirk the fact that the game has to be abolished. And any political outfit that tried it on would have about as much chance of power as the chief executive of BP has in taking over from Oprah Winfrey.

Eagleton is unambiguous that soccer is a tool of crass 'class warfare', thus preventing workers from seeing their authentic (that is, miserable) conditions. He insists the following about soccer: 'No finer way of resolving the problems of capitalism has been dreamed up, bar socialism'.

Eagleton hints that there might be a trace of rebellion left in the working classes with respect to soccer, or what he calls a 'supporters revolt against the corporate fat cats who muscle in on their clubs'. Yet he ends his piece with the same depressing tone that soccer is 'the opium of the people'. In short, Eagleton sees little redemption in soccer and is thus a proponent of the Soccer War discourse. That is, soccer is the 'crack cocaine' of the masses, as well as a defender of capitalism, big business, extreme nationalism, the status quo and authoritarianism.

In the United States, the Soccer War discourse is reinforced by soccer haters, who suggest that soccer is un-American, European, leftist, communitarian, pro-immigrant, and rife with violence and hooliganism. Disdain for soccer was captured by Tom Weir in a 1993 *USA Today* article, when he insisted that 'hating soccer is more American than apple pie, driving a pickup, or spending Saturday afternoons channel surfing with the remote control'.[21] Such rhetoric mirrors what I call the Soccer War discourse: ultra-nationalistic, exclusionary, anti-immigrant and xenophobic.

## The Nobel Prize discourse

Ignoring the Soccer War, one Swedish parliamentarian believes that soccer is a positive force for the international community. In 2001, soccer was nominated for the Nobel Peace prize by Swedish parliamentarian Lars Gustafsson. 'Soccer has and will continue to play an important role in the global arena, when it comes to creating understanding between people',[22] opined Gustafsson in his nomination letter to the Norwegian Nobel Committee in Oslo. Furthermore, Gustafsson argued that soccer had survived two world wars and numerous ethnic and regional conflicts, while 'hostile nations' could meet on the pitch when other contact would be impossible.

Markovits and Rensmann could in part support Gustafsson's Nobel Prize discourse.[23] They insist that soccer increasingly acts as a cosmopolitan force for inclusiveness through the principle of merit at both club and country. They argue that 'people love good players' on the national team, no matter their origins'.[24] Multiethnic national teams such as France and the USA allegedly unite the nation across social boundaries and embody the ethnic and cultural diversity of those countries.[25] Kofi Annan, the former United Nations Secretary General, could state the following in 2006 when his native Ghana qualified for the World Cup in Germany:

> For any country, playing in the World Cup is a matter of profound national pride. For countries qualifying for the first time, such as my native Ghana, it is a badge of honor.

For those who are doing so after years of adversity, such as Angola, it provides a sense of national renewal. And for those who are currently riven by conflict, like Côte d'Ivoire, but whose World Cup team is a unique and powerful symbol of national unity, it inspires nothing less than the hope of national rebirth.[26]

Soccer might also help to heal internal divisions within a state. As Laurent Dubois commented, 'the mass communion that took place in the streets in 1998' after France won the World Cup liberated 'many from the shackles of their own uncertainty about their place in French society' and 'should serve as a charter for a different way of being French.'[27] Soccer provides a venue to express inclusive conceptions of nationalism. When France won its only World Cup in 1998 under its talisman captain Zinedine Zidane, a Marseille-born superstar of Berber, Algerian roots, it was imagined that France could become a more multicultural, inclusive and egalitarian society. According to this logic, change in the soccer stadium could precipitate changes in values and practices in government, business, media and civil society in general.

## The Gramscian discourse

While the first two discourses in relation to soccer are unambiguous (that is, the extreme poles of the negative Soccer War discourse and the optimistic Nobel Prize discourse), the Gramscian discourse is more ambiguous about the possibilities for soccer as it straddles between defence of power and social change. Gramsci could see soccer as a tool to promote the dominant ideology, but also a mechanism to challenge hegemonic thought through counter-hegemonic initiatives in civil society.

Unlike orthodox Marxists who see culture as a direct reflection of dominant socio-economic relations, Gramscians view culture as a critical terrain of social struggle. Gramsci insisted that liberal capitalism is cemented as the ruling ideology in the West because of the 'common sense' support it receives from the masses in civil society, rather than the 'repressive state apparatus' (for example, the police and army).[28] One of the gravest errors that we make as human beings, argued Gramsci, 'is the belief about everything that exists, that it is "natural" that it should exist, that it could not do otherwise than exist'.[29] For Gramsci, 'common sense' is informed by 'everyday experience' and is the 'traditional popular conception of the world'.[30] In short, common sense is an uncritical and 'largely unconscious way of perceiving and understanding the world' that has become 'common' in any historical epoch.[31] Ultimately, common sense limits our mental horizons and thus stunts the creation of alternative political futures. Common sense is forged in relation to our ideas about the state, market, culture and even soccer matches.

Gramsci argued that while soccer was a reflection of competitive and individualistic values associated with capitalism, it was simultaneously wedded to the ethics of fair play, official rules and 'human loyalty'.[32] Writing in *Avanti!* on 27 August 1918, Gramsci noted that soccer is 'a model of individualistic society. It demands initiative, competition and conflict. But it is regulated by the unwritten rule of fair play'.[33] Thus, for Gramsci soccer can simultaneously support or subvert dictatorships, extreme nationalism or excessive commercialization.

Through Gramsci we might reflect on whether professional soccer, like other realms of culture, imbues us with what he called 'common sense', which privileges more powerful nations and classes above less powerful ones. Gramsci saw soccer as part of the struggle for ideological hegemony in any society, whether dominated by socialist or liberal values. Gramsci pointed out that the course of history depends on the country, the constellation of hegemonic and counter-hegemonic forces in civil society, and the interaction of material interests, dominant ideas, and political, military and 'strategic' powers.[34]

Ideological hegemony, argues Gramsci, seeks to defend capitalism and liberalism through the support of the masses. For Gramsci, soccer is a reflection of the values of liberal capitalist societies. On the one hand, capitalism demands 'initiative, competition and conflict', as a few capitalists own the means of production and the vast majority of workers (including professional soccer players) worldwide must sell their labour in order to earn a wage and survive. On the other hand, there is the ideal of 'human loyalty' to club and country. In addition, laws are created by the liberal state to protect capitalism, the bourgeoisie and private property. These laws also ensure equal rights for all ('fair play') in the public sphere as a consequence of the legacies of the American and French revolutions in the late eighteenth century (for example, citizenship laws, periodic elections, equality before the law and later equality between the sexes and various ethnic groups).

Gerhard Vinnai, a German social psychologist, wrote *Fussballsport als Ideologie* (1970) about soccer as an ideology and its mass psychology.[35] In this work, Vinnai interprets soccer as a game in which the goals that are scored are scored 'against the dominant'. For cultural theorist Stuart Hall, culture (including soccer) is a 'critical site of social action and intervention, where power relations are both established and potentially unsettled'.[36] Both of these thinkers echo the Gramscian discourse. Soccer is a site of contestation between different class interests, and on numerous occasions soccer goals have more often been scored on behalf of the dominant soccer continents, nations, clubs and social classes. Professional clubs and national teams advance the interests of capitalism and serve to legitimize and recreate the inequalities of their respective societies. Yet, soccer clubs, national teams and their fans might also, as Vinnai posited, score goals 'against the dominant'.

Let me highlight some examples of this Gramscian discourse. The first soccer clubs in England in the late nineteenth century were often built by factories and were arguably designed to stop the spread of worker unity and burgeoning socialist ideals. The British colonial authorities, as well as English gentlemen, soldiers, sailors and businessmen all played roles in spreading soccer worldwide. Yet, as Patrick Hutchison pointed out, soccer could also be used to organize and create resistance again empires through the erection of national teams.[37] For example, Algeria's National Liberal Front – FLN – organized national matches beginning in 1958 before the country's independence from France in 1962.

International soccer matches can also legitimize populists or dictators. As Markovits and Rensmann observe, 'Throughout the twentieth century dictatorships of various kinds utilized the charismatic power of sports for their own, often nefarious, causes'.[38] Italy won two World Cups in 1934 and 1938 during Mussolini's Fascist dictatorship and three-time Italian Prime Minister Silvio Berlusconi is the owner of AC Milan, Italy's biggest 'media empire', and founded a political party, *Forza Italy*, which is named after a soccer chant meaning Go Italy! In a sardonic tone, in his *The Soccer War* Kapuściński quotes an exiled Brazilian colleague after Brazil's third World Cup victory in 1970: 'The military right-wing can be assured of at least five more years of peaceful rule'.[39] Kapuściński underscores the dual use of some Latin American soccer stadiums, particularly during the military dictatorships in the 1970s and 1980s: 'In peacetime they are sports venues; in war they turn into concentration camps'.[40] Chile's national soccer stadium was used to imprison and torture opponents of Augusto Pinochet's military regime, while the regime also engaged in 'an era of terror' against amateur soccer clubs and neighbourhood and civic associations.[41]

Yet, Gramsci could see the power of civil society, including soccer, to challenge authoritarian regimes, or liberal capitalist society. Influenced by Gramsci, Del Burgo argues that soccer can be a vehicle for social change. He argues that soccer is a 'social phenomenon in its own right, which may in turn have implications for the world beyond the game'.[42] Soccer can be used as a tool to 'enter into a dialogue with society at large'[43]; heal divided societies; promote anti-racism; tackle neglected societal issues (for example, authoritarianism and militarism, sexism, homophobia, poverty, environmental problems, or ethnic and religious sectarianism); and conceivably transform the hearts and minds of millions of followers worldwide.[44]

In 2013, nation-wide Brazilian protests against government corruption, excessive World Cup and Olympic Games spending (for the public, this meant less government spending on education, welfare and poverty reduction) and high transportation prices during the Confederations Cup won the hearts of numerous Brazilian national team players and fans. In the same year, rival Turkish fans from Istanbul (Galatasaray SK, Fenerbahçe SK and Beşiktaş JK) put aside their differences to unite in street protests against the authoritarian tendencies of Prime Minister Recep Tayyip Erdoğan. James Dorsey could write the following about Egyptian soccer during the 'Arab Spring': 'The newly-found solidarity among supporters of Al Ahly and its arch rival Al Zamalek SC' allowed them to forge 'a bridge across diametrically opposed political and social poles'.[45] Soccer fans, Dorsey argues, were 'emboldened by their role in protests that deposed Egyptian President Hosni Mubarak after 30 years in office' and later sought to alter the politics of their country's 'beautiful game' and democratize Egyptian society.[46]

Following Del Burgo and Gramsci, the communist, anarchist and anti-capitalist identity of hardcore fans associated with German club FC St. Pauli or Italian team A.S. Livorno Calcio, as well as fan-owned clubs, challenge the ownership and capitalist logic of our society. Brenda Elsey points out that Chilean amateur soccer clubs connected the working class to political parties; served as venues for critique; and played a role in the turn away from the dictatorship and the democratization of the public sphere.[47] Based in England, the Hackney Laces are 'a community supported and run football club for girls who want to play football and learn new skills, on and off the pitch'.[48] The club's manifesto states that it is a 'football family' interested 'in enthusiasm not scorelines'.[49]

In *The World Through Soccer: The Cultural Impact of a Global Sport*, I offer support for the Gramscian discourse.[50] I use the examples of soccer clubs during the rise of the industrialized working class, the Soccer War, Silvio Berlusconi's (and Paolo Maldini's AC Milan and Italy) and Salvador Mariona's FC Alianza and El Salvador to demonstrate that, from a neo-Marxist perspective, the 'ideological state apparatus' engenders mass support in defence of capitalism and social control. Yet, I simultaneously advance the argument that world soccer is not merely a space for extreme nationalism, rampant commercialism and defence of dictatorial regimes. Rather soccer also enhances positive values and possibilities for social change.[51] Soccer can be the site for generosity, fair play, and initiatives for social change.

FIFA awards Fair Play prizes each year in order to promote positive values such as fair play. Soccer has also enhanced leadership skills. Soccer allowed anti-apartheid activists to learn leadership skills in prison through the Makana Football Association from 1966–1973, a league created and run by anti-apartheid prisoners, including current South African President Joseph Zuma.

Soccer provided a venue for the dreams of countless boys and girls around the world, including the former US international Julie Foudy, who now runs her own leadership school for girls and young women.[52] Samuel Eto'o, a Chelsea star, Cameroonian international and the African Player of the Year winner a record four times, dreamed of being the new Roger Milla (a World Cup star for Cameroon in 1982, 1990 and 1994) as a child.[53]

Soccer is used by states to promote soft power.[54] For example, Uruguay won two World Cups as 'soccer pulled this tiny country out of the shadows of universal anonymity',[55] in the words of Uruguayan writer Eduardo Galeano. Galeano also argues that Uruguay built many soccer fields and participated in international soccer tournaments as early as the 1920s as part of a positive nation-building scheme.[56] The strategy has paid off for Uruguay with greater international recognition as a result of its overachieving performances at major soccer tournaments. Uruguay is the smallest country in the world to have won a World Cup: it had less than two million people when it won the first World Cup in 1930. It won the 1950 World Cup in Brazil. In addition, Uruguay has won a record 15 *Copa América* titles. Already in the 1920s and 1930s, Uruguay fielded black players and thus engaged in anti-racism work long before it became mainstream.

Soccer supports anti-racism initiatives such as Kick It Out and Show Racism the Red Card. Soccer has been involved in efforts for social change such as the Homeless World Cup. In 2013, Los Angeles Galaxy star Robbie Rogers was widely supported by his team and fans when he came out as the first openly gay player in Major League Soccer. Soccer stars have challenged authoritarian regimes. Brazilian soccer legend Sócrates openly defied the military regime in the 1980s and attempted to democratize both his club Corinthians and the wider Brazilian society.

Discourses surrounding national teams can also be Gramscian. Joshua H. Nadel points to numerous narratives related to the Honduran national soccer team throughout history. When Honduras won matches, blacks were praised, but they were also blamed when the nation lost. 'Black Hondurans have remained barely visible in representations of the country over the past century, largely as a result of conscious decisions made by national political and intellectual leaders', writes Nadel.[57] Although black Hondurans make up merely 2% of the Honduran population and face serious racial discrimination, poverty and lower educational and social mobility rates compared to mestizos or whites, more than half of the players on the national team at the 2010 World Cup were of black African descent. Thus, soccer is one of the few domains in Honduras where national unity can be engendered and racism can be challenged through the racial composition of the national team. In 2011, black Honduran national team players led by defender Osman Chávez, including David Suazo, Maynor Figueroa, Hendry Thomas and Wilson Palacios, challenged racist discourses in the state, the stands, on Web postings, and in civil society.[58]

A national soccer team can unite or divide the nation, depending on whether you are a civic or ethnic nationalist, to borrow the distinction made by Hans Kohn.[59] National soccer teams can also exclude not merely because one needs to be a citizen of the country to play for it, but also as a result of societal pressures to field ethnically or religiously homogeneous squads. This latter perspective is known as *ethnic nationalism*, which stresses the predominance of tribal solidarity, an emotional and mystical connection to an idealized past and national development.[60] In contrast, *civic nationalism* focuses on liberal universalism, rationality, individual rights and self-transcendence, and a community of numerous sovereign states living in harmony.[61] This type of nationalism is, in theory, more cosmopolitan and colourless than ethnic nationalism and based on shared republican values. Hence, civic nationalists would want players not just from the dominant ethnic group on the pitch, but all citizens of the state (irrespective of their ethnic or biological origins) united by merit and shared liberal values. Gianluigi Buffon, an Italian national goalkeeper with neo-fascist sympathies, is the teammate of Mario Balotelli, an Italian descended from an African father and raised by a Jewish mother. They inspire different nationalist visions of what it means to play for the Italian national team.

Soccer is, to use Robert Putnam's notion of 'bridging capital', an 'integrative force among different groups and their cultural boundaries'.[62] So, for example, there are a high number of Israeli Arabs in Israeli professional soccer.[63] Tamir Sorek points out the high number of Israeli Arabs playing professional soccer and even on the national soccer team, insisting that sport is 'the only public sphere in which Arab excellence is tolerated by the Jewish majority'. The Israeli Government posits a different discourse, namely that Israeli Arab citizens of Israel have equal opportunities and the proof is that they are populated in the world beyond the soccer pitch as parliamentarians, mayors, judges, diplomats, university professors and business owners. Israeli Arabs challenge this official discourse and argue that they are 'second-class citizens'.

Yet, a team of ethnically diverse players does not completely undermine what Putnam calls 'bonding capital', or 'a hardening of boundaries among different constituencies and their cultures'.[64] Ukrainian soccer fans in Lviv held up banners of the Nazi collaborator Stepan Bandera. On 22 January 2010, the outgoing President of Ukraine Viktor Yushchenko awarded Bandera the title of Hero of Ukraine (posthumously), but was roundly condemned by Russian, Polish, Jewish and other international community groups, as well as the European Parliament.

## Conclusion

This paper has traced three prevalent discourses related to soccer: the Soccer War, the Nobel Prize and the Gramscian. The Soccer War discourse cautions us to the dangers of soccer's manipulation by extreme nationalists and authoritarian regimes. The Nobel Prize nomination for soccer demonstrates that soccer can contribute towards building more diverse societies, as well as promote values such as fair play and anti-racism. The Gramscian discourse highlights the way soccer is used to maintain existing power relations, but how soccer can also be a vehicle for social change.

I do not claim that soccer officials, fans, the media and states do not disseminate other discourses related to soccer. Soccer discourses can also include the use of soccer fans' discourses in daily life in order to challenge established state discourses to soccer clubs in Corsica as sites of national identity.[65] Yet, to what extent might we be able to fit these discourses under the ambit of the three main discourses highlighted in this paper?

How can we promote soccer as a positive rather than negative force around the world? It is clear that soccer is a reflection of society, both its ugliness and possibilities for change.

Contemporary soccer can increase negative tendencies in human societies: extreme nationalism, sexism, racism, anti-Semitism and hooliganism. Professional soccer includes other serious problems: a win-at-all-costs philosophy (including game-fixing rings)[66]; corruption scandals such as Qatar's 2022 World Cup bid; turning a blind eye to dictators that host World Cups (Argentina in 1978 and more recently Russia in 2018 and Qatar in 2022); and non-recognition as with the refusal of Arab and most Muslim states to play soccer competitions against Israel.

FIFA has also been accused of 'opportunistic nationalism'.[67] FIFA recognizes 209 national federations, whereas there are only 193 member states of the United Nations. FIFA receives fees for every international match, even from 'nations' that are not sovereign states such as Kosovo and Gibraltar. FIFA thus contributes to enhancing nationalistic tensions between existing states and national federations. FIFA cares little about Kosovo or Gibraltar, but is interested in the marketing potential and revenue base associated with structuring soccer along nationalistic lines. In short, Scotland vs. England, Serbia vs. Croatia, Iran vs. the United States or perhaps one day Israel vs. Palestine sells for FIFA.

Yet, soccer can also be an educational tool and a mechanism for social transformation. In response to a banana thrown on the field in a Spanish league match in 2014, Dani Alves ate the banana before taking a corner kick. The incident went viral and led to widespread support by soccer players, coaches and fans around the world. Cesare Prandelli, the former manager of the Italian national team, took a photo eating a banana and it was distributed through social media. The racist offender against Alves was banned from the stadium in Villareal for life, although Alves called for leniency on the fan and stressed the importance of education in the struggle against racism.

In general, professional soccer has been far too light on racists, anti-Semites and hooligans in stadiums, particularly in Europe. As Gavin Jones noted in relation to Italian soccer, 'Repeated promises by politicians to crack down on soccer violence have proven ineffective, often resisted by the clubs themselves as well as their organized supporters'.[68]

The former French international captain Lilian Thuram, who won the 1998 World Cup and is at the forefront of anti-racist education struggles, has suggested that we are not born with racism but rather learn it; soccer is a useful terrain for anti-racist struggle because it reaches millions of people; and soccer authorities need to ban racists from soccer stadiums.[69] I agree with Thuram. By ostracizing and shaming racists, we send a powerful message that racism will not be tolerated in the twenty-first century. Education in civil society is fundamental in fighting racism in the stadiums. It will not be easy, particularly in Europe, where anti-immigrant, extreme right-wing political parties are now mainstream and have participated in numerous coalition governments in the 1990s and 2000s.[70] In 2012, Sarah L. de Lange pointed out that radical right-wing populist parties participated in five different national governments in western Europe in the new millennium (Austria – 2000/2003, Denmark – 2001/2005/2007, Italy – 2001/2005/2008, the Netherlands – 2002, and Norway – 2001) and four different national governments in eastern Europe in the 1990s and new millennium (Estonia – 1992/1994, Poland – 2006, Romania – 1993, and Slovakia – 1992/1994/2006).[71]

To the extent that soccer is played by people of all genders, colours, nations and faiths, it is talent and merit that ultimately matter. Or, the joy or passion of the game, particularly for amateurs, as highlighted by the example of the Hackney Laces. Kuper and Szymanski are correct to point out that English soccer clubs largely abandoned their racism once they realized that black players could help teams attain success.[72]

Perhaps no player had greater talent and merit in soccer history than Pelé. Pelé's popularity in his native Brazil was so breathtaking that in 1995 Brazilian president Fernando Henrique Cardoso dubbed him 'Extraordinary Minister for Sport'. World leaders longed to be photographed with Pelé; the former Shah of Iran waited for three hours at an international airport to speak with him, and Nigeria declared a two-day truce in its war with Biafra to allow the combatants to see him play.[73]

In 2014, Pelé released his third book, *Why Soccer Matters*,[74] further cementing his role as the greatest ambassador of the game worldwide. Like his first book published in the late 1970s, *Why Soccer Matters* advances a discourse that I have called the Nobel Prize discourse. Soccer is the 'beautiful game', filled with passion, creativity and joy; it engenders unity across classes, nations, ethnic groups and religions; and it can humanize national 'enemies' through matches. In *Why Soccer Matters*, Brazil's defeat to Uruguay in the 1950 World Cup final is interpreted by Pelé in positive terms as promoting national unity through shared experiences:

> Standing around the radio, and suffering together on July 16, 1950, gave Brazilians a shared experience. For the first time, rich and poor alike had something in common, something they could discuss with anybody on the street corner, whether they were in Rio, Bauru, or deep in the Amazon.

> We take this sort of thing for granted now; but it was very important back then, in creating a common story of what it meant to be Brazilian. We weren't strangers anymore. And I don't think we ever really were again.[75]

Yet, even Pelé could be criticized within his own country as a 'traitor' when in 2013 during protests being held in Brazil during the Confederations Cup he told his compatriots to 'forget all the commotion and remember how the Brazilian squad is our country and our blood'.[76] Some things such as democracy and dissent are much more important than soccer. Yet, soccer might ironically be that mass appeal vehicle that gets the soccer community and other authorities listening to the concerns of people around the world. The debates and criticisms of Russia and Qatar hosting the 2018 and 2022 World Cups will hopefully make us more sensitive to the nature of World Cup bids, corruption, kickbacks and the lack of transparency in FIFA. If soccer is to be a force for social change, FIFA will need to be on board. In 2006, it was estimated that FIFA would have been the 19th largest economy in the world if it was a sovereign state.[77] Issues surrounding worker rights also need to be tackled by FIFA. Many foreign labourers have died in building projects for Qatar's World Cup, while forced labour has been widely reported.

We might also ask questions about whether authoritarian regimes should ultimately host World Cups. While I am in general against boycotts in sports (with the exception of the most heinous regimes such as apartheid South Africa and Nazi Germany), having such debates highlights the power of global sports and enhances democratic accountability. Yaya Touré, the Manchester City star and Ivory Coast international, suggested that black players boycott the World Cup in Russia because of the anti-black racism in Russian stadiums. I profoundly respect his position, but slightly disagree. We should attempt to ban racists from stadiums and Yaya Touré should lead the Ivory Coast to a World Cup victory. Both scenarios would silence the racists, in the stadiums at least. Thus, the slogan of the 2012 Homeless World Cup, 'One ball can change the world',[78] will become a reality.

## Disclosure statement

No potential conflict of interest was reported by the author.

## Notes

1. Bryla, 'FIFA World Cup History'.
2. FIFA.com, 'FIFA World Cup Group Stages Break New Ground in TV Viewing'.
3. Nadel, *Fútbol!: Why Soccer Matters in Latin America*, 1.
4. See Markovits and Hellerman, *Offside: Soccer and American Exceptionalism*.
5. Dionne Jr., 'Clinton Swipes the GOP's Lyrics; The Democrat as Liberal Republican'.
6. A discourse is: 'A formal discussion of a topic in speech or writing,' or 'Written or spoken communication or debate.' See Oxford Dictionaries, 'discourse'.
7. Tuathail, 'Thinking Critically About Geopolitics', 1–12.
8. In reference to the Italian Marxist thinker Antonio Gramsci (1891–1937).
9. For soccer as a pagan religion, see Villoro, *Dios es redondo*. For the relationship between soccer and tribalism, see Villoro, *Los once de la tribu*.
10. Desmond Morris, *The Soccer Tribe*.
11. Shankly, 'Own Words'.
12. For soccer as a pagan religion in Mexico, see Bar-On, 'El Tri: A Pagan Religion for All'.
13. Kapuściński, *The Soccer War*, 182.
14. Ibid. and Durham, *Scarcity and Survival in Central America: Ecological Origins of the Football War*.
15. Cuscatla, 'LA GUERRA DEL FÚTBOL 1969'.
16. The French Marxist Louis Althusser (1918–1990) made a distinction between the 'repressive state apparatus' and the 'ideological state apparatus,' both of which serve the ruling economic class. The 'repressive state apparatus' is based on violence and the logic of obey and command: the heads of state, government, police, courts and the army. The 'ideological state apparatus,' on the other hand, includes all of civil society outside the ambit of the state: the family, the media, religious organizations, the education system, culture and sporting contests. From this perspective, soccer clubs and national teams are also part of the 'ideological state apparatus.' According to Althusser, the 'repressive state apparatus' acts in favour of the ruling class through covert and overt forms of violence. The 1969 Soccer War between Honduras and El Salvador is as an example of the use of the 'repressive state apparatus.' Yet the 'repressive state apparatus,' insisted Althusser, also functions through ideology and it heavily favours dominant social classes. The 'ideological state apparatus' functions principally through a dominant ideology and the intimation of symbolic violence as it can call for the support of the 'repressive state apparatus.' Louis Althusser, 'Ideology and Ideological State Apparatuses', In *Lenin and philosophy, and other essays*, 121–176.
17. Althusser, 'Ideology and Ideological State Apparatuses'.
18. Friedman, *The Next 100 Years: A Forecast for the 21st Century*.
19. Sobek, 'Rallying Around the Podesta: Testing Diversionary Theory Across Time', 29–45.
20. Orwell, 'The Sporting Spirit'.
21. Quoted in Fisher, 'The American Spectator and Soccer's Vaudevillian Culture'.
22. ABC News, 'Game of Soccer Gets Nobel Peace Nomination'.
23. Markovits and Rensmann, *Gaming the World: How Sports are Reshaping Global Politics and Culture*.
24. Ibid., 12, 31.
25. On the French national team after it won the 1998 World Cup, see Dubois, *Soccer Empire: The World Cup and the Future of France*.
26. Annan, 'How We Envy the World Cup'.
27. Dubois, *Soccer Empire: The World Cup and the Future of France*, 169.
28. Gramsci, *Selections from the Prison Notebooks*.
29. Ibid., 367.
30. Ibid., 433.

31. Hoare and Smith, *Selections from the Prison Notebooks*, 625.
32. Bell, 'Philosophy Football'.
33. Quoted in Galeano, *Soccer in Sun and Shadow*, 34.
34. Gramsci, *Selections from the Prison Notebooks*.
35. Vinnai, *El fútbol como ideología*. The book was translated into English as *Football Mania* (1973), while the Spanish translation's title stayed true to the original German.
36. Procter, *Stuart Hall*, 2.
37. Hutchison, 'Breaking Boundaries: Football and Colonialism in the British Empire'.
38. Markovits and Rensmann, *Gaming the World: How Sports are Reshaping Global Politics and Culture*, 8.
39. Kapuściński, *The Soccer War*.
40. Ibid., 159.
41. Elsey, *Citizens and Sportsmen: Fútbol and Politics in Twentieth-Century*, 242–3.
42. Del Burgo, 'Don't Stop the Carnival: Football in the Societies of Latin America', 69.
43. Ibid.
44. Bar-On, *The World through Soccer: The Cultural Impact of a Global Sport*, particularly Chapter 4 entitled 'One Ball Can Change the World', 61–82.
45. Dorsey, 'Emboldened Fans Rewrite the Politics of Egyptian Soccer'.
46. Ibid.
47. Elsey, *Citizens and Sportsmen: Fútbol and Politics in Twentieth-Century*.
48. Hackney Laces, 'About'.
49. Hackney Laces, 'Manifesto'.
50. Bar-On, *The World Through Soccer: The Cultural Impact of a Global Sport*, in particular Chapter 3 entitled 'Winning Hearts and Minds: Soccer, Ideological Hegemony, and Class Warfare', 39–59.
51. On possibilities for social change, see Bar-On, *The World Through Soccer: The Cultural Impact of a Global Sport*, 61–82.
52. Julie Foudy Sports Leadership Academy.
53. Nexdim Empire, 'Samuel Eto's's Letter to Roger Milla'.
54. By soft power, Joseph S. Nye means neither the use of money, nor force to achieve state foreign policy goals. Nye, *Soft Power: The Means to Success in World Politics*.
55. Galeano, *Soccer in Sun and Shadow*, 45.
56. Ibid.
57. Nadel, *Fútbol!: Why Soccer Matters in Latin America*, 153.
58. Ibid., 155–6.
59. Kohn, *The Idea of Nationalism: A Study in its Origins and Background*.
60. Ibid., 574.
61. Ibid.
62. Markovits and Rensmann, *Gaming the World: How Sports are Reshaping Global Politics and Culture*, 2.
63. Sorek, 'Arab Football in Israel as an "Integrative Enclave"', 431; and Sorek, *Arab Soccer in a Jewish State: The Integrative Enclave*.
64. Markovits and Rensmann, *Gaming the World: How Sports are Reshaping Global Politics and Culture*, 3.
65. Levin, 'Soccer Discourses and the Daily Life of Adolescents in a Small Israeli Town', 83–96; and Győri Szabó, 'Identity and Soccer in Corsica', 36–55.
66. See, for example, Hill, *Juego sucio: Fútbol y crimen organizado*.
67. Gameros, 'Las goles de la FIFA', 127.
68. Jones, 'Italy Arrests Man Over Cup Final Shootings, Bemoans Football Violence'.
69. See Lilian Thuram's *Fondation*, http://www.thuram.org/.
70. Bar-On, *Rethinking the French New Right: Alternatives to Modernity*, 8–9.
71. De Lange, 'Radical Right-Wing Parties in Office', in *Right-Wing Extremism in Europe: Current Trends and Perspectives*, 173, 192.
72. Kuper and Szymanski, *Soccernomics*, 95–110.
73. Pelé (with Fish), *My Life and the Beautiful Game: The Autobiography of Pelé*, 12.
74. Pelé (with Winter), *Why Soccer Matters*.
75. Ibid.
76. Rainbow, 'Pele Defends Himself after Being Branded "Traitor of the Century"'.

77. Bar-On, *The World through Soccer: The Cultural Impact of a Global Sport*, 127–8. Also see Gameros, 'Las goles de la FIFA', 126.
78. Bar-On, *The World through Soccer: The Cultural Impact of a Global Sport*, 61–82.

## References

ABC News. 'Game of Soccer Gets Nobel Peace Nomination'. January 23, 2001. http://abc news.go.com/International/story?id=81640 (accessed August 18, 2014).

Aderet, Ofer. 'WATCH: Hungarian Soccer Fans Disrupt Israeli Anthem with Anti-Semitic Slurs'. *Haaretz.Com*, August 19, 2012. http://www.haaretz.com/jewish-world/jewish-world-news/watchhungarian-%20soccer-fans-disrupt-israeli-anthem-with-anti-semitic-slurs-1.459251 (accessed October 27, 2012).

Althusser, Louis. *Lenin and Philosophy, and Other Essays*. New York: Monthly Review Press, 1971.

Annan, Kofi A. 'How We Envy the World Cup'. *United Nations*, June 2006. http://www.un.org/sport2005/newsroom/worldcup.pdf (accessed July 15, 2013).

Bar-On, Tamir. 'El Tri: A Pagan Religion for All'. *Monkey Cage: The Washington Post*, June 4, 2014. http://www.washingtonpost.com/blogs/monkey-cage/wp/2014/06/04/el-tri-a-pagan-religion-for-all/ (accessed August 18, 2014).

Bar-On, Tamir. *Rethinking the French New Right: Alternatives to Modernity*. Abingdon: Routledge, 2013.

Bar-On, Tamir. *The World through Soccer: The Cultural Impact of a Global Sport*. Lanham, MD: Rowman and Littlefield, 2014.

Bell, Jack. 'Philosophy Football'. *The New York times Soccer Blog*, April 30, 2010. http://goal.blogs.nytimes.com/2010/04/30/philosophy-football/?_php=true&_type=blogs&_r=0 (accessed September 20, 2013).

Bryla, Mac. 'FIFA World Cup History'. *Eye See Data*, December 3, 2013. http://eyesee data.com/fifa-world-cup-history/.

Caparrós, Martin, and Juan Villoro. *Ida Y Vuelta: Una Correspondencia Sobre Fútbol*. 1st ed. México, D.F.: Seix Barral, 2012.

Cuscatla. 'LA GUERRA DEL FÚTBOL 1969'. *Cuscatla.Com*, n.d. http://www.cuscatla.com/la_guerra.htm (accessed August 21, 2014).

De Lange, Sarah L. 'Radical Right-Wing Parties in Office'. In *Right-Wing Extremism in Europe: Current Trends and Perspectives*, eds. Uwe Backes and Patrick Moreau, 171–94. Göttingen: Vandenhoeck and Ruprecht, 2012.

Del Burgo, Maurice Biriotti 'Don't Stop the Carnival: Football in the Societies of Latin America'. In *Giving the Game Away: Football, Politics, and Culture on Five Continents*, ed. Stephen Wagg. London: Leicester University Press, 1995.

Dionne, E.J. 'Clinton Swipes the GOP's Lyrics; The Democrat as Liberal Republican'. *The Washington Post*, July 21, 1996.

Dorsey, James. 'Emboldened Fans Rewrite the Politics of Egyptian Soccer'. *The Turbulent World of Middle East Soccer Blog*, March 6, 2011. http://mideastsoccer.blogspot.mx/2011/03/emboldened-fans-rewrite-politics-of.html (accessed May 11, 2014).

Dubois, Laurent. *Soccer Empire: The World Cup and the Future of France*. Berkeley: University of California Press, 2010.

Durham, William H. *Scarcity and Survival in Central America: Ecological Origins of the Football War*. Stanford: Stanford University Press, 1979.

Eagleton, Terry. 'Football: A Dear Friend to Capitalism'. *The Guardian*, June 15, 2010. http://www.guardian.co.uk/commentisfree/2010/jun/15/football-socialism-crack-cocaine-people (accessed September 2, 2012).

Elsey, Brenda. *Citizens and Sportsmen Fútbol and Politics in Twentieth-Century Chile*. Austin: University of Texas Press, 2011.

FIFA.com. 'FIFA World Cup Group Stages Break New Ground in TV Viewing'. *FIFA*, June 28, 2014. http://www.fifa.com/worldcup/news/y=2014/m=6/news=fifa-world-cuptm-group-stages-break-new-ground-in-tv-viewing-2388418.html (accessed August 18, 2014).

Fisher, U.J. 'The American Spectator and Soccer's Vaudevillian Culture'. *Swol*, April 18, 2014. http://swol.co/the-american-spectator-and-soccers-vaudevillian-culture/33982 (accessed August 15, 2014).

Fondation Lilian Thuram. 'Fondation Lilian Thuram – Education contre le racisme'. n.d. http://www.thuram.org/ (accessed August 21, 2014).

Friedman, George. *The Next 100 Years: A Forecast for the 21st Century*. New York: Anchor Books, 2010.

Galeano, Eduardo. *Soccer in Sun and Shadow*. Trans. Mark Fried. London: Verso, 2003.

Gameros, Manuel. 'Los goles de la FIFA' [The goals of FIFA]. *Foreign Affairs En Español* 6, no. 3 (Julio–Septiembre 2006): 121–31.

Goldblatt, David. *The Ball is round: A Global History of Soccer*. London: Viking, 2006.

Goldblatt, David. *Brazil: The Curious Rise of the Futebol Nation*. New York: Nation Books, 2014.

Gramsci, Antonio. *Selections from the Prison Notebooks*. Ed. and trans. Quentin Hoare and Geoffrey Nowell Smith. London: Lawrence and Wishart, 1971.

Hackney, Laces. 'Our Manifesto'. *Hackney Laces*, n.d. http://www.hackneylaces.co.uk/?p= 919 (accessed May 11, 2014).

Hill, Declan. *Juego sucio: fútbol y crimen organizado* [Dirty game: Soccer and organized crime]. Trans. Concha Cardeñoso Sáenz de Miera and Francisco López Martín. Barcelona: Alba, 2010.

Hutchison, Patrick. 'Breaking Boundaries: Football and Colonialism in the British Empire'. *Student Pulse* 1, no. 11 (2009). http://www.studentpulse.com/articles/64/breaking-bound aries-football-and-colonialism-in-the-british-empire (accessed July 26, 2013).

Jones, Gavin. 'Italy Arrests Man over Cup Final Shootings, Bemoans Football Violence'. *Reuters*, May 4, 2014. http://uk.reuters.com/article/2014/05/04/uk-soccer-italy-cup-vio lence-idUKKBN0DK0G920140504 (accessed May 11, 2014).

July Foudy Sports Leadership Academy. n.d. http://www.juliefoudyleadership.com/ (accessed October 4, 2012).

Kapuściński, Ryszard. *The Soccer War*. Trans. William Brand. London: Granta, 1990.

Kohn, Hans. *The Idea of Nationalism: A Study in Its Origins and Backgrounds*. New Brunswick, NJ: Transaction Publishers, 1998.

Krauze, León. 'México y Estados Unidos: identidad y fútbol' [Mexico and the United States: identity and soccer]. *Foreign Affairs En Español* 6, no. 3 (Julio–Septiembre 2006): 147–51.

Kuper, Simon, and Stefan Szymanski. *Soccernomics: Why England Loses, Why Germany and Brazil Win, and Why the U.S., Japan, Australia, Turkey and Even Iraq Are Destined to Become the Kings of the World's Most Popular Sport*. New York: Nation Books, 2014.

Levin, David. 'Soccer Discourse and the Daily Life of Adolescents in a Small Israeli Town'. *Soccer and Society* 13, no. 1 (2012): 83–96.

Markovits, Andrei S., and Steven L. Hellerman. *Offside: Soccer and American Exceptional-ism*. Princeton, NJ: Princeton University Press, 2001.

Markovits, Andrei S., and Lars Rensmann. *Gaming the World: How Sports Are Reshaping Global Politics and Culture*. Princeton: Princeton University Press, 2010.

Morris, Desmond. *The Soccer Tribe*. London: Cape, 1981.

Nadel, Joshua H. *Fútbol!: Why Soccer Matters in Latin America*. Gainesville: University Press of Florida, 2014.

Nexdim Empire. 'Samuel Eto's's Letter to Roger Milla'. June 1, 2010. http://nexdimem pire.com/samuel-etoos-letter-to-roger-milla.html/ (accessed November 9, 2013).

Nye Jr., Joseph S. *Soft Power: The Means to Success in World Politics*. New York: Public Affairs, 2004.

Orwell, George. 'The Sporting Spirit'. *Tribune*, December 1945. http://orwell.ru/library/arti cles/spirit/english/e_spirit (accessed July 22, 2013).

Oxford Dictionaries. 'Discourse'. http://www.oxforddictionaries.com/definition/english/dis course (accessed August 15, 2014).

Pelé (with Brian Winter). *Why Soccer Matters*. New York: Celebra, 2014.

Pelé (with Fish, R.L.). *My Life and the Beautiful Game: The Autobiography of Pelé*. Garden City, NY: Doubleday, 1977.

Procter, James. *Stuart Hall*. London: Routledge, 2004.

Rainbow, Jamie. 'Pele Defends Himself after Being Branded "Traitor of the Century"'. *World Soccer*, March 17, 2014. http://www.worldsoccer.com/world-cup-3/pele (accessed May 11, 2014).

Shankly, Bill. 'Own Words'. *Bill Shankly – This Website is a Part of LFCHistory.Net*, n.d. http://www.shankly.com/article/2517 (accessed May 21, 2014).

Sobek, David. 'Rallying around the Podesta: Testing Diversionary Theory across Time'. *Journal of Peace Research* 44, no. 1 (2007): 29–45.

Sorek, Tamir. 'Arab Football in Israel as an "Integrative Enclave"'. *Ethnic and Racial Studies* 26, no. 3 (May 2003): 422–50.

Sorek, Tamir. *Arab Soccer in a Jewish State: The Integrative Enclave*. Cambridge: Cambridge University Press, 2007.

Szabó, Róbert Győri. 'Identity and Soccer in Corsica'. *Soccer and Society* 13, no. 1 (January 2012): 36–55.

Tuathail, Gearóid Ó. 'Thinking Critically about Geopolitics'. In *The Geopolitics Reader*, eds. Gearóid Ó Tuathail, Simon Dalby, and Paul Routledge, 1–12. London: Taylor and Francis, 2003.

Villoro, Juan. *Dios es redondo* [God is round]. México D.F.: Editorial Planeta Mexicana, 2006.

Villoro, Juan. *Los once de la tribu* [Eleven of the tribe]. México D.F.: Punto de Lectura, 2005.

Vinnai, Gerhard. *El fútbol como ideología* [Soccer as ideology]. México D.F.: Siglo XXI, 2003.

Zirin, David. 'Boycott Sochi?'. *Grantland*, August 1, 2013. http://grantland.com/features/gay-rights-sochi-boycott-movement/Do (accessed May 11, 2014).

# Civic integration or ethnic segregation? Models of ethnic and civic nationalism in club football/soccer

Glen M.E. Duerr

This essay evaluates the ways that soccer has been used by various actors in the promotion of both ethnic and civic forms of nationalism throughout the world. By focusing on domestic soccer, this paper further investigates the phenomenon of nationalism in the world and provides broader theoretical and practical answers to the questions of integration and ethnic identity. This essay starts by examining the issue of ethnicity in historic and contemporary football, provides a review of the academic literature on ethnic and civic nationalism and then discusses the role of ethnic and civic models of identity within club football. Most notable is a discussion of five categories, which best explain why ethnic nationalism persists, and why it was initially mobilized. The essay then moves to a discussion of why most soccer clubs in the world have made the transition to a more civic form of nationalism. Finally, conclusions are drawn on the issue of ethnic nationalism in domestic football.

## Introduction

Even a cursory survey of the Barclays Premier League (BPL), La Liga, Serie A or the Bundesliga reveals among every team in these divisions, a virtual United Nations of players coming from all over the globe. Heterogeneity on the soccer field has become ubiquitous, especially in the top leagues around the world, but virtually every league, regardless of the country, has been touched by globalization and the need to find the best players whatever their nation or state of origin. It is very common, for example, to see Brazilians playing professionally everywhere in the world. But it has become equally common to see American players plying their trade in Europe, Africa and Asia. The sight of a foreign coach is a normal occurrence everywhere around the world and is not a rarity, as was the case a couple of decades ago even in the BPL.

Yet, despite these changes, there are several clubs across the world that have ignored these changes and have chosen to retain a strong connection to an ethnic identity. The question being addressed in this essay is why? Why has an ethnic form of nationalism persisted in club football/soccer in various different contexts around the world?

The question is a large one that can look dramatically different based on different national and political contexts, but is one that seeks to examine – with the goal of decreasing – discrimination based on racial and ethnic a priori characteristics that any one person may possess. Since association football has become so popular around the world, the sport itself can be used as a tool to impact lives – in either positive or negative ways. On the issue of race and ethnicity, what happens on the soccer field, as is alluded to in this essay, often precedes changes in the political realm. For instance, in order for a person to accept someone of a different racial or ethnic background in his/her neighbourhood, it helps to see a player of that same racial or ethnic background playing for his/her local football club. This does not hold true in all circumstances because there are obvious exceptions on virtually every continent, but this type of interaction can establish better relationships between people of different ethnic and racial backgrounds.

The linkages between football/soccer and various forms of nationalism have long been overt. As nationalism scholar Eric Hobsbawm, once famously noted, 'the imagined community of millions seems more real as a team of eleven named players. The individual, even the one who only cheers, becomes a symbol of his nation himself'.[1] Of course, Hobsbawm borrows the term 'imagined community' from another scholar of nationalism, Benedict Anderson, who uses the term as a way of describing the connections between people who live in a given country, but yet will never meet each other.[2] For example, for a person living in the United States, will she ever meet all of the 318 million other Americans living in the country? The answer is rhetorical because it is impossible for one person to meet over 300 million other people. So, in being an American, Anderson argues, there is a sense of national envisioning and a sense of national imagining that takes place.

A national entity owes a lot to its sporting heroes who represent the country on the global stage, and help in instil feelings of belonging, pride and patriotism. If the question was asked as the following: When does one feel American? Or French? Or Cameroonian? Or Polish? Or Japanese? The answer to the question is often on national holidays, with the celebration of a monarch, in listening to the national anthem, watching a military parade or, invariably, watching a sporting event. Since soccer is so popular in many parts of the world, the sport becomes a mobilizer of national feelings itself. The sport itself is merely a tool, it is agnostic, but can be manipulated for a variety of causes.

To cite one example, the very first international match played between England and Scotland in 1872 still has a political impact in the contemporary nationalist debate in the United Kingdom.[3] Since both entities belong to the same country, the distinction between the English and the Scottish is often highlighted at events like football matches wherein the two subnational entities are treated as different. So the sport of soccer has impacted the issue of nationality, in various ways, for over 140 years.

This article specifically examines the role of club football on the issue of race/ ethnicity. From an examination of numerous ethnic nationalist 'mini-cases', five distinct categories emerge with an explanation as to why an ethnic form of nationalism persists as the club level. This article starts with an examination of the ethnic–civic nationalism dichotomy (defined in the next section) and then moves on to a more detailed description of the ethnic nationalist interplay through football.

The research is based largely on a mix of primary and secondary sources, in addition to archival resources, but also on field research playing, watching and studying the sport in a range of different countries. The thinking behind the research has been supplemented by years of playing and watching football in Europe, North and Central America, and Asia. Previous informal field research has impacted the discussions of Chivas USA, Chivas Guadalajara, Rangers/Celtic and Athletic Bilbao, especially.

The motivation behind this section of the essay is twofold. First, it is designed to be an academic compliment to a documentary aired on HBO (a TV station in the USA), which investigated allegations of racism on the part of former Chivas USA players who claimed discrimination by the club. In the documentary, MLS journeyman, James Riley, who is of mixed African-American and Korean ancestry, argues that he was discriminated against by the club and was traded because he is not Mexican or Mexican-American.[4] The second motivation comes from an article on the website of ABC Univision written in the aftermath of the documentary, which examines the issue of race and ethnicity in club football. Most of the teams discussed in the club football section of the paper are drawn from this article.[5]

## Competing models of ethnic and civic nationalism

Nationalism, according to numerous scholars, is a modern phenomenon.[6] That is, the concept of nationalism and the idea that human beings organize themselves in separate states are relatively new. Several states have long histories, but, for most countries, this concept of nationalism is a fairly recent notion from the last few centuries. This is helpful to the discussion because it provides an underpinning of how human beings group themselves, and who belongs in these groups. Other scholars disagree,[7] arguing that nationalism is ancient, but if the argument is followed that nationalism is a modern phenomenon, soccer can be thought of as a tool that can affect how different countries approach the issue of nationalism. The subject of nationalism can be taken as a binary – between ethnic and civic forms. French scholar Ernest Renan was the first to make this distinction arguing that, in the aftermath of the Franco-Prussian War (1870–1871), a civic and inclusive French nationalism stood in stark contrast to the ethnic Prussian/German exclusive nationalism (ethnic).[8] The definitions of ethnic and civic nationalism have changed over time, but civic nationalism has become much more prominent since the rise of globalization with its related component part – migration – increasing around the world, wherein people move for work, asylum, or to seek a better/different life. Virtually every country in the world has thousands of people residing within its borders who are non-citizens, or new citizens, which makes this subject very important.

Ethnic nationalism is based on an allegiance to a homogenous nation that represents the political unit of the state. It is 'an individual's deepest attachments are inherited, not chosen'.[9] In essence, in order to be recognized as a member of the state, a person must have a given ethnic background that is often defined in tandem with linguistic and/or religious unity. There are many examples of ethnic nationalism. Perhaps the most prominent is Nazi Germany in the 1930s and 1940s wherein membership in the German state was based on being defined within the German 'volk'. Many people who did not fit within the model of an ethnic German were removed from the state or discriminated against – often through violent and destructive means. Ethnic nationalism does not necessarily have to be this violent, but membership within a state is limited to people with specific ethnic characteristics and is not open to those who do not possess said ethnic characteristics.

Civic nationalism is a very different approach. In essence, civic nationalism is more inclusive wherein ethnicity plays a very little role in the identification of the state. Citizenship is what matters to national belonging.[10] Anyone can join the nation (and the state), which is not closed based on ethnicity, language or heritage. Civic nationalism is held together by legal tradition, and by a given person obtaining a particular set of values in the state.[11] There are many examples of civic national-ism today. Although the United States is far from a perfect model, membership in the country is based on citizenship, which can be obtained by anyone regardless of ethnic or religious characteristics.

There is, however, a significant debate on the applicability and/or viability of civic nationalism as a useable academic model.[12] Nicholas Xenos argues that civic nationalism is, by its very nature, an oxymoron. Nationalism, it is argued, is an oxy-moron because, by its very definition, it requires a component of ethnicity.[13] Like-wise, Bernard Yack argues that the very conceptualization of civic nationalism is based on liberal scholarship from the developed world and implicitly does not have universal applicability.[14] Ethnic nationalism is longstanding, however, because the concept of the ethnic group is much more of an important factor around the world. Furthermore, as Daniel Weinstock argues, there is a level of instability inherent within civic nationalism. He notes that after periods of instability, the tendency is to revert back to ethnic nationalism – in essence, civic nationalism will only ever be short-lived, at best.[15] Finally, Kai Nielsen argues that nationalism is actually cultural, and not subject to a dichotomy of ethnic or civic types.[16] Nielsen argues, using the case of Quebec in Canada, that it is actually the culture of Quebec that perpetuates nationalism and not an ethnic or civic base. Obviously, this is contested and, some argue, is simply a cover for ethnic nationalism.[17]

With any dichotomy, there are problems with categorization especially if the model is applied globally. Nonetheless, there are basic means of categorization when investigating whether or not people from ethnic minority backgrounds are accepted within a given state. The dichotomy may have cultural biases, but evidence can be collected on the way that people and governments treat minority populations.

As it relates to domestic, club-level football, civic and ethnic forms of national-ism provide a vital distinction in how newcomers or minorities are treated in any society. In this article, football serves as a bridge to society. Where fans accept and include people from different backgrounds, this facilitates the political process of welcoming new people – assuming legality – into the country. If newcomers and minorities are welcomed, the process can be very good; if not, the process can not only lead to xenophobia and discrimination, but also violence targeting minority groups.[18]

## Why does ethnic nationalism persist?

An important question was posed at the outset of this article: why has an ethnic form of nationalism persisted in club football/soccer in various different contexts around the world? The interplay between globalization and tribalism is a strong answer to the question, but it does not provide a holistic answer. On the one hand, the forces of globalization are shrinking the world, while, on the other hand, many people have a desire to protect their native language and culture in the face of increased homogeneity.[19] Similarly, globalization has created 'winners' and 'losers' through economic competition. Where one ethnic group is perceived to have gained in the era of globalization, sometimes ethnic hostilities arise.[20] Paradoxically, global-ization and tribalism have both become stronger forces in the world in the twenty-first century. This is evident to some degree on the soccer field, albeit that globalization is certainly more powerful.

This subject is too broad to simply examine every club around the world that retains a level of ethnic distinction. There are dozens of teams still in existence, but fewer and fewer clubs have chosen to retain this level of homogeneity, especially in a globalized era wherein their opponents will attract better players from all over the world. The economic reality is that in order for a team to be successful, a team should select the best players from anywhere in the world, regardless of national origin. Only in rare cases have teams successfully retained a homogenous profile and stayed within the top level of their domestic league.

In answering the question, five major categories have been created to show where and how various clubs around the world maintain an ethnic form of nationalist identity. Each category provides at least one example, but there are several more in many of these categories – an exhaustive study is simply not feasible in an article. These groups are not exclusive. Sometimes a given club might fit into two (or more) of these categories, but they have been assigned to the category that fits most closely with the motivations and ambitions of the category.

### Category 1: military connection

In specific parts of the world, many football clubs have an explicit connection with the military forces of the country. Most notably, 'Nacional' clubs in Latin America have this tie to their home military. On other occasions, the Nacional name is used to denote that the team was founded by people from the home country rather than by British people or other foreigners, but, in many cases, the tie between the club and the military. Major Nacional clubs exist in Ecuador, Mexico, Brazil, Colombia and Uruguay.[21] There is a major connection then with ethnic nationalist policies. For example, in Ecuador, Nacional is known as 'puros curollos' – the pure natives. Obviously, given the nature of colonialism in Latin America, and the intermarriage of people from many different countries, it is very hard to make the claim that anyone is of a 'pure' background. But, nonetheless, it has been mobilized by supporters of the team.

In some countries around the world, the military may also own soccer clubs depending on the situation. In Egypt, for example, 'about half of the Egyptian Premier League's 16 teams are owned by the military, the police, government ministries or provincial authorities'.[22] If a country is heterogeneous, then a team owned by the military could be based on civic nationalism. It is best analysed on a case-by-case basis, but it depends on the complex web of how citizenship is defined in different countries throughout the world.

Ethnic nationalism may persist then through soccer teams connected to the military. There is an important purpose here, in presenting a defence of the national state. The question is whether this support is based on ethnicity. This example is a double-edged sword because a military provides defence to a territory and a people, but, if citizenship is based on ethnicity (rather than a constitution), then it can lead to xenophobia, exclusionism, discrimination and possibly violence.

To build on the earlier example, Club Deportivo El Nacional, a team from Ecuador, is partly owned by the Ecuadorian air force. Historically, the team only used to play members of the air force. This policy changed, but the club strictly plays players from Ecuador.[23] This mini-case provides a slightly different light to the ethnic–civic debate. In some ways, national security necessitates homogenous hiring practices. Since there is only a historical link to the air force, the club could easily change, but there is still an overt tie to the military in Ecuador. Any change would be difficult because the culture and history of the club cling to the protection of Ecuador by its armed forces. El Nacional's team is a reinforcement of ethnic nationalism, but the caveat is that this policy is tied to the historic connection with Ecuador's military.

## Category 2: selling ethnic nationalism

The second category includes clubs that try to market towards ethnic nationalism. For example, Chivas USA of MLS at times tried to rally Mexican-American fans to the cause of the team by selecting players primarily from Hispanic backgrounds. (There were many periods of time when Chivas USA had players from various types of ethnic backgrounds, but the team has been accused of seeking to promote Hispanic players over others.)[24] The incentive here in this category is to 'sell' the team as something more narrow, in contrast to the rest of the teams in the league that have brought in players from different countries to improve their chances of victory. A team will take a business approach to ethnic nationalism by trying to gain financially on the basis of doing the opposite of the rest of the teams. There may well be a core ideology behind the team that it committed to an ethnic group, but the question, then, is why is a soccer team used to promote the idea rather than a political or social organization?

The most recent example of potential ethnic segregation has been the case of Chivas USA, or at least via allegations recently ascribed at the team. Surveying the roster since the team's founding in 2005, Chivas USA has been made up of players from many different ethnic backgrounds.[25] The allegations by some players including MLS veteran, James Riley, point to discrimination against non-Mexican heritage players. Recently, HBO's Real Sports investigation examined these allegations. The results are, at this point, inconclusive, but several former Chivas USA players continue to argue that they were discriminated against by the club. The team has always had a roster of people of different ethnic and national groups, but there was a short period of time in 2011 and 2012 that can be debated as to the civic inclusiveness of the club.

Club Deportivo (Chivas) Guadalajara is the 'parent' club of Chivas USA and is also known for largely playing and selecting only Mexican players. Occasionally, Mexican-American players have played for Chivas Guadalajara, but the club was set-up to play only Mexican players. This is a more obvious case of ethnic nationalism in that there is exclusivity in the club that does not allow for a more civic sense of openness. All of Chivas' players are Mexican, and this policy has been a long-standing tradition with the club – it is an obvious case of the ethnic segregation model.

## Category 3: sectarianism

Sectarianism essentially means that there is some form of religious-based divide in a society. Ethnicity usually plays a major role in the sectarian divide as the lines between the two terms often overlap. Therefore, sectarian-based teams typically exist in deeply divided societies. Competing forms of identity in the society play against each other and are mobilized through soccer. Teams in Scotland, Northern Ireland, Israel and Lebanon all fit into this category, as do many others from similar type societies elsewhere in the world.

A useful place to start when discussing ethnicity and segregation is in Glasgow. The sectarian divide in Scottish football – between Rangers and Celtic in Glasgow, but also between Hearts and Hibernian in Edinburgh – was along Protestant and Roman Catholic lines.[26] This rivalry speaks to the issue of ethnic and religious identity versus another group. It has a financial component as well in that, it is argued, the rivalry was kept alive by club owners in order to make a profit.[27] In recent years, the sectarian divide has decreased quite dramatically in Glasgow. Both teams now sign players from a range of different backgrounds, and the sectarian issue is no longer a major point of distinction between the players (although it is still a major point of distinction between fans). There is still a sectarian component to this rivalry, but the ethnic nationalist distinctions have decreased in recent decades.

Another example comes from Israel. One of the most prominent clubs in the country, Beitar Jerusalem, has never played an Arab player.[28] Periodically, some Muslim players have played for Beitar Jerusalem, but it is rare. For example, two players of Chechen origin were signed as well as a Nigerian Muslim, but all of these players did not stay on the team for a long period of time.[29] This issue, in part, is due to the highly political nature of ethnicity in Israel between Israelis and Palestinians. In particular, this team values Jewish symbols – the Menorah is on the team's crest – such that it tries to promote a predominantly Jewish identity within the club.[30] There are a range of opinions of how to manage – and solve – the Israeli/Palestinian issue, one of which is to retain a level of ethnic segregation between the two communities. In conclusion, then, the exclusivity of Beitar Jerusalem is discriminatory against Arabs, but not based solely on ethnic nationalism.

After all, the current Beitar Jerusalem team is made up of the allowed five foreigners in the Israeli league. Beitar's five foreigners are from South America and Europe.[31] The issue of nationalism as it relates to Beitar should be taken in context of civic nationalism – in that it includes people from different parts of the world – but also ethnic nationalism – in that it excludes people from certain groups. (The caveat here is that a player has to be good enough to play for a team and fit well in the playing style and formation.)

## Category 4: the protection of an ethnic minority

In many heterogeneous societies across the world, the issue of minority rights remains highly important. In some areas, there is a desire to mobilize a minority and to protect a small group. The use of a soccer team can assist in the process of maintaining the distinctness of a given ethnic group.

There are some examples throughout the world, but the most prominent is Athletic Bilbao.[32] The policy of ethnic separation has been in place at Athletic Bilbao since the club's founding in 1919.[33] Perhaps most notably, players from the club signed up to fight in the Spanish Civil War (1936–1939) against the coming fascist regime of Francisco Franco (who ruled Spain until his death in 1975).

Athletic Bilbao, paradoxically, has been by some metrics, successful in their use of ethnic kin. The team is one of three (the other two are Real Madrid and FC Barcelona) to never have been relegated from La Liga. The team won the championship on eight occasions, most recently in 1983–1984. And, the team made the final of the UEFA Cup in 2012 only to lose to Atletico Madrid.

Interestingly, the team accepts any Basque player, which, given the boundaries of the ethnic group, includes people in the north of Spain as well as a small section of the south of France. So, while the idea of protecting an ethnic minority fits into a broad definition of ethnic nationalism, some of the lines are sufficiently blurred to make categorization difficult.

The Basque region has significant cultural differences from Spain; in fact, Spain's 1978 Constitution recognizes the Basque region as one of three special communities within the country. Even the name of the team, Athletic, is in English and not in Spanish, which speaks to the idea of maintaining a specific cultural identity.[34] Under former dictator, Francisco Franco, the name of the club was a major political issue; in fact, under Franco, it was changed to Atletico Bilbao in line with the requirements of his intentions to create a country centred on a Castilian Spanish identity.[35]

Since 1919, Athletic Bilbao's Board of Directors has upheld a strict policy of playing Basque players only.[36] These players can come from both France and Spain, but all must be of Basque ethnicity.[37] As a result of this longstanding policy, Athletic Bilbao has retained a policy of ethnic nationalism as it relates to supporting players of Basque ethnicity only. The Basques are a small minority in Spain and have been discriminated against historically. The question, however, is whether it is acceptable for the team to promote a policy of ethnic segregation in order to promote the ethnic minority?

## Category 5: building the youth system

For many countries around the world, it is difficult to compete with the entrenched favourites in the world's game. Large, experienced countries such as Brazil, Germany and Italy have distinct advantages, statistically, when it comes to winning soccer games.[38] The question, then, is how do smaller countries compete? There are a range of different answers such as playing against regular high-level competition,[39] or creating very strong youth teams that will hopefully develop into strong national and club teams.

Deportivo Saprissa is one of Costa Rica's best teams. Founded in 1935, the team used to hire only Costa Rican players. This practice changed long ago, but its historic practice of only hiring Costa Rican players was a longstanding part of the tradition of the team. (Even in the 1950s, the team signed Brazilian and Argentinian players to the roster.) The major reason for this was to build the team's youth academy. Since Costa Rican players made up the academy, it was more natural that the first team was eventually filled by Costa Rican players who moved through the youth system. However, especially in recent years, this policy has changed somewhat as the current roster of players is drawn from several different countries.[40] For a period of time in the 2000s, Saprissa was even owned by Mexican businessman, Jorge Vergara (who also happens to own Chivas Guadalajara and was the operator-investor of the Chivas USA MLS franchise), so there has been a natural shift away from its roots of hiring only Costa Rican players. Today, Deportivo Saprissa has adopted a more civic form of national identity in its team selection with more players drawn from other countries. Nonetheless, the category of maintaining ethnic nationalism as a means of building a particular brand of football has utility in that it explains why some clubs have historically resisted the movements towards a more open sense of identity for the team.

## What does this mean for club football?

As noted at the outset of the article, the top clubs from the top leagues around the world have players from all over the world. This is not to say that the world of football is completely open and inclusive to people of all ethnic backgrounds, but that most owners and teams want the best players to play for them. This has, especially in the last twenty years with the proliferation of globalization, led to much greater ethnic and racial diversity on the football pitch.

Depending on the soccer fan, support for one's club can be as important – if not more important – than support for one's national team. For the vast majority of teams around the world, fans accept – and support – almost any player that wears the club shirt. This has not always been the case, but recent years have borne testament to the changing international norm on players who come from all corners of the globe. Owners generally want to win more matches in order to make more money, and so, logically, will look to sign the best available players regardless of ethnic or racial background. Fans might not necessarily accept said player; in fact, there are many cases where players of different ethnic backgrounds may be taunted by their own fans for racial reasons. This is where the models of civic integration or ethnic segregation come into play.

As private businesses, each team has a right to decide which players to hire, and which players not to hire (although this is subject to national laws). The international norm of non-discrimination should be followed, but the prerogative remains with the business owner on who can participate for the team. There is, however, a risk in choosing not to sign an excellent player who can help a team win matches, if he is not from a particular ethnic group. Clubs may choose the model of ethnic segregation, but it does not make financial sense, and this choice does oppose the international norm of non-discrimination.

There are a small minority of teams around the world that will only accept players from a particular background. This distinction is not necessarily ethnic, it may well be tied to a particular identity in which any person can belong provided that one parent has the a priori, blood relationship to the ethnic nation. So, the policy might not necessarily be racist, it may have political motivations. The policy might still be discriminatory, though.

Table 1. Select cases of ethnic nationalism.

| Team | Ethnic nationalism? | Category |
| --- | --- | --- |
| Celtic | Decreased since the 1990s | Sectarianism |
| Rangers | Decreased since the 1990s | Sectarianism |
| Deportivo Saprissa | Up until the 1950s | Build up the youth academy |
| El Nacional | Yes | Military connection |
| Beitar Jerusalem | Selective ethnic/religious | Sectarianism |
| Athletic Bilbao | Yes | Protect minority group |
| Chivas Guadalajara | Yes | Business |
| Chivas USA | Limited, but it depends on the time | Business |

Table 1 selects eight clubs that have historical ties to ethnic-based separation. This model is more closely aligned with ethnic exclusivity. Three of the clubs definitely uphold the ethnic nationalism model. However, some of these clubs have definitely transitioned to become much more open with a model of civic integration. The evidence is more difficult for some clubs like Chivas USA, and perhaps Celtic and Rangers, but even some of the most exclusive clubs have become more open and have opted for a policy of civic integration. The lines are certainly blurred even for clubs that profess to stick to a certain ethnic rigidity in their team selection.

What is also worth considering is that these are selective teams, which shows that, at least in club football, the norm of civic openness has become quite ubiquitous. These cases were selected specifically for examination because of their historic policies of ethnic segregation. By its absence, it also shows that the vast majority of major clubs around the world have a policy of civic integration – in line with the international norm.

## Transitioning away from ethnic nationalism

In more recent years, many teams around the world have transitioned away from ethnic nationalism. The reasons for this change are numerous. First, football is a business. There is a pragmatic side to the sport, which, in most circumstances, is to make money. Better players on the field typically lead to a better product, as well as a winning team. If better players can be found overseas, or in neighbouring countries, there is an incentive to buy (or trade for) foreign players. Second, in an era of globalization, when virtually any form of good can be bought or sold, the world has seemingly shrunk. With greater contact with other people comes a greater tendency to interact, and to view others differently – typically with greater understanding. Third, norms have changed. With the creation of the United Nations, the European Union and other international organizations, several norms have become an entrenched part of the international system. The 1975 Helsinki Accords codified the idea that borders should not change – with the exception of secession, which is only really granted on a case-by-case basis.[41] Other norms such as respect for ethnic minorities in heterogeneous states have also played a role in the transition away from ethnic nationalism. In essence, where ethnic nationalism was once seen as acceptable, it has become much less so in recent years. Ethnic nationalism tends to lead to a range of social ills such as xenophobia, animosity towards others and rampant nationalism. This can be better avoided with a greater openness to people from other countries and cultures. Fourth, many countries around the world are heterogeneous in nature. It makes better sense on the field to include players regardless of their ethnic backgrounds. Finally, in order to compete in major international tournaments with massive financial incentives for winning, teams must assemble a large squad in order to play a large number of games. This means relying on a larger pool of players to be successful at both domestic and international levels. A small national or ethnic group is less likely to provide many skilled players that can compete at the highest levels.

Ultimately, any decision to transition from ethnic nationalism to civic nationalism takes significant affirmative actions towards buying or signing the best players regardless of ethnicity.[42] Change does not occur without effort, otherwise lingering resentments, hostilities and prejudices may remain. Institutional and ideational changes are most important. For example, FIFA's 'Say no to racism' campaign presents the idea that racism is not acceptable in football. Prominent players read statements, banners are flown, and decision-makers do their best to persuade people to adopt the norm of anti-racism.

The transition from ethnic nationalism to civic nationalism is difficult. Raymond Breton notes that the transition from ethnic to civic nationalism is ultimately a long road and requires much time and work to change the thinking of the layperson, because they must become more accepting of people who are different.[43] Discussing the case of Quebec, he argues that the province is in the process of transitioning to civic nationalism, but faces many difficult questions with regard to its ideology and stance vis-à-vis other groups.[44]

## Discussion and conclusions

In many respects, soccer may be a driver of ethnic equality throughout the world. While there are numerous examples of problems and issue revolving around the issue of ethnicity, the idea of racial parity has become more popular and has helped change the way minority groups are perceived in a range of different societies. The sport of soccer has done much to help people integrate into their new societies and to foster a greater sense of harmonious race relations, in many cases. More work needs to be done in order to foster a more cosmopolitan environment where people, who have obtained legal visas to enter and work in a given country, are then able to become citizens. Obviously, legality differs from one country to another, but political leaders must make decisions on other situations with undocumented persons residing within a border. Each country also has the right – as a sovereign state – to create laws that best suit the culture and the desires of said state, which could entrench ethnic nationalism. Even though the present author disagrees with this idea, it is a component of international politics that should be respected assuming that it does not contradict the tenets of international law, such as the Responsibility to Protect.

The big question is whether people are able to integrate into a society, and whether they are welcome to become members of the society. Migration is a component of human history, some countries were formed bridging two (or more) ethnic groups, and so the treatment of minority groups is important. As the world's most popular sport, football can play a dynamic role in this discussion. Soccer is a tool, which can be mobilized in either positive or negative ways, but the game itself is neutral.

As discussed in the section on the role of club football in the ethnic–civic dichotomy, there are various clubs from different parts of the world that maintain (or used to maintain) strict rules on who could play for the club. There are differing reasons for these policies, but even then, most teams have an openness to players from all over the world. Moreover, the cases discussed are selective and representative of clubs that have historically been described as more closed. Some of the most ethnically exclusive clubs have even begun to change, which shows that civic inclusivity has become more the norm in club football. The sport of soccer, then, for the most part, has been used as a tool to fight non-discrimination, which is a positive step. It is still incomplete, especially since some fans retain racist urges, but progress is being made.

## Disclosure statement

No potential conflict of interest was reported by the author.

## Notes

1. Hobsbawm, *Nations and Nationalism since 1780*, 143.
2. Anderson, *Imagined Communities*, 1990.
3. Duerr, *The Goal of Independence*, 60–1.
4. HBO, *Chivas USA*.
5. ABC Univision, 'Six Major Teams that Don't Hire Foreigners'.
6. The best known sources are Anderson, *Imagined Communities*; Gellner, *Nations and Nationalism*; and Hobsbawm, *Nations and Nationalism since 1780*.
7. Most notably, Smith, *The Ethnic Origins of Nations*.
8. Renan, 'Qu'est-ce qu'une nation?'.
9. Ignatieff, *Blood and Belonging*, xv.
10. Greenfeld, *Nationalism*.
11. Ignatieff, *Blood and Belonging*, xiv–xv.
12. These include Nielsen, 'Cultural Nationalism'; Xenos, 'Civic Nationalism: Oxymoron?'; Weinstock, 'Is there a Moral Case for Nationalism?'; and Yack, 'The Myth of Civic Nationalism'.
13. Xenos, 'Civic Nationalism: Oxymoron?'.
14. Yack, 'The Myth of Civic Nationalism'.
15. Weinstock, 'Is There a Moral Case for Nationalism?'.
16. Nielsen, 'Cultural Nationalism'.
17. MacPherson, *Is Blood Thicker Than Water?*
18. For example, see Buford, *Among the Thugs*, on the propensity towards violence in football.
19. Barber, *McWorld vs. Jihad*.
20. Chua, *World on Fire*.
21. Galleano, *Soccer in Sun and Shadow*.
22. Dorsey, 'Soccer: A Middle East and North African Battlefield', 5.
23. ABC Univision, 'Six Major Teams that Don't Hire Foreigners'.
24. HBO, 'Chivas USA'.
25. Duerr, 'Becoming Apple Pie', 153.
26. Finn and Giulianotti, 'Scottish Fans, Not English Hooligans!', 192.
27. Ibid., 40.
28. ABC Univision, 'Six Major Teams that Don't Hire Foreigners'.
29. Ibid.
30. Beitar Jerusalem.
31. Ibid.
32. See, for example, MacClancy, 'Nationalism at Play'; and Carlos, 'Play Fresh, Play Local'.
33. Gonzalaez-Aja, 'Spanish Sport Policy in Republican and Fascist Spain', 104.
34. MacClancy, *Sport, Identity and Ethnicity*, 182.
35. Murray, *Football*, 162.
36. Gonzalaez-Aja, 'Spanish Sport Policy in Republican and Fascist Spain', 104.
37. Athletic Club.
38. Kuper and Szymanski, *Soccernomics*.
39. Duerr, 'Caribbean Teams in North American Professional Soccer'.
40. Saprissa.
41. See Buchheit, *Secession*.
42. See Duerr, 'Talking with Nationalists and Patriots'.
43. Breton, 'From Ethnic to Civic Nationalism'.
44. Ibid., 100.

## References

ABC Univision. 'Six Major Teams That Don't Hire "Foreigners"'. http://abcnews.go.com/ABC_Univision/major-soccer-teams-hire-foreigners/story?id=19749247 (accessed July 23, 2013).

Anderson, Benedict. *Imagined Communities: Reflections on the Origin and Spread of Nationalism*. London: Verso, 1990.

Athletic Club (Bilbao). 'Home Page – English'. http://www.athletic-club.net (accessed April 5, 2014).

Barber, Benjamin R. *Jihad Vs. McWorld*. New York: Ballantine Books, 1995.

Beitar Jerusalem. 'Home Page'. http://www.beitarfc.co.il/ (accessed February 23, 2014).

Breton, Raymond. 'From Ethnic to Civic Nationalism: English Canada and Quebec'. *Ethnic and Racial Studies* 11, no. 1 (1988): 85–102.

Buchheit, Lee C. *Secession: The Legitimacy of Self-determination*. New Haven, CT: Yale University Press, 1978.

Buford, Bill. *Among the Thugs*. New York: Vintage Books, 1991.

Carlos Castillo, Juan. 'Play Fresh, Play Local: The Case of Athletic De Bilbao'. *Sport in Society* 10, no. 4 (2007): 680–97.

Chua, Amy. *World on Fire: How Exporting Free Market Democracy Breeds Ethnic Hatred and Global Instability*. New York: Anchor Books, 2004.

Dorsey, James M. 'Soccer: A Middle East and North African Battlefield'. *Qantara*, 2009: 1–32.

Duerr, Glen. 'Becoming Apple Pie: Soccer as the Fifth Major Team'. In *Soccer Culture in America: Essays on the World's Sport in Red, White and Blue*, ed. Yuya Kiuchi. Jefferson, NC: McFarland, 2014: 143–59.

Duerr, Glen 'Caribbean Teams in North American Professional Soccer: Time for a New Direction?' *Recreation and Society in Africa, Asia, and Latin America* 5, no. 1 (2014): 1–15.

Duerr, Glen. 'The Goal of Independence: Secessionist Movements in Europe and the Role of International Soccer'. M.A. thesis, The University of Windsor, 2005.

Duerr, Glen. 'Soccer's Own Goal: Immigration, Economics, and the Decline of American Soccer in the Early 1930s'. In *American History through American Sports: From Colonial Lacrosse to Extreme Sports*, vol. 1, ed. Danielle Coombs, and Bob Batchelor. Santa Barbara, CA: Praeger, 2013: 217–27.

Duerr, Glen M.E. 'Talking with Nationalists and Patriots: An Examination of Ethnic and Civic Approaches to Nationalism and Their Outcomes in Quebec and Flanders'. PhD diss., Kent State University, 2012.

FIFA. www.fifa.com (accessed March 1, 2014).

Finn, Gerry, and Richard Giulianotti. 'Scottish Fans, Not English Hooligans! Scots, Scottishness and Scottish Football'. In *Fanatics!: Power, Identity, and Fandom in Football*, ed. Adam Brown. London: Routledge, 1998: 189–202.

Foer, Franklin. *How Soccer Explains the World: An Unlikely Theory of Globalization*. New York: HarperCollins, 2004.

Galeano, Eduardo. *Soccer in Sun and Shadow*. Trans. Mark Fried. New York: Nation Books, 2013.

Gellner, Ernest. *Nations and Nationalism*. Ithaca, NY: Cornell University Press, 2008.

Gonzalez-Aja, Theresa. 'Spanish Sport Policy in Republican and Fascist Spain'. In *Sport and International Politics: Impact of Fascism and Communism on Sport*, ed. Pierre Arnaud, and Jim Riordan. E & FN Spon, 1998: 97–113.

Greenfeld, Liah. *Nationalism: Five Roads to Modernity*. Cambridge, MA: Harvard University Press, 1992.

HBO. 'Chivas USA: Real Sports with Brian Gumbel', 2014.

Hobsbawm, Eric J. *Nations and Nationalism since 1780: Programme, Myth, Reality*. Cambridge: Cambridge University Press, 2012.

Ignatieff, Michael. *Blood and Belonging: Journeys into the New Nationalism*. Toronto: Random House, 1993.

Kuper, Simon. *Ajax, the Dutch, the War*. New York: Nation Books, 2012.

Kuper, Simon. *Football against the Enemy*. London: Phoenix, 1996.

Kuper, Simon, and Stefan Szymanski. *Soccernomics: Why England Loses, Why Germany and Brazil Win, and Why the U.S., Japan, Australia, Turkey – And Even Iraq – Are Destined to Become the Kings of the World's Most Popular Sport*. New York: Nation Books, 2009.

MacClancy, Jeremy. 'Nationalism at Play: The Basques of Vizcaya and Athletic Bilbao'. In *Sport, Identity and Ethnicity.* 1996: 181–199.

MacClancy, Jeremy. *Sport, Identity and Ethnicity.* Herndon, VA: Berg, 1996.

McPherson, James M. *Is Blood Thicker than Water?: Crises of Nationalism in the Modern World*. Toronto: Random House, 2011.

Montague, James. *Thirty-One Nil: On the Road with Football's Outsiders: A World Cup Odyssey*. New York: Bloomsbury, 2014.

Murray, Bill. *Football: A History of the World Game*. Aldershot: Scolar Press, 1994.

Nielsen, Kai. 'Cultural Nationalism, Neither Ethnic Nor Civic'. *Philosophical Forum* 28, nos. 1–2 (1997): 42–52.

Renan, Ernest. 'Qu'est-Ce Qu'une Nation?' [What is a nation?]. Conférence Faite en Sorbonne, le 11 mars 1882. Calmann Lévy, 1882.

Saprissa. 'Jugadores Lista'. http://www.saprissa.cr/jugadoresLista.php (accessed March 13, 2014).

Smith, Anthony D. *The Ethnic Origins of Nations*. Oxford: Blackwell, 1986.

Weinstock, Daniel M. 'Is There a Moral Case for Nationalism?' *Journal of Applied Philosophy* 13, no. 1 (1996): 87–100.

Xenos, Nicholas. 'Civic Nationalism: Oxymoron?' *Critical Review* 10, no. 2 (1996): 213–31.

Yack, Bernard. 'The Myth of the Civic Nation'. *Critical Review* 10, no. 2 (1996): 193–211.

# The 1883 F.A. Cup Final: working class representation, professionalism and the development of modern football in England

James R. Holzmeister

The 1883 F.A. Cup Final has long been viewed as a seminal event in the rise of professional football and an example of the class/culture conflict thought to characterized later Victorian sport. Recent scholarship has improved understandings of the larger contexts surrounding the match but diminish the importance of the 1883 Final as a catalyst for wider change. Little has been done to reconcile traditional understandings with this new, and more complex, view of the motivations for cultural change within the F.A. Utilizing new perspectives on the traditions and character of English sporting culture more generally, this article seeks to recast the 1883 Final within a post-colonial discourse concerning identity and representation. Through this perspective, traditional interpretations can be reconciled with contemporary understandings and the 1883 Final can be re-imbued with a sociocultural significance that more recent perspectives tend to neglect.

Within popular sporting culture, the 1883 F.A. Cup Final has long been recognized as a noteworthy event within the early history of high-level, organized, football (soccer) in England. Any history of the English Football Association generally or the F.A. Cup specifically would seem remiss without some acknowledgement of Blackburn Olympic's 2–1 victory over Old Etonians in the spring of that year, an outcome that represented a first in F.A. Cup history. In the traditional narrative, Olympic's victory signified the ascendency of a sporting culture, a challenger to the F.A.'s staid iteration of the game. The game Olympic played has been alternately referred to as northern, working class, industrial, professional, county or any number of differing lexical variations upon these basic themes. Despite the evident confusion concerning just what Olympic might have represented, their 1883 Final victory nonetheless stands as a seminal moment for a club of their type, and as such, their victory was viewed as a critical turning point in the history of the Football Association. When tied to larger process of transformation in English football and English sport more generally, Olympic's victory has been forwarded as an example of a general process of class/cultural transformation occurring in the later nineteenth century as older Victorian ideals were gradually replaced by a modern, capitalized culture of sport. Regardless of how one might refer to the 'kind' of team Olympic was or whether we agree with the traditional manner in which the 1883 Final has been presented, there are obvious reasons for seeing the match as a seminal moment in the history of the F.A. Cup, an event which marks a literal dividing in the historical record.

Within the competition's first decade of existence, all of the Cup holders had clear associations with English military or public schools, and as such, evidenced a mid-Victorian sporting culture accentuating amateurism and membership drawn from the upper class. After 1882, however, the names of Cup winners utilize a more familiar, geographically based, nomenclature – Blackburn Rovers, West Bromwich Albion, Aston Villa – and many others from the decades of the 1880s and 1890s are instantly recognized as sides still competing in the sport's highest levels today. In name, Blackburn Olympic and all the rest of the post-1883 champions are clearly differentiated from the champions that preceded them and this obvious distinction hints to a much wider gulf between the two eras. Yet like any aspect of history, and despite the obvious evidence that initially propelled the 1883 Final to a point of prominence, the traditional narrative surrounding the match has been subject to a great deal of scrutiny. Confusion certainly exists concerning the issue of how the match relates to or represents processes and interests within football (and sport more generally) in the later nineteenth century and many have questioned whether the match still serves as an apt metaphor for larger sociocultural contexts. In the wake of revision and uncertainty, there remains a real need to interrogate the 1883 F.A. Cup Final further; the basic evidence that supports the match's importance has not changed nor evaporated; it is still there and should not be ignored. From that evidence, a real argument for the significance of the 1883 Final remains and within it lays the possibility of coming to a greater understanding of critically important issues concerning the sociocultural significance of modern football and modern professional sport more generally.

Much of the interest generated by the 1883 Final – for both Victorian and modern audiences – stems from the basic assertion that a difference existed between Blackburn Olympic and Old Etonians. When classified through class or geography, the match held a rich metaphoric potential through the pitting of two cultures against each other on the field of play. Drawn largely from the contemporary Victorian accounts and assumptions of the culture surrounding the match, the traditional narrative clearly accentuated features of class and geography as a means to rationalize the match, alternately presenting Olympic as a working class team who took on and defeated the affluent casuals of Eton or a match which pit northern industrial soccer against a southern, schoolyard form of the game. These interpretations obviously sought to present the match as a metaphor for the more general discourse concerning English sport and a means for sport to represent the class/culture conflict that is thought to imbue many facets of late Victorian life. Within these approaches, the match was generally forwarded as an example of the ascendency of common or working class culture within a regulating body (the F.A.) that had, up to that time, been dominated by the English upper class, a significant event within the assumed context of the later nineteenth century.

Yet despite the many reasons why the 1883 Final has gained a place in the popular lore of English soccer and the elegance of the narrative that has emerged from the event, through the latter half of the twentieth century critical perspectives have thrown considerable doubt on traditional readings by calling into question the perceived nature of the sociocultural conflicts which the match supposedly signified and challenging the level of attention the match has traditionally received. Initially, historians sought to refine assumptions concerning the manner in which the match might represent opposing cultures in English sport, a move that shifted focus from class and geography to centre on the key issue of professionalization. Geoffrey Green's mid-century *History of the Football Association* further complicated things using the issue of professionalism to illustrate that the divide in English Football was not easily defined by a simple dichotomy between north and south or high class and working. In actual fact, stances on the issue of professionalism reflected a much more diverse and pragmatic approach within soccer's organizational structure.

Green's assertions suggest that traditional representations of the 1883 Final, then, were based upon an oversimplification of the cultural field surrounding the Football Association. To put the match forward as evidence of those cultural conflicts would only further such error. In order to view the match in a more accurate light, therefore, sociocultural and economic contexts needed to be understood more completely.[1]

Given the substantial revision that has taken place concerning our understanding of the 1883 F.A. Cup Final over the past half century, Matthew Taylor's recent discussion of the match in *The Association Game* provides perhaps the best synopsis of the results of this work undertaken by Wray Vamplew and others. Diminishing the importance of class and geographic divides within the match, Taylor asserts that 'the significance of the result [in the 1883 Final] was not that it symbolized the end of public school domination and the rise of the working class game' but rather that the match asserted the rise of a 'new, professional approach'. Drawing upon Wray Vamplew's extensive discourse on the subject, Taylor utilizes a now familiar explanation of change in soccer's competitive culture as a gradual 'drift towards professional football' inaugurated by the 'decisions of individual sports entrepreneurs responding to the economic stimuli which underpinned the growth of late nineteenth-century commercialized leisure'.[2] Taylor stresses the significance of these individual actors by asserting that the improving fortunes of soccer in England, and its continued popularity, were not inherent or inevitable, but rather resulted from the deliberate actions of individuals who sought to promote the game and its role as a spectator attraction. While Taylor may find the 1883 Final significant to be worth mentioning, the match warrants little attention within his overall discussion and this general diminishment of the match's significance marks a trend within recent perspectives. Indeed, for Taylor and a number of other sporting historians, the machinations of English sport's transition to professionalism were occurring far from the field of play and were largely the result of business rather than sport itself, and as a result, the 1883 Final has been relegated to a footnote within the general history.

It is impossible to deny that the 1883 F.A. Cup Final occurred within a much larger context surrounding the adoption of professionalism in English soccer. Critical perspectives have been greatly improved by situating the match more completely within a much larger history of organized sport and the development of the Football Association. Yet the overt accentuation of professionalism – in place of everything else – as the key point of differentiation between the alternate cultures represented by Blackburn Olympic and Old Etonians is as useful as it is potentially dangerous. In the hands of many, the issue of professionalism has served as a means to obscure or ignore key issues rather explain them. In the hands of a generation of economic historians that have followed in Vamplew's wake, the overly economized perspective inspired by the focus on professionalism has not only served to diminish the importance of the 1883 Final itself, but in so doing has left critical questions concerning aspects of the transition in English sport unanswered and unaddressed. Economic historian Stefan Szymanski's 2006 article 'Football in England' amply demonstrates the inherent danger in these omissions. Within the article, Szymanski presents English soccer as a monoculture directly derived from the public school traditions of the mid-century and accentuates the primacy of the F.A. as the chief vehicle for the promotion of the game in England. Based on this perspective, football's expanding popularity in England through the course of the later nineteenth century is argued to be a direct the result of F.A. itself – primarily through the invention of the knock-out competition with the F.A. Cup and regulation of international competition.[3] Though Szymanski is correct in his assertion that the F.A. was indeed an important and primary motivator within the spread of soccer in England during the nineteenth century, it is impossible to deny the F.A.'s heavy investment in amateur traditions, nor the alternate football organizations whose popularity represented a real challenge to the F.A.'s sole authority. Despite the fact that the F.A.'s support for amateur competition was an opinion not uniformly held by all of the F.A.'s member clubs, the organization itself evidenced a strong aversion to professionalism and clearly differentiated themselves from teams such as Blackburn Olympic who were thought to be associated with professional culture. Beyond this, there is ample evidence to suggest that the F.A.'s public school brand of amateur soccer did not elicit tremendous public interest. The fact that alternate, professional competitions such as the Football League and the Lancashire Cup could exert such pressure on the F.A. throughout the late 1870s and early 1880s attests to professional soccer's popular appeal. If the popularity of football is conceived as a tendency that is not based in class or geography, then some explanation must be given for the different levels of spectation and support between the F.A. Cup and alternate forms of competition.

It is precisely within this question of football's popularity that the 1883 Final retains significance. Whether we view the 1883 Final as a catalyst or merely a symbol of change, the match provides an opportunity to understand, rather than merely note, the complex human motivations and desires that resulted in soccer's increasing popularity through the close of the nineteenth century and a critical motivation in the F.A.'s eventual adoption of professionalism. In this respect, it is perhaps more correct to forward the F.A. and its Cup as the truly symbolic elements in the equation. The F.A. Cup's seemingly indelible position in English popular culture illustrates the considerable influence that both the Football Association and the F.A. Cup have exercised. It is reasonable, given the tournament's prominence, to assert that the F.A. Cup exerts influence not merely over competition on the field, but also within the general culture of the sport, serving a critical role within the dissemination and organization of competitive culture to the larger English population. Thus, it is natural that through the course of the F.A. Cup's first two decades of existence, the competition became a locus in which the wider cultural discourse concerning sport in England was adjudicated and dominant cultural forms crystallized. As the primary arbiter of organized football in England, the F.A.'s influence on the larger culture of English football was critical even if their control over the game was not always absolute. Thus, changes in the F.A. must be recognized for both their significance and their reach. If the F.A. Cup served in this prominent role of cultural definition and mediation generally throughout the period, there is no more important period for the F.A. in this respect, than the years surrounding the 1883 Cup Final and no more important issue than that of professionalism. While we might rightly view the F.A.'s eventual adoption of professionalism as the most important event in a long process of cultural and organizational change, we cannot cast the F.A. as the originator of the action. The F.A. originated as an amateur body, and for much of their early history, they exhibited a stubborn desire to resist change when it came to the issue of paying players.

From its inception, the English Football Association promoted a competitive model derived from the ideals of the public school sporting tradition popularized by Thomas Arnold's Rugby School, the novels of Thomas Hughes, and the mandates of Muscular Christianity. The teams that made up the backbone of the Football Association and the bulk of teams who contested for the F.A. Cup through the first decade of Cup competition represented a continuation of the schoolyard sporting culture popularized by mid-Victorians and evidenced in team names and affiliations. More importantly, these teams participated within a culture characterized by the gentlemanly ideals of disinterested competition and the mentality of the casual player. While the F.A. might have thought their brand of soccer ideologically pure, there was an obvious dissonance between this competitive culture and the kind of competition inaugurated by the F.A. Cup. Cup play naturally insinuates an interest in the outcome and clearly the teams that participated in the competition during its first decade of existence must have evidenced some desire and will to win. Perhaps partially due to this underlying contradiction, the brand of play in the early years of the F.A. Cup seemingly did little to make the game accessible or appealing to a spectating audience. Indeed, through the first decade of the F.A. Cup's existence, the tournament inspired modest public interest at best.

Challenges to the F.A.'s authority came early and often as alternative competitive cultures sought to establish their own concerns in the space left by the F.A. The alternative culture that proved most popular and durable evidenced a level of popularity amongst spectators that enabled competitions to be both self-sustaining and profit generating. While professionalism might be seen as the primary difference between the F.A. and this alternate culture, it cannot solely account for the difference in public interest. The practice of professionalism retains significance certainly, but its inclusion also insinuates an even deeper level of contrast. Professionalism in sport is never the sole invention of the enterprising businessmen; it is also always contingent upon a demand and a set of expectations. If there was not a desire deep enough to motivate individuals to pay for the privilege of witnessing a match, if competitive sides had not proven to motivate increased public interest, then there would have been little reason for entrepreneurs to field teams, enclose grounds, hold practices or pay for improved on-field talent. Thus, the desires of both working class players and spectators of all classes must be recognized as influential features within the development of the business of soccer in England.

As the popularity of professional soccer can be seen as a primary motivation for the F.A.'s transition to professionalism in 1885, it is critical to interrogate and understand how both professionalism and the 1883 Final itself inspired greater public interest and acclaim. Although difficult to measure with certainty, the 1883 Final has long been presented as a match that evidenced a marked increase in both attendance and public interest.[4] This uptick in interest directly inspired by the match would buoy the tournament's cultural standing over the next several years and reiterated a point that the F.A. had most certainly already acknowledged – change would be necessary for the F.A. to remain relevant. The marked increase in public interest surrounding the 1883 Final acts as an indicator of the match's social resonance but there was something more to this isolated groundswell. History shows, of course, that the increase in public interest inspired by the 1883 Final was a phenomenon that would only expand as time went on as did the expansion of professional influence itself. The Blackburn side and the fans that supported them represented a culture that had not before been seen in such a ostentatious and public manner to that point. It was an emergent football culture that represented a different way to play the game and a different way to support that play in the grandstands, on the training ground, and the club's front office. It was an approach to football that uniformly earned positive responses from audiences as the gradual transition to professionalism evidences efforts to meet that demand.[5]

The F.A., of course, did not accept professionalism until well after the 1883 Final. At the time of the F.A. Cup Final of 1883, every side in the competition had to adhere to a strict code of amateurism to participate. With the increasing involvement of working class clubs in competition through the 1870s, the F.A. addressed the financial stress encountered by clubs and players along with the influence this financial stress might play in promoting professionalism. Envisioning professionalism as something of a Pandora's box, the F.A. was active in stemming the tide of professionalism by investigating and sanctioning clubs. The F.A. did allow players to be compensated for time missed at their regular employment, but required that it could not exceed their normal working rate. This system was easy to exploit however, and many teams did. Like nearly every other club with working class associations, Olympic would face accusations of having paid players throughout the early 1880s. A letter to the editor of *Bell's Life in London and Sporting Chronicle* in September of 1884 expresses the general consensus concerning the assumed presence of professionalism within working class teams:

> It is pretty well understood amongst Association football men that not only are Blackburn Rovers, Blackburn Olympic, Bolton Wanderers, Great Lever, North End, [etc.], guilty of professionalism to a greater or less extent, but so also are many of the Midland clubs, such as Notts County and Aston Villa, whilst in Scotland it is well known that prominent players are not averse to 'earning an honest penny' by their proficiency in the football field.[6]

Although the debate over professionalism had lain under the surface of F.A. competition since its inception, the increasing influence of working class teams within the F.A. Cup competition brought the issue into greater prominence. The restrictions obviously provided upper-class Victorian sides with an advantage, if only by keeping superior competition off the field. On the field, Victorian sporting ethics also tried to hold working class play in check. Denounced with cries of 'hacking' and other fouls, working class teams were generally accused of playing too rough, perhaps another way of simply saying they tried too hard to win or perhaps worked too hard for their compensation. In these and many other subtle ways, the F.A. sought to define an attitude and style in the game that most certainly had an impact on quality of play.

The code of conduct for amateur athletics greatly downplayed the importance of victory or the effort and exertion required to attain it. Based within a larger historical logic that saw Victorian regulation of sport as the means to refine and civilize the childish and dangerous practices of England's rough past, the softening of football was perceived as a moral as well as sporting mission. The desire for victory and the partisanship that came with it were seen as detrimental to both the game and larger English society.[7] Common tactics for improving on-field performance – training, organized practice and fitness development – were not only viewed as unnecessary, their utilization was antithetical to the amateur ideal. On-field performance should be unpracticed and effortless according to the Victorian aesthetic, and the concern for spectative interest was virtually non-existent. The point was to simply play. Whether someone wanted to watch was completely beside the point. The Victorian ethic of disinterestedness was professed so fervently that it most certainly impacted performance on the field and, in turn, characterized the brand of soccer played by upper-class sides. Richard Holt recounts the behaviour of the Corinthian Casuals in *Sport and the British* as an extreme example of a team whose on-field adherence to the ethics of fair play was taken to a preposterous extent. Citing a gentlemanly code of ethics, the Casuals were known for removing their goalkeeper whenever the opposing team was awarded a penalty shot; to leave the keeper in, they argued, even with only the barest chance of deflecting the ball, was not in the spirit of the ruling.[8]

By contrast, through the course of the 1870s, a number of tournaments based on the F.A. model emerged in England and many of them catered to local areas, particularly in the industrial heartland of the North. County championships and intercity matches provided a training ground for the emergent working class clubs and offered a challenge to the F.A. Cup in terms of public interest. While Old Etonians and other upper-class sides might evidence a level of competency honed through decades of formal matches, it was only in the later 1870s that teams from outside the public school league began to develop the match experience necessary to viably compete at the highest levels. Yet with improving play and increasing success in the F.A. Cup, professional clubs not only proved their ability to win on the pitch, but also at the gate. As organized football's popularity spread in England, clubs emerging from England's industrial heartland came to represent a serious threat to the F.A.'s southern, public school, style of play and the F.A.'s position as the head of the game.

Olympic's 2–1 victory over Old Etonians was not the prettiest or most convincing victory; they won largely due to the fact they faced only eight opponents by match's end due to injury or exhaustion. The victory stood as a testament to Olympic's fitness if nothing else. And yet improved fitness and stamina were one of the traditional qualities attributed to working class professionals. The next several years would see working class soccer develop well beyond simple improvements in fitness and basic skill, gradually, and over time, the old school style of play would be supplanted by a faster, more complex and more physically demanding form of the game. While the culture needed a few years to develop, the impetus for such development was laid in Olympic's success in the 1883 Final. While it was clear that a more competitive version of football garnered greater public interest, the Victorian F.A. model was in little position to take advantage of it. Throughout the F.A. Cup's early years, ties had generally drawn small crowds. Finals crowds ranged in the low thousands. Prominent inter-county or interschool matches might draw in the thousands as well. The organizers of these matches charged nominal admission to cover the cost of staging the match, but there was always the question of what to do with any profit. In grand Victorian fashion, amateur sides were generally expected to donate gate proceeds to charity – another stipulation that sought to combat professionalism but was widely exploited. As the crowds at F.A. Cup matches became larger, the problem and temptation presented by the volume of interest were apparent, as was the public's obvious preference for the soccer played by clubs suspected of circumventing the rules concerning professionalism – the shamateurs.[9]

Recognizing professionalism in soccer as an inevitable and potentially beneficial addition to the game, the F.A. eventually legalized professionalism in 1885 after a long series of debates concerning its operation and regulation. While the Football Association's acceptance of professionalism certainly helped to solidify their hold on English soccer, the acceptance of professional culture helped to develop high-level competition in a number of tangible ways. Professional culture helped foster a new found competitiveness on the field, but also established a level of professionalism within the organizational culture of clubs as well. Although not a tremendously common occurrence, there are several published incidents of amateur sides forced to forfeit F.A. Cup ties because they could not field a team.[10] When faced with the prospect of thousands of paying spectators, it was unthinkable that a match might have to be cancelled, much less that one would have to worry about the respective teams showing up to play. In this and many other small ways, professionalism recognized the place of the fans and supporters within the performance and the economy of football. While the needs of recreation and exercise were certainly important parts of sport culture and would remain so, the culture of professional soccer tapped into an alternate sporting culture, one not necessarily predicated upon sporting practice. This again demarcated a clear point of difference with the upper-class game, but one that might ultimately prove more significant than any other point of differentiation. While spectation certainly presented a different means of engaging with sport, the product of that engagement was different as well. Rather than simply regularizing behaviour and ethics through structured performance, spectation accentuated that social and discursive aspects of sport, the mixing of peoples and ideas from diverse points in the sociocultural spectrum.

With working class club organization in England and its association with local geography and populations, the emergence of devoted partisanship should have come as an expected result. Beyond the 1883 Final's impact on the game on the pitch and in the front office, the major story behind the contest lay back in Blackburn. For weeks (even years) after the fact, newspapers in England would write of the jubilant crowds who greeted the Olympic players upon their return and the novelty of such a display.[11] Within this emergent fan culture there was exhibited an energy and enthusiasm likened to participation on the field, but directed towards spectation, support and adulation. Centred around travel and game attendance, or vicarious celebration from a distance, fan culture not only served to offer movement to various English populations, it also served to plug them into popular culture in a way they previously had not been. Contemporary sporting historian Jeffrey Hill writes of the significance of travel within the early professional English sporting narrative. Through his explorations of sporting press accounts of the FA Cup Final during the later nineteenth century, Hill highlights the fact that the press circulated stories centred on the experiences of sporting fans travelling to London to witness their teams in England's premier football competition. Replicating the narrative proclivities of the pilgrimage tale, these accounts accentuate sociocultural differences within the English population as local identities come into contact through travel. Removed from their localities through the liminal journey to the capital, the fans often exhibit behaviours of excess, the foibles of the traveller in a foreign city, and the eventual re-accentuation of local identity upon their return. There is one particular story that Hill relates that is of particular relevance here. It involves a fan from Burnley who visits the Crystal Palace during his stay in London for the FA Cup Final. As Hill relates:

> There was, of course, nothing to compare with [the Crystal Palace] in Burnley, and it
> was therefore a 'must.' The visitor, careful (as northerners are) with his money, had ini-
> tially demurred at paying an additional entrance fee to the Crystal Palace over and
> above the price of his match ticket. But he was later forced to acknowledge that the
> price had been worthwhile; the glass structure was certainly an impressive experience.
> He added, though, as a summation of the whole experience: 'By gum, aw wouldn't
> like to go and mend a brokken pane up theer.'[12]

In his extended musings on this story, Hill accentuates the strange mixture of cultural cues and social identities encapsulated within the visitor's experience and utter-
ance. Hill contends that the visitor 'is undoubtedly impressed' by the structure and
yet infuses his experience with the consideration of the practical concern of maintenance, a means of expressing his refusal to get carried away by the grandeur of the
national symbol. The delivery of the line in dialect is clearly a means to highlight
the rustic local identity of the visitor, but also 'reminds us that the nation is composed of a variety of people, with different habits, cultures, and speech patterns'.
Hill also contends that readers of the story back in Burnley (or ostensibly other
regions of the north of England) 'would have recognized the irony contained in the
sentiments and marked it down as capturing their own mentality'. The remark comes
to represent the mentality of the 'everyman' and the 'relationship between provinces
and metropolis'. Finally, and most crucially, Hill questions the origins of the story
and the author of the remark, doubting 'its literal truth', and an expression of the
'myth of the north'. But despite this, Hill will also contend:

> ... the newspaper reporter who composed that section of the paper no doubt felt that
> the remark had a ring of truth. His readers would undoubtedly have expected someone
> to have said something like this, in this particular situation. The pleasure experienced
> by the reader in the story derived from the way it both presented and confirmed a
> vision of the self.[13]

But the 'vision of the self' that the FA Cup fan presents is a complex one, in part an
expression of the grandeur of Victorian culture represented in the awe inspiring
potential of the Crystal Palace but also the down to earth, working class practicality
that agonizes over the building's maintenance. England's society had always been
composed of these two iterations of identity, culture, and perspective, but national
culture had, by and large, been determined by and directed towards only one seg-
ment of that wider personality. Within iterations of later nineteenth century sporting
culture, it is possible to witness the emergence of a wider recognition of a broader,
more populist character in English society and an early instance of the more
inclusive social culture that would come to characterize the modern era.

Beyond providing a reiteration of David Russell's presentation of late Victorian
soccer as a site of cultural hybridity and compromise, a harbinger of twentieth century social development, Jeffrey Hill's work with Victorian periodical evidence is
significant for understandings of the 1883 Final – an event whose traditional meanings have, in large part, been drawn from periodical accounts. Although Hill certainly questions whether the events described in the press are truly accurate, he also
contends that representation was a much more complex issue within these common
sporting narratives than simple veracity. Thus, while it is important to understand
that periodical accounts of the 1883 Final may not have been completely representative of the truth, they were able to capture a sense of how various populations
viewed themselves and the events which occurred around them. Whether the 1883
Final actually pit industrial workers against public school dandies is beside the

point, what is important is the fact that fans noticed a difference between the teams and sought to rationalize that difference in similar ways; within the popular narrative that emerges, there lies a key to determining the desire and intent of the represented personality. What is even more intriguing within this context is the similarity that exists not merely within popular accounts of the 1883 Final, but the manner in which the popular narrative of Olympic's victory matches up with other contests in English sporting history that have been defined as clashes of culture or class – particularly within the post-colonial contexts of the British Commonwealth. Whether one considers test cricket or international rugby, colonial victories over the mother country have always held significant positions within local sporting cultures analogous to the importance traditionally appended to the 1883 Final. Beyond this, one of the further common features these cross-class/culture meetings in sport have spawned is a tendency to identify areas where alternative cultures have added to or altered English games. From Australian fast bowling to the All Blacks integration of Maori elements into rugby, these alternate cultures have always been represented initially as threats and then gain gradual acceptance over time. The reason for these common representations and responses is linked to the complex manner in which colonial experience structures identity and leads to the development of particular desires surrounding the issue of visibility and representation.

Franz Fanon and Homi Bhabha have both appended considerable significance to the subject of colonial identity as a means for understanding the psychic effects of colonial culture. Key to their interrogation is the tendency of colonial structures to create a sense of dual or competing identities within the colonial subject and the representation of either hold significant and often detrimental implications for the individual.[14] The colonial subject can recognize obvious benefits within assimilation to the colonizer's parent culture, yet also recognizes the implications of relinquishing the intrinsic, native, self and impossibility of complete identity conversion. Conversely, a desire to retain authentic identity relegates the subject to a diminished sociocultural position. Given these options, it is not surprising that narratives of invisibility and desires for visibility tend to dominate within colonial cultures. Within this complex social and cultural context, colonial subjects found a common point of discourse within the conception of visibility and valuation. Ideally, the colonial subject should be able to present themselves as authentically different, and yet for that difference to be recognized as at least a neutral if not beneficial characteristic rather than a detriment. Given colonial attitudes, such as the F.A.'s adherence to amateurism, and the depth to which they were established in social expectations and valuations are not easily altered however, and thus, conflict becomes not only a necessary means of rationalizing the struggle for authentic representation, but also serves to provide the means through which colonial subjects might achieve their ends. In order for attitudes to be changed, big, public displays of native ability and equivalency were deemed necessary by colonized populations and the sporting field has proven to provide a prime venue where these conflicts might be both enacted and resolved in constructive and socially affirming ways. Thus, it is not only possible to see elements of colonial thinking in the manner in which the F.A. sought to promote soccer in England as has been noted by J.A. Mangan, but those similar tendencies carry over into the resolution of the colonial situation as well.[15] Ultimately, the utilization of colonial and post-colonial discourse provides the means to understand conflict as a crucial element within cultural reconciliation, but also a vehicle for presenting sport as a venue with the capacity to address and alleviate real-world problems associated with disenfranchisement and social inequality. From this perspective, it seems only fitting that the 1883 F.A. Cup Final retains a position of importance in the historical record and remains a viable means for understanding cultural modification in late Victorian sport.

The years that have passed since the 1883 F.A. Cup Final have seen soccer's emergence as the most popular sport in the world. Although amateur soccer continues to be played at the amateur level in sandlots, suburban fields and schoolyards across the globe, the game is culturally dominated by high-level professional competition. As kids play, they see themselves as their professional heroes; they attempt to play the game in the professional manner. Although there were a host of factors playing into the transformation of soccer in the late-nineteenth century, it is clear that the F.A. Cup Final of 1883 acts as harbinger of change and a signal of the culture that would become dominant in English sport. Blackburn Olympic, like the amateur ideals they helped to displace, may have slipped from their once prominent position, but the impact of their storied victory and the culture the victory helped to popularize is most certainly still with us.

## Disclosure statement

No potential conflict of interest was reported by the author.

## Notes

1. Green, *The History of the Football Association*, 19–33; and Russell, 'From Evil to Expedient: The Legalization of Professionalism in Football, 1884–85', 43–4.
2. Taylor, *The Association Game*, 43–4.
3. Szymanski, 'Football in England', 459.
4. For discussion of the increase in public interest inspired by the F.A. Cup Final, see 'Sports and Pastimes', 4; 'Football Matches Yesterday', 1; 'Football', 1; 'News of the Day', 1; 'Football', 4; 'Blackburn Olympic v. Old Etonians: The Association Challenge Cup', 1; and 'The Football Association Challenge Cup', 1.
5. A letter to the editor of the Blackburn Standard in March of 1882 supports the idea that working class fans were particularly critical of the performance of their teams and demanded effort from the players. Within the letter, the fan chastises the Olympic side for 'sulking in the field' and employing poor tactics (dribbling rather than passing) in a match against an inferior opponent. Additionally, the author ties the quality of soccer on the field to the team's popularity amongst the fans. As he writes: 'I am sure it is no satisfaction to their supporters to go to the field and see [Olympic] play so miserably as they have done on several occasions'. Sentiments such as these, when paired with the exponential growth of soccer's popularity in England over the course of the later nine-teenth and early-twentieth centuries, support the idea that the brand of soccer on the pitch was responsible, in no small way, for encouraging or discouraging public interest in the game. 'The Blackburn Olympic Football Team', 8.
6. 'Letter to Editor', 3.
7. For more on this topic see: Holt, *Sport and the British*, 98–102; 'Football Reform', 3.
8. Richard Holt, *Sport and the British*, 99.
9. It seems that nearly every northern, working class team experienced accusations of professionalism. For discussion of the case against Preston North End see: 'Football', 26 January 1884, 3; against Bolton Wanderers see: 'Football', 20 October 1883, 4; for sanctions enacted on individual players see: 'Football', 27 October 1883, 3.
10. For instances of this phenomenon see: 'Football: Torquay v. Dartmouth', 4; and 'Football: Association Cup Tie', 5.
11. For descriptions of the celebration see: 'Summary', 1.
12. Hill, 'Anecdotal Evidence: Sport, the Newspaper Press, and History', 117–30.

13. Ibid., 125.
14. Bhabha, *The Location of Culture*, 57–64; and Fanon, *Black Skin, White Masks*, 157–8.
15. Mangan, *'Manufactured' Masculinity*, 409–15.

## References

Bhabha, Homi K. *The Location of Culture*. New York: Routledge, 1994.

'The Blackburn Olympic Football Team'. *The Blackburn Standard*, March 18, 1882.

'Blackburn Olympic v. Old Etonians: The Association Challenge Cup'. *London Morning Post*, Monday, April 2, 1883.

Fanon, Franz. *Black Skin, White Masks*. London: Pluto, 1986.

'Football'. *Bell's Life in London and Sporting Chronicle*, Saturday, April 7, 1883.

'Football'. *Bell's Life in London and Sporting Chronicle*, Saturday, October 20, 1883.

'Football'. *Bell's Life in London and Sporting Chronicle*, Saturday, October 27, 1883.

'Football'. *Bell's Life in London and Sporting Chronicle*, Saturday, January 26, 1884.

'Football'. *The Graphic*, Saturday, April 7, 1883.

'The Football Association Challenge Cup'. *Leeds Mercury*, Monday, April 2, 1883.

'Football: Association Cup Tie'. *Reading Mercury, Oxford Gazette, Newbury Herald, and Berks County Paper*, Saturday, December 19, 1885.

'Football Matches Yesterday'. *Lloyd's Weekly*, Sunday, April 1, 1883.

'Football Reform'. *The Standard*, London, Tuesday, February 8, 1870.

'Football: Torquay v. Dartmouth'. *The Devon and Exeter Daily Gazette*, Monday, November 8, 1886.

Green, Geoffrey. *The History of the Football Association*. London: Naldrett, 1953.

Hill, Jeffrey. 'Anecdotal Evidence: Sport, the Newspaper Press, and History'. In *Deconstructing Sport History: A Postmodern Analysis*, ed. Murray G. Phillips, 117–30. New York: State University of New York Press, 2005.

Holt, Richard. *Sport and the British: A Modern History*. Oxford: Oxford University Press, 1989.

'Letter to Editor'. *Bell's Life in London and Sporting Chronicle*, London, England, Saturday, September 13, 1884.

Mangan, J.A. *'Manufactured' Masculinity: Making Imperial Manliness, Morality, and Militarism*. New York: Routledge, 2012.

'News of the Day'. *Birmingham Daily Post*, Monday, April 2, 1883.

Russell, Dave. 'From Evil to Expedient: The Legalization of Professionalism in Football, 1884–85'. In *Myths and Milestones in the History of Sport*, ed. Stephen Wagg. New York: Palgrave MacMillan, 2011.

'Sports and Pastimes'. *Supplement to the Nottinghamshire Guardian*, March 30, 1883.

'Summary'. *Manchester Courier and Lancashire General Advertiser*, Tuesday, April 3, 1883.

Szymanski, Stefan. 'Football in England'. In *Handbook on the Economics of Sport*, ed. Wladimir Andreff and Stefan Szymanski. Northampton, MA: Edward Elgar, 2006.

Taylor, Matthew. *The Association Game: A History of British Football*. New York: Routledge, 2007.

# The British isolation from world football in the middle decades of the twentieth century – a myth?

Paul Wheeler

The popular impression of British soccer's relationship with the rest of the world until the late 1950s was one of selfish, arrogant, isolation. The reality, however, was quite different with frequent and multi-dimensional contact between the 'Home Nations' and the rest of the soccer world. This paper acknowledges their self-imposed absence from the FIFA and as a consequent their non-participation in the first three World Cups. However, it demonstrates that at almost every other level, Britain remained at the centre of world soccer, as regards the laws, playing international matches, club tours and the migration of players and referees. It reflects on the circumstances that helped substantiate the myth, focusing on an attitude of superiority, the ban on foreign professionals being 'employed' in British soccer and the alleged inferior style of foreign soccer and refereeing standards. This is in contrast to the globalized product that is today's English Premier League.

In a recent interview with BBC Radio 5 Live, the incoming FA Chairman Greg Dyke identified that one of his biggest challenges is to increase the number of young English players being represented in the English Premier League (EPL). Opta statistics show that in the 2012/2013 season, only 36% of the players in the EPL were actually English which compares very unfavourably with the other top European leagues. In Spain, the previous World and current European champions, their top league 'La Liga' had a significantly higher proportion of Spanish players at 61%, whereas in Germany, the figure was 47% and in Italy it was 46%.[1]

Data on the nationalities for the 64% of the overseas players (overseas meaning non-British) reveals that there were 69 different nations represented in the EPL including players from every continent and all the major footballing nations. The highest representation was from France with 31, Spain at 25, followed by Holland 13 and 12 each from Belgium and Brazil but also one each from the historically weak footballing nations of Iran and the Philippines.[2] This compares with the first week of the Premier League in 1992 when there were a total of 11 players from countries outside of the four home nations and the Republic of Ireland.

The global links between the British game and the rest of the world are equally apparent in terms of exporting the 'product', with EPL TV rights having been agreed with countries in every continent providing the league with an income of over £1.4 bn in the period 2010–2013.[3] British teams, and those from the EPL in particular, frequently travel around the world for high-profile and highly lucrative friendlies in countries that previously had very little footballing pedigree or culture. This allows the EPL and the clubs to interact with supporters in these countries in a much closer relationship than ever before, enabling them to generate an international fan base. This is evidenced by Manchester United who have been reported to have over 50 million supporters around the world.[4] Most overseas supporters will now have either seen them play live or have watched their games on TV rather than just having heard about the exploits of Charlton or Best as they would have 40 years ago.

These examples demonstrate the current cosmopolitan nature of the EPL and how football in Britain has come to reflect the globalization of football. This essay will demonstrate how the current situation contrasts with the past, when football in Britain for large periods isolated itself from the rest of the world. However, a further intention of this essay is to show that this position can be misleading or over exaggerated and how British football was always collaborating with countries around the world in different ways in terms of dissemination, governance, competition and through player and coaching migration.

As identified by Hill, the term 'globalization' has been applied to a wide range of international developments including sport.[5] This essay examines the concept of 'globalisation' with reflections on the political, economic and cultural approaches that Britain has taken towards football at home and abroad since the FA was formed over 150 years ago. This will support the views of other writers, that these globalization developments are significant and on a scale never before experienced in the history of the game.[6] Yet, there are those including McGovern who challenge the statement that true globalization has occurred, preferring to suggest that while the market for professional footballers has become more international, football remains a number of steps short of being fully globalized.[7]

Although there are many examples of ball games that were played throughout the world, it is accepted and summarized by Kitching that the originators of what we now know and accept as modern football were the British.[8] How and why the British came to export the game is the subject of considerable debate amongst historians. All agree that the British were instrumental in the early development and establishment of the game at the end of the nineteenth and early twentieth centuries. Sport was often used by the British to provide a certain measure of influence over other countries either by direct or indirect means, even if these countries were independent in political terms like Argentina. There was a significant British trading presence in Argentina and certain sports like polo, football and rugby became popular with the 'local' population after first being played by the British migrants.[9] This supports the views taken by many historians including Lincoln Allison who noted that the game was first played abroad by British bankers, entrepreneurs and engineers who played matches between themselves.[10] Britain at this time was the dominant world power in industry and commerce and its professionals were in high demand around the world. Along with their professional skills and expertise, they brought their sports, including football. Britain and all things British, including its sports, were seen as modern and the local elite were keen to adopt them as a way to become modern themselves. Allison notes that the sports were introduced to institutions like public schools and gentlemen's clubs as the second step in the internalization of the game. The third step was the adoption of the game by the country's working classes. As a simple game that required little equipment other that a ball, two goals and an area of open space, football was more accessible to the working classes and also easier to understand than other potential competing British exports like rugby and cricket.[11] However, Allison's model has been contested by academics including Beck and Lanfranchi and Taylor who argue that it assumes that the British were making a conscious effort to spread football to the citizens from other countries whether they were the elite or the masses.[12] This essay recognizes that there would often be resistance by a country's leaders, the church and patriots to 'foreign games' being adopted. Holt has described that even within the British Isles, Gaelic games were used as resistance to English culture in Ireland.[13] This essay also acknowledges that there was some development of local variations or styles of football. However, the desire to associate with modernity and games like football is considered to have been very strong amongst the local inhabitants in those countries where the British were playing 'their games'.[14] There may not have been a premeditated or formal plan on behalf of the British to persuade the world to play football, but like many other aspects of British life, there was an arrogance or confident self-belief in the British way of life including its sports. This was a period of imperial enthusiasm and total confidence in Britain's position in the world, as Birley notes 'there was a belief that games were essential for leadership and that the British were uniquely gifted in both'.[15]

The influence of the British either formally by design or informally by accident in the development of football worldwide is not disputed and is witnessed by many sources through the 'Anglicised' names given to the newly formed teams, Grasshoppers and Young Boys in Switzerland and AC Milan, not Milano, in Italy.[16] Similarly, the language of sport was English, it was used when playing the game or when organizing the game.[17] The Italian football federation's name originally included the English word 'Football' in the title, but this was changed to 'Calcio' in 1909 to emphasize the Italian nature of the game.[18] It is therefore incorrect to say that Britain was excluded or isolated in the formation of the game in Europe as they were wholly integrated with the game's development, even if there was no formality to it or a centralized plan.

Once sports are established in countries, domestic matches and leagues are formed and then there is a natural progression to international competition. Again, the template for this came from Britain with the creation of the (English) FA in 1863 and the other three home countries having formed their own associations and competitions by the 1890s.[19] The first international match was held in 1872 between England and Scotland and within 12 years, an annual championship was held between the two nations and Wales and Ireland, (Northern Ireland after partition).[20] The internationalization of sport was not unique and was just one example of political and economic developments between nation states in the late nineteenth and early twentieth centuries.[21] It was in this period that the International Olympic Committee (IOC) was formed in 1894 at the Paris International Convention, the brainchild of Frenchman Pierre de Coubertin.[22]

Within two years, the first modern Olympic Games were held in Athens in 1896 in an attempt to not only bring the world's athletes together but to also attempt to foster world peace.[23] Football was not played in the first games but did make an appearance in the Paris Games in 1900 and was actually won by Upton Park FC from Britain. Although it is unclear why they were chosen by the English FA to attend the Games on behalf of Great Britain, it may have been, in part, because they were a resolutely amateur club.[24] The Olympic football competition will be addressed in more detail later, but it is important to concentrate on the creation of the Federation Internationale de Football Association (FIFA) which was established in 1904. The first international match between two non-British teams was played the previous year when Hungary beat Bohemia 2–1. According to Hill, there were two principal objectives for its formation: to regulate the trend towards international matches and to standardize the laws of the game. A later responsibility was to oversee the international transfer of players.[25] However, unlike the IOC, there was no British representation amongst the initial eight countries that formed FIFA. Significantly FIFA, like the IOC, was formed in Paris and not a British city. Indeed there was a very definite lukewarm approach from Britain to the whole concept of an international football organization, although the FA did join in 1906 and were followed by Scotland, Wales and Ireland by 1911. For a short period, there was a cooperative approach to British integration into the administration of world football (South Africa joined in 1908 and Argentina and Chile in 1912). Britain's leading position in world football, even as a late comer to FIFA, was evidenced by each of the home countries having their own representative on the FIFA board rather than having just one British member. Indeed this was one of the reasons for the other home countries' belated entry, after FIFA initially had difficulties accepting them under the federation's one member one country principle.[26]

FIFA was not the first organization created to oversee the governance of the game because initially the laws for actually playing the game varied from country to country and it was accepted practice that the home team (country's) laws would apply. To overcome this, the International F.A. Board (IFAB) had been created in 1886 by representatives from the four home nations to standardize and supervise the laws. With the four home nations becoming members of FIFA, the IFAB was increased to five organizations in 1913, with FIFA having the fifth seat, in addition to those original four. With this development, Britain ensured that it had control over the laws of its game with any changes having to be agreed by a four-fifths majority.[27]

British representation in FIFA was however short-lived and continued to reflect a superior attitude consistent with being founders of the game. As Fredrick Wall, the FA Secretary, wrote in his memoirs, 'we want to govern ourselves both on and off the pitch'.[28] Indeed as Russell identifies it was for 'off the field reasons' that in 1920, after the First World War, the four home nations withdrew from FIFA over FIFA's desire to resume relations with ex-enemy countries. A brief return was made in 1924 before they withdrew for a significantly longer period in 1928. Russell further explains that the principal reason given related to definitions of amateurism, this concerned the participation of players in the Olympics for which FIFA now had responsibility for organizing the football element of the Games.[29] However, a much deeper and insular reason was the ongoing belief that FIFA should not have total control over individual national associations. 'We should be free to conduct our affairs in the way our long experience has shown them to be desirable' was the FA's opinion.[30] Or as Mason identified, 'no one could tell them anything about football'.[31]

Formal relationships with FIFA were then ended in 1928 until 1946. However, in reality, this did not mean a period of isolation from international football for British teams. Despite being outside of FIFA, the four British FAs enjoyed a type of virtual membership with constant dialogue with FIFA via the attendance by FIFA officials at matches in the Home International Championships, with the continuance of the overwhelming British presence on the IFAB and most importantly, the continuation of friendly internationals.[32] Beck writing on Britain's relationship with FIFA during the inter-war years notes that on the pitch itself, England in particular continued to play international 'friendlies' across Europe, despite the technicality of not being eligible to play matches against FIFA-associated countries. The challenge of playing against the masters of football was too strong for the continental teams to resist or sensible for FIFA to enforce. England generally enjoyed successful results in these matches, beating and drawing with the 1934 and 1938 World Cup winning Italy and beating Germany in 1935 and 1938. There were defeats, including a 4–3 reverse in Spain in 1929, but generally, the public and the press accepted the absence from the first three World Cups and considered that the real test remained the annual Home International Championships.[33]

For both parties, maintaining cordial relations was important. FIFA needed British support to retain their creditability as the international governing body for a world sport and this they achieved by having a close association with of the founders of the game even if it was informal. Two examples of this association were the lifting of the ban on British referees officiating in FIFA-organized matches from 1931 and then the recognition of the 75th anniversary of the FA in 1938 when a Rest of Europe team lost 3–0 at Highbury, London.[34] The most significant example of this informal relationship was the courting of the four British FAs by FIFA officials including their General Secretary Ivo Schricker to participate in each of the first three World Cups, despite their absence from FIFA. FIFA's objective in inviting the British teams and especially England was to increase the credibility of their tournament. However, the invitations appear to have been unsuccessful for a number of reasons: although there is little documented evidence to support this, they are thought to include the general feeling of superiority and a 'Little Englander' attitude, together with the real logistical issues associated with travelling to and playing in the inaugural World Cup in Uruguay in 1930. Indeed only four European teams made the journey across the Atlantic. These logistical challenges were supported by a report from Chelsea FC who had toured South America in 1929 but had identified many difficulties and dangers of playing on that continent, which only helped back up the entrenched views of non-involvement held by the FA.[35] Chelsea's tour however is another example in itself to counter the total isolation view of British football from the rest of the world during the inter-war years. Prior to the second World Cup that was held in Italy in 1934, FIFA officials attended the 1933 England v Scotland game to investigate the possibility of both countries' involvement. They even offered direct entry into the completion, no pre-qualifying would be required and expenses would be paid to cover travelling and accommodation costs. Both FAs again said no, but ironically, both countries played friendlies on the continent during the summer of 1934 prior to the World Cup matches.

A similar approach was made in 1938 in the lead up to the finals in France and even an offer to enter a United British Team made. This was not surprisingly rejected by the British FAs as it was considered to potentially set a precedent for future international team involvement and end the independence of each of the four FAs to run its own team. This would be a recurring theme for the following 70 years and one that was controversially revisited in the lead up to the 2012 London Olympics, with long and heated debates in the press and between the respective home nation FAs and the British Olympic Association (BOA) about the merits and challenges of a Team GB playing at the Games.[36] As in 1934, England and Scotland played games in Europe in 1938 in the lead up to the World Cup and England actually played in Paris in the World Cup final stadium just nine days before the tournament started and attracted a bigger crowd than any game of the World Cup. There was also a move towards greater co-operation off the field with the 1938 meeting of the IFAB switched from its original venue in Northern Ireland to Paris so that officials could also attend World Cup matches and events. However, there was still little enthusiasm from the British press or the public for the World Cup, with little coverage in the newspapers for this foreign tournament.[37] Far more coverage was given to England's 6–3 victory in the same year against Germany when as Russell reports *The Daily Mail* proclaimed, 'Once again England are proved to be the leading football nation in the world', although this game is most famous for the English players giving the Nazi salute before the kick-off.[38] The political significance of the game was reported to audiences that in Berlin, 'England beat Nazis … restoring British soccer prestige on the continent'.[39]

Following the Second World War, a change of attitude saw Britain keen to establish itself a role in a post-British Empire world and so it became more enthusiastic to be included in world organizations. This new reality was recognized by Stanley Rous, the FA secretary from 1934 to 1961, who saw football as a chance for Britain to retain some influence over world culture.[40] So in 1946, two years before the Olympic Games were staged in London, the four home nations rejoined FIFA but only on their terms. This meant ensuring they were still represented as four separate nations on the pitch and in the committee room with each 'nation' having its own single vote in FIFA and also ensuring they had 50% of the votes on the IFAB.[41] IFAB was now to have four representatives from FIFA and one each from England, Scotland, Wales and Northern Ireland – an abiding acknowledgement of the historic significance of the British associations in world football. A three-quarters majority was required for any item to be passed.[42]

Once returned to FIFA, progress and results were mixed for the previously superior England football team. The first foreign team to play at Wembley were Argentina who were beaten 2–1 in 1951, but this was only one year after the highly embarrassing 1–0 defeat by the USA in the 1950 World Cup in Brazil, the first time that any of the home nations had competed in the tournament. Greater humiliation followed in 1953 with the infamous 6–3 defeat by Hungary at Wembley which shattered once and for all the pretensions about English dominance in international football, a position that six months later was reinforced to an even greater depth when the Hungarians beat England 7–1 in Budapest. These defeats and the lowering of England's position in the world order of football might also be seen to be symptomatic of Britain in the 1950s, a country still struggling with rationing and having lost its position as the most dominant power and economic force in the world.[43] There was one significant return to a position of the previous ascendancy when in 1966 with Rous now as the president of FIFA, England hosted and won the World Cup beating the West Germany 4–2 after extra time at Wembley Stadium.[44] However, since then, England has failed to repeat this success and indeed failed to even qualify for the final stages three times in 1974, 1978 and 1994.

Even in the second decade of the twenty-first century, there is an argument that nothing has changed regarding the feelings in Britain towards FIFA. There were signs of mistrust at best and claims of bias and corruption levelled at FIFA following the discussion to award the 2018 World Cup to Russia and the 2022 competition to Qatar rather than to England.[45] Calls were made for England to leave FIFA and set up an independent rival organization. This echoes the comments of a previous Football League President Charles Sutcliffe from the beginning of the twentieth century who stated 'an organisation where Uruguay, Paraguay, Egypt and Bohemia are equal with England has little appeal and is an example of magnifying the midgets'.[46]

Returning to Olympic football, it is worth highlighting the performance of the British team in the Games, and its participation which was not continuous and broadly in line with British membership of FIFA. Britain actually won gold in 1900, 1908 and again in 1912, but in 1920, a weakened team representing a tired nation after the First World War was beaten in the first round. This possible threat of further humiliation, the fear of international football in general being linked to increased levels of nationalism and finally concerns with payments to players, a situation that to the British with their strong amateur values was a complete compromise of the values and ideals of the Olympic Games, saw no British participation in the 1924 and 1928 Games.[47] There was no football competition in the 1932 Los Angeles Games, but the 1936 Berlin Games did see the return of a British team to play in the Olympics when they lost in the quarter finals to Poland.

Away from international football, there was a significant record of British professional club sides participating in overseas tours with an increasing frequency shown by reports from the 1920s.[48] However, these adventures were not always positive or likely to foster good impressions likely to encourage closer international ties, with reports of rough play, poor interpretation of the laws by poor and even biased referees.[49] However, once again, this provides evidence that British football associations were not totally against engaging with foreign teams or even travelling to and playing them in their country. One of the major developments in football after the Second World War was the installation of floodlights at a number of the top English football teams' grounds. One of the first was Molineux home of Wolverhampton Wanderers. This was in 1954 and to launch this development, the club embarked on a series of 'floodlit friendlies'; two of the first teams to visit were Spartak Moscow and Honved of Hungary.[50] The Honved match saw Wolves prevail 3–2 against one of the strongest teams in Europe, a team that included many of the Hungarian national team who had recently beaten the England national side. The success of these games prompted Gabriel Hanot the editor of L'Equipe, the main sports paper in France, to encourage the Union of Europe Football Associations (UEFA) to organize a European Club championships. This was approved and started the following season in 1955, but despite the obvious success of the Wolverhampton experiment, there was no English entry into the first competition with the Football League Secretary Alan Hardaker refusing to let the current English champions Chelsea enter as he did not believe it was in the best interests of English football to be a part of it.[51] The Scottish league however were more enlightened and permitted Hibernian to enter, not that they were Scottish Champions but because they had floodlights at their ground and it was thought their participation would generate interest across Europe. Hibernian actually progressed to the semi-finals before losing to the French team Stade Reims.[52]

English teams could not be denied the place in the competition for long and the next year, the exclusion was challenged by Matt Busby who entered Manchester United without the support of the league, but who in the first year of entering also made the semi-finals before losing to the great Real Madrid side.[53] Despite this success, the league were still sceptical about English club participation and this was shown in their reluctance to help the clubs with accommodating their overseas fixtures including a requirement that teams had to return to England a full day before they were scheduled to play their next domestic fixture. This possibly contributed to the urge to return home promptly after Manchester United's quarter final game in Belgrade in February 1958, for fear of possible fines. The players and team officials boarded the plane in Munich in extremely dangerous and snowy conditions before the now infamous crash that left eight players and three officials dead.[54]

Despite this tragedy, British teams continued to embrace the European club football tournaments which were expanded to three annual competitions by the beginning of the 1960s. Tottenham Hotspur became the first English team to triumph in Europe, winning the Cup Winners Cup in 1963 before Celtic became the first British team to win the European Cup in 1967 beating Inter Milan 2–1.[55] Manchester United with Munich Air Crash survivors' Matt Busby, Bobby Charlton and Bill Foulkes present followed Celtic to win the European Cup in 1968.[56] This began a dominant era for English and Scottish teams through the 1970s and 1980s with a total of 23 wins in the three major European competitions including six straight winners of the European Cup from 1977 to 1982. This run of success was ended in 1985 after the Heysel stadium disaster when Liverpool played Juventus and 39 fans were killed after crowd unrest. This lead to the expulsion of English teams from European competition for five years as a punishment. On this occasion, the isolation was not instigated by the British, but it meant the clubs were excluded from international football. The ban was lifted in 1990 and it was Manchester United who again led the way back by winning the Cup Winners Cup in 1991 and becoming the first English team to win the European Champions League in 1999 beating the German side Bayern Munich in a thrilling 2–1 extra time win in Barcelona's Camp Nou.[57]

The role of the individual, especially players but also coaches can help support the isolationist viewpoint, but research has also demonstrated that a significant amount of migration occurred with Britons plying their trade at overseas clubs, more than is often assumed. In recent years, there has been an increasing importation of foreign players, coaches and owners to provide further evidence of the cosmopolitan nature of the British game.

It has already been established how the British were instrumental in creating an interest in football around the world and how they were central to the creation of new teams. Naturally, British players were part of this process; FC Barcelona formed in 1899, included the Witty brothers in their early teams.[58] However, the brothers were more a representation of Britons living and working in Barcelona with a passion for football, rather than regular British players displaying economic migration tendencies seeking to ply their footballing trade abroad. While there were examples of British footballers playing overseas, as Lanfranchi and Taylor observed, they were not natural travellers. The push and pull effect of playing abroad was weak. Why would successful players want to leave the most prestigious and competitive league in the world to play in less well-developed and less challenging alternatives?[59] Indeed, this is still partly true today, given the economic advantages of playing in the EPL even if the quality level is often debated.

There were however a significant minority of players who did take the opportunity to play abroad and one of the attractions of British players for foreign teams during the inter-war period, in addition to their playing ability, was there was no official requirement to negotiate and pay transfer fees to the British clubs. This was because with the self-imposed exile from FIFA, it meant the home country FAs had considerably less control over players' rights and registration requirements if overseas clubs approached them.[60] During this period, there were a number of players who enjoyed long and successful careers abroad, in France in particular. However, this situation did represent a threat to the Football Leagues' status and these players risked being banned from returning to play in the British leagues if their 'transfer' had not received the consent of their English clubs prior to their defection. It reached a pinnacle in April 1932 when the Football League President John McKenna announced that any players going to France 'would cease to have the right to play (football) again in this country', although this threat had little impact on player migration to France.[61]

After the Second World War, some players took the opportunity to move to Columbia to play football, influenced no doubt by the chance to receive significant payments far in excess of the maximum wage that players in the British game were still being paid. Two of the highest profile players were Manchester United's Charlie Mitten and Stoke's Neil Franklin. Franklin had to break his contract with Stoke to play in Bogota, could not settle in Columbia and found that, as with the situation of footballers playing in France before the war, when he returned home, the Football League took punitive action banning him for a year and suspending from the England team indefinitely.[62] Later in the early 1960s, further high-profile British footballers had short spells in Italy and this included Denis Law and Jimmy Greaves. However, for most of these players, they found it difficult to fit in with the culture, the food and even the training encountered in Italy and quickly returned to Britain.[63] This is supported by Lanfranchi and Taylor who identified the absence of the traditional English drink and pub culture as reasons why Greaves and then more recently Gascoigne failed to adapt to the accepted Italian footballers' lifestyle.[64] One notable exception to this trend was John Charles who enjoyed considerable success during the late 1950s and early 1960s playing for Juventus and Roma. He embraced the Italian way of life and this is perhaps one of the reasons for his success and he has been considered to be one of the most successful British footballing exports and one of the finest foreign players in Italy.[65] At the end of the twentieth and into the early twenty-first century, Lanfranchi and Taylor suggest that with few exceptions, the world finest players were migrants.[66] Yet, only a small percentage of these successful talented migrant players have been British, with most of them still preferring to stay at home.

Another notable footballing British export throughout the first half of the twentieth century as Taylor has identified was the migrant British coach who played an important role in the development of the game in the rest of the world. Taylor describes how these migrant coaches have become known as the second footballing wave following on from the early touring teams and were employed by overseas teams to teach them the British game. Detailed records do not exist, but he estimates there were in excess of 100 British coaches working across Europe in the inter-war years. This is particularly relevant, for it was the period when the British FAs were mainly outside of FIFA and indeed of the 16 teams at the 1934 World Cup in Italy, 3 had English managers.[67]

In terms of today's footballing imports to Britain, this essay has already identified the multi-national or even saturated nature of the EPL and has also described how this has increased throughout the EPL's existence. While this essay has argued and identified that British football has not been as isolated as some might suggest, it is unquestionable that as far as allowing players from outside of the Britain and Ireland, most foreign professionals had effectively been banned from the English game between 1931 and 1978. The only foreigners allowed were amateurs, students, those with family Commonwealth ties, POWs or those who arrived for other reasons (non-football work) and achieved resident status after two years.[68] It is interesting to note that while the 1948 Immigration Act confirmed that Colonial-born players were free to enjoy unrestricted entry into Britain, few players were actually attracted or encouraged to play here.[69] This contrasted with the French approach that used sport as a process of cultural assimilation creating the concept of the 'Black French-man'.[70] However, for players coming from outside of the British Empire, there was very strong resistance and even hostility. When in the 1930s Arsenal, who were the leading team of the time, tried to sign an overseas player, the then FA President Sut-cliffe said 'it was repulsive to clubs, offensive to British players and an admission of weakness in club management'.[71]

The 1970s witnessed two significant developments which instigated a change of regulations and attitudes. The first was Britain's entry into the European Economic Community (EEC) in 1973 and the subsequent impact on employment law. The second in 1978 saw the self-imposed ban lifted when the Professional Footballers Association (PFA) agreed to lift the ban on overseas players after UEFA had agreed with the EEC that it was unlawful to discriminate against footballers from other EEC countries. This led to a season of star arrivals including Muhren and Thijssen.[72] Initially however, when the ban was lifted, the Department of Employment would only issue work permits to players from non-EEC countries that were capped and could in their opinion 'make a contribution to the national game'.[73] A further restriction that was imposed in England was a limit of only two foreign players per team which was set at the beginning of the 1980s.[74] This restriction was relaxed in 1991 after a 'Gentleman's Agreement' between UEFA and the EEC resolved that football was in breach of European Employment law regarding the freedom of movement of work-ers between member states. This led to the adoption of a compromise and the so-called '3+2' rule where up to five non-nationals could be part of every matchday squad.[75] This agreement remained in place until 1995 when after five years of pro-ceedings, the pivotal 'Bosman' ruling from the European Court of Justice decreed that football should not be treated differently to any other industry and that the sport was in breach of the Treaty of Rome by restricting the number of EU footballers (workers) able to move and therefore play for a club within the EU.[76] This was the last significant barrier to any isolation for English football with unlimited access to players from across the 27 EU member states. A more relaxed attitude to the 'im-port' of players from across the world has seen the EPL transformed. This is best illustrated by *The Daily Mail* reporting the examples of Chelsea and Arsenal who have, respectively, fielded a team of 11 non-English players and a full matchday squad of 16 non-English players in EPL games.[77]

Finally, some consideration of the political, geographical, economic and cultural factors that attract international players to the EPL is required. These reasons have been identified by Maguire in his work on the typologies of sport labour migration where he has shown that the motivations and experiences can vary considerably.[78] It is clear however that in economic terms, the EPL is one that can offer a footballer a substantial salary. A succession of lucrative TV deals between the EPL and Sky TV has significantly increased the salaries paid to footballers, making a transfer to a top English team a very attractive proposition.[79] This equates to Maguire's theory of 'following the money'.[80] There are also a number of cultural reasons why players might decide to come and play at 'the home of football'. For the northern Europeans in particular, McGovern states that integration is often relatively easy, most speak English as their second language.[81] This is supported by Lanfranchi and Taylor who add the climate is similar and they are familiar and comfortable with a 'British way of life' with similar political, religious and culinary experiences to which they are used to at home.[82]

The EPL, since it was formed in 1992, has accelerated the globalization of English football with the top English clubs now being regarded as global brands as much as just football clubs representing the local community. This is reflected in the international nature of their shirt and ground sponsorships deals. Arsenal are a classic example playing in the Emirates Stadium, managed for 16 years by Frenchman Arsène Wenger, a prolific buyer on the global transfer market and in 2012 having 12 different countries represented in their regular matchday squad in addition to the few English players.[83] Wenger is currently one of the 8 foreign managers in the EPL and one of the 33 who have managed in the league since it was formed. It is important to note that in the league's inaugural season, none of the then 22 clubs had foreign managers in charge, although Aston Villa had previous employed the first non-British-born manager to take charge of a team in England's top league when Jozef Venglos was appointed for one season in 1990/91. This reflects the changing trend in the EPL and potentially is linked to the increased globalization of the league and the increase in overseas owners. In terms of managerial success, there has also been a swing towards foreign managers with only six trophies having been won by clubs managed by an English-born manager of the 70 major trophies in English football that have been won during the existence of the EPL compared with 27 trophies won by clubs with foreign-born managers.[84] Of course, over this same period, Sir Alex Ferguson collected 20 trophies during his reign at Manchester United, continuing a long history of successful Scottish managers in the English league.

Another development is an ever-increasing amount of foreign ownership of clubs in the EPL.[85] The two most successful English football clubs in terms of league titles won, Manchester United and Liverpool, have American owners and Manchester United are actually listed on the New York Stock Exchange rather than the London equivalent. The most recent progression in these trans-Atlantic ownership partnerships has seen Manchester City, another club from the north west of England, although now owned by the billionaire Sheikh Mansour of Abu Dhabi, form a business partnership with the New York Yankees Baseball organization to form a new Major League Soccer franchise in New York.[86] This development, if successful, could lead to even greater collaboration between English clubs and sporting clubs from foreign countries, not necessarily from the same sport, working together to create international brands and business partnerships.

As pioneers of the game, the British, as with most of their cultural products and values, were keen to share, export and sometimes impose football on countries around the world wherever they ventured. Initially and informally, there was always a high level of integration rather than isolation between the 'home of football' and the rest of the world. There were however two notable and high-profile exceptions to this rule which have given the impression of an isolationist policy. These have been identified as the reluctance to join and then remain part of FIFA and the acceptance of foreign players into the British leagues. This essay has not sought to deny either of these very well-documented facts and has highlighted and discussed material to support both of these positions; it has endeavoured to show that behind the mask of a policy of isolationism, there has always been a significant level of co-operation and contact between individuals, clubs and even associations from Britain and the rest of the world. This contact and Britain's historical, economic, cultural and social positions have all contributed to the situation today where the EPL is the richest, most watched and most culturally diverse league in the world. A situation that fans often argue is to the detriment of the development of home-grown British players and to the potential for success of England or any of the home nations at international team competitions. It even goes to the very fabric of the game with the majority of the famous and most successful teams 'enjoying' foreign ownership and involvement.

## Disclosure statement

No potential conflict of interest was reported by the author.

## Notes

1. BBC, *FA's Dyke Wants More English Youngsters in Premier League*, http://www.bbc.co.uk/sport/0/football/22680882.
2. Transfermarket, *Premier League England, Foreign Player Statistics 2012–13*, http://www.transfermarkt.co.uk/en/premier-league/gastarbeiter/wettbewerb_GB1.html.
3. The Guardian, *Premier League TV Rights Set to Top £5 bn for First Time*, http://www.guardian.co.uk/football/2012/nov/12/premier-league-tv-rights-5-bn.
4. Hill, *Sport in History an Introduction*, 116–17.
5. Ibid.
6. Lanfranchi and Taylor, *Moving with the Ball*, 7.
7. McGovern, 'Globalization or Internationalization?' 38–9.
8. Kitching, '"Old" Football and the "New" Codes', 1733–49.
9. Hill, *Sport in History an Introduction*, 124.
10. Mason, 'Football and the Historians', 136–41.
11. Birley, *Sport and the Making of Britain*, 260.
12. Lanfranchi and Taylor, *Moving with the Ball*, 33.
13. Holt, *Sport and the British*, 238.
14. Lanfranchi and Taylor, *Moving with the Ball*, 19–22.
15. Birley, *Sport and the Making of Britain*, *328*.
16. FIFA, Clubs inspired by foreign flavours, http://m.fifa.com/newscentre/news/newsid=2210154/index.html.
17. Lanfranchi and Taylor, *Moving with the Ball*, 20.
18. Ibid., 22.
19. Ibid., 39.
20. Holt, *Sport and the British*, 255.
21. Hill, *Sport in History an Introduction*, 133.
22. Coakley and Pike, *Sports in Society*, 445.
23. Hill, *Sport in History an Introduction*, 135.
24. Moore, 'Football and the Olympics'.
25. Hill, *Sport in History an Introduction*, 134.
26. Beck, 'Going to War', 113–34.
27. Ibid.
28. Ibid., 118.
29. Russell, *Football and the English*, 91.
30. Tomlinson and Whannel, *Off the Ball: The Football World Cup*, 89.
31. Mason, 'Football', *Sport in Britain*, 176.
32. Beck, 'Going to War', 118.
33. Ibid., 116–17.
34. Ibid., 120–1.
35. Ibid., 122.
36. Ewen, 'Team GB, or No Team GB', 302–4.
37. Beck, 'Going to War', 123–4.
38. Russell, *Football and the English*, 123.

39. Huggins, 'Projecting the Visual', 80–102.
40. Tomlinson, 'FIFA and the Men Who Made It', 55–71.
41. FIFA, 'Info Plus'.
42. FIFA, *Info Plus – Form and Function*, http://www.fifa.com/mm/document/fifafacts/organisation/ip-100_04e_ifab_9481.pdf.
43. Holt, *Sport and the British*, 273.
44. Tomlinson, 'FIFA and the Men Who Made It', 60.
45. BBC, *English Media Angry at FIFA World Cup Voting 'fix'*, http://news.bbc.co.uk/sport1/hi/football/9253692.stm.
46. Goldblatt, *The Ball is Round*, 240.
47. Ibid.
48. Taylor, 'Football's Engineers?' 38–163.
49. Beck, 'Going to War', 122.
50. Charlton, *My Manchester United Years*, 110.
51. Ibid.
52. UEFA, *History, Football's Premier Club Competition*, http://www.uefa.com/uefachampionsleague/history/index.html.
53. Charlton, *My Manchester United Years*, 116–21.
54. Ibid., 151.
55. UEFA, 'Champions League History', http://www.uefa.com/uefachampionsleague/season−1966/.
56. Charlton, *My Manchester United Years*, 286–99.
57. UEFA, 'Champions League History', http://www.uefa.com/uefachampionsleague/season=1998/index.html.
58. Burns, *Barca*.
59. Lanfranchi and Taylor, *Moving with the Ball*, 51.
60. Ibid., 51–3.
61. Ibid., 53.
62. Russell, *Football and the English*, 147–8.
63. Hill, *Sport in History an Introduction*, 132.
64. Lanfranchi and Taylor, *Moving with the Ball*, 234.
65. Hill, *Sport in History an Introduction*, 133.
66. Lanfranchi and Taylor, *Moving with the Ball*, 229.
67. Taylor, 'Football's Engineers?' 138–63.
68. McGovern, 'Globalization or Internationalization?' 28–9.
69. Lanfranchi and Taylor, *Moving with the Ball*, 169.
70. Hill, *Sport in History an Introduction*, 126.
71. The Independent, *Home and Away*.
72. Taylor, 'Global Players? Football, Migration and Globalization, c. 1930–2000', 25.
73. Lanfranchi and Taylor, *Moving with the Ball*, 129.
74. Ibid., 218–19.
75. Ibid., 220–1.
76. Ibid., 213–14.
77. Daily Mail, *English Football's Trailblazing Foreigners*, http://www.dailymail.co.uk/sport/football/article-337865/English-footballs-trailblazing-foreigners.html.
78. Maguire, 'Blade Runners: Canadian Migrants', 335–60.
79. Millward, 'New Football Directors', 1–16.
80. Ibid.
81. McGovern, *Globalization or Internationalization?* 33 .
82. Lanfranchi and Taylor, *Moving with the Ball*, 233–4.
83. Magee and Sugden, 'The World at Their Feet'.
84. The Independent, *English Managers are Becoming Poor Relations of the Top Flight*, http://www.independent.co.uk/sport/football/premier-league/english-managers-are-becoming-poor-relations-of-the-top-flight-8611880.html.
85. Hill, *Sport in History an Introduction*, 137.
86. BBC, *Manchester City form MLS Franchise with New York Yankees*, http://www.bbc.co.uk/sport/0/football/22615026.

# References

Beck, Peter. 'Going to War, Peaceful Co-Existence or Virtual Membership? British Football and FIFA 1928–46'. *The International Journal of the History of Sport* 17, no. 1 (2000): 113–34.

Birley, Derek. *Sport and the Making of Britain*. Manchester: Manchester University Press, 1993.

British Broadcasting Corporation. 'English Media Angry at FIFA World Cup Voting "Fix"'. http://news.bbc.co.uk/sport1/hi/football/9253692.stm.

British Broadcasting Corporation. 'FA's Dyke Wants More English Youngsters in Premier League'. http://www.bbc.co.uk/sport/0/football/22680882.

British Broadcasting Corporation. 'Manchester City Form MLS Franchise with New York Yankees'. http://www.bbc.co.uk/sport/0/football/22615026.

British Broadcasting Corporation. 'Premier League: English under-21s Reaches New Low'. http://www.bbc.co.uk/sport/0/football/22687663.

Burns, Jimmy. *Barca: A People's Passion*. London: Bloomsbury, 1998.

Charlton, Bobby. *My Manchester United Years*. London: Headline Publishing Group, 2007.

Coakley, Jay, and Elizabeth Pike. *Sports in Society: Issues and Controversies*. Maidenhead: McGraw-Hill, 2014.

Daily Mail. 'English Football's Trailblazing Foreigners.' http://www.dailymail.co.uk/sport/football/article-337865/English-footballs-trailblazing-foreigners.html.

Ewen, Neil. 'Team GB, or No Team GB, That is the Question: Olympic Football and the Post-War Crisis of Britishness'. *Sport in History* 32, no. 2 (2012): 302–24.

FIFA. 'Clubs Inspired by Foreign Flavours'. http://m.fifa.com/newscentre/news/newsid=2210154/index.html.

FIFA. 'Info Plus – Form and Function'. http://www.fifa.com/mm/document/fifafacts/organisation/ip-100_04e_ifab_9481.pdf.

Goldblatt, David. *The Ball is round: A Global History of Football*. London: Viking, 2006.

Hill, Jeffrey. *Sport in History an Introduction*. London: Palgrave McMillan, 2011.

Holt, Richard. *Sport and the British*. Oxford: Clarendon Press, 1989.

Huggins, Mike. 'Projecting the Visual: British Newsreels, Soccer and Popular Culture 1918–39'. *The International Journal of the History of Sport.* 24, no. 1 (2007): 80–102.

Kitching, Gavin. '"Old" Football and the "New" Codes: Some Thoughts on the 'Origins of Football' Debate and Suggestions for Further Research'. *The International Journal of the History of Sport* 28, no. 13 (2011): 1733–49.

Lanfranchi, Pierre, and Matthew Taylor. *Moving with the Ball: The Migration of Professional Footballers*. Oxford: Berg, 2001.

Magee, Jonathan, and John Sugden. 'The World at Their Feet'. *Journal of Sport and Social Issues* 26, no. 4 (2002): 421–37.

Maguire, Joseph. 'Blade Runners: Canadian Migrants, Ice Hockey and the Global Sports Process'. *Journal of Sport and Social Issues* 21, no. 3 (1996): 335–60.

Mason, Tony. 'Football and the Historians'. *The International Journal of the History of Sport* 5, no. 1 (1988): 136–41.

Mason, Tony. *Sport in Britain: A Social History*. Cambridge: Cambridge University Press, 1989.

McGovern, Patrick. 'Globalization or Internationalization? Foreign Footballers in the English League, 1946–95'. *Sociology* 36, no. 1 (2002): 23–41.

Millward, Peter. 'New Football Directors in the Twenty-First Century: Profit and Revenue in the EPL's Transnational Age'. *Leisure Studies* (2012): 1–16. doi:10.1080/02614367.2012.673130.

Moore, Kevin. 'Football and the Olympics and Paralympics'. *Sport in Society* 17, no. 5 (2014): 640–55.

Russell, David. *Football and the English: A Social History of Association Football, 1863–1995*. Preston: Carnegie, 1997.

Taylor, Matthew. 'Global Players? Football, Migration and Globalization, C. 1930–2000'. *Historical Social Research* 31, no. 1 (2006): 7–30.

Taylor, Matthew. 'Football's Engineers? British Football Coaches, Migration and Intercultural Transfer, C.1910–C.1950s'. *Sport in History* 30, no. 1 (2010): 138–63.

The Guardian. 'Premier League TV Rights Set to Top £5bn for First Time'. http://www.guar dian.co.uk/football/2012/nov/12/premier-league-tv-rights-5-bn.

The Independent. 'English Managers Are Becoming Poor Relations of the Top Flight'. http:// www.independent.co.uk/sport/football/premier-league/english-managers-are-becoming-poor-relations-of-the-top-flight-8611880.html.

The Independent. 'Home and Away: How Arsenal's Imports Changed the Landscape'. http:// www.independent.co.uk/sport/football/news-and-comment/home-and-away-how-arsenals-im ports-changed-the-landscape-6152409.html.

Tomlinson, Alan. 'FIFA and the Men Who Made It'. *Soccer & Society* 1, no. 1 (2000): 55–71.

Tomlinson, Alan, and Garry Whannel. *Off the Ball: The Football World Cup*. London: Pluto Press, 1986.

Transfermarket. 'Premier League England, Foreign Player Statistics 2012–13'. http:// www.transfermarkt.co.uk/en/premier-league/gastarbeiter/wettbewerb_GB1.html.

UEFA. 'History, Football's Premier Club Competition'. http://www.uefa.com/uefachampi onsleague/history/index.html.

UEFA. 'Champions League History'. http://www.uefa.com/uefachampionsleague/season= 1966/.

UEFA. 'Champions League History'. http://www.uefa.com/uefachampionsleague/season= 1998/index.html.

# 'To Cross the Skager Rack'. Discourses, images, and tourism in early 'European' football: Scotland, the United Kingdom, Denmark, and Scandinavia, 1898–1914

Matthew L. McDowell

This article examines the footballing relationship between the UK and Scandinavia during the period 1898–1914, specifically that between first-tier Scottish football clubs and the Danish Football Association (*Dansk Boldspil Union*, DBU) and the middle-class Copenhagen clubs which dominated it. The strictly amateur DBU and its city clubs invited British football clubs to Denmark on summer tours of the country to learn how to play the game; and, in turn, British clubs typically received a payment to come over. This article examines the common themes in both the Scottish and Danish press accounts of these tours, particularly the use of sketches, cartoons and other imagery. Then, the political context of British and Scandinavian football during the period is examined, including Scotland's anomalous relationship with FIFA, the new governing body of world football. Finally, this article looks at the touristic accounts of Scots whilst in Denmark, ones which typically sought out the familiar.

## Introduction

This article will examine the interrelationships between European clubs and associations during some of the early years of competitive association football.[1] Its specific focus will be on the journeys of British football clubs to Scandinavia during the period 1898–1914, with a particular examination of Scottish clubs' summer presence in Denmark during the time period. Whilst newspapers and club insiders were faintly cognizant of the future potential of club football as competition, Scottish clubs' pre-First World War tours to Denmark largely had three purposes: (1) the procurement of technical football knowledge, especially *from* professional Scottish clubs; (2) money: both for the clubs who visited, and for the Danish Football Association (*Dansk Boldspil Union*, DBU) and the middle-class, amateur Copenhagen clubs which dominated its governance during the pre-War period; and (3) relaxation and enjoyment after the stresses of the domestic league and cup seasons. Nevertheless, the broader meanings of these tours, which have largely been undiscussed within the English-language historiography of football, will also be analysed: namely, the media treatments of the events – including the cartoons, etchings and photography used for the occasions – as well as some media accounts (typically written by the players themselves) which emphasized the fraternal and touristic aspects of the trip. Tourism was especially important, as football's entry into

Denmark came on the back of well-established transport and trade links between the country and the UK's North Sea ports, and thus precedents already existed for the well-trod paths that British footballers would take towards discovering Denmark, its landscape, and its 'history'. Here, then, the early years of 'international' club football in Europe can be viewed as a lens for viewing late nineteenth- and early-twentieth century British attitudes toward the idea of 'the Continent', and possible futures for the game. They also reveal elements of political insecurity within the broader British, Scandinavian and European contexts, in these the earliest years of world football governance.

This piece builds upon an earlier work by the author, which examined the first three tours of Denmark by Scottish and British clubs: those of Glasgow's Queen's Park FC in 1898, 1900 and 1903.[2] Yet this is one of the few articles in the English-language historiography of football which examined British clubs and pre-War European tours to any great extent. In the case of Denmark, this is perhaps especially surprising, as the nation was one of the first to face off against British national teams in a significant men's football finals: those of the 1908 Olympics in London and the 1912 Olympics in Stockholm, where 'Great Britain' squads, comprised of English amateurs, beat Denmark in the gold medal match.[3] Very shortly after Stockholm, Nils Middleboe would become the first Dane to emigrate to British football.[4] Grønkjær and Olsen believed that these tours, especially Queen's Park's first appearance in Copenhagen in 1898, indeed had a galvanizing effect on the development of competitive football, non-professional in Denmark.[5]

### The origins of Danish football?

The early years of Danish football certainly had their fair share of connections to the UK, as has been previously discussed in the English-language historiography on the history of world football.[6] One of the working myths on the foundation of Denmark's (and continental Europe's) first official association football club, Københavns Boldklub (KB) – a body founded in 1876 – involves the father of one pupil at Zealand's Sorø Akademi, who in 1877 received a football as a birthday gift from his father, a merchant based at Hull. By 1878, he and other boys from Sorø Akademi and several other nearby schools began playing football in 1878 a winter activity in lieu of cricket. Scottish footballers worked on the premise of a different myth: previous to Queen's Park first 1898 tour, Queen's Park's Alexander Hamilton credited Dundee man JT Smart, a former KB member whilst resident in Copenhagen, as having introduced the game.[7]

The truth is difficult to pinpoint: KB had its fair share of British members, in part due to the movement of people and goods which occurred between Denmark and the UK after the former's defeat by Germany in 1864 at the end of the Second Schleswigian War. During the late nineteenth century, Denmark's cities, especially Copenhagen, benefitted both from the explosion of the agricultural industry and easy access to international sea lanes. Copenhagen quadrupled in population to over half a million people by the end of the period.[8] Families from well-to-do backgrounds would often send their children on tours of Britain, while some Danish companies had employees trained in the UK: it is therefore not likely that one single person, British or Danish, introduced association football to Denmark.[9] Part of what made Denmark and a logical location for early continental forays amongst British clubs, in fact, was its easy access from Edinburgh, Newcastle-upon-Tyne, Hull and the north-east coast of the UK. The Leith, Hull and Hamburg Steam Packet Company was founded in 1836, and established a regular service between Copenhagen, Kristiansand, Hamburg, Hull and Leith shortly after its management was taken over by James and Donald Currie in 1862. From the outset of these sailings, the company's boats carried Danish exports of cattle to the UK; and, in the coming years, more state-of-the-art ships had special compartments fitted for the transportation of butter, eggs and bacon.[10]

Queen's Park's 1898 visit to Denmark was the first trip to continental Europe made by a Scottish football club, and the second tour by major UK football clubs beyond British and Irish shores in as many years; in 1897, London's Corinthians visited South Africa. Queen's Park and Corinthians were the self-styled amateur clubs of Scotland and England, respectively, and their visits abroad took on 'missionary' connotations for commentators of the time. For Corinthians, their 1897 tour of South Africa was meant to solidify the bonds of British imperialism.[11] England's Clapton FC are widely acknowledged as the first to make the trip to the continent, having made a trip to Belgium in 1890, though it is probably difficult to identify who was first with any certainty.[12] Queen's Park, however, were interested primarily in what they thought of as education, and in communing with the broad church of European amateur sport.[13] Danish football would remain staunchly amateur until 1978.[14]

## The tours and their sources

Queen's Park FC's first visit to Denmark in 1898 was arranged through the visit of a Mr. Knudsen (often spelled with other variations) to the Scotland-Wales international at Fir Park, Motherwell on 19 March 1898. This set off a chain of correspondence between the club and the Danish Sports Federation (*Dansk Idræts-Forbund*, DIF), which negotiated the club's attendance at the International Festival of Sports and Gymnastics (*Den Internationale Gymnastik-og Idrætsfest*), held in Copenhagen from 30 May to 2 June of that year.[15] Essentially, Queen's Park's attendance at this staunchly amateur festival was a show of solidarity: Danish athletic and gymnastics culture at the time was militantly amateur and overwhelmingly middle-class, as were QP, who maintained their staunch anti-professionalism in the face of a Scottish and English football establishment that had been forced by clubs to accept professionalism.[16] But there was also cynical edge to this, as the Festival sold Queen's Park's amateurism towards a more deliberate end: gate receipts, needed to make the event profitable after an initial grant from the Danish government.[17] Queen's Park would return in 1900 and 1903; but, despite the role played by the Glasgow club in instituting these contests – and they would continue to come over to Denmark in the coming years – the DBU was interested in better clubs, one which represented the professional vanguard of British football. Even by 1903, for their third clash against Queen's Park, the DBU hired a professional coach: David Mitchell, formerly of Rangers and Kilmarnock, the first of a long line of British coaches who migrated abroad.[18] When Newcastle United and Southampton arrived in Copenhagen in 1904 to participate in the Regatta Cup, it ushered in a highly lucrative era for Copenhagen's ostensibly amateur city clubs. This was a self-perpetuating cycle which helped Copenhagen clubs maintain firm control over the DBU: most of association's select squads which faced Queen's Park were made up of members of KB, Akademisk Boldklub

(AB), Frem, and Boldklubben 1893 (B93). These clubs drew from a highly middle-class, educated circle; and, aside from filling their coffers, British clubs' tours of Denmark strengthened the power and prestige of the Copenhagen clubs.[19]

By 1914, Queen's Park was far from the only ones to have travelled down the Øresund. During the late 1900s and early 1910s, Copenhagen had become a popular closed-season destination for British football clubs, and not just ones based immediately on the North Sea coast. Table 1, derived from the DBU's annual reports based in the Danish State Archives (*Rigsarkivet*), shows the extent to which British and Danish football interacted, specifically during the period 1910–1914.

Major Scottish clubs such as Celtic, Rangers and Hearts were common visitors, as were big English sides such as Newcastle United, Liverpool and Middlesbrough. The teams assembled to play the visitors, as before 1910, were typically a mix of players from KB, B93, AB and Frem, with the odd DBU select squad. Matches against British clubs were a part of busy summer programmes, and were typically sandwiched around matches at home and away against a variety of mostly Swedish and German sides. Unlike their continental counterparts, Danish clubs and select teams, previous to 1914, were not recorded as making a return journey. After Queen's Park's second visit to Denmark, in 1900, Scottish newspapers suggested inviting a DBU select team to the 1901 Glasgow International Exhibition, but this never happened.[20]

Taylor has recently argued that historians, unlike those working within other disciplines within the broad umbrella of 'sport studies', have been relatively slow to embrace transnational research.[21] To that end, a few precedents for transnational, bilingual research exist within the broad body of work on media accounts of mega events: specifically, the work of von der Lippe and MacLean, as well as Boyle and Monteiro.[22] Additionally, Kowalski and Porter provide another rough template for this work in their historical examinations of football during the cold war.[23] Several other articles discuss the influence of British football on later Nordic playing styles, but little English-language work has attempted to examine the transnational development of late nineteenth–early twentieth century European club football (inclusive of the UK) on two sides of the linguistic coin.[24]

Research for this paper was performed via contemporary newspapers located in the Mitchell Library in Glasgow, the National Library of Scotland in Edinburgh, and the Danish Royal Library (*Det Kongelige Bibliotek*) in Copenhagen. At the same time, it utilizes governing bodies' documents housed in the Scottish Football Museum in Glasgow and the Danish State Archives in Copenhagen. The Scottish and British newspaper accounts of these trips were written by the players and officials of the clubs, and this inevitably influences their content and primary motifs; thus, it is necessary to obtain accounts of these events from different provenances, primarily Danish ones. After all, as Brown has recently stated regarding the assumed link by Anglophone historians between the 'informal Empire' of Britain and the origins of South American association football, an assumed model of outward British diffusion typically ignores sources in languages other than English, as well as national contexts for sporting and cultural development.[25]

Sport was a popular topic in Scottish newspapers by the late nineteenth and early twentieth centuries. While the best coverage of Scottish football was initially based in weekly or bi-weekly sports-only titles such as *Scottish Referee* and *Scottish Sport*, by the 1890s populist dailies like Glasgow's *Evening Times* were beginning to make heavy inroads into the field, so much so that their sales were increasingly being

Table 1. International team and international club interactions between with Denmark the UK, 1910–1914. *International matches*.

| Date | Location | Danish team/club (goals scored) | British team/club (goals scored) |
|---|---|---|---|
| *05 May 1910* | *Copenhagen* | *Denmark (2)* | *England Amateurs (1)* |
| 16 May 1910 | Copenhagen | B93 and KB (2) | Manchester City (3) |
| 18 May 1910 | Copenhagen | B93 and KB (5) | Manchester City (2) |
| 22 May 1910 | Copenhagen | B93 and KB (3) | Liverpool (0) |
| 24 May 1910 | Copenhagen | B93 and KB (0) | Liverpool (1) |
| 01 June 1910 | Copenhagen | AB and Frem (1) | Notts County (1) |
| 03 June 1910 | Copenhagen | AB and Frem (2) | Notts County (4) |
| 05 June 1910 | Copenhagen | AB and Frem (1) | Notts County (2) |
| 07 May 1911 | Copenhagen | AB and Frem (1) | Middlesbrough (1) |
| 09 May 1911 | Copenhagen | AB and Frem (1) | Middlesbrough (1) |
| 12 May 1911 | Copenhagen | AB and Frem (1) | Middlesbrough (2) |
| 14 May 1911 | Copenhagen | AB and Frem (2) | Bradford City (4) |
| 16 May 1911 | Copenhagen | AB and Frem (2) | Bradford City (2) |
| 25 May 1911 | Copenhagen | B93 and KB (2) | Sheffield Wednesday (3) |
| 26 May 1911 | Copenhagen | B93 and KB (2) | Sheffield Wednesday (3) |
| 28 May 1911 | Copenhagen | B93 and KB (2) | Sheffield Wednesday (3) |
| 08 June 1911 | Copenhagen | B93 and KB (1) | Rangers (1) |
| 11 June 1911 | Copenhagen | B93 and KB (1) | Rangers (3) |
| 08 September 1911 | Copenhagen | DBU Select (6) | Wanderers (2) |
| *21 October 1911* | *London* | *Denmark (0)* | *England Amateurs (3)* |
| 03 May 1912 | Copenhagen | AB, B93, Frem, and KB (2) | Civil Service (Edinburgh) (0) |
| 05 May 1912 | Copenhagen | AB, B93, Frem, and KB (2) | Civil Service (Edinburgh) (1) |
| 10 May 1912 | Copenhagen | AB, B93, Frem, and KB (3) | Clapton Orient (3) |
| 12 May 1912 | Copenhagen | AB, B93, Frem, and KB (0) | Clapton Orient (4) |
| 19 May 1912 | Copenhagen | AB, B93, Frem, and KB (1) | Heart of Midlothian (1) |
| 21 May 1912 | Copenhagen | AB, B93, Frem, and KB (2) | Heart of Midlothian (0) |
| 02 June 1912 | Copenhagen | AB, B93, Frem, and KB (1) | Celtic (3) |
| 05 June 1912 | Copenhagen | AB, B93, Frem, and KB (4) | Celtic (1) |
| *04 July 1912* | *Stockholm (1912 Olympics, Gold Medal Match)* | *Denmark (2)* | *Great Britain (4) (referred to as 'England')* |
| 01 May 1913 | Copenhagen | AB, B93, Frem, and KB (1) | Birmingham (0) |
| 04 May 1913 | Copenhagen | AB, B93, Frem, and KB (5) | Birmingham (4) |
| 12 May 1913 | Copenhagen | AB, B93, Frem, and KB (1) | Newcastle United (4) |

*(Continued)*

Table 1. (*Continued*).

| Date | Location | Danish team/club (goals scored) | British team/club (goals scored) |
|---|---|---|---|
| 15 May 1913 | Copenhagen | AB, B93, Frem, and KB (2) | Newcastle United (3) |
| 18 May 1913 | Copenhagen | AB, B93, Frem, and KB (1) | Newcastle United (1) |
| 01 June 1913 | Copenhagen | AB, B93, Frem, and KB (1) | London Caledonians (3) |
| 03 June 1913 | Copenhagen | AB, B93, Frem, and KB (7) | London Caledonians (1) |
| 05 June 1913 | Copenhagen | AB, B93, Frem, and KB (1) | Rangers (2) |
| 08 June 1913 | Copenhagen | AB, B93, Frem, and KB (1) | Rangers (1) |
| 23 June 1913 | Copenhagen | KFUMs Boldklub (YMCA Sports Club) (2) | YMCA, England (4) |
| 26 June 1913 | Copenhagen | KFUMs Boldklub (YMCA Sports Club) | YMCA, England (0) |

driven by interest in sport.[26] But Queen's Park's first three tours of Denmark, despite their novelty, were given very little coverage by both the sports papers and dailies. 1898 and 1903 featured some run-up and post-tour coverage, while 1900s tour competed for column space with the relief of Mafeking during the Second South African War.[27] Scottish newspaper accounts of the trips, even those written by travelling club members, often did not list names of the opposing team's players, or sometimes even the name of the club beyond 'the Danish team'; the term 'Boldklub' (football club or ball club) was used interchangeably between different sides. Football supporters were not alone in facing this particular issue with regard to Danish affairs: the 1910 annual report of the British legation in Copenhagen noted a void in British papers' coverage of Denmark:

> There is still no British correspondent in Copenhagen, and the British press continues to get its Danish news either from Danish correspondents … (some of whom are undoubtedly good), or from the German Press. Regret is frequently express in Danish journalistic circles that the British press is not better supplied with Danish news.[28]

Given this deficiency, it would be unrealistic to expect the likes of the *Evening Times* to cover these tours thoroughly, let alone *Scottish Referee*. In fact, in many respects, *Referee*'s lack of a travelling correspondent meant reducing the Danes to crude stereotypes: Figure 1 shows a cartoonist's perception of Queen's Park's 1903 tour, one that sufficiently illustrates Denmark to be a 'Viking' land across an ocean. For British newspapers, Boolean searches through digitally available help only so much with getting around this black hole in coverage: since the best accounts of these tours were written by the players and administrators of these clubs, they ended up appearing in smaller, more sympathetic newspapers. In Glasgow, for instance, the *Glasgow Observer*, the city's Catholic weekly, contained a great deal about Celtic's post-1905 tours of Europe; for cross-town rivals Rangers, it was the Unionist title the *Glasgow News*. However, *Politiken*, the daily liberal Copenhagen broadsheet, devoted front pages towards these visits, often with sketches of the matches them-

Figure 1. *Scottish Referee's* view of Queen's Park's 1903 voyage Denmark.
Source: *Scottish Referee*, 29 May 1903.

selves. For instance, Figure 2 shows not just the match itself between Middlesbrough and a DBU select in Copenhagen on 9 May 1907, but also the surrounding media scrum, complete with photographers sitting on the touchline at goal. When Celtic visited Copenhagen in June that year, all three of their matches got sketches of their own (Figures 3–5).

Some of *Politiken*'s sketches were admittedly humorous, such as Queen's Park's playing in the rain during their May 1908 visit, as shown in Figure 6. Others still display a clever use of reportage: for example, the paper's numbered account of Rangers' 1911 exploits against a side featuring KB and B93 members, as shown in Figure 7. Meanwhile, the illustration of Civil Service FC's visit in May 1912, as shown in Figure 8 came with a far larger account than was given in the hometown *Edinburgh Evening News*.[29] But if one looks beyond just the coverage of the stories themselves, and onto adverts for the games, one begins to notice certain patterns. Take, for instance, Celtic's journey to Copenhagen to play a select team of KB, B93, Frem and AB members, part of a longer journey around Scandinavia and continental Europe. Celtic were advertised as a 'professional' club; and, after general entry to their first match cost one kroner, the price fell to 50 øre for the second match (Figures 9 and 10). Meanwhile, Rangers' June 1913 visit to the new Idrætsplads ground at Fælledparken in Østerbro, Copenhagen, offers an opportunity to view *Politiken*'s photographs of the match itself, and the well-dressed crowds which attended it. Hearts' tour the year previous noted the 'colossal' size of the new ground, costed at £40,000: Jimmy Duckworth, Hearts' trainer, was reported as

Figure 2.   Middlesbrough vs. a DBU select in Copenhagen.
Source: *Politiken*, 10 May 1907.

saying that he had 'never seen any track that comes near this one'.[30] Two days later, an Edinburgh paper referred to the exclusivity of the crowd, stating: 'The crowd included many members of the Danish Government and civic dignitaries seated in the Tribune as the reserved section is called. It was half men and half women. Very few of the working class attend football'.[31]

Beyond just information, however, both Scottish and Danish newspapers' accounts of the trips served as an opportunity to further build upon pre-existing sporting identities; or, in some cases, as a means of displaying the 'otherness' of their foreign opponents. Scottish football clubs were certainly perceived to be upholding their own unique traditions, and this included Glasgow's 'Old Firm', Rangers and Celtic.[32] Rangers, shown in Figure 11 marching off to the continent for their 1913 tour of Scandinavia, are drawn to look distinctly like Orange marchers, not-so-subtly hinting at the club's close relationship at the time with employees of the staunchly Protestant Harland and Wolff shipyards on the River Clyde.[33] The narrative of the Norwegian leg of Celtic's 1912 tour, meanwhile, featured as one of its centrepieces Roman Catholic mass at St. Olav's Cathedral in Christiania (now Oslo).[34] (In contrast to Celtic's mass, given in Latin, a Protestant service in Christiania went well over the head of Hearts that same year; they had to settle for unintelligible Norwegian speakers and Bibles.[35]) But the reputation of Queen's Park as Scottish football's middle-class tastemakers did not mesh with the Danish sketch

Figure 3.   Sketch from Celtic's tour of Copenhagen, 1907.
Source: *Politiken*, 4 June 1907.

artists' perceptions of them. Upon playing the first match of their May 1900 tour to Denmark – which was played in front of the Danish royal family, including Prince Christian (the future King Christian X), Princess Maud, Prince Carl (the future King Haakon VII of Norway) and Princess Aleksandrine – *Politiken*'s artists drew a decidedly more common, somewhat foreign Queen's Park lining up to meet Prince Christian, as seen in Figure 12. The Danish press, then, like their Scottish/British counterparts, viewed the 'other' as something a bit more alien.

**Political football?**

The presence of royalty and other Danish government officials at these matches means that they cannot be considered wholly apolitical. Hearts, during their May 1912 tour to Denmark, even witnessed the funeral of King Frederick VIII, whose death forced the postponement of their first match.[36] Yet, whilst the Scottish newspapers accounts of the post-1905 matches noted the presence of the British ambassadors and other diplomatic staff at these events, records of the British embassies in Copenhagen, as well as those in Oslo and Stockholm – housed at the National Archives in Kew – barely mentioned football in any context. This apparent lack of explicit political interest in football did not mean that the context of these visits did

Figure 4.   Sketch from Celtic's tour of Copenhagen, 1907.
Source: *Politiken*, 8 June 1907.

not exist within a greater political context – far from it. Wider European geopolitics were creeping into football by this point. The formation of the Federation Internationale de Football Association (FIFA) in 1904 featured both Denmark and Sweden, but none of the home nations. England joined only when Daniel Woolfall was made FIFA president in 1906, and applications by the Scottish Football Association (SFA), the Football Association of Wales (FAW) and the Irish Football Association (IFA) were rejected by FIFA members who feared a precedent for similar 'stateless nations' – Germany's states, in particular – being admitted into the Federation.[37] The SFA, the FAW and the IFA were not admitted until 1910, largely through a grandfather clause, and FIFA sought to protect this distinction: for instance, in 1911, SFA member club Aberdeen was warned by FIFA not to participate in summer friendly matches against teams affiliated with the Bohemian Football Association.[38] Before Hearts' voyage 1912 voyage to Scandinavia, the *Edinburgh Evening News* made reference to Celtic, Rangers and Aberdeen, who the year before had 'taken advantage of the raising of the embargo upon Continental tours by Scottish clubs'.[39] Even at this point, Scottish clubs had their first taste of FIFA's attempts to establish governance of world football, and the complexities of the UK's unique privileges complicated Scottish participation in international football against the Nordic coun-

Figure 5.   Sketch from Celtic's tour of Copenhagen, 1907.
Source: *Politiken*, 10 June 1907.

tries: whilst a bitter professional/amateur feud raged within the British Olympic Association (BOA) in the run-up to the 1912 Olympics in Stockholm, the BOA vetoed a plan from 1912 organisers which would have allowed England, Scotland, Wales and Ireland to compete separately in the competition's football tournament. As in 1908, Great Britain's Olympic football team comprised of English players selected solely by the English Football Association (FA).[40] Quite tellingly, within the DBU's 1913 annual report, Denmark's gold medal match at the 1912 Olympics against Great Britain (which the Danes would lose 4–2) is recorded as being against 'England'.[41] Whilst Danish newspapers clearly recognized that Scottish clubs were 'Scottish', Scotland itself had a long way to go as being recognized as a separate sporting polity outside the UK.

Beyond this, war and muscular statecraft were certainly motifs in the Scottish accounts of these tours. While the press accounts of Queen's Park's first 1898 tour are sparse, the build-up in *Scottish Sport* made no bones about Glasgow's middle-class amateurs crossing into a friendly enemy's territory:

> [Queen's Park] cross the foam on Thursday from Leith to one of the finest cities in the north of Europe. It is strongly fortified, and is enclosed by a wall, the circuit of which is five miles, but though the Q.P. are carrying war into an enemy's country, we fancy the gates will be opened quickly enough to them. Within the walls they can study the

Figure 6.    Queen's Park in Copenhagen in 1908.
Source: *Politiken*, 16 May 1908.

arts of peace, and a visit to the royal library and museum, if for nothing else but to see Thorwaldsen's sculptures, will repay them.[42]

Upon their return to Scotland, one of *Scottish Sport*'s columnists, 'The Misanthrope', even joked about a future where war was sublimated in favour of football:

> I'd rather have a jolly good old-fashioned war any day to a modern football match, and surely nations would never sink so low as to prefer the latter to the former. But, mark you, that is the direction in which things are tending.[43]

*Scottish Referee* was more explicit about the martial context. Upon Queen's Park's return home, in a piece headlined 'Scots Wha Hae!':

> As we anticipated, Queen's Park have nobly upheld their own and their country's honour in the land of the Dane. Our cablegrams from our correspondent at the seat of the War tell of victory all along the lines, goal, penalty, and touch, and utter subjugation, if not annihilation of the enemy.[44]

A decade later, *Referee* saw reasons for optimism in Queen's Park's 1908 voyage, especially as Queen's Park's draw in its first match was held up as an indication that Danish football was pulling level, stating:

Figure 7.   Action shots of Rangers during their 1911 tour.
Source: *Politiken*, 9 June 1911.

> The time may come when we will have many international contests, and so assist to
> preserve the 'entente cordiale' with all countries, and any disputes which could not be
> settled at The Hague might be quite well decided on the football field. The question of
> reduction of armaments would also be solved.[45]

Events in Europe, however, would quickly render such feelings obsolete, and
perhaps in retrospect look dangerously naïve.

   Beyond just Denmark, and within the regional context of Scandinavian football,
Scottish clubs noted that trips to Norway in particular *were* political, at least in the
minds of their Norwegian hosts, whose union with Sweden broke up in 1905. The
Norwegian Football Association (*Norges Fotballforbund*, NFF) was not formed until
1902, and the government was keen to promote sport as a means of competing inter-
nationally against Sweden, the primary barometer by which Norwegian sport (especially football) was judged.[46] At that point, Norway had hired their own British
coach, former Manchester United man Vincent Hayes.[47] *Glasgow News* noted during

**Fra den skotsk-danske Fodboldkamp i Gaar.**

Figure 8.   Civil Service FC in Copenhagen, 1912.
Source: *Politiken*, 6 May 1912.

Rangers' 1911 visit to Christiania that: 'There is a big effort being made here to make the game popular, the Government giving a grant of £50 to help towards the expenses of the two games'.[48] The next year, when Celtic visited, *Glasgow Observer*'s 'Man in the Know', quite probably a high-ranking club official, stated:

> I may say that there is the most intense jealousy between Norway, Sweden and Denmark in matters political and imperial, and this feeling extends to football. The game was introduced to Norway only ten years ago, and had but a brief spell of life, languishing and dying in the short space of two years. But when the natives saw the progress made by Swedes and Danes, they took heart, engaged English professionals as coaches, fitted up a tidy enclosure, and went into the pastime with as much zest as they impart to their great winter games of skiing and skating.[49]

The storm clouds were already on the horizon. In one of the few references to competitive sport in the records of Britain's Nordic embassies, Sir Cecil Spring-Rice, the British ambassador to Sweden (future envoy to the US), reflected establishment concerns about the country's poor performance at the 1912 Olympics in Stockholm:

Figure 9. The price advertised for tickets for Celtic's second 1912 match in Denmark is cheaper than the first.
Source: *Politiken*, 1 June 1912.

Although British subjects were successful in what we should generally consider as the most important events, lawn tennis, football, swimming, shooting, rowing, the mile and the marathon races, they failed in those competition which required long technical training of a highly specialized characters and the system of scoring adopted in the Olympian games by which each event is of equal value, results in what appears to be a rather ignominious conclusion for England. Consequently our prestige has suffered to a certain extent, especially in the military competition in which, partly to bad luck, our representation did not obtain distinction. The question naturally presents itself – is it worthwhile to go through the trouble and expense of completion unless the British competitors can be trained to the same extent and degree as their foreign rivals? This question will naturally be carefully considered by the military authorities [by] the next Olympic meeting which will take place in Berlin.[50]

At least partially, then, the post-1918 treatments of these Scottish tours (or lack thereof) can be explained by the First World War, and the shifting geopolitics of football at the time. Richard Robinson's flawed 1920 history of Queen's Park, for instance, saw the club's failed attempts during the period to initiate friendly matches with German clubs as clairvoyant; it was hard to imagine, stated Robinson, 'that the classic slopes of Hampden [could have ever] been desecrated by the foot of a Hun … The vileness of the race was not then known, or even suspected'.[51] Waquet and Vincent state that it was not until the creation of inter-allied tournaments during the Great War that football and rugby became truly international sports.[52] The period 1898–1914, then, was a highly awkward time in the broader narrative of international association football.

Figure 10.   The price advertised for tickets for Celtic's second 1912 match in Denmark is cheaper than the first.
Source: *Politiken*, 4 June 1912.

Figure 11.   Rangers, marching to Scandinavia for their 1913 summer tour.
Source: *Scottish Referee*, 30 May 1913.

## Tourism

By the late 1900s, Denmark was no longer the only stopping point for most British clubs who made their way to continental Europe. Nevertheless, the footballers who visited Denmark and other countries were not there solely for footballing reasons.

Skotterne præsenteres for Prins Christian.

Figure 12.   Queen's Park meet the future King of Denmark, 1900.
Source: *Politiken*, 23 May 1900.

Aside from the commercial and cultural reasons football clubs made these trips, these trips were also recreational: they served as players' rewards for a hard-fought season in the top tiers of British football. Tours and holidays had long been a hall-mark of Victorian football, at least in Scotland: whilst many matches were deliber-ately arranged with major English sides in order to secure significant crowds and gate receipts (and occasionally to laud Scots who had become professional foot-ballers in England), other winter and summer tours were planned specifically with relaxation and occasionally hedonism in mind. Football in Victorian Scotland, after all, existed in a highly masculine, fraternal context which encouraged after-match (over)sociability.[53] In fact, not all tours were so lucrative for the travelling teams: the *Edinburgh Evening News*'s 'Diogenes' even hinted that Hearts' 1912 Scandina-vian tour – hurt at least somewhat by the death of Frederick VIII – was not primar-ily for money:

> [Hearts'] trip was pre-eminently a holiday outing, intended more for this than anything else, to give players a change of air and scene after a very arduous season. It was not a money-making business; in fact so far as I can gather it will cost the club a trifle. How-ever, it was, within limits, a great success. The members of the party saw some strange sights, they made some friends, they played some good football.[54]

It is not surprising then that in Scottish newspaper accounts of the trips, the sea voy-ages themselves, as well as the destinations visited along the way, were a part of players' and administrators' narratives of what occurred. Huggins states that, despite the 'sporting tour' being a common theme of the historiography of British and Irish sport (particularly in an imperial context), the opportunity of players to enjoy themselves as tourists in these places has been left mostly unexamined.[55] This theme is currently being developed further by Taylor, who recently gave a paper on accounts of foreign tourism in interwar British football players' autobiographies.[56]

With the lack of English-language scholarly historiography of British tours of Denmark during the period, it can be difficult to find evidence of what exactly the common routes of travel were for Britons, including Scots, who found themselves on Zealand's Øresund coast. It is doubtful, however, that these Scottish footballers went too far off of the beaten tourist path. The Leith, Hull and Hamburg Steam Packet Company's 1896 tourist guide to its destinations included a map of Copenhagen's, as well as description of its sights:

> Copenhagen, the capital of Denmark, with 300,000 inhabitants, is very beautifully situated on the Sound. The principal attractions are: – the Thorvaldsen Museum, built in the form of a hollow square, with the grave of the great sculptor in the quadrangle, and containing all his principle works and many paintings and relics illustrative of his life; the Fruekirke (sic), with Thorvaldsen's Christ and the Twelve Apostles; the famous Museum of Northern Antiquities,; the Ethnographical Museum of Northern Antiquities; the Danske Folke-Museum; the Royal Picture Gallery; the Castle of Rosenborg, with a chronological collection illustrative of the reigns of the Danish kings from the 16th century; and, in the evening, the Tivoli Gardens – the favourite place of entertainment for all Copenhagen. Go up also to the top of the Round Tower of the Trinity Church by winding ascent that Peter the Great is said to have ridden up on horseback. The view from the summit is a very interesting one.[57]

Whilst the guide did recommend voyages outside of Copenhagen, they were typically confined to the immediate environs of the Danish capital, particularly those destinations based on the Øresund:

> Interesting excursions can be taken to the Deer Park (Dyrehave), Charlottenlund, Klampenborg, the palace of Frederiksborg, arranged as a National Historical Museum, and by rail or carriage through the pleasant meadows and shady beech woods of Zealand, so often described in the stories of Hans Christian Anderssen. A very pleasant trip can be made taking the steamer to Elsinore, where Hamlet's grave may be visited, and returning by the railway. Roskilde also, with its fine old Cathedral and pleasant surroundings, is well worth a visit.[58]

Scottish clubs' tours of the sights and sounds whilst in Denmark did not deviate far beyond these contours. In fact, at least in part, Queen's Park's first visit can be described as part of a package holiday. The organisers of the International Festival gave participant athletes free entry and travel to a variety of attractions and destinations in Copenhagen, and on Zealand's west coast. The awards ceremony of the Festival was held in the Arenatheatret of Tivoli Gardens, the opulent amusement park located in central Copenhagen and the delegates were each given a ticket for free entry.[59] Delegates were also given steamship tickets to the Festival's after-party, held at Skodsborg, just north of Klampenborg.[60] Robinson's accounts of the Skodsborg dinner – and another dinner in Copenhagen the night before – featured Queen's Park in the central role, with Carl Melchior, one of the DIF's top officials, proposing a toast to the 'Scottish Football Team', and Charles Campbell, after a speech, toasting the Danish football squad with 'Highland honours, much to the astonishment and amusement of the Danes'.[61]

It was the environs north of Copenhagen, such as the leafy, well-to-do holiday villages of Skodsborg and Klampenborg, as well as footballers' first approaches into Copenhagen from the north of the Øresund (via Hull and Kristiansand), that Scottish commentators attempted to place within the framework of the familiar. For the west of Scotland's footballers, the Øresund and its shores were used as a stand-in for the Firth of Clyde and its coast, one of Scotland's premier tourist regions and a short distance from its largest city, Glasgow.[62] The region certainly had its fair share of activities, and many of them were shared by the different footballers who went there, including: deer hunting on the King of Denmark's land, based around his grand hunting lodge, Eremitageslottet (The Hermitage); nearby golfing at Københavns Golf Klub; and fun and games at the nearby Dyrehavsbakken ('The Deer Park Hill'), an amusement park located on the royal estate. The golf course, in 1911, in fact had as its professional a Musselburgh native.[63] At the start of Celtic's June 1912 voyage to Scandinavia, 'Man in the Know' noted that: 'even our invalids were able to crawl up on deck a few hours before landing and view the glories of the Sound, which was just our own Firth of Clyde over again'.[64] Of Queen's Park's first journey to Denmark, Robinson wrote of 'Skotsborg' as being 'doon the water'.[65] *Scottish Referee*, on Celtic's 1912 trip to Denmark, referred to 'Scotsbord' as 'A LOVELY WATERING PLACE'. Rangers, on their 1913 trip to the country, walked from Skodsborg, 'a delightful holiday resort', into the forests south of the town going towards Klampenborg. 'It was a really delightful walk through vast wooded territory', proclaimed the author for the *Glasgow News* piece, 'which, had it not been for the beeches instead of firs, would have reminded us of Bonnie Scotland'. On that same trip, Rangers' players, along with their hosts, drove to Lyngby, and from there sailed to Frederiksdal.[66] One can read too much into this recognition, however: the familiarity of landscape was not reserved solely for Denmark. After the Danish leg of Celtic's 1912 tour of Scandinavia, Celtic's visit to Norway prompted similar observations. The member of Celtic's party who gave his thoughts to *Scottish Referee* wrote that 'cruising in and out of the islands which make up the fjords is a perfect treat, and makes one think of the Kyles of Bute at their best in midsummer'.[67] (In general, this participant was more convinced of the kinship between Scotland and Norway, also stating that: 'The people here are much the same as "oor ain folks", and are much more reserved than the Danes, quieter in all their actions and ways'.[68])

The sights and sounds of Copenhagen itself were taken in more on their own terms, though even here, the footballers did not stray far beyond the well-established tourist routes. After its use in the International Festival in 1898, Tivoli Gardens certainly featured in these accounts. Hearts were entertained at the De Strasse Hotel opposite the Gardens after their defeat to their Danish hosts in May 1912.[69] The Celtic team would meet up with their Danish opposites at the amusement park a month later, during their tour.[70] Rangers' members, along with their hosts, certainly enjoyed Tivoli Gardens whilst in the city in June 1913: 'most of our time', stated the *Glasgow News*' correspondent 'was spent on the Joy Wheel, [with] players of both sides trying their luck to the amusement of everybody around'.[71] The clubs mentioned other sites in their travels, such as the Royal Library and the Thorsvalden Museum.[72] Rangers' players' June 1913 account of their shopping even hints at the highly gendered, masculine environment these tours took part in:

> On Saturday we spent the morning looking for presents to take home. This is about the worst job – after flittings. I may tell you we are two minutes' walk from the 'Buchanan Street of Copenhagen' [a major Glasgow shopping thoroughfare], and it took the best of two hours to make our purchases.[73]

But no other Copenhagen location was as central to the narratives of the footballers and their charges as the Carlsberg Brewery. Rangers, during their 1911 visit, were given a tour of the Brewery by one of its employees, Mr. Hennison, 'who was born in Greenock, and has a warm side to Scotland'.[74] When Hearts visited Denmark in May 1912, they too received a tour, despite the death of the King Frederick VIII a few days before.[75] Celtic, in their visit to the Brewery a month later, were noted as taking a special interest to its 'wonderful machinery', with several members of 'The Trade' being present. (Quite a few of Celtic's members continued to be associated with the public house or whisky trades.) Celtic's members also noted the philanthropic aims of the Jacobsen family, who owned the Brewery, and patronized various projects of the Danish government.[76]

## Conclusion

Scottish commentators at the time sensed that there was a possible future in this kind of international football. Even after Queen's Park's 1898 tour, *Scottish Sport*'s A Misanthrope had a prophetic vision of a globalized game, albeit within a highly regional, European context:

> ... before long we will have clubs advertising for players thus: – 'No one need apply who cannot speak every European language; preference given to those who can swear at a referee in Gaelic, and tell a linesman he's a blanketty blank of blank in the various German dialects.' We're getting on; we're getting on![77]

Celtic manager Willie Maley, meanwhile, was far more explicit in foreseeing a future where international club football played a central role. However, whilst Maley remembered Celtic's pre-First World War tours fondly, his ultimate dream was a very different one, which he fulfilled in 1931:

> [Aside from various sites in Europe] Celtic have also visited America and Canada, where in 1931 they made a tour of New York, Baltimore, Chicago, Brooklyn, Boston, Fall River, Detroit, Pawtucket, Toronto, and Montreal.

> This tour had been the dream of the early Celtic pioneers, and those privileged to travel on this occasion can never forget the hearty welcome received from their exiled friends from Scotland and Ireland. It was a real breath of home to those folks over the water and an event that will be a life-long memory to all concerned.[78]

So, while Maley could certainly see the wider commercial potential of such tours when targeted to the right audience, 'European' football, even as late as the 1930s, was still not yet seen a prize worth fighting for, or anything beyond a recreational opportunity for Scotland's and the UK's major clubs.

This article, while examining what could be described as a dead end in the history of 'European' football, has nevertheless established that British football culture, by 1900, was increasingly beginning to acknowledge and seek sporting contacts with an 'outside world', towards a variety of ends. It also establishes that Danish and other Scandinavian football clubs and associations had their reasons for seeking out highly lucrative and occasionally politically important relationships with the UK's major clubs. Perhaps most importantly, however, it establishes that forms of cultural exchange took place amongst the British and Scandinavian footballers who interacted with each other: be this through pragmatic footballing knowledge, tourism or in mutual critiques of foreigners' otherness which existed in the newspapers of respective countries. Given the diverse summer programmes assembled by Copenhagen's major football clubs by the early 1910s, and given the other destinations visited by British clubs during this period, one can assume that this article is a highly incomplete example of what is out there with regard to the potential of transnational research during this period of football's history.

## Disclosure statement

No potential conflict of interest was reported by the author.

## Acknowledgements

This research was funded through the Annie Dunlop Endowment at the University of Glasgow, School of Humanities.

I am very grateful to Allan Bennich Grønkjær for all of his assistance with this project. I am also grateful to David Speed, historian of Heart of Midlothian FC, for lending me some of the club's historical materials. I am also indebted to the following people for their help with this piece: Dr. Catriona M.M. Macdonald and Dr. Martin MacGregor at the University of Glasgow; Dr. Kay Schiller at Durham University; Professor Matthew Taylor at De Montfort University; Professor John Bale and Professor Verner Møller at Aarhus University; Roy Hay at Deakin University; and Richard McBrearty at the Scottish Football Museum.

## Notes

1. Quote from *Evening Times*, June 3, 1914. This paper also uses elements from a previous conference paper by the same author: 'Scottish Football, Europe, and "North Sea" Cultural Exchange', given at the annual meeting of the British Society of Sports History, Glasgow, September 2012.
2. McDowell, 'Queen's Park FC'.
3. Porter, 'London Football'; and Llewellyn, 'A Tale of National Disaster', 719, 721.
4. Lanfranchi and Taylor, *Moving with the Ball*, 47.
5. Grønkjær and Olsen, *Fodbold*, 38–9.
6. Murray, *The World's Game*, 22–3; and Walvin, *The People's Game*, 97.
7. *Scottish Sport*, 17 May 1898.
8. Jespersen, *A History of Denmark*, 161–4.
9. Grønkjær and Olsen, *Fodbold*, 14.
10. Glasgow University Archive Service (GUAS), UGD255/4/34/1, Anon. Company history, *C.K. Hansen Co.* ('the first establishment of the service looked after the interests in the line in Denmark').
11. Bolsmann, 'Amateurs, Pioneers, and Profits'.
12. The Friends of Clapton FC, 'The Friends of Clapton FC'.
13. McDowell, 'Queen's Park FC in Copenhagen'.
14. Olsen and Grønkjær, 'Dansk fodboldshistorie'.
15. McDowell, 'Queen's Park FC in Copenhagen'.
16. Jørgensen, 'Order, Discipline, and Self-control', 340, 346–8; McDowell, *Cultural History*; Murray, *Old Firm*, 7; Vamplew, *Pay up*, 51–153; and Crampsey, *Game*.
17. McDowell, 'Queen's Park FC in Copenhagen'.
18. *Scottish Referee*, May 25, 1903; *Scottish Referee*, June 8, 1903. For more on the migration of British coaches during the first half of the twentieth century, see Taylor, 'Football's Engineers?'.
19. Olsen and Grønkjær, 'Dansk fodboldshistorie'.
20. *Scottish Referee*, April 23, 1900; and *Evening Times*, May 28, 1900.

21. Taylor, 'Sport, Transnationalism, and Global History'.
22. Boyle and Monteiro, 'Euro 2004'; and von der Lippe and MacLean, '1954 Football World Cup'.
23. Kowalski and Porter, 'Moscow Dynamo in Britain'.
24. Larson, 'Charles Reep'; and Sund, 'The British and Continental Influence on Swedish Football'.
25. Brown, 'British Informal Empire', 1–14.
26. McDowell, *Cultural History*, 307–46.
27. McDowell, 'Queen's Park FC in Copenhagen'.
28. The National Archives, Kew (TNA), FO211/276, British Legation in Denmark, Foreign Office Correspondence, 1910: 1 January 1910 report to Foreign Secretary Sir Edward Grey.
29. *Edinburgh Evening News*, May 11, 1912.
30. Unknown Edinburgh newspaper clipping from 17 May 1912, in possession of Heart of Midlothian FC (HOMFC).
31. Unknown Edinburgh newspaper clipping from 19 May 1912, in possession of HOMFC.
32. Murray, *Old Firm*; Finn, 'Racism, Religion and Social Prejudice I'; Finn, 'Racism, Religion and Social Prejudice II'; Bradley, *Ethnic and Religious Identity in Modern Scotland*; and Walker, '"Glasgow Rangers"'.
33. Murray, *Old Firm*.
34. *Glasgow Observer*, June 15, 1912.
35. Unknown Edinburgh newspaper clipping from 12 May 1912, in possession of HOMFC.
36. Unknown Edinburgh newspaper clippings from 15 May 1912 and 17 May 1912, in possession of HOMFC.
37. Beck, *Scoring for Britain*, 50–8; and Tomlinson, 'FIFA and the Men Who Made It', 55–7.
38. Scottish Football Museum (SFM), Minutes of the Scottish Football Association Ltd., (May 1911–May 1912), May 9, 1911, May 23, 1911, May 30, 1911; and *Scottish Referee*, June 2, 1911.
39. *Edinburgh Evening News*, April 20, 1912.
40. Llewellyn, 'A Tale of National Disaster', 719, 721.
41. Rigsarkivet (Danish State Archives, RAK), 10519, Dansk Boldspil Union (DBU) (Danish Football Association), Årsberetninger (annual reports) (1910–1969), *DBU Aarsberetning 1913*. See Table 1.
42. *Scottish Sport*, May 24, 1898.
43. *Scottish Sport*, June 10, 1898.
44. *Scottish Referee*, June 3, 1898.
45. *Scottish Referee*, May 22, 1908.
46. Goksøyr, 'Football, Development and Identity in a Small Nation'; Goksøyr, 'The Popular Sounding Board'; and Goksøyr, 'Phases and Functions of Nationalism'.
47. *Scottish Referee*, June 14, 1912.
48. *Glasgow News*, June 5, 1911.
49. *Glasgow Observer*, June 22, 1912; Murray, *Old Firm*, discusses possible sources of 'Man in the Know': 50–1, 58, 70.
50. TNA, FO188/300 1912, British Legation in Sweden, Political Correspondence with the Foreign Office, 25 June 1912 letter from Sir Cecil Spring-Rice to the Private Secretary. For more on the 1912 Olympics and the establishment reaction to them, see Llewellyn, 'National Disaster'; and Llewellyn, 'A Nation Divided'.
51. Robinson, *Queen's Park*.
52. Waquet and Vincent, 'Wartime Rugby and Football'.
53. McDowell, '"Enterprise with Vengeance"'.
54. *Edinburgh Evening News*, June 1, 1912.
55. Huggins, 'Sport, Tourism, and History'.
56. Taylor, '"The World's My Football Pitch"'.
57. GUAS, UGD255/4/34/1, Anon. *Summer Tours from Leith*, 25.
58. Ibid.

59. RAK, 10366, Danmarks Idræts-Forbund (DIF) (Danish Sports Federation), Komité for 1. Internationale Gymnastik- og Idrætsfest I København (KFIGIK) (Committee for the first International Gymnastics and Sports Festival in Copenhagen), 'Festen i Arenatheatret, Adgangskort til Tivoli' (Celebrations in Arenatheatret, Admission to Tivoli).
60. RAK, 10366, DIF, KFIGIK, 'Dampskibsbillet, Kjøbenjavn – Skodsborg, Adgangskort til Festen paa Skodsborg' (Steamship Ticket, Copenhagen – Skodsborg, Admission to the festival on Skodsborg).
61. Robinson, *Queen's Park*.
62. Durie, *Scotland for the Holidays*, 86–123.
63. *Glasgow News*, June 14, 1911; *Scottish Referee*, June 10, 1912; and *Glasgow News*, June 11, 1913.
64. *Glasgow Observer*, June 8, 1912.
65. Robinson, *Queen's Park*.
66. *Glasgow News*, June 11, 1913.
67. *Scottish Referee*, June 14, 1912.
68. Ibid.
69. *Edinburgh Evening News*, May 25, 1912.
70. *Scottish Referee*, June 10, 1912.
71. *Glasgow News*, June 11, 1913.
72. *Scottish Sport*, May 24, 1898; and *Glasgow News*, June 14, 1911.
73. *Glasgow News*, June 11, 1913.
74. *Glasgow News*, June 14, 1911.
75. *Edinburgh Evening News*, May 25, 1912.
76. *Scottish Referee*, June 10, 1912.
77. *Scottish Sport*, June 10, 1898.
78. Maley, *The Story of the Celtic*, 29–30.

# References

Anon. *Dansk Boldspil-Union: Aarsberetning, 1910 (Annual Report)*. Copenhagen: Chr. Christensens Bogtrykkeri, 1911.

Anon. *Dansk Boldspil-Unions: Aarsberetning, 1911*. Copenhagen: Chr. Christensens Bogtrykkeri, 1912.

Anon. *Dansk Boldspil-Unions: Aarsberetning, 1912*. Copenhagen: Chr. Christensens Bogtrykkeri, 1913.

Anon. *Dansk Boldspil-Unions: Aarsberetning, 1913*. Copenhagen: Chr. Christensens Bogtrykkeri, 1914.

Anon. *Dansk Boldspil-Unions: Aarsberetning, 1914*. Copenhagen: Chr. Christensens Bogtrykkeri, 1915.

Anon. *Summer Tours from Leith to Norway, Denmark & Germany: The Leith, Hull & Hamburg Steam Packet Co., James Currie & Co., Managers, Leith*. Leith: William Nimmo & Co, 1896.

Beck, P.J. *Scoring for Britain: International Football and International Politics, 1900–1939*. London: Frank Cass, 1999.

Bolsmann, C. 'South African Football Tours at the Turn of the Twentieth Century: Amateurs, Pioneers and Profits'. *African Historical Review* 42, no. 1 (2010): 91–112.

Boyle, R., and C. Monteiro. '"a Small Country with a Big Ambition": Representations of Portugal and England in Euro 2004 British and Portuguese Newspaper Coverage'. *European Journal of Communication* 20, no. 2 (2005): 223–44.

Bradley, J.M. *Ethnic and Religious Identity in Modern Scotland: Culture, Politics and Football*. Aldershot: Avebury, 1995.

Brown, M. 'British Informal Empire and the Origins of Association Football in South America'. *Soccer and Society* 16, no. 2–3 (2015): 169–82.

Crampsey, R.A. *The Game for the Game's Sake: The History of Queen's Park Football Club*. Glasgow: The Queen's Park Football Club Ltd., 1967.

Durie, A. *Scotland for the Holidays: A History of Tourism in Scotland, 1780–1939*. Edinburgh: John Donald, 2006.

Finn, G.P.T. 'Racism, Religion and Social Prejudice: Irish Catholic Clubs, Soccer and Scottish Society – I the Historical Roots of Prejudice'. *International Journal of the History of Sport* 8, no. 1 (1991): 70–93.

Finn, G.P.T. 'Racism, Religion and Social Prejudice: Irish Catholic Clubs, Soccer and Scottish Society – II Social Identities and Conspiracy Theories'. *The International Journal of the History of Sport* 8, no. 3 (1991): 370–97.

Goksøyr, M. 'Phases and Functions of Nationalism: Norway's Utilization of International Sport in the Late Nineteenth and Early Twentieth Centuries'. *The International Journal of the History of Sport* 12, no. 2 (1995): 125–46.

Goksøyr, M. 'Football, Development and Identity in a Small Nation: Football Culture, Spectators and Playing Styles in Twentieth Century Norway'. *Football Studies* 1, no. 1 (1998): 37–47.

Goksøyr, M. 'The Popular Sounding Board: Nationalism, 'the People' and Sport in Norway in the Inter-War Years'. *The International Journal of the History of Sport* 14, no. 3 (1997): 100–14.

Grønkjær, A.B., and D.H. Olsen. *Fodbold, Fair Play Og Forretning [Football, Fair Play, and Business]*. Aarhus: Turbine Forgalet, 2007.

Huggins, M. 'Sport, Tourism and History: Current Historiography and Future Prospects'. *Journal of Tourism History* 5, no. 2 (2013): 107–30.

Jespersen, K.J.V. *A History of Denmark*. Basingstoke: Palgrave Macmillan, 2011.

Jørgensen, P. '"Order, Discipline and Self-control": The Breakthrough for the Danish Sports Federation and Sport 1896–1918'. *The International Journal of the History of Sport* 13, no. 3 (1996): 340–55.

Kowalski, R., and D. Porter. 'Political Football: Moscow Dynamo in Britain, 1945'. *The International Journal of the History of Sport* 14, no. 2 (1997): 100–21.

Lanfranchi, P., and M. Taylor. *Moving with the Ball: The Migration of Professional Football*. Oxford: Berg, 2001.

Larson, O. 'Charles Reep: A Major Influence on British and Norwegian Football'. *Soccer and Society* 2, no. 3 (2001): 58–78.

von der Lippe, G., and M. MacLean. 'Brawling in Berne: Mediated Transnational Moral Panics in the 1954 Football World Cup'. *International Journal of the History of Sport* 43, no. 1 (2008): 71–90.

Llewellyn, M.P. 'A Nation Divided: Great Britain and the Pursuit of Olympic Excellence, 1912–1914'. *Journal of Sport History* 35, no. 1 (2008): 73–97.

Llewellyn, M.P. '"A Tale of National Disaster"'. *The International Journal of the History of Sport* 28, no. 5 (2011): 711–29.

Maley, W. *The Story of the Celtic*. Westcliff on Sea: Desert Island Books, 1996.

McDowell, M.L. *A Cultural History of Association Football in Scotland, 1865–1902*. Lampeter: Edwin Mellen, 2013.

McDowell, M.L. '"Enterprise with Vengeance": Parties, Performances, Excursions, and the Development of Early Scottish Football, 1865–1902'. *Recordé: Revista De História Do Esporte* 5, no. 1 (2012): 1–39.

McDowell, M.L. 'Queen's Park FC in Copenhagen, 1898–1903: Paradoxes in Early Transnational Amateurism'. *Idrottsforum* (published online 14 May 2014).

Murray, B. *The Old Firm: Sectarianism, Sport, and Society in Scotland*. Edinburgh: John Donald, 1984/2000.

Murray, B. *The World's Game: A History of Soccer*. Chicago: University of Illinois Press, 1998.

Olsen, D.H., and A.B. Grønkjær. 'Dansk fodboldshistorie: Var der fodbold før 1980?' [Danish football history: was there football before 1980?] *Idrottsforum* (published online 8 April 2009).

Porter, D. '"Coming on with Leaps and Bounds in the Metropolis": London Football in the Era of the 1908 Olympics'. *The London Journal* 34, no. 2 (2009): 101–22.

Robinson, R. *History of the Queen's Park Football Club, 1867–1917*. Glasgow: Hay Nisbet and Co.

Sund, B. 'The British and Continental Influence on Swedish Football'. *International Journal of the History of Sport* 14, no. 2: 163–73.

Taylor, M. 'Football's Engineers? British Football Coaches, Migration and Intercultural Transfer, C.1910–C.1950s'. *Sport in History* 30, no. 1 (2010): 138–63.

Taylor, M. 'Editorial – Sport, Transnationalism, and Global History'. *Journal of Global History* 8 (2013): 199–208.

Taylor, M. '"The World's My Football Pitch": Travelling Tales, Cultural Encounters and the Life Stories of British Professional Footballers, 1920–1958'. Unpublished conference paper given at Football 150, Manchester, September 2013.

Tomlinson, A. 'FIFA and the Men Who Made It'. *Soccer and Society* 1, no. 1 (2000): 55–71.

Vamplew, W. *Pay up and Play the Game*. Cambridge: Cambridge University Press, 1988.

Walker, G. '"There's Not a Team like the Glasgow Rangers": Football and Religious Identity in Scotland'. In *Sermons and Battle Hymns: Protestant Popular Culture in Modern Scotland*, ed. G. Walker and T. Gallagher, 137–59. Edinburgh: Edinburgh University Pres, 1990.

Walvin, J. *The People's Game: The History of Football Revisited*. Mainstream: Edinburgh, 1994.

Waquet, A., and J. Vincent. 'Wartime Rugby and Football: Sports Elites, French Military Teams and International Meets during the First World War'. *The International Journal of the History of Sport* 28, nos. 3–4 (2011): 372–92.

# Soccer clubs and civic associations in the political world of Buenos Aires prior to 1943

Joel Horowitz

The article examines how in the years from 1912 to 1943 emerging football clubs and other civic associations in Greater Buenos Aires were part of a movement by the city's inhabitants to create their own institutions to fulfil needs that they perceived the larger society did not satisfying (in the case of football, opportunities for recreation). It also examines how the political system pushed successful organizations to look to politicians to enable long-term success. In examining football clubs and other civic associations, it becomes clear that the theories developed by Robert Putnam, among others, based on the writings of Alexis De Tocqueville, simply do not work for Argentina. They cannot be considered the schools for democracy that some writers have envisioned. Rather they became part of a clientelistic- and patronage-oriented political world. The average citizen could not obtain aid from the government without dependence on the powerful.

## Introduction

During the first decades of the twentieth century, the inhabitants of greater Buenos Aires created innumerable civic associations. To a large extent, they were attempting to fill vacuums created by a rapidly expanding city and a weak government that could not or would not provide what the inhabitants wanted. The most striking example was the founding of hundreds of football clubs. For the first time, a large percentage of the young male population had the time and the desire to play sports, and that sport was football. No existing institutions offered the opportunity to do so, and those who wanted to play soccer created their own opportunities. This type of activity was mirrored, though often slightly later, by a myriad of other types of civic associations attempting to fulfil other needs. However, the civic associations never played the role laid out for them by Alexis de Tocqueville or Robert Putnam. Many became cogs in the political system or were dominated by important individuals.

During the end of the nineteenth century and the first three decades of the twentieth, immigrants poured into Argentina, especially the capital. The latter's population practically doubled between 1909 and 1936,[1] with immigration playing a heavy role in this growth. As public transportation improved and as developers created and sold lots to those eager to move away from the crowded centre city, inhabited areas rapidly spread across the city's territory. This intensified serious deficiencies in public services.

Immigrants and citizens frequently lacked social services or recreational opportunities. Indeed, they often did not have basic city services. Combined with the problems created by rapid growth was the lack of truly democratic elections, which limited the need for politicians to concern themselves with these issues. A new Argentine political system emerged with the passing of a law in 1912 that required voting for male citizens and made voter fraud harder to commit. However, reforms to the political system did not bring a real elective city council until 1917. This meant that nitty-gritty urban problems could be easily ignored. Civic associations were created largely to fill the gap that the state had left in the world of social services. Perhaps the best example of this is the lack of libraries provided for the general reader by the city government. In 1935, there were just three public libraries intended for the general reader plus six kiosks in public spaces. In 1941, public money was given to 124 libraries created by private groups that met certain criteria. Many more such privately run libraries existed.[2] Clearly, there existed institutional vacuums.

Since the time of Alexis de Tocqueville's *Democracy in America*, the existence of citizen controlled formal and informal organizations has been seen by many as a crucial element for the success of democracy. Recently, Robert Putnam has even worried that in the United States people bowled alone.[3] De Tocqueville argued that associations were necessary for the continuation of democracy in societies, especially as they became less aristocratic. The argument is essentially that interest and participation in government has to be placed in a network of social and mutual relationships. Formal and informal associations teach the skills and attitudes necessary for the development of democracy. They can also mediate between the world of politics and the larger society.[4] Although other commentators have given more importance to the design of institutions or socio-economic factors, certainly the existence of civic organizations has been seen as playing a crucial role in creating the atmosphere for healthy democracies. Such organizations mediate between the citizen and the state, and give the citizen experience in democracy.[5]

Starting in the 1980s, as Argentina emerged from a horrific military dictatorship, historians and others started examining civic associations in an attempt to rediscover Argentina's democratic or perhaps proto-democratic roots.[6] More recently, there has been a questioning of the link between democracy and the creation of civic associations. In Argentina, this has been joined by even some of the pioneers of the study of such associations.[7]

Whatever the impact of civic associations in other countries, in Argentina civic associations, despite generally operating with annual assemblies and elected officials, frequently became tied to politicians or other men who had wide influence within the society. Why? Groups of ordinary citizens lacked the ability to obtain things from the state without help. The clientelistic nature of Argentine politics contributed. Aspiring politicians used the organizations to build coteries of friends and potential supports.

Why did many politicians see civic associations as vital to creating a political base, especially in the city of Buenos Aires? The most successful political party during the period after 1912, the Radical Party, was non-programmatic. In saying that one is not necessarily agreeing with its enemies who claimed that the Radicals stood for little, if anything. What this meant, however, was that ideas were not how politicians tended to build a following. Even in parties such as the Socialist Party, in which ideas were considered important, the structure of the party helped make other issues important. These two parties, the dominant ones in Buenos Aires, created party structures in each of the city's 20 wards. The district party apparatus organized campaign events and other activities. They sent representatives to conventions, and candidates for office were supposedly selected openly. If new men were to emerge from these district organizations they had to build local political followings. This was certainly the pattern in the 1920s among the Radicals and seems to be true to a lesser extent also among the Socialists. Politicians built support in an electoral ward and used that base to become powerful enough to obtain office.[8] The party organization in each ward provided the workers necessary for the extensive pre-electoral spectacles of the pre-1943 era.[9]

How did politicians and parties get that kind of support? No doubt recipients of patronage were expected to reciprocate the help that they had received. Politicians looked elsewhere as well. If we examine the largest civic associations, football clubs, politicians from all political parties held key offices in a number of them.

By involving themselves with civic associations, politicians built political capital or a network of friends, followers and acquaintances that could provide a base of support. This is parallel to what sociologists call social capital. As Mario Small stated:

> Social capital theory argues that people do better when they are connected to others because of the goods inherent in social relationships. These goods-the social capital-include the obligations that people who are connected may feel toward each other, the sense of solidarity they may call upon, the information they are willing to share, and the services they are to perform. People who are socially connected therefore have recourse to a stock of 'capital' they can employ when needed.[10]

Politicians developed friends and associates who could help with a political career. People are more likely to vote for someone that they know and that they think of as being like them, sharing basic identities. They could also provide the labour for political activities. In return, politicians provided patronage jobs or help with the bureaucracy. Such patronage activity was extremely common.[11]

Leadership in civic associations also tied politicians to their neighbourhood. They helped lead an organization or obtained from the city government street lights or a paved street. They were making the lives of a portion of a barrio's population slightly better and raised the hopes of others. Thus, they created a sense of reciprocal obligation, though obviously people are not always grateful.

Becoming president of a large civic association, such as a soccer club, could also bring substantial citywide publicity. For example, the popular newspaper *Crítica* frequently referred to football clubs by the names of their president, meaning that their name would become known citywide. An article in 1922 said 'Nueva Chicago [a football club] or better said the club of Don Ghio ...'[12] Fernando Ghio was an activist in the barrio of Nueva Chicago, also known as Mataderos. He participated in a wide range of civic associations from social clubs, local development associations to community newspapers, as well as the football club Nueva Chicago. When his brother died, this appeared in *Crítica*

> The home of the councilor of associations and the leader of the Club Nueva Chicago señor Ghio is in mourning. A brother of his has died ... Señor Fernando Ghio has had the opportunity to value in this emergency how much sympathy can be won in the sporting world where the unfortunate occurrence is painfully understood.

Ghio was a Socialist Party militant who had helped form the party's local committee and as early as 1914 had been elected to a party congress. He sat on the city council of Buenos Aires in the early 1930s. Ghio's activities in his barrio clearly built him a coterie of people who liked and respected him, and his leadership of the football club Nueva Chicago made him known across the city. Ghio also built personal connections through helping people. He reputedly taught people how to read and lent books from his large library.[13] These types of connections and personal debts were useful for politicians attempting to win votes, both within the party contests and in general elections. Mataderos, where Ghio built his support, had a complex web of civic associations. María Teresa Sirvent has found that between 1915 and 1945, 6 sociedades de fomento (development societies); 10 libraries and cultural centres; and 12 social and athletic clubs were created.[14]

## Football clubs

Football came to Argentina with its large British community. In the last years of the nineteenth century, they began to form clubs in which soccer was played. However in the first two decades of last century young men, both immigrants from other regions and Argentine born, created their own opportunities to play soccer, and their clubs rapidly surpassed those of the introducers of the game.[15] It has been argued that schools did not provide opportunities to play football. However, considerable evidence exists that some learned about the game at schools. Several founders of the iconic clubs, Boca Juniors and River Plate, established in a working-class barrio, learned soccer at school.[16] However, most working-class youth did not continue beyond primary school and men in their early 20s also played. They needed to create their own institutions to indulge their passion for the game.

Although the accounts of the founding of clubs are largely based on stories written down several decades afterwards, almost all of the literally hundreds of clubs established in the first decades of the twentieth century in greater Buenos Aires were created by young men who wanted to play football. They got together in cafes, plazas or private homes and set up a structure, chose a name, colours for their shirts, etc. By 1912, there were 482 clubs in greater Buenos Aires.[17] Some had outside sponsors from the beginning. Most famously, San Lorenzo de Almagro was sponsored by a Salesian priest, Lorenzo Massa.[18] The importance of sponsors can be seen in the nearby provincial capital of La Plata, which was a new city and still small. When in 1905 high school and university students founded Estudiantes, the initial meeting was held in Félix Díaz's store, which sold shoes and sporting goods. Díaz supplied their first shirts and he and other older men helped the club meet expenses. When it needed a place to play, the members made Nazario Roberts president, apparently because he was in charge of the large park in La Plata, and the team received land in the park. Because La Plata was a company town, its business being the capital of the province, the club's leaders were tightly tied to provincial politicians who frequently were members, making the situation somewhat unusual.[19]

The vast majority of clubs were ephemeral, ceasing to exist because of declining interest, internal rivalries, financial issues or a myriad of different problems. Many more clubs than one would think still survive. Today 250 neighbourhood clubs exist in the city.[20] Soccer clubs were membership organizations with elected authorities and at least theoretically power residing in the club's members. The larger clubs also offered a wide range of sporting-related activities as well as cultural and social opportunities.[21]

Clubs that wanted to compete in the officially recognized leagues needed to find places to play. This was nearly impossible in the more built up neighbourhoods, as there was little park land and usually organized sports were not permitted. In other sectors, land to rent was difficult to locate and even harder to buy. In many cases, people with political connections or those with the desire and the financial where-withal to provide the money needed to intervene.

Until 1931 soccer was technically amateur but well before this date, players were paid or were given jobs, most of which were sham. Politicians and business owners provided the jobs.[22] Even within the first division, the clubs' income varied tremen-dously. In 1929, Boca Juniors received 79,779 pesos from admissions while Argenti-nos del Sud received just 2464.[23] Clearly, true competition was difficult. The turn to professionalism intensified this trend as the teams with the most money could more easily obtain the best players and five teams dominated the sport. By the late 1920s, soccer had become a spectator sport. This meant that ambitious clubs needed to have a stadium. The size of stadiums varied tremendously. For example, in 1930 the sta-dium of San Lorenzo de Almagro held 73,500 while that of the Boca Juniors 55,000, Vélez Sarsfield almost 16,000 and the Chacarita Juniors just 8000.[24] When shortly thereafter Chacarita was forced by the league to expand its stadium (to some 25,000), it spent almost 168,000 pesos for construction.[25]

This problem was compounded because of the limited area from which most clubs drew their fans. In 1931, the year of professionalization, the first division had 18 teams, all in greater Buenos Aires.[26] Teams were still barrio (neighbourhood) based, with the exception of River Plate and partially Boca Juniors.[27] This meant that they had a relatively limited geographical base, though as the decade of the 1930s went on, this decreased somewhat. Although the number of club members grew, it remained relatively small for the demands placed on the clubs. Argentinos Juniors claimed 1200 members in 1926, 669 in 1930 and 2246 in 1934, while Chacarita had 978, 1346 and 5840. The larger clubs such as Boca Juniors had in those years, 3022, 7728 and 22,095, while River Plate had 3661, 15,686 and 27,195.[28]

Finding a place to play was not a one-time event. Most clubs moved at least several times before 1943. Independiente played in four locations before reaching its current location, while for Boca it was five.[29] It is only through the help of major figures that most clubs could afford to do such things. The role of wealthy individu-als in helping to secure fields is illustrated by events in the 1930s for the Argentinos Juniors. In the 1920s, the team played in the first division and rented land on which it built a stadium holding more than 10,000 people. After the adoption of profession-alism, the team had trouble meeting its financial obligations, and the landowner expelled the team and seized the material that composed the stands. The team was also relegated to the second division. The membership had sunk from more than a thousand to a hundred, when in 1939 the team's treasurer suggested electing as pres-ident Gastón García Miramón, who was not a club member and was out of the coun-try. Upon his return and with his own money, García Miramón rented land for a stadium, settled the club's debts and began the process of rebuilding the stands. The new stadium opened in 1940.[30]

Similarly when All Boys was founded, their field and installations were made possible by a gift of 1800 pesos from the Club Floresta, which had been founded in

1899 with the idea of spreading the game of pelota; it was also a social organization. In addition, Leopoldo Rígola ceded some land for eight years at no charge and he also paid for the first stands.[31]

The role of wealthy individuals was intensified because the soccer clubs were controlled by elected officials who could not be paid.[32] As clubs got larger and the role of president became more complex, only those who could spare the time could afford to be president, which basically limited the job to the wealthy and to politicians. Club presidents were rarely members of the traditional upper class. Why did businessmen want to play roles in soccer clubs? Leaving aside passion for the club and football, practical reasons existed. Local businessmen could win the gratitude and loyalty of those from the barrio who supported the club. Simón Bruschtein, an owner of a local pharmacy, gave the club Nueva Chicago its first bocce court. He had opened his pharmacy in 1921 and became embedded in his community. He served on honorary commissions for two local sociedades de fomento (neighbourhood development associations) and he supported their publications by placing numerous advertisements for his business.[33] In other words, he supported his neighbourhood and in return undoubtedly won the business of some. For businessmen who operated on a larger scale, soccer clubs were a way of making a series of wider contacts that could prove useful. Janet Lever has argued that in Brazil holding office in soccer clubs functioned as a way to further careers. In all probability that was true in Argentina as well.[34]

## Politicians and football clubs

The role of politics in aiding soccer clubs can be seen in the case of Almagro (not to be confused with San Lorenzo de Almagro). It was somewhat unusual in that politics was present in the club from its beginnings and was largely the reason for its existence. Almagro was founded in 1916 after a split in a club between Radical and Conservative Party members. Almagro was of considerable size, claiming some 400 members in 1924 and 1053 in 1926. In 1930, it had the sixth largest stadium in Buenos Aires.

One of Almagro's founders and a dominant figure from its creation until at least 1927 was Miguel Ortíz de Zárate, a Radical politician who won election to the Chamber of Deputies in 1928 and 1938. According to a 1924 article in the sports magazine El Gráfico, Ortiz de Zárate controlled the local Radical organization through his ability to mobilize Almagro members; almost all Almagro's founders were Radicals and the party's influence was expanding. Ortiz de Zárate was also famous for tying the loyalty of Buenos Aires's newspaper venders (canillitas) to the club, partly through sponsoring a football championship for teams of canillitas. The club, like the Radical Party, distributed clothes and toys to children on New Year's Day and Three Kings Day. Since the club and Ortiz de Zárate were tightly tied together, he would benefit politically from gratitude to the club.

Political connections served the club well. In 1921, Almagro levelled its playing field using the city of Buenos Aires's only road grading machine with city workers and oxen. A Socialist city councillor asked the executive branch for information, and it became clear that the club would have to reimburse the city for the costs but the city had given its approval for what was a loan based only on the word of Rómulo Trucco. Trucco sat on the city council for the Radicals and was the official first member of Almagro and at various times served as its president. From the discussions in the council, it was clear that political influence had been important, since not all clubs could have the use of such equipment. The club never paid the money it owed, as the council voted to wave the fee with no discussion. The five-man committee that presented the motion included Trucco and Virgilio Tedín Uriburu. The latter later served as president of the football club Chacarita Juniors and of the Asociación Argentina de Football. This was not Trucco's only public service for the club. When Almagro sought a subvention from the city of 5000 pesos to build stands, it asked Trucco to try to obtain it.[35] Direct political intervention by club officials who were politicians was not unique. Radical Party city councillor Pedro Bidegain, who was also vice president of San Lorenzo de Almagro, joined with Trucco and another city councillor to ask for a subvention for San Lorenzo.[36] The political nature of Almagro's leadership did create friction when the Radical Party splintered. Tensions threatened to split the club.[37] Still, Radical Party politicians continued to be active in the club. For example in 1940, the future Argentine president Arturo Frondizi was nominated for a position with the football federation by Almagro.[38] Numerous other football clubs, such as Racing and Independiente, had ties to political parties through their leaders.[39] In fact, almost all the major clubs had connections to the political system through individual politicians.

Politicians aided football clubs by helping run them and by obtaining some of the material advantages that they needed. However, they were also serving their own needs by building a coterie of friends and followers who felt that they owed the politician something.

## Other civic associations

The rapid development of other types of civic associations occurred for much the same reasons as the development of football clubs. The city's inhabitants perceived needs that governmental structures did not provide and took steps to fill the gaps. It is impossible to fully sketch the growth of civic associations since they were common and could be defined to include mutual-aid societies, immigrant associations and unions.

As the city's inhabitants pushed further away from the compact city centre with the improvement in public transportation and the creation of housing lots by real estate developers, city amenities were frequently lacking.[40] As neighbourhoods developed, sociedades de fomento (neighborhood development societies) were created to overcome these needs. Not surprisingly they tended to develop in the outlying regions of the city. Of the 151 recognized by the city government at the beginning of 1942, almost none existed in the downtown region.[41]

A key function of the sociedades de fomento was to lobby the municipal government for improvements in the neighbourhood that they served, but they also acted on their own. For example, the Sociedad de Fomento de Versailles during one year in the late 1920s got the city to put in 21 street lights of various types and it had promises for others. It also planted 1250 trees most of which it received from the national government. It also cleaned vacant lots and pulled weeds. It had an employee to do much of the work.[42]

The Asociación de Fomento de Villa Pueyrredón Norte in its report on its activities in 1937 listed a number of different petitions that it had made to the municipal authorities. These included: installing a first-aid station in a location that had been set aside for that and which had already been promised; the paving of various streets; the opening of others; the lighting of a street; and the paving of a sidewalk in a plaza. The city did do some of these.[43] The Sociedad de Fomento of Villa Lugano had an employee who cleaned streets and ditches and a tractor to level streets.[44] Only the wealthier sociedades could afford to have employees let alone tractors.

Given the sizeable needs of the city and the size of budgets, a significant percentage of requests for municipal action could not be met. If influential figures intervened, the organizations would more likely have their requests granted. In most case, this would have not been visible to outsiders. More common are examples that seem to indicate that someone had connections. For example, after several complaints by the Asociación de Fomento of Villa Devoto regarding a serious flooding problem (a problem not uncommon in Buenos Aires, then or now) a delegation met with the *intendente* [mayor] José Luis Cantilo, who then visited the sociedad de fomento and spent an hour touring the neighbourhood. He promised to take action. Given the sheer number of requests, it is unlikely that Cantilo would have made the trip without some type of intercession. It most likely came through the efforts of the organization's president, who by 1938 had been both a local police chief and a justice of the peace. Both were highly political positions.[45]

The response to the sociedades de fomento was frequently tied to politics. According to Luciano de Privitellio, Mariano de Vedia y Mitre, Buenos Aires's *intendente* between 1932 and 1938, used the societies as a way around the political parties. The actions of his secretary of public works Amílcar Razori and the man in charge of dealing with the sociedades de fomento, Francisco Traba, had an impact. A significant percentage of petitions brought to the city were satisfied and many sociedades de fomento, especially those furthest from the centre, responded favourably. On several occasions, sociedades de fomento held celebrations honouring Razori and Traba. They were frequently praised extravagantly. Traba was made an honorary president of one sociedad de fomento. The sociedades de fomento were responding to very real actions. Razori regularly received delegations from sociedades de fomento and promised action on their grievances. He even helped one organization acquire building material for the construction of its headquarters. He also travelled to barrios to inspect conditions or to help inaugurate new facilities either municipal built or those of the societies themselves. This did not mean the associations became blind exponents for the intendente's policies. The Asociación Manuel Belgrano combined support for Razori and Traba with joining opposition campaigns against government policies and invitations to Socialist city councillors to visit the barrio.[46]

An alternative to petitioning, the city's executive branch (intendentes were presidential appointments and therefore not necessarily overly responsive to public opinion) was to appeal to the city council or individual councilmen. For example, in 1928 two sociedades de fomento asked the council to force a railroad company to pull up some tracks that were a nuisance and no longer necessary.[47] In the same year, a counsellor, José Penelón, presented a motion asking that a road be constructed through the property of the Facultad de Agronomía (School of Agriculture) so that workers would not have to walk the five blocks around it. He did so after visiting the site at the suggestion of a sociedad de fomento.[48] Such actions served two purposes. At times the council passed legislation forcing executive branch action but in other cases it just shined a light on the problem and therefore placed pressure on the government.

Most development associations were small. Their membership frequently ranged between 100 and 200 and that might include institutions and companies.[49] How did these small organizations have influence? Leaving aside political connections, many members were local business owners and professionals. The Sociedad de Fomento Asociación Belgrano R. published a list of 97 member merchants with their type of business and addresses. These ranged from flower stores and newspaper distributers to jewellery stores, opticians and garages. Unfortunately, the total number of members was not given. Dues were one peso a month, not a particularly large sum but one that was considerable because in most cases there was little immediate return.[50] The barrio's wealthier members and those who had a vested stake in its flourishing were those most likely to belong. Still, the improvements pushed by these associations were the type that a significant percentage of the inhabitants of a barrio would want and therefore a sociedad de fomento could rally popular support.

Influential individuals often played an oversized role. The Asociación General Alvear de Fomento Edilicio was founded in 1922 to serve the northern portion of the still underdeveloped middle-class barrio of Caballito. From its very beginning, the Dagnino family, which had moved to the neighbourhood in 1912, played a key role. The father of the family, José, initially allowed the nascent organization to operate from his home. According to his son Lorenzo, José also personally recruited more than a hundred members by going door to door. He, two of his sons and a son-in-law served as its president. Particularly influential was one son, the journalist, geography professor and urbanist, Lorenzo Dagnino Pastore. In 1938 he was president of the organization, while a brother and a brother-in-law served on the board. Crucial to the organization's success in this period appears to be its connection to José Rouco Oliva, a city council member who had belonged to the Independent Socialist Party but had become a Conservative. He was also active in the Amigos de la Ciudad, an organization interested in the design of the city, of which he was president in 1939. Dagnino Pastore had been on its board of directors from 1925 to 1930. In the 1930s, Rouco Oliva presented close to 30 projects of the Asociación General Alvear to the city council. He played a crucial role in getting one of the organization's principal long-time goals achieved, the opening of Acoyte Avenue. What did Rouco Oliva get out of his efforts? He received a great deal of publicity in the organization's periodical; it gave him a public reception and he was made the organization's first honorary member. In other words, he received significant favourable publicity. Others in the sociedad de fomento also had political connections. Eduardo Robirosa, who served as president and as editor of the organization's periodical, owned a local paper *El Baluarte*. Jorge Robirosa, who was almost undoubtedly a relative, was a politician who ran for office as a Progressive Democrat and was close to Leandro de la Torre, the party's founder. The sociedad de fomento's periodical even praised his appointment as economic minister of the Province of Buenos Aires, a highly unusual step. David Beltran Núñez, who also served as president of the sociedad de fomento, had been a successful politician in the province of Santiago del Estero and he undoubtedly still had connections.[51]

Despite the need that sociedades de fomento had for dealing with the political system, the politicians' roles are often much less visible than in soccer clubs. Sociedades de fomento were numerous, had few members, and for a politician dedicating a lot of time to one might have little advantage. The role of aspiring politicians is also difficult to see. Frequently politicians did not direct the organizations but provided aid. A good example is Florencio Arias who was active in the Radical Party in the distant first ward and won election to the city council in 1922. Arias was a doctor who had lived in the ward since 1909 when it was still largely undeveloped. He cared for many poor patients despite the bad roads. He served as president of the local school board (consejo escolar), and as president of the equivalent of the local PTA. He also served on the honorary commission of the football club Nueva Chicago. In addition, he aided the sociedades de fomento. For example, he was honorary president of the Sociedad de Fomento José Enrique Rodó. According to its periodical, the sociedades de fomento 'always received the ardor of his wise advice, the knowledge of his constant and effective cooperation and gracious contribution of his influence and goodness ...'[52]

The Sociedad de Fomento Asociación Belgrano R, in submitting a report to its members, thanked among many others, four members of the city council, especial José Claisse, an Anti-Personalist Radical with these words: 'great friend and collaborator who is virtually our legal advisor and to whom we owe a great part of the work that we have done.'[53] In other words, the politicians helping and getting the recognition may not even have belonged to the organization, making their roles more difficult to assess but just as vital.

Connections came in many forms. In the late 1920s, the Sociedad de Fomento de Versailles sought the placing of cobblestones in several streets and thanks to the intervention of two men, José Guerrico and Tomas R. Cullen, it felt that it was close to attaining its goal. Guerrico, an honorary member of the society, was a conservative politician who served off and on for two decades on the city council and was in 1930 appointed *intendente* by the government that seized power in a coup. Perhaps more importantly he was a land developer who had named the barrio. According to a contemporary journalist, Guerrico was one of the magicians who had transformed the barrio after the first subdivision was made in 1912. Cullen was a member of the traditional elite, a conservative and former cabinet member. Guerrico's interventions also helped the sociedad de fomento get a school placed in the barrio.[54]

Some politicians did hold office in such organizations. An example is the well-known historian and politician Emilio Ravignani, who clearly followed a strategy of building political capital. In the 1920s, he served in an important administrative position in the Buenos Aires municipal government and became the centre of a web of patronage, obtaining personal I.O.U.s. He had an extraordinarily active career in the academic world. He also played a role in civic associations. He sat on the board of the Automovil Club Argentino and in 1935–1936 he was elected as president of the Sociedad de Fomento Tte. General Luis María Campos. In 1936, he ran for the governing board of the elite sporting club Gimnesia y Esgrima de Buenos Aires on a list that unsuccessfully challenged its seemingly eternal president Ricardo C. Aldao. In 1936, he was elected to congress on the Radical Party list.[55] Clearly part of Ravignani's strategy for creating political capital was through associations.

Remigio Iriondo also helped his political career through involvement in local organizations. He moved to the Villa Crespo neighbourhood in 1896 and began a career in education, founding schools. He also ran a periodical. From the last years of the nineteenth century, he was active in civic associations. These include a local development society, founded directly after the beginning of the new century, which he served as its president and which was later named after him. He was also active for more than 30 years in a popular library and presided over it from 1934 to 1940. When the Universidad Popular Florentino Ameghino was founded in Villa Crespo in 1926 to serve as a source of adult education, its first rector was Iriondo and its classes met in his school. He was active on the boards that oversaw education in two districts and he served in municipal posts before the political reform in the capital. After the reform, he was elected to the city council in 1921 on the list of the Progressive Democrats.[56] Clearly, political capital could be won by being active in civic associations of any type.

## Conclusion

Civic associations were created in great numbers in the first decades of the last century. They provided things that governmental structures simply did not. Their founders displayed tremendous abilities in providing what local inhabitants felt they needed and in creating institutions, many of which proved long-lived. However, the civic associations were created as a new political system emerged. The system of politics that developed contained strong elements of clientelism. Aspiring politicians attempted to build political capital by playing a crucial role in helping civic associations interface with the state. This provided politicians with the neighbourhood bases needed to become important politically.

Civic associations no matter what their size, even the large football clubs, had a hard time approaching the government without powerful intercessors. Most civic associations needed help from the government for land, stadiums, books or neighbourhood improvements. Only those with good connections could seemingly obtain them. This meant that civic associations could not perform like the Tocquevillean model of a school for democracy, rather they became part of a wider system of politics in which those with personal clout carried more weight than the average inhabitant. Although civic associations in Buenos Aires vastly improved the quality of life of many of its inhabitants, they cannot be considered schools for democracy in the De Tocquevillean sense.

## Disclosure statement

No potential conflict of interest was reported by the author.

## Acknowledgements

I would like to thank Brenda Elsey for the invitation that produced the first version of this article and St. Bonaventure University for partially funding the research.

## Notes

1. Walter, *Politics and Urban Growth*, A1.
2. Miranda, *Las bibliotecas*, 31; and Comisión Protectora de Bibliotecas Populares, *Nómina de las bibliotecas*, 5–10.
3. De Tocqueville, *Democracy in America*; and Putnam, *Bowling Alone.*
4. Putnam, *Bowling Alone*, esp. 19, 338–9, 345–6; and Sabato, *The Many and the Few*, esp. 12.
5. Putnam, *Making Democracy Work*, esp. 10–1, 90–1, 183; Almond and Verba, *Civic Culture*, esp. 245. For the importance of civic culture in the democratic tradition of Latin America, Forment, *Democracy in Latin America.*
6. PEHESA, '¿Dónde anida la democracia?'; and Sabato, *The Many and the Few.*
7. Riley, *The Civic Foundations*; De Privitellio and Romero, 'Organizaciones de la sociedad', 1–34; and Di Stefano et al., *De las cofradías.*

8. Walter, *The Socialist Party*, esp. 59–60; Rock, 'Machine Politics'; and Horowitz, *Argentina's Radical Party*.
9. For a Radical campaign *La Epoca*, March 12–22, 1919. See *La Prensa* during any electoral season for campaigns by other parties.
10. Small, *Unanticipated Gains*, 6.
11. Horowitz, *Argentina's Radical Party*, 65–94.
12. *Crítica*, October 19, 1922. For other examples, October 10 and November 1, 1922.
13. *Crítica*, December 31, 1921; *La Vanguardia*, May 23, 1914; Vecchio, *Mataderos*, esp. 58, 149, 177, 190–201; 'Aquí Mataderos-Revista Social, Cultural y Deportiva de Mataderos', http://www.r-aquimataderos.com.ar/nueva_chicago_1911.htm (accessed July 6, 2009); Bucich Escobar, *Buenos Aires*, 219–21; 'Sitios de Interés Cultural, Bar "Oviedo"', www.bibleduc.gov.ar/areas/cultura/cpphc/sitios/detalle.php?id=102 (accessed February 16, 2007); 'Don Fernando Ghio', *Foro de la Memoria de Mataderos*, February 4, 2008, www.forommataderos.blogspot.com/2008/02/don-fernando-ghio.html (accessed February 11, 2010); and Cutolo, *Historia de los barrios*, I, 522.
14. Romero, 'El estado y las corporaciones', in *De las cofradías*, 173.
15. For soccer's early history, Frydenberg, *Historia social*; Iwanczuk, *Historia de fútbol amateur*; Lorenzo (Borocotó), *Historia del fútbol argentino*. This is not intended to be comprehensive.
16. Frydenberg, *Historia social*, 26–8; Rosatti, *Cien años*, vol. 1, 41–7; *El Gráfico*, January 19, 1935, 21; and Bertolotto, *River*, 25–9.
17. Frydenberg, 'Redefinición del fútbol', 51.
18. The role of a priest in the founding of San Lorenzo makes it unique but partially explains Pope Francis's support for the club.
19. *El Gráfico*, August 17, 1935, 14–5; 'Historia de C.A. Estudiantes', www.taringa.net/posts/deportes/6868259/Historia-deC_A_-Estudiantes.html (accessed November 22, 2011); *La República*, February 22, 1938; Club Atlético Estudiantes (La Plata), *Memoria 1928–1930*, 9–11; and *Memoria 1938–1940*, 10–11.
20. *La Nación*, December 24, 2013. Not all play soccer and many were founded after the period under examination.
21. Horowitz, 'Football Clubs', 557–85.
22. *La Vanguardia*, April 5, 1916; *El Gráfico*, November 17, 1928, 12, January 4, 1930, 19, September 22, 1934, 22, 38. For where players worked, *El Gráfico*, November 3, 1928, 8.
23. Asociación Amateurs Argentina de Football, *Memoria 1929*, 165.
24. Iwanczuk, *Historia de fútbol amateur*, 243.
25. Club Atlético Chacarita Juniors, *Memoria 1932*, 17–20 and *Memoria 1933*, 11; 'Historia del Club Atlético Chacarita Juniors', http://www.oocities.org/colosseum/track/5717/homechaca.html (accessed July 7, 2014).
26. Two teams were in La Plata, slightly beyond greater Buenos Aires.
27. Horowitz, 'Football Clubs'.
28. Asociación Amateurs Argentina de Football, *Memoria 1926*, n.p.; and Asociación de Football Argentino, *Memoria 1934*, 130.
29. Julio David Frydenberg, 'Espacio urbano y práctica del fútbol, Buenos Aires, 1900–1915', www.efedeportes.com/efd13/juliof.htm (accessed January 31, 2007).
30. Asociación Atlético Agentinos Juniors, Sitio oficial, 'Historia', http://www.argentinosjuniors.com.ar/club/historia/historia/1920-1940 (accessed August 8, 2014).
31. C.A. All Boys, 'Historia del Albo', www.albocapo.com.ar/historia.htm; 'La Historia de All Boys', *La Floresta*, www.la-floresta.com.ar/historia_albo.htm (accessed January 16, 2012); Archivo Intermedio (Buenos Aires). Fondo Inspección General de Justicia. Registro de Asociaciones Civiles, Caja 61, no. 351436, Club Floresta (no longer accessible).
32. Scher and Palomino, *Fútbol*, 20.
33. Vecchio, *Mataderos*, *104*; *Acción Comunal*, June 1937, April 1938, June 1939, October/November 1940; *Liniers*, May, October 1940, April/June 1941.
34. Lever, *Soccer Madness*, 57.
35. Sitio Oficial Club Almagro, 'Historia en tres colores', www.calmagro.com.ar/historia.htm; ' Club Almagro', http://es.wikipedia.org/wiki/Club_Almagro (accessed August 7,

2014); 'Cuando Almagro estuvo en Parque Chas', www.parquechasweb.com.ar/par quechas/notas/Nota_almagropch.htm (accessed January 29, 2007); *La Epoca*, August 30, 1920; Scher and Palomino, *Fútbol*, 106; Iwanczuk, *Historia de fútbol amateur*, 243; Concejo Deliberante de la Municipalidad de Buenos Aires, *Actas*, April 12, 1921, 267, May 10, 1921, 585, May 13, 1921, 644–8, November 17, 1921, 2438–9; *La Prensa*, November 3, 1924; Bucich Escobar, *Buenos Aires*, 215; and H. Cámara de Diputados de la Nación, *Nómina de Diputados*, 103, 112 (no longer accessible).

36. Concejo Deliberante, *Actas*, May 12, 1921, 609.
37. *Crítica*, January 4, 13, April 14, 19, October 31, November 21, 1922.
38. *La Hora*, May 9, 1940.
39. Horowitz, 'Football Clubs'.
40. For example Scobie, *Buenos Aires*; and Gorelik, *La grilla y el parque*.
41. *Censor Edilicio*, February/March 1942, 12–13.
42. Sociedad de Fomento de Versailles, *Memoria 1927–1928*, 5–8.
43. Asociación de Fomento de Villa Pueyrredón Norte, *Memoria 1937*, 11–18.
44. *El Progreso*, July 1931, 5.
45. *Boletín de la Asociación de Fomento de Villa Devoto*, February, March and April 1930; *Caras y Caretas*, December 3, 1938, 86.
46. De Privitelio, *Vecinos*, esp. 123–47; Razori, *La obra de la intendencia*; *Manuel Belgrano*, October 1935, 1–2, May 1935, 5–7, June 1936, 3, July 1937, 2, October/November 1937, 1–2, January/February 1938, 1–2, March/April 1938, 1, June 1938, 1–2; *El Fomento de Flores Sud órgano oficial de la Asociación Fomento y Cultura Flores Sud y Biblioteca Popular Gral. Juan Martín Pueyrredón*, August 1935, 3–4, September 1935, 14, January 1936, 2, 12, April 1936, 2–7; *Los Olivos*, April/May 1936, 10, June/July 1936, 9–11, August/September 1936, 8, Flier inside April/June 1937; and *Acción Comunal*, July 1937, 8–9, August 1937, 2.
47. Concejo Deliberante, *Actas*, June 30, 1928, 1169–71. For another example, November 9, 1929, 2318–9.
48. Ibid., May 29, 1928, 477–8.
49. For examples, *Manuel Belgrano*, August 1935, 3; Asociación de Fomento de Villa Pueyrredón Norte, *Memoria 1937*, 4; *Los Olivos*, February/March 1936, 17–18; *Censor Edilicio*, June/July 1942, 5; and *El Fomento de Flores Sud*, July 1937, 6.
50. *Verdades*, October, November/December 1939.
51. Dagnino Pastore, ed., *Casi un siglo*, esp. 276–8, 305–6; *Caballito: Informativo de la Asociación General Alvear de Fomento Edilicio*, July 1938, inside front cover, August 1938, 2–5, October 1938, 4–5, September/October 1939, 1, 4–7, November/December 1939, 11, March/April 1940, 3–4, 14–15, July/August 1940, 4–6, December 1940, 11; Sanguinetti, *Los socialistas independientes*, esp. 258; *Nueva Era*, March 1922, 1; *Boletín de los Amigos de la Ciudad*, January 1939, 51; and Rogelio Alaniz, 'Los duelistas', *El Litoral.com*, August 14, 2013, http://www.ellitoral.com/index.php/id_um/91850-los-duelistas (accessed June 20, 2014).
52. Acción Comunal, April 1937, August 1939; Bucich Escobar, *Buenos Aires*, 217; 'Su historia', http://r-aquimataderos.com.ar/nueva_chicago_1911.htm (accessed August 8, 2014).
53. *Verdades*, November/December 1939.
54. Sociedad de Fomento de Versailles, *Memoria 1927–1928*, 7, 11; Walter, *Politics and Urban Growth*; 'Plazas de Versalles', http://plazas.faggella.com.ar/versalles.htm (accessed June 10, 2014); 'Tomás Cullen', http://es.wikipedia.org/wiki/Tomás_Cullen (accessed July 10, 2014); and *Caras y Caretas*, December 6, 1930, 169–71.
55. Horowitz, *Argentina's Radical Party*, 76–7; Library of the Instituto Ravignani (Buenos Aires), Colección Emilio Ravignani, esp. Arv. 9, no. 7, 8; Arv. 29, no. 231, 232 234, Arv. 32 no. 59–75; and 'Gimnesia y Esgrima de Buenos Aire', http://en.wikipedia.org/wiki/Gimnasia_y_Esgrima_de_Buenos_Aires (accessed July 9, 2014).
56. Del Pino, *El barrio de Villa Crespo*, 76–7; La Universidad Popular Florentino Ameghino, *La Universidad Popular*, 6, 9, 15; Library of the Instituto Ravignani, Colección Emilio Ravignani, Arv 37, no. 38, 54; 'Barrio Villa Crespo-habitantes notables', http://www.lugaresgeograficos.com.ar/verCiudad.php?id=3427458&idtexto=1006#.U8WmI LE4dI0 (accessed July 1, 2014).

# References

Almond, Gabriel A., and Sidney Verba. *Civic Culture: Political Attitudes and Democracy in Five Nations*. Boston, MA: Little, Brown, 1965.

Asociación Amateurs Argentina de Football. *Memoria y balance general, correspondiente al ejercicio de 1926* [Report and general balance sheet, corresponding to the fiscal year 1926]. Buenos Aires: Guillermo Kraft, 1927.

Asociación Amateurs Argentina de Football. *Memoria y balance general, correspondiente al ejercicio 1929 [Report and general balance sheet, corresponding to the fiscal year 1929]*. Buenos Aires: Geronimo J. Pesce, 1930.

Asociación de Fomento de Villa Pueyrredón Norte. *Memoria y balance del ejercicio 1937* [Report and balance sheet, corresponding to the fiscal year 1937]. Buenos Aires: Asociación de Fomento de Villa Pueyrredón Norte, 1937.

Asociación de Football Argentino. Memoria y balance general 1934 [Report and general balance sheet 1934]. Buenos Aires: Asociación de Football Argentino, 1935.

Bertolotto, Miguel Angel. *River: El campeón del siglo* [River: The champion of the century]. Buenos Aires: Oceano/Temas, 2000.

Bucich Escobar, Ismael. *Buenos Aires ciudad* [The city of Buenos Aires]. Buenos Aires: Editorial Tor, 1936.

Club Atlético Chacarita Juniors. *Memoria y balance general 1932* [Report and general balance sheet 1932]. Buenos Aires: Club Atlético Chacarita Juniors, 1932.

Club Atlético Chacarita Juniors. *Memoria y balance general 1933* [Report and general balance sheet 1933]. Buenos Aires : Club Atlético Chacarita Juniors, 1933.

Club Atlético Estudiantes (La Plata). *Memoria del ejercicio 1928–1930* [Report on the period 1938–1940]. La Plata: Club Atlético Estudiantes, 1930.

Club Atlético Estudiantes (La Plata). *Memoria 1938–1940* [Report 1938–1940]. La Plata: Club Atlético Estudiantes, 1940.

Comisión Protectora de Bibliotecas Populares. *Nómina de las bibliotecas populares protegidas* [List of the favored popular libraries]. Buenos Aires: Comisión Protectora de Bibliotecas Populares, 1941.

Cutolo, Vicente Osvaldo. *Historia de los barrios de Buenos Aires* [History of the neighbourhoods of Buenos Aires] vol. 1. 2nd ed. Buenos Aires: Editorial ELCHE, 1998.

Dagnino Pastore, José María, ed. Casi un siglo: Lorenzo Dagnino Pastore [Almost a century: Lorenzo Dagnino Pastore]. Buenos Aires: Editorial Dunken, 2000.

De Privitelio, Luciano. *Vecinos y ciudadanos: Política y sociedad en la Buenos Aires de entreguerra* [Neighbours and citizens: Politics and society in Buenos Aires between the wars]. Buenos Aires: Siglo XXI, 2003.

De Privitellio, Luciano, and Luis Alberto Romero. 'Organizaciones de la sociedad civil, tradiciones cívicas y cultura política democrática: el caso de Buenos Aires, 1912–1976' [Organizations of civil society, civic traditions and the culture of democratic politics: The case of Buenos Aires, 1912–1976]. *Revista de Historia (Mar del Plata)* 1, no. 1 (inicios de 2005): 1–34.

De Tocqueville, Alexis. *Democracy in America*. Trans. Henry Reeve. New York: Bantam Classics, 2000.

Del Pino, Diego A *El barrio de Villa Crespo* [The neighbourhood of Villa Crespo]. Buenos Aires: Municipalidad de La Ciudad de Buenos Aires, 1974.

Di Stefano, Roberto, Hilda Sabato, Luis Alberto Romero, and José Luis Moreno. *De las cofradías a las organizaciones de la sociedad civil* [From confraternities to the organizations of civil society]. Buenos Aires: Gadis, 2002.

Forment, Carlos A. *Democracy in Latin America 1760–1900: Volume I, Civic Selfhood and Public Life in Mexico and Peru*. Chicago: University of Chicago Press, 2003.

Frydenberg, Julio D. *Historia social del fútbol: Del amateurismo a la profesionalización* [The social history of football: From amateurism to professionalization]. Buenos Aires: Siglo XXI, 2011.

Frydenberg, Julio D. 'Redefinición del fútbol aficionado y del fútbol oficial. Buenos Aires 1912' [Redefinition of amateur football and of official football. Buenos Aires 1912]. In *Deporte y sociedad*, eds. Pablo Alabarces, Roberto Di Giano, and Julio Frydenberg, 51–65. Buenos Aires: EUDEBA, 1998.

Gorelik, Adrián. *La grilla y el parque: Espacio público y cultura urbana en Buenos Aires, 1887–1936* [The grid and the park: Public space and urban culture in Buenos Aires, 1887-1936]. Bernal: Universidad Nacional de Quilmes, 2004.

H. Cámara de Diputados de la Nación. *Nómina de Diputados de la Nación por distrito electoral: Periodo 1854–1991* [List of national deputies by electoral district: Period 1854–1991]. Buenos Aires: Secretaría Parlamentaria, Dirección de Archivo, Publicaciones y Museo, 1991.

Horowitz, Joel. *Argentina's Radical Party and Popular Mobilization, 1916–1930.* University Park: The Pennsylvania State University Press, 2008.

Horowitz, Joel. 'Football Clubs and Neighbourhoods in Buenos Aires before 1943: The Role of Political Linkages and Personal Influence'. *Journal of Latin American Studies* 46, no. 3 (August 2014): 557–85.

Iwanczuk, Jorge. *Historia de fútbol amateur en la Argentina* [History of amateur football in Argentina]. Buenos Aires: Centro de Investigación de la Historia del Fútbol, 1992.

La Universidad Popular Florentino Ameghino. *La Universidad Popular Florentino Ameghino en su XV aniversario* [The Popular University Florentino Ameghino on its 15th anniversary]. Buenos Aires: Universidad Popular Florentino Ameghino, 1941.

Lever, Janet. *Soccer Madness: Brazil's Passion for the World's Most Popular Sport.* Chicago: University of Chicago Press, 1983.

Lorenzo, Ricardo (Borocotó). *Historia del fútbol argentino* [The history of Argentine football]. 3 vols. Buenos Aires: Editorial Eiffel, 1955.

Miranda, Arnaldo Ignacio Adolfo. *Las bibliotecas públicas municipales de la Ciudad de Buenos Aires* [The municipal public libraries of the city of Buenos Aires]. Buenos Aires: Cuadernos de Buenos Aires, 1996.

PEHESA. '¿Dónde anida la democracia?' [Where is democracy nested?]. *Punta de Vista* 15 (1982): 6–10.

Putnam, Robert D. *Making Democracy Work: Civic Traditions in Modern Italy.* Princeton University Press: Princeton, 1993.

Putnam, Robert D. Bowling Alone. *The Collapse and Revival of American Community.* New York: Touchstone Books, 2000.

Razori, Amílcar. *La obra de la intendencia municipal en los barrios suburbanos de la ciudad de Buenos Aires durante los años 1932–1935* [The work of the municipal intendency in the suburban barrios of the city of Buenos Aires during the years 1932–1935]. Buenos Aires: Peuser, 1935.

Riley, Dylan. *The Civic Foundations of Fascism in Europe: Italy, Spain and Romania, 1870–1914.* Baltimore, MD: Johns Hopkins University Press, 2010.

Rock, David. 'Machine Politics in Buenos Aires and the Argentine Radical Party, 1912–1930'. *Journal of Latin American Studies* 4, no. 2 (November 1972): 233–56.

Rosatti, Horacio. *Cien años de multitud: Historia de Boca Juniors, una pasión argentina* [A hundred years of the multitude. The history of the Boca Juniors, an Argentine passion]. Vol. 1. Buenos Aires: Galerna, 2008.

Sabato, Hilda. *The Many and the Few: Political Participation in Republican Buenos Aires.* Stanford: Stanford University Press, 2001.

Sanguinetti, Horacio. *Los socialistas independientes* [The Independent Socialists]. Buenos Aires: Editorial del Belgrano, 1981.

Scher, Ariel, and Héctor Palomino. *Fútbol: Pasión de multitudes y de elites: Un estudio de la Asociación de Fútbol Argentino (1934–1986)* [Football: A passion of multitudes and elites: A study of the Argentine Football Association]. Buenos Aires: Documento del CISEA, 1988.

Scobie, James R., and Buenos Aires. *Plaza to Suburb, 1870–1910.* New York: Oxford University Press, 1974.

Small, Mario Luis. *Unanticipated Gains: Origins of Network Inequality in Everyday Life.* New York: Oxford University Press, 2009.

Sociedad de Fomento de Versailles. *Memoria y balance 1 de abril de 1927–31 Marzo de 1928* [Report and balance sheet April 1, 1927–March 31, 1928]. Buenos Aires: Talleres Gráficos Pfeifer, 1928.

Vecchio, Ofelio. *Mataderos mi barrio* [Mataderos my barrio]. Buenos Aires: Editora "Nueva Lugano", 1981.

Walter, Richard J. *Politics and Urban Growth in Buenos Aires: 1910–1942*. Cambridge: Cambridge University Press, 1993.

Walter, Richard J. *The Socialist Party of Argentina, 1890–1930*. Austin: University of Texas Press, 1977.

# The history of the Zenit Soccer Club as a case study in Soviet Football Teams

Karina Ovsepyan

In this article, an attempt is made to look at how the Soviet football team was organized. 'Zenit' is now a rich and successful Russian football team, but during the Soviet era, it was an ordinary team that introduced the city of Leningrad to the USSR football league. By using rare archival materials and some other sources, we try to understand how it was managed and what was hidden.

## Introduction

The study of sports of the USSR history is impeded by the ambivalence of the official explanation of the status of both the athletes and organizations (clubs) that united them. Formally, athletes that achieved high results were called amateurs, and clubs, in the form that they were social organizations on a voluntary basis. But in fact, the first were professionals, and the second governmental organizations. Professional sport in the USSR was associated with Western commercial and bourgeois sport where players were like commodities that were bought and sold. The reality was rather carefully disguised, and the available documentation reflects almost exclusively the official perspective on the subject. Largely, the everyday life of Soviet football players remains unexplored for this reason. Reconstruction of these details will help to show some characteristic features of its organization and the role it played within the Soviet state.

The history of football (first of all in Russia) is a field where the authors are most often not historians but sport journalists and other sport functionaries. Recently, however, scientific publications about sports and football in particular have appeared. They considered the history of certain football teams problematized in accordance with social, political, ethnic conditions.[1] Today, there are few studies about the club Zenit (dedicated to the events that led to cups) and all are documentary or popular.[2]

So in this essay, an attempt is made to look at the history of the Soviet football team, not through the prism 'scores-goals-trophies', but through official documents and memoirs. In focus is the Leningrad[3] (now St. Petersburg) football team Zenit, and the peculiarities of its organization. One of the goals of the article is to examine how the football team, which played in the Soviet football championship (Vysshaya Liga) functioned.

**Some organizational features of the Zenit team**

The football team Zenit now is the only St. Petersburg team playing in the Premier League – the Russian football championship. Zenit has become a very popular, famous, rich and successful team in Russia, especially since Gazprom Company became its main sponsor. And it is a favourite of city residents. During the last 10 years, it has been the champion of the Russian football league several times. In Europe, it earned recognition after winning the UEFA and Super UEFA Cups in 2008. But during the Soviet period, the team received only a few awards and was not as famous and popular as it is now. Nevertheless, the club can be considered typical of Soviet organization for Masters' (elite or top-flight) sport teams, and we can examine it through official documents, such as annual reports and budgets. The Masters' team Zenit played in the national championship in football with more or less success, while other famous Leningrad football teams like Dynamo, Admiralteets and Spartak ceased to exist and finally didn't save there place in championship.

At the same time, Zenit was a kind of sport hallmark for the city of Lenin along with the basketball team Spartak, the volleyball team Avtomobilist and the hockey team SKA. There was something like a secret list of 'representation' of the Union republics in the highest football league in the Soviet Union: Moscow was represented by four teams (Spartak, CSKA, Dynamo and Torpedo). Lokomotiv entered in the League and left this group periodically and was the so-called 'the fifth wheel of the Moscow cart'. Ukraine, as the largest and most important of the Union republics, was first represented by Dynamo Kiev and Shakhter, which corresponded to the spirit of competition between the capital and the industrial east of the republic. Periodically (as a form of flirting with the local elites), Karpaty (Lvov), Tavria (Simferopol) and Zarya (Voroshilovgrad) were allowed in the big leagues. Belarus was represented by Dynamo (Minsk), Armenia by Ararat (Erevan), Azerbaijan by Neftyanik, Uzbekistan by Pakhtakor, Kazakhstan by Kairat. Several times Torpedo (Kutaisi), and once Nistru (Kishinev), entered the highest football league. Other Soviet republics represented in the first division were Pamir (Dushanbe, Tajikistan), Alga (Frunze, Kyrgyzstan), Daugava (Riga, Latvia), Zhal'giris (Vilnius, Lithuania), Kalev (Tallinn, Estonia). So, playing for a club such as Zenit meant belonging to elite sport, the opportunity to be well known throughout the country.

Officially, the football club Zenit traces its history back to 1925. This date is disputed, as evidence has been provided by historians of the club themselves. Without questioning this date, we will pay attention to the post-war period in the history of the club (1950s–1980s) when Soviet League football resumed and became stable. Not that the team collected titles in the Soviet period; triumphs were limited to the USSR Cup in 1944, a third-place finish in the league table in 1980, and just one league championship (first-place finish) in 1984.

The beginning of the 1950s was a period of searching for optimal solutions for the organization of mass football competition in the city. This was a large event that included a large number of players that voluntary sports societies and offices (vedomstva) conducted. In the 1950–1960s, the city football championship was a notable sporting event where Leningrad plants and factories fielded football teams of different ages (children, youth and men's teams). It is important to note that the city championship had not only the aim of promoting health and the physical development of workers, or of developing football at grassroots sport organizations, but as an active search of football talent: increasing of sport skill of the players and identifying capable and promising players for the replenishment of the Zenit team or other masters' teams. Football players who played in the Soviet football championship (called 'masters') could be overused and play in city football just before or after their playing for their masters' team. In the 1970–1980s, the picture changed – the Leningrad championship was not so popular or well attended, and the selection of talented football players for the country championship was not through the city championship, but through specialized sport schools.

In the early 1950s, management of the football team masters Zenit was carried out by the Leningrad Regional Council and the Central Committee of the Voluntary Sports Society[4] Zenit and by the trade union organization. According to the report, they provided economic and financial assistance to the team. The Bureau of Leningrad Regional Party Committee also patronized the team and in the case of strong dissatisfaction with its performances, or more specifically, its final standings, would cause the Voluntary sport society to change the coach, etc. As the sport (more correctly – achieving athletes) was an important indicator of the 'effectiveness of the party leadership' in the district, city and regional committees of the CPSU closely monitored it to ensure that their territory was well represented at the appropriate level of competition. Successes in this area became an important position in Party reporting.

Meanwhile, the funding, which could be provided to the team by master class 'A' Voluntary sports society, and which came from revenues from the games, was obviously not enough. In addition, the team did not have a training base, and the administration of the city and Leningrad office of Voluntary sport society set the team the task to keep its place in class 'A'. Vladimir Ageevets, the former team chief, notes that at that time, for the team to have a plant as the 'rear' was an important factor, and 'not only because the plant or any other structure had the opportunity, if necessary, to support their team material, but also because after football career players could get any manufacturing specialty or, being a fellow of the plant, to get proper education'.[5] This prompted him and the head coach to contact the General Director of the optical-mechanical plant (large and known company in the city at that time, later LOMO), Michael Panfilov with the proposal to move the team from Leningrad office of Voluntary sport society 'Zenit' to under the protection of the plant. And in 1958, plant number 412 (Leningrad optical-mechanical plant) took the team on its balance sheet and registered the state of the football team 'Zenit' in the amount of 25 people from 1 September 1958 and became its main financial sponsor. From this time forward, the budget of the maintenance of the team was calculated by the plant's accountant.

From 1958, the football team 'Zenit' was attached to the trade union committee of the Leningrad optical-mechanical plant (later Association LOMO) and had a special position. For example, its financial report and team budget were formulated separately from those of the other personnel staff. To understand the opaque structure of management of the Soviet masters team and the hierarchy of power in it is not so easy. Here is how it was written in the report (1962) for the above voluntary sport society, the formulation was given quite ornately: 'The supervision of the team is carried out directly by the factory Committee and the Board of the sports club GOMZ named OGPU, supervises and provides necessary assistance of the CPSU, the party organization and the management of the plant. All the activities of the football team are under the control of the Leningrad Regional Council of voluntary sport society 'Trud' (Labour). In addition, the football team, in their training work and participation in competitions was accountable to the Leningrad city Council of the Union of sport societies and organizations of the city and to its football section. The regional party Committee, the city Committee of the Communist party and the Komsomol, the Executive Committee of the city council of people's deputies control the team and provide necessary assistance in the work'.[6] The report of 1965 made it clearer:

> The football team 'Zenit' is subordinate to the trade union LOMO. The management team, Chairman of the trade union, sports club and the Bureau of the football section associations lead the team and provides effective assistance to the work of the team.[7]

However, the team almost rarely met with players of the factory team, which participated in the championship of the city, if only occasionally in training. The masters had their own schedule, regime and they did not work at the plant, but would sometimes visit to meet with workers. In this connection, the lack of communication between team management and players with the work collective of LOMO is noted.[8] A meeting of workers with the football players of 'Zenit' in 1964 was described in the factory newspaper:

> A good tradition has appeared now at football team 'Zenit' – to report to the workers for games in the previous national championship. The meeting, which was held recently in the Palace of culture 'Progress', attracted many fans of the team. 'Zenit' was the only Leningrad team in the highest League, and therefore its successes and failures always excite the huge army of fans.[9]

The meeting was opened by the speech of the team chief, honoured coach of the USSR Valentin Fyodorov, who spoke about the performances of 'Zenit' players in the League and had the shared plans for the future. Many questions were asked to the players and the coach, honoured coach of RSFSR I. Afanas'ev. In conclusion of the meeting, young Leningrad poet Evgeny Kuchinsky recited funny poems addressed to the players.

According to the staff schedule, 'Zenit' football players were divided into three categories and their wages differed depending on the category. Players of the first two categories received allowances (Table 1).[10] The head coach and team chief had the highest salaries. Besides, players in this soviet football team had a senior coach, deputy head of the team in administrative and economic issues, trainer and masseuse (a woman). One of the famous goalkeepers of the team, Leonid Ivanov, also remembered the bootmaker who went with the team.

Annual reports, the budget and interviews with former players indicate that their conditions differed from the conditions of training factory players, which trained at the factory stadium. The team's budget included the expenses on wages of the players, on winter and spring training camps, railway transportation, food, accommodation, daily allowance in the way, automobile expenses, the purchase of new sports training forms and inventory (also for its repair and washing), buying magazines and newspapers, lectures and museums. Interestingly, financial reports could also include the cost of purchasing souvenirs for the opposing teams when going out abroad for friendly games. In 1958, 32 wool suits, 64 woollen shirts, 64 pair of gaiters, 64 pair of trunks, 64 cotton T-shirts, 44 balls should have been purchased for the team.[11] This means that each football player in 'Zenit' was given two sets of the uniform for the season.

Table 1. Staffing of football team 'Zenit' in 1959 (before the monetary reform)[a].

| N | The name of the position | The number of units | Salary | The premium for skill | Monthly payroll |
|---|---|---|---|---|---|
| 1 | Head of team | 1 | 2000 | – | 2000 |
| 2 | Head coach | 1 | 2000 | 100 | 2100 |
| 3 | Coach | 1 | 1600 | 100 | 1700 |
| 4 | Administrator | 1 | 1000 | – | 1000 |
| 5 | Massage therapist | 1 | 900 | – | 900 |
| 6 | Players of the first category | 15 | 1600 | 150 | 25,500 |
| 7 | Players of the second category | 6 | 1300 | 100 | 7900 |
| 8 | Players of the third category | 6 | 1100 | – | 6600 |
|   | Total | 32 |  | 1800 | 47,700 |

[a]TsGASPb, f.2187, op.7, d.220, l.1.

## Annual report of the team (1962) as a source

Annual reports are for us a source for the formation of ideas about the features of the functioning of the team. They allow us to reconstruct some peculiarities of the Soviet masters' team players' lives.

The report section on political-educational work is of a special interest. It suggests that the team had its own Komsomol and trade union organizations, where Communist Party group leaders as komsorg (Komsomol organizer) and proforg (trade union organizer), and also partgruporg (Party organizer) were appointed. In the report, it was necessary to show what measures were taken to deal with violations, to feedback on organized cultural programs, meetings with workers, etc. The reports included the main elements of the proper education and behaviour of the Soviet sportsmen, who before all were Soviet citizens (and as recognizable personalities, they were to serve as a good example to Soviet society), organized cultural trips to the cinema, wall newspapers (fotogazety) issue, collective reading of newspapers, the establishment by team management of communication with parents and relatives of players, etc.

The Presidium of the city Council of Sport union (Sportsoyuza), drawing attention to violations of the regime and 'immoral acts', noted the bad condition of the political-educational and educational training work in teams. As defined, this has led to a decrease in sport results:

> Practice has shown that we should not be limited to lectures, readings of newspapers and punishment of the offenders. To the questions of education applies correct calendaring competitions, competent planning of educational-training work, enhancing the role of trade unions and Komsomol organizations in the everyday lives of players.[12]

To change the situation, the coaches of the teams were asked to pay special attention to improving the individual technical skills as the foundation for rapid upsurge of class game, increasing the sport loads, thereby improving the versatile physical training of players, education of diligence and increasing theoretical knowledge.[13]

Political news in the country did not pass over the sport, at least in reports. The annual report of the year 1962 was particularly politicized:

In 1962 the team worked and lived in the period of radical changes in the life of our country caused by the XXII Congress of the CPSU. All political-educational work was aimed at further improving the ideological-educational, cultural level of the players, education of patriotism and devotion to Motherland, implementation of the principles of the moral code of communism builders. The team has constantly studied all the materials of 1962 related to the CPSU and USSR Government. The team is familiarized with Khrushchev's speeches during the political information and lessons.[14]

It seems that general words about party news or quotes from Marxism–Leninism were one of the essential features of an official report or public report. From the report, it was stated that on the basis of their work teams and the guidelines of football Federation of the USSR, decisions of the higher sports organizations and trade unions were approved. In doing this, all the provisions and regulations were taken to unconditional execution and brought to the consciousness of every member of the team (kollektiv). The party Committee of GOMZ, named OGPU, heard the results of the work team for the first round on the party-economic asset. The team reported to the Board of the sports club with 'involving a wide asset'. In 1962, the team had 16 general meetings, trade unions and Komsomol meetings, where the plans and results of the team's work for various periods were discussed. There, reports of players on education were provided, the norms of behaviour on the field, fulfilment of the coaching staff's tasks, and violations of discipline and behaviour were discussed.[15]

Gradually, the report came to a situation that was closer to reality. The author of the report, which, most likely, was the head coach of the team, was told that in 1962, there was an improvement of discipline of players, a sharp reduction of cases of violations of the regimen, increased responsibility for the general education and special education. There was a shift towards a friendly collective (*druzhnyi kollektiv*), as evidenced by the results of the first round. He wrote, 'The sharp fall of the results in the second round and unsure game in the final stage is telling about serious shortcomings in educational team training and about moral violations in team training'.[16]

In 1965, seven players were dismissed from the team for the following reasons: unauthorized departure from the collective, bad attitude towards training work, drunkenness, and decrease in athletic performances.[17] These violations were not isolated. We can only guess the reasons for the lack of discipline.

In 1962, based on the report, 13 lectures on various topics, 15 general and the Komsomol meetings, 18 general visits to the theatre, cinema, and excursions were held. The editorial board released wall and photo newspapers, designed a colourful album from the results of 1962. In addition, the players were trained using video equipment; part of the games were filmed and seen in order to be used as visual aids for analysis; for these purposes, two movie cameras 'Neva' and 'Leningrad' were acquired.[18]

Obviously, specifications were drawn up by the head coach of the team and contained estimates of the fitness of the players (physical, technical, tactical, volitional training), and also how they spent the season (discipline, personal characteristics, behaviour in the team and so on). The description of the player of Zenit in 1964 can help us to understand the attributes that were important while evaluating football players, and therefore, those qualities for which the Soviet player has been approved/was condemned:

In the main staff of the team [the player] was introduced from mid-season this year. Tactical trainer's tasks he performs satisfactorily. Technique helps him to play in defending confident, well connected to the attack, but he is not always included in the game. This shortcoming should be removed. [He is] disciplined, well-trained. He is useful member of the team (kollektiv). Studying in school for trainers.[19]

Among these assessments, we meet rather curious ones: 'always thinking of something else', 'often trained without a twinkle', 'abuse of stroke', 'he spent the season well, having given up his shortcomings', 'hasn't given the team what he can', 'broke ties with the unhealthy environment that surrounded him last year, he became a healthy family man'.

In winter, the team began to prepare for the season. The first part of the preparation of 'Zenit' was held in Leningrad, for example, in 1962, six days a week:

Monday – Gymnastics on the equipment and with shells, acrobatics with an average load (the sports hall of the Textile Institute);

Tuesday – technical elements isolated from football games and gaming exercises with an average load (winter stadium arena);

Wednesday – elements of athletics: starts, jumping, repeated and variable (pere-mezhny) running with a heavy load (winter stadium arena);

Thursday – elements of the techniques and tactics of football with an average load (ice rink);

Friday – physical training outdoors (skiing, hockey, cross-country with an average load);

Saturday – sided game on a snowy field of normal size with a heavy load;

Sunday – a day of rest.

Each lesson in football technique was given 30 min of time for any work with the ball, where players improved their favourite techniques and partly to eliminate their weaknesses.[20] As we can see, the training schedule was intense.

The main period for the team was games in the USSR championship in the class 'A' (which lasted roughly from May to the end of November).

Zenit for a long time did not have its own base, and they had to train on leased sites. Therefore, it was believed that the away conditions were sometimes better than in its hometown Leningrad. In one of the reports, there were complaints that players with the necessary level of skill did not go to 'Zenit', because the material conditions (at other teams) were better than what 'Zenit' could offer.[21] They had to rent a sports arena for training. Only in 1963, one was built for the team in its own base in Udelnaya.

Obviously, the revenue to some extent depended on the sale of tickets, as in 1964, the report reported: 'This year, the revenue estimates of the team are much worse compared with the previous year. The reason – a bad team play in the first round, when the team failed to comply with the plan.'[22]

Quarantine for players in part served the purpose of controlling them before the game. One of the players recalled his quarantine experience in the 1980s negatively:

Championship games were held on Saturdays. Sunday was a day off, we go home. On Monday we already had training, on Tuesday – two trainings, and from Wednesday began quarantine. We were locked up for four days, and we sat at the base. This is mind-boggling! Cards, billiards, dominoes, we couldn't look at each other. Even after the game we moved on base – pool, sauna, and only in the morning we have to go home. It was a madhouse. It was hard. I would look at current players if they sat for four days at the base.[23]

There were other football teams in Leningrad, but they mostly did not play in the highest football championship; they were created mainly to serve as a reserve for main teams like Zenit. As a former Zenit player remembered in the 1950s, Dynamo Leningrad were the 'eternal rival' team of Zenit. It is interesting that in 1970–1980s, the situation changed – after Dynamo Leningrad was revived, it became a kind of reserve to Zenit, where players often came from and where they would go to get game experience and/or training of military service.

## Social status of the Soviet players

Athletes that were called amateurs, in fact, were professionals, as they played for a major league team (in our case) and provided them with wages[24] and full employment (the inability to combine with any other work).But it did not guarantee them a future after finishing playing for the masters team. Thus, the professional status of players officially was not recognized, but in fact, it was presented. Also, nobody loudly declared that the players were amateurs.

It is important how one of the Zenit veterans described professional sport: 'However, we don't have professionals in the Western bourgeois sense of the word. Every athlete has some more fundamental cause in life, which engages in full and starts, only stepping down from the sport'.[25] Apparently, professionalism 'in the Western, bourgeois sense of the word' was inherent in active marketing, contracts, advertising, buying/selling of players, which certainly was negatively assessed by the Soviet leadership and the press. The Soviet press, in turn, represented the bourgeois players as disenfranchised goods.

There were 20 players on the team in December 1952 and they were of different professions, such as fitters, turners, chauffeurs, collectors, radio operators, cabinet-makers, patternmaker, borer. Among them, in the annual report, there were only two football coaches. None of the players were available for higher education; there was an average of two, one–two years of college.[26] Georgy Lasin, a Zenit player of 1940s, studied at the Institute of Physical Education. So, he surprised a lot of people because at that time, football players seldom studied in the Institute. Some people just did not believe that football could be combined with successful studies at the institute. There were those who believed that the great players did not need higher education. But gradually, especially starting in the 1960s, Zenit players began to receive education, mostly sports education in the Lesgaft Institute.

## Conclusion

Football competitions held in the framework of the Leningrad office of Voluntary sport society Zenit were held not only with the aim of promoting health and the physical development of workers, or of developing of football at grassroots sport organizations, but also with the purpose of increasing of sport skill of the players and identifying capable and promising players for the replenishment of the team Zenit.[27] And the main purpose of the teams that competed in the city championship was the supply of personnel for Zenit and Dynamo, and the search for talented players. The best players of the teams that won other championships were invited to the masters team, which obviously meant greater status.

The football team Zenit was subordinate to the voluntary sport society Zenit, but from 1958 was in charge of the trade union committee LOMO. The analysis of the sources containing information about the team Zenit has allowed us to conclude that it existed separately from the LOMO as a whole: players as they played on the team of masters did not work at the plant, just sometimes participated in meetings organized with the labour collective of the plant. First of all, LOMO acted as a patron, sponsor, and football players could go there to work after ending their playing career. This was one of their strategies of existence, because they did not have any retirement benefits once they stopped playing for the masters team.

In general, the budget, some details of the report, staffing and other sources show that the Soviet football team (where 'Zenit' was my case study) existed practically autonomously as a body within a body and functioned essentially as a professional club in which the profession of the players, as well as its financing and governance were veiled.

## Disclosure statement

No potential conflict of interest was reported by the author.

## Notes

1. See Edelman, 'A Small Way of Saying "No"'; Bradley, 'Celtic Football Club, Irish Ethnicity, and Scottish Society'; Mills, 'Velez Mostar Football Club and the Demise of "Brotherhood and Unity" in Yugoslavia, 1922–2009'; Zeller, 'Our Own Internationale'; and Edelman, 'Romantitki-neudachniki: "Spartak" v zolotoi vek sovetskogo futbola (1945–1952)'.
2. Butusov and Dolganov, *Zenit*; Korshak, *Nash 'Zenit'*; Izmailov, *V alyh futbolkah – leningradtsy*; Doganovskii, *Zenit. Istoria v litsah*; Lukosyak, *Letopis' FK 'Zenit'*; Pogorelov, *17 stupenei k kubku UEFA*; Pogorelov, *Kak vozrozhdali 'Zenit'*; Jurinov, *Zolotoi marshrut. Isroria odnoi komandy*; and Rabiner, *Pravda o Zenite*.
3. The second most important city in the RSFSR.
4. Voluntary sports societies were created in the mid-1930s in order to develop mass physical culture, sport and tourism, training people in system 'Ready for Labor and Defense of the USSR', athletes dischargers, masters of sport and improve the skills of the athletes.
5. Ageevets, *'Zenit'*, 33.
6. Tsentral'nyi gosudarstvennyi arhiv Sankt-Peterburga (TsGA SPb), f.687, op.1, d.113, l.137.
7. TsGA SPb, f.687, op.1, d.199, l.140.
8. TsGA SPb, f.687, op.1, d.199, l.100.
9. 'Vstrecha s 'Zenitom', *Znamya progressa*.
10. But players also received awards and were able to have informal payments. That was slightly more than the average wage of a worker in the USSR, but nevertheless could not provide them a future.
11. TsGA SPb, f.2187, op.7, d.199, l.10.
12. 'Esche raz o futbole. Na prezidiume gorodskogo soveta Sportsoyuza', *Sportivnaya nedelya Leningrada*.
13. Ibid.
14. TsGA SPb, f.687, op.1, d.113, l.119.
15. Ibid.
16. Ibid., 120.
17. TsGA SPb, f.687, op.1, d.197, l.135.

18. Ibid., 121.
19. TsGA SPb, f.687, op.1, d.176, l.57.
20. TsGA SPb, f.687, op.1, d.113, l.124.
21. TsGA SPb, f.687, op.1, d.176, l.56.
22. TsGA SPb, f.687, op.1, d.176, l.102.
23. 'My igrali dotemna', *Sankt-Peterburgskie vedomosti*.
24. For example, state schedule football team 'Zenit' in 1958 contains the list of players and their wages//TsGA SPb, f.2187, op.7, d.198, l.3.
25. Ivanov, *V vorotah Zenita,* 147.
26. TsGA SPb, f.4588, op.1, d.41, l.1.
27. TsGA SPb, f.4588, op.4, d.123, l.70.

# References

Ageevets, Vladimir. *'Zenit' (fragmenty istorii)* [Zenit (fragments of history)]. 2nd ed. St. Petersburg: Shaton, 2005.

Bradley, J.M. 'Celtic Football Club, Irish Ethnicity, and Scottish Society'. *New Hibernia Review* 12, no. 1 (2008): 96–110.

Butusov, M., and A. Dolganov, eds. *Zenit.* Leningrad: Soyuz sportivnyhobschestviorganizatsii Leningrada, 1959.

Doganovskii, Dmitriy. *Zenit. Istoria v litsah* [Zenit. History in persons]. St. Petersburg: Ivan Fedorov, 2004.

Edelman, R. 'Romantitki-neudachniki: "Spartak" v zolotoi vek sovetskogo futbola (1945–1952)' [Romantics-losers: 'Spartak' during the Gold age of Soviet football (1945–1952)]. In *Rossiiskaya imperia chuvstv: Podhody k kul'turnoi istorii emotsii* [The Russian Empire of the senses. Approaches to the cultural history of emotions]. Moscow: Novoe literaturnoe obozrenie, 2010.

Edelman, R. 'A Small Way of Saying "No": Moscow Working Men, Spartak Soccer, and the Communist Party, 1900–1945'. *The American Historical Review* 107, no. 5 (December 2002): 1441–74.

'Esche raz o futbole. Na prezidiume gorodskogo soveta Sportsoyuza'. [Again about the football. At the presidium of the city council of sports union]. *Sportivnaya nedelya Leningrada*, January 6, 1962.

Ivanov, Leonid. *V vorotah Zenita* [In the Gate of the Zenit]. Leningrad: Lenizdat, 1986.

Izmailov, Al'bert. *V alyh futbolkah – leningradtsy* [In Scarlet t-shirts are Leningraders]. Leningrad: Lenizdat, 1986.

Jurinov, Vladimir. *Zolotoi marshrut. Isroria odnoi komandy* [The gold route. The story of one team]. St. Petersburg: OLMA Media Group, 2009.

Korshak, Juriy, ed. *Nash 'Zenit'* [Our Zenit]. Lenizdat: Leningrad, 1985.

Lukosyak, Yuriy. *Letopis' FK 'Zenit'* [The chronicle of FC Zenit]. St. Petersburg: Alexandr PRINT, 2007.

Mills, R. 'Velež Mostar Football Club and the Demise of 'Brotherhood and Unity' in Yugoslavia, 1922–2009'. *Europe-Asia Studies* 62, no. 7 (2010): 1107–33.

'My igrali dotemna' [We played till the dark], *Sankt-Peterburgskie vedomosti*, November 20, 2009.

Pogorelov, Fedor. *17 stupenei k kubku UEFA* [17 steps to the UEFA Cup]. St. Petersburg: Amfora, 2008.

Pogorelov, Fedor. *Kak vozrozhdali 'Zenit'* [How the Zenit was revived]. St. Petersburg: Amfora, 2009.

Rabiner, Igor. *Pravda o 'Zenite'* [The truth about Zenit]. St. Petersburg: OLMA Media Group, 2009.

Zeller, M. 'Our Own Internationale', 1966 Dynamo Kiev Fans between Local Identity and Transnational Imagination'. *Kritika: Explorations in Russian and Eurasian History* 12, no. 1 (2011): 53–82.

# Can Hong Kong Chinese football players represent their 'Fatherland'? The Cold War, FIFA and the 1966 Asian Games

Chun Wing Lee

During the Cold War years, both the Chinese regimes in Beijing (PRC) and Taipei (ROC) claimed to be the sole representative of the Chinese nation, thus giving rise to a battle over which regime should be recognized by the international sporting community. The issue of recognition, however, was not the only source of contention among supporters of the two regimes during the Cold War years. This paper documents how pro-PRC forces and members of the British expat community in Hong Kong, despite their different political allegiances, formed an alliance to stop Hong Kong football players from representing the ROC in the 1966 Asian Games. This attempt was not successful, partly because of the role played by then-FIFA President Stanley Rous, and the saga eventually offered the pro-ROC forces in Hong Kong the opportunity to strengthen the identification of the Chinese population in Hong Kong with the regime.

## Introduction

Despite coming under British colonial rule in the 1840s, athletes from Hong Kong have always represented China since China first began participating in international sporting competitions during the early twentieth century. From the 1910s to the 1930s, the Republic of China (ROC) won nine straight football titles in the Far East Games, due in large part to the contribution of players based in Hong Kong. The ROC national football team was arguably one of the best in Asia during the 1950s and 1960s. They qualified for the 1960 Olympic Games in Rome, won the prestigious Merdeka Cup in 1963 and shared the title with South Korea in the 1965 Merdeka Cup. Most importantly, the ROC team won gold medals in the 1954 and 1958 Asian Games. Such achievements, usually made by squads made up entirely of players from colonial Hong Kong, allowed the ROC national team to become an important icon of the ROC regime in the Chinese communities in Hong Kong and elsewhere in South-East Asia.[1]

Although the practice of having players based in Hong Kong represent the ROC began in the early twentieth century, the political and sporting context of the 1950s and 1960s was very different from that of the previous decades. The ROC regime, led by the Chinese Nationalist Party (KMT), was defeated in the Chinese Civil War in the late 1940s and therefore had to retreat to the island of Taiwan, which did not have much of a football tradition. The establishment of the People's Republic of China (PRC) in Beijing in 1949 by the communists caused the two Chinese regimes to begin to battle for legitimacy and recognition among Chinese people overseas and the international sporting community. In other words, Hong Kong players no longer represented a Chinese regime that was widely recognized as the only legitimate Chinese regime.

With regard to the sporting context, the existence of two Chinese regimes and their unwillingness to follow the 'Two Koreas' or 'Two Germanies' model meant that the International Olympic Committee (IOC) and many international sporting federations had to determine which Chinese regime they would recognize when deciding whether to accept the sporting association from mainland China or Taiwan into their membership. Also important to the present study is the fact that the Hong Kong Football Association (HKFA) joined FIFA in 1954 and began to participate in official international competitions with the 1954 Asian Games. Many ethnic Chinese players in Hong Kong were therefore eligible to represent either colonial Hong Kong or the ROC in international competitions. In the 1950s, most top ethnic Chinese players in the Hong Kong league represented the ROC, with the Hong Kong team widely regarded as a B team of the ROC team[2].

While the ROC faced little opposition when calling up Hong Kong players in the 1950s, such was no longer the case in the 1960s. Several attempts were made by members of the Hong Kong football community to prevent Hong Kong players from playing for the ROC. By far the most dramatic and publicized attempt occurred in December of 1966, when the HKFA refused to permit the 16 Hong Kong players called up by the ROC to participate in the 1966 Asian Games held in Bangkok. Thirteen players opted to defy the HKFA and flew to Bangkok to play three matches for the ROC over three days. Upon the players' return to Hong Kong, they were charged of misconduct by the HKFA. Eventually, however, the charges were dropped after the HKFA received a letter from then-FIFA President Stanley Rous.

In addition to documenting this dramatic event, this paper will discuss how various political allegiances influenced different forces' attitudes towards the issue. More specifically, by examining how the issue was reported and discussed in pro-ROC newspapers, pro-PRC newspapers and English-language newspapers targeting the British expatriate community in colonial Hong Kong, the relationships between the various political allegiances and their varied understandings of the practice of Hong Kong players representing the ROC will be explained. Moreover, this paper offers insight into FIFA's position regarding issues caused by the existence of two competing Chinese regimes when Rous presided over the organization.

## Forbidding the players from playing for the ROC/Taiwan

From the 1950s to the 1960s, the practice of calling up players based in Hong Kong to represent the ROC proceeded as follows: first, the ROC Football Commission would invite the Chinese Amateur Athletic Federation of Hong Kong (CAAF), which claimed to be the governing body of ethnic Chinese sports in colonial Hong Kong, to select players from Hong Kong. The CAAF would then invite the Chinese Football Association of Hong Kong (CFA), a member organization of the CAAF made up of ethnic Chinese clubs playing in the HKFA league, to select the players. Thereafter, the ROC would write to the HKFA, asking the HKFA to release the players because according to Article 11 of the HKFA rules: 'No club or player shall be allowed to compete in any charity, representative or other competition without the permission of the Council'.[3]

Approximately two weeks before the start of the Asian Games, which were due to start on 10 December 1966, the practice described above commenced. On 2 December, the CFA selected 16 players to represent the ROC, and it was on the agenda for the HKFA Council meeting on 6 December to discuss the letter from the ROC Football Commission concerning the release of the players. For the first time ever, however, the HKFA decided not to release the players after a vote resulted in 8–6 votes against the release of the players.

Three days later, on 9 December 1966, an emergency HKFA Council meeting was held to reconsider the issue after a telegram signed by FIFA President Stanley Rous, who was in Bangkok, and General Torsakdi, the President of the Thailand Football Association and an official of the Asian Football Confederation (AFC), reached the HKFA on 8 December. The message from Rous and Torsakdi read as follows:

> News of China's probable withdrawal received here with great regret. Fixtures were arranged specially to permit them to complete league matches in Hongkong. All officials here request urgent reconsideration. Hopefully await your cable giving approval for participation.[4]

Nevertheless, the HKFA Council again decided not to release the 16 players called up by the ROC after a vote of 9–5.

The distribution of these two votes, which is presented in Table 1, is revealing. At that time, the HKFA Council was comprised of one chairman, who was elected in the Annual General Meeting; one representative from each First Division Club; six representatives who were elected by clubs from the junior divisions and one representative each from the CAAF, the CFA and the Hong Kong Army Sports Board. In the 1966–1967 season, there were 12 First Division clubs. Thus, the council was made up of 22 persons. Nineteen members attended the 6 December meeting, and 16 attended the emergency meeting on 9 December. The ROC cause obtained support from no more than six council members in the two meetings. Aside from the representative of CAAF and Hussain, who was of Indian descent, only four representatives from First Division clubs voted in favour of the release of the players. These four clubs were all ethnic Chinese clubs, each of which had players called up to represent the ROC. Representatives from two other ethnic Chinese clubs in the First Division, Happy Valley and Tung Sing, voted against the release of the players. Happy Valley was well known for being a pro-PRC club, which gave rise to a huge controversy when the club visited mainland China under the name of Tung Cheung in 1964. Tung Sing was a club presided by Henry Fok, a businessperson with close ties with the PRC regime.[5] Other council members who voted to block the players' participation in the Asian Games were either representatives of clubs run by British expatriates, such as the Rangers, Army and Hong Kong Football Club, or representatives of clubs playing in the junior divisions. It is worth noting this fact, as non-Chinese clubs were still a major force in the lower divisions in the mid-1960s. In other words, those who voted against releasing the 16 players represented the pro-PRC forces and the British expatriate community in colonial Hong Kong.

## Making sense of the rejection

Judging from discussions in the two council meetings, as well as a statement released by the HKFA after the 13 players defied the HKFA by participating in the

Table 1.   How the members of the HKFA Council voted when deciding whether or not to release the HKFA registered players to play for the ROC/Taiwan in the 1966 Asian Games.

| Voting decisions at the 6 December meeting | | |
| --- | --- | --- |
| For the release of the players (6 votes) | Against the release of the players (8 votes) | Present but did not vote or abstained (5 persons) |
| (1)  CK Woo (CAAF) | (1)  FC Chan (Junior League) | (1)  Ian Petrie (Junior League; acting chairman), |
| (2)  Gordon Wu (South China) | (2)  CY Lai (Happy Valley) | (2)  Joe Toole (Hong Kong Football Club) |
| (3)  LY Yuen (Sing Tao) | (3)  MC Tse (Tung Sing) | (3)  WD White (Junior League) |
| (4)  T Lui (Kowloon Motor Bus) | (4)  PM Kwok (Junior League) | (4)  CC Lo (Yuen Long) |
| (5)  ST Wong (Eastern) | (5)  Colin Green (Junior League) | (5)  PW Chan (Police) |
| (6)  Jindoo Hussain (Junior League) | (6)  Maj. W Perritt (Army) | |
| | (7)  Maj. N Connally (Army) | |
| | (8)  M O'Brien (Rangers) | |

| Voting decisions at the 9 December meeting | | |
| --- | --- | --- |
| For the release of the players (5 votes) | Against the release of the players (9 votes) | Present but did not vote or abstained (2 persons) |
| (1)  Gordon Wu (South China) | (1)  FC Chan (Junior League) | (1)  Ian Petrie (Junior League; acting chairman) |
| (2)  LY Yuen (Sing Tao) | (2)  MC Tse (Tung Sing) | (2)  PW Chan (Police) |
| (3)  T Lui (Kowloon Motor Bus) | (3)  PM Kwok (Junior League) | |
| (4)  ST Wong (Eastern) | (4)  Colin Green (Junior League) | |
| (5)  Jindoo Hussain (Junior League) | (5)  Maj. W Perritt (Army) | |
| | (6)  Maj. N Connally (Army) | |
| | (7)  M O'Brien (Rangers) | |
| | (8)  WD White (Junior League) | |
| | (9)  Joe Toole (Hong Kong Football Club) | |

Source: 'The HKFA Forbids Us to Take Part in the Asian Games' [in Chinese], *Hong Kong Times*, 7 December 1966, 8; 'HKFA Council Urgent Meeting Rejects Rous' Request to Release Players' [in Chinese], *Hong Kong Commercial Daily*, 10 December 1966, 5; 'Yesterday's HKFA Meeting Stopped Chiang from Snatching Players' [in Chinese], *Wen Wei Pao*, 7 December 1966, 6.

Asian Games for the ROC, the main reason that the players were not released was to protect the integrity of domestic competitions. Newspapers reported that council members who opposed the release of the players tended to legitimize their stance during the two council meetings by referring to the impact on domestic competitions. In addition, the HKFA statement stated that if the players were released and therefore missed any domestic fixtures, it would not have been fair to Hong Kong soccer fans, nor would it have been in accordance with HKFA rules regarding the fielding of full-strength sides, to have allowed vital championship and relegation league matches to have been played in Hong Kong during this period by under-strength first division sides.[6]

Interestingly, among the six clubs that would have lost out because of the absence of the 16 players, five clubs (South China, Kowloon Motor Bus, Sing Tao, Eastern and Tung Wah) made it clear to the HKFA Council that they would allow the players to participate in the Asian Games. Nevertheless, the pro-PRC press was quick to frame the issue as a classic 'club vs. country' conflict and had no hesitation in defending the interests of the clubs playing in the Hong Kong league. For example, previewing the HKFA Council meeting on 6 December, a column in the pro-PRC newspaper *Wen Wei Pao* argued that releasing the players would be detrimental to the clubs and players of the Hong Kong league, as well as the fans in Hong Kong:

> If these players go [to Bangkok], would the league fixtures be affected? Even though no matches are rescheduled … the matches would no longer be proper matches when the big name players are not available, would it be a loss to fans … Would it affect the gate? Would some clubs and players therefore suffer?[7]

Obviously, ensuring that the big-name players would appear in domestic competitions can hardly explain why the HKFA's decision to keep the players in Hong Kong was described by *Wen Wei Pao* as a 'good thing which pleases many people' and by another pro-PRC newspaper, the *Hong Kong Commercial Daily*, as a decision that 'defends the dignity and sovereignty of the HKFA'.[8] For the pro-PRC forces, the major goal of the HKFA's decision was to embarrass the archrival of the PRC regime, the ROC regime. According to *Wen Wei Pao*, Taiwan's selection of Hong Kong football players should not have continued for both sporting and political reasons. With regard to sports, the practice meant that the HKFA was merely a 'Football Department of Taiwan'.[9] Politically speaking, by calling up Hong Kong players, 'Taiwan's Chiang Bandits' were 'implementing the "two Chinas" policy and using the players as political tools'.[10]

Like the pro-PRC press, the English-language press, which reflected the opinions of the British expatriate community, applauded the HKFA decisions. I.M. MacTavish wrote in *China Mail*, 'Everybody who genuinely has the wellbeing of Colony football at heart will applaud the decision'.[11] MacTavish did not bother to discuss the potential disruption of local fixtures if the players were released in his columns. Instead, he chose to back up his stance by emphasizing the viewpoint that Taiwan had no right to select players from Hong Kong:

> Since the change of regime in China, Hong Kong football has suffered mercilessly at the hands of Taiwan whose officials have unashamedly ravaged the Colony's ranks for their own covetous and totally unrealistic, prestige-hunting ends.

> It is difficult to know why this blatant poaching has been tolerated by the Hong Kong Football Association and also in fact, by the Hong Kong Government, which surely cannot remain indefinitely indifferent to such activities … activities which really amount – as has just been demonstrated – to a complete disregard of football's legal and established order in this British colony.[12]

In other words, in spite of the eligibility of Chinese players to represent the ROC, they ought to play for the British colony. Also, Taiwan's long-held practice of calling up Hong Kong players was regarded as detrimental to the interests of Hong Kong because Hong Kong could have fielded a much stronger team if there had been no 'poaching' from Taiwan. The decisions by the HKFA, which effectively blocked the players from representing the ROC, were thus 'in the best interests of HONGKONG FOOTBALL' (capital letters original) because 'The HKFA has no responsibilities, implied, real or imaginary, to further the distorted soccer affairs of Taiwan', according to MacTavish.[13]

A column from the *South China Morning Post* also criticized Taiwan for the 'constant "piracy" of *our* players' (emphasis added) and bemoaned the fact that despite the decision not to release the players, certain HKFA Council members had 'show(n) their true colours' by voting to allow the players to play for the ROC, meaning that they were working for the interests of Taiwan at the expense of Hong Kong.[14] The anonymous columnist therefore reminded these council members that 'Surely, any individual who accepts a seat on the Council should put the interests of Hong Kong first and foremost'.[15] Likewise, MacTavish singled out Hussain, the only non-ethnic Chinese HKFA council member who supported the players' participation in the Asian Games, for criticism (without revealing his name) because Hussain had 'stood up as one of the chief orators for the wider interests of Taiwan'.[16]

The pro-PRC forces and the British expatriate community in Hong Kong undoubtedly had very different political allegiances, with the former forces being loyal to the PRC regime and the expatriate community pledging their loyalty to colonial Hong Kong. Despite this obvious difference, in this matter, the two forces formed a strategic alliance against the pro-ROC forces. For the pro-PRC forces, the absence of an ROC team in the Asian Games would signal a defeat for the ROC regime, which was still competing for legitimacy against the PRC regime in Hong Kong and in the overseas Chinese community. While such a stance was clearly motivated by political concerns, the pro-PRC press also regarded itself as a defender of the interests of Hong Kong football in order to make sense of their anti-Taiwan attitude regarding this issue. As for the expatriate community, the fixture problem was clearly not really an important consideration. Much more crucial was the understanding that players based in Hong Kong should remain loyal to Hong Kong by representing Hong Kong, and the past success of the ROC Team in international competitions was thus believed to have been obtained as a result of sacrificing the interests of football in colonial Hong Kong. The HKFA was thus doing the right thing because it was, albeit belatedly, defending the interests of the colony.

## Chinese should represent China

Unlike the pro-PRC and English-language newspapers that welcomed the HKFA decisions in early December, the pro-ROC press greeted the decisions of the HKFA with anger. The *Hong Kong Times* blamed the pro-PRC forces for influencing the HKFA Council members: 'There is no justice within the HKFA, which is now controlled by the evil red forces.'[17] Meanwhile, the *Kung Sheung Daily News* used the following title to report the first vote of the HKFA Council: 'HKFA Dares to Reject China's Notification.'[18]

While pro-PRC forces branded the calling up of the players as a political act and the English-language press referred to the players as 'our' Hong Kong players, who therefore should not represent Taiwan, the pro-ROC forces argued that the players' loyalty should lie with the ROC because they were ethnic Chinese. George Sim, then-CAAF President and team manager of the ROC football team, explained his identification when releasing a statement to defend himself and the 13 players who defied the HKFA: 'Although I am a citizen of Hong Kong, I am also an ROC national. As an overseas Chinese person living away from home (*qiaoju*), one has the obligation and right to stay loyal to one's country'.[19]

In other words, residing in Hong Kong did not oblige an ethnic Chinese person to be loyal to the colony, as an ethnic Chinese person residing in Hong Kong was merely a Chinese person living away from his or her home country, China. Because pro-ROC forces viewed the ROC regime as the only legitimate Chinese regime, an ethnic Chinese person in Hong Kong ought to be loyal to the ROC regime.

Both the *Kung Sheung Daily News* and the *Hong Kong Times* shared this position and therefore attacked Lee Fuk Shu, the HKFA President at the time, who had only a symbolic role, according to the HKFA Constitution, after the pro-PRC press reported that Lee wanted to see Hong Kong players represent Hong Kong.[20] A columnist writing in the *Hong Kong Times* reminded Lee Fuk Shu of his own ethnicity and the contribution that Chinese people have made to Hong Kong football:

> The HKFA President, Mr. Lee Fuk Shu, is a yellow-faced Chinese person. At this moment, he should answer the questions I want to ask from the standpoint of a Chinese person. When the Chinese represent their fatherland in the Asian Games, which colonial laws have they violated? If there were no Chinese players in Hong Kong, would Lee Fuk Shu have become the HKFA President? Today's Hong Kong football is the football of the Chinese. Those who watch football are Chinese fans. If there are no Chinese fans, how can the HKFA survive?[21]

The above quotation not only sought to remind readers and Lee Fuk Shu of their national/ethnic identity but also to emphasize the fact that ethnic Chinese people had made meaningful contributions to Hong Kong football. This expression of nationalistic sentiment also serves as a rebuke of the British expat community, as it stressed the idea that football successes in the British colony actually hinged on the efforts and contributions of the colonial subjects, rather than of their colonial masters.

The *Kung Sheng Daily* even challenged Lee Fuk Shu in an editorial:

> We now ask Mr. Lee Fuk Shu the following: Hong Kong is not an 'independent state'. Hong Kong Chinese players have represented China in the Asian Games and the Olympic Games for a long time. The Hong Kong government has never intervened. In fact, it has no right to intervene. You are the HKFA President. You were elected because of the support of the ethnic Chinese clubs. How dare you provide such a ridiculous 'instruction' to the HKFA Council?[22]

One reason why the above quotation deserves our attention is that the editor also reminded Lee Fuk Shu that Hong Kong was not an independent state. In fact, similar reminders could also be found in the *Hong Kong Times*, which condemned the pro-PRC forces for urging the HKFA not to release the players: 'These bandits ... seem to think that they belong to the "Hong Kong state"; that's just shameful'.[23] Moreover, the argument presented by the English-language press, which wanted the 'Hong Kong people to represent Hong Kong', was explicitly rejected because 'Until Hong Kong becomes an independent state, we are all Chinese who are living away from home in Hong Kong'.[24] In other words, the pro-ROC press, in addition to using the ethnic identity of the players and the target readers to defend the right to play for the ROC, exhibited the world view that everyone should belong to a nation and that each nation should be represented by its own sovereign state. Because Hong Kong was not an independent state but a city under colonial rule, it did not make sense to ask the Chinese people residing in Hong Kong to identify with Hong Kong. The hegemony of the 'inter-state' world view was thus enforced.[25]

In sum, the pro-ROC forces felt that the ethnic Chinese people residing in Hong Kong should be loyal to the ROC, as they believed that the Chinese people residing in colonial Hong Kong should put their national identity first and that the ROC was the only legitimate regime of the Chinese people. Playing for the ROC was therefore regarded as a means of displaying such loyalty; thus, no one should deprive the players of the right to play for their fatherland. Ethnic Chinese people, such as Lee Fuk Shu and the pro-PRC forces, who were against Hong Kong players' long-held practice of representing the ROC were thus effectively betraying their Chinese identity. The 13 players who defied the HKFA were thus hailed by the *Hong Kong Times* as '*zhuangshi*', or 'fighting heroes', not only because they had 'crushed the Chinese Communist bandits into pieces' by flying the ROC flag in the Asian Games despite the efforts of the pro-PRC forces to force them to remain in Hong Kong but also because they were 'struggling for the right to represent the fatherland for the next generation of overseas Chinese people in Hong Kong'.[26]

## The role of FIFA and Stanley Rous

As previously noted, after the HKFA Council decided not to release the players, a cable from Stanley Rous prompted the HKFA Council to hold another meeting to discuss the issue. His role in this episode did not end here, however. It was reported that the players only agreed to take part in the Asian Games after being assured by Stanley Rous that they would not be breaking any FIFA rules or regulations upon their arrival in Bangkok.[27] Ultimately, Rous played an instrumental role in ensuring that the 13 players were not punished by the HKFA. Acting as the legal advisor for the 13 charged players, solicitor Woo Po Sing flew to England on 3 February 1967 to meet with Stanley Rous. He returned to Hong Kong on 6 February and then handed over a letter signed by Rous to the HKFA special commission that was set up to deal with the incident. Rous's major argument was that approval from the HKFA was not needed for the players to play for the ROC because they were amateur players. In the letter, Rous wrote the following:

> As I told your Chairman in Bangkok, I feel sure that FIFA will consider taking the appropriate action against your association if the players are punished for playing for their national association, and your status as a national association of FIFA might well be reviewed ... No permission or consent is required from the Hongkong FA for its registered players to play for their national country so long as they are amateurs ... I greatly hope that the charges against the players and officials concerned will be dropped.[28]

Upon receipt of the letter, the special commission duly dropped the charge against the players on 7 February 1967.

Clearly, Rous was effectively championing the ROC cause. In fact, in addition to depriving the ethnic Chinese people of their right to play for their 'fatherland', another 'crime' committed by the HKFA, according to the pro-ROC press, was that the HKFA disobeyed FIFA. When the HKFA Council rejected the ROC's request to release the players for a second time after receiving the cable sent by Rous, the *Kung Sheung Daily News* criticized the HKFA for 'not respecting' Rous and the AFC and 'ignoring the FIFA constitution'.[29] The result of the second vote prompted the following angry response in the form of a column in the *Hong Kong Times*:

> It is no longer the time to reason with the FA. Since the FA has decided to disobey the law ... and challenge FIFA, it is useless for anyone to attempt to correct the FA's stupidity and mistakes. We must complain to FIFA and wait for sanctions according to the FIFA constitution.[30]

The pro-ROC forces thus appealed to the legitimacy of FIFA to advance their cause.

While the pro-ROC press criticized the HKFA for ignoring the legitimacy of FIFA, from the perspectives of the pro-PRC press and the English-language press, the party that had broken rules and regulations was not the HKFA but rather the 13 players who had defied the HKFA. The English-language press called the 13 players 'rebels' and demanded that the HKFA suspend the players or even cancel the players' registration.[31] The pro-PRC press described the case as a case of 'disobedience'.[32] Unlike the pro-ROC press, the pro-PRC press defined the interventions of Stanley Rous as unreasonable and illegitimate. The *Hong Kong Commercial Daily* not only claimed that the pro-Taiwan figures were using FIFA to 'persecute' the HKFA,[33] but also one column on its sports page explicitly rejected the legitimacy of Rous and argued that he should not play a role in this affair:

> This order from Rous is obviously a means of using the position of the FIFA Presidency to pressure the HKFA to release the players, and ... Torsakdi is also bullying the HKFA in an arrogant manner. They are treating the HKFA as their own joint venture. This not only harms the dignity of the HKFA but is also a humiliation. How can Rous and Torsakdi be entitled to intervene in the internal affairs of the HKFA?[34]

Another pro-PRC newspaper, *Wen Wei Pao*, even refused to recognize the position held by Rous, calling him the 'so-called "FIFA President"' and referring to FIFA as the 'so-called international football federation'.[35] The 9 December meeting was therefore described as a test to determine whether the HKFA

> could be independent and use its own power depending on the local situation. If ... [the HKFA] still bows to the pressure and forces from organizations outside Hong Kong, then the Chiang bandits will increase their pressure and cause trouble in the football community.[36]

Again, the pro-PRC press was making sense of its stance by promoting the interests of Hong Kong, but in this context, the parties threatening the HKFA were FIFA and Rous.

The English-language papers were also unhappy about Rous's intervention. MacTavish, for example, described the February letter from Rous as an example of 'injustice' and bemoaned that the letter had 'in fact handed out to a group of international pot-hunters a flimsy judgment which is an open license to pirate Hong Kong players'.[37] However, unlike the pro-PRC press, the English-language press did not reject the authority of Rous and FIFA. Instead, their discontentment with FIFA and Rous and their respect for the international football order headed by Rous and FIFA were negotiated by emphasizing that Rous took a pro-ROC stance because he had been misled. A column from the *South China Morning Post* stated that Rous was 'not presented with the true facts of the situation'.[38] MacTavish also suggested that the telegram from Rous was sent because his stance was formulated 'based on the "advice" given to him on the spot'.[39]

Who misled Rous? Both newspapers mentioned the name of Lee Wai Tong, even though they stopped short of explicitly claiming that Rous wrote the cable and the February letter because of Lee Wai Tong. This legendary figure was born in Hong Kong and played the majority of his amateur football career in Hong Kong. He was a member of the ROC national team prior to the Second World War and also managed the team after the war. He was well known for his pro-ROC stance, and in 1966, he was the vice-president of FIFA. He represented the ROC in the AFC and FIFA while residing in Hong Kong. Blaming Lee Wai Tong for offering Rous biased advice implied that Rous and FIFA were not the culprits, as it was a Hong Kong resident who was championing the Taiwanese cause at the expense of the interests of the British colony who was to be blamed.

Rous's interventions in this saga, which favoured the ROC, forced the Hong Kong press to present the international football order in very different ways. The pro-ROC press respected and reinforced the legitimacy of FIFA by condemning the HKFA for defying Rous. However, the pro-PRC press rejected the legitimacy of FIFA and argued that the HKFA should stand firm against Rous's intervention. Despite their similar stance on the release of the players, there was an obvious difference between the pro-PRC press and the English-language press regarding FIFA and Rous. The English-language press did not agree with Rous's stance but did reluctantly respect the authority of FIFA and Rous by placing the blame on Lee Wai Tong. Such a difference is understandable because Rous, like the majority of the expat community in Hong Kong, was British. For the pro-PRC forces, the PRC had left FIFA in the late 1950s,[40] and the PRC, in the mid-1960s, became heavily involved in the Games of the New Emerging Forces (GANEFO), a movement that challenged the role played by the Olympic Movement and other international sporting federations dominated by the Capitalist Bloc of the west.[41] As there was little doubt that the European capitalist states were the major force within FIFA, which stood by the interests of Taiwan, the pro-PRC forces found no reason to recognize the legitimacy of FIFA and its president, Rous.

## The Cold War, political allegiances and FIFA

By reviewing the saga of the ROC football team's participation in the 1966 Asian Games, this paper demonstrates the relationship between political allegiance and attitudes towards the practice of having Chinese players from Hong Kong representing the ROC. The pro-ROC forces in Hong Kong displayed their loyalty towards the ROC regime by condemning the HKFA and supporting the 13 players who defied the HKFA. For them, the national identity of the Chinese people residing in Hong Kong was of the utmost importance. In addition, because the ROC regime was recognized as the sole legitimate regime of China, representing the ROC was regarded as the right and obligation of the ethnic Chinese people residing in Hong Kong. Those Chinese people who did not adopt this position were thus criticized for betraying their national identity.

The forces loyal to the PRC regime, on the other hand, perceived the ROC regime as their archrival. The ROC's participation in the Asian Games was therefore seen as a political act that could increase the legitimacy of the rival regime. The pro-PRC forces thus applauded the HKFA's decision not to release the players. They also attempted to present their stance by making an apolitical argument referring to the interests of local football, which somehow brings the pro-PRC forces in line with the British expatriate community in Hong Kong. Because the British expatriate community pledged its loyalty to colonial Hong Kong, they regarded the ROC's practice of calling up Hong Kong Chinese players to be at the expense of the interests of Hong Kong.

The world of sports became an important platform in which different political forces aimed to demonstrate their respective superiority during the Cold War years.[42] Under the framework of Cold War politics, colonial Hong Kong and the ROC belonged to the Capitalist Bloc, which was the enemy of communist China. Nevertheless, the peculiar situation of colonial Hong Kong and the state of football in Taiwan served as a basis for pro-PRC forces and the British expatriate community to become strategic allies in this case.[43] Moreover, because of the makeup of the HKFA Council and the earlier decision of the HKFA Council not to send a team to take part in the 1966 Asian Games, the pro-ROC forces suffered a defeat when the pro-PRC council members and other council members representing the British expat community united and voted not to release the players.

Although the pro-ROC forces lost out in the battle within the HKFA, the saga itself may have actually helped them secure more sympathy, at least among the football fans in Hong Kong. The West German side Eintracht Frankfurt was scheduled to play two matches in Hong Kong during the Christmas period in 1966: the first match was against the Hong Kong Representative Team, and the second match was against Hong Kong XI. After the HKFA decided not to release the players, the *Hong Kong Times* effectively began a campaign against the HKFA. On 14 December 1966, just eight days after the HKFA had first rejected the release of the 16 players, the *Hong Kong Times* claimed that it had received more than 300 letters from readers concerning the issue.[44] From 10 December to 24 December, the day on which Eintracht Frankfurt played its first match in Hong Kong, the *Hong Kong Times* published a total of 33 letters from readers that supported the ROC players and management or condemned the HKFA/pro-PRC forces for failing to give permission to the players to play in the Asian Games. Many of these letters openly called for a boycott of the HKFA in the form of refusing to watch the Eintracht Frankfurt matches. On the day on which Eintracht Frankfurt played its first match of the tour, the *Hong Kong Times* offered a very short preview of the match with the following title: 'The Hong Kong Representative Team to Play the Germany Team Today under Calls for Boycott from all Hong Kong Football Fans; Anger all over the Place, Lots of Tickets Available'.[45] Ultimately, the turnout for both matches was poor. Less than 5000 spectators watched the first match, and less than 10,000 attended the second match in a stadium capable of holding 28,000 spectators. Both the English-language press and the pro-PRC press conceded that the boycott campaign initiated by the *Hong Kong Times* was effective.[46] The HKFA, for which one of the major revenue streams is gate receipts from matches against foreign teams, thus suffered a great financial loss of approximately HK\$20,000.[47]

In addition to the effective boycott campaign initiated by the *Hong Kong Times*, another indicator shows that the entire saga may have actually reinforced sympathy for the ROC regime and the form of political identity that it promoted. After the special commission that dealt with the 13 players who defied the HKFA began to meet, the *Sing Tao Daily*, a newspaper that supported the ROC regime in a relatively moderate manner in comparison with the *Hong Kong Times* and the *Kung Sheung Daily News*, found it necessary to ask its readers not to call the newspaper to ask about the special commission's decision: 'The players have not broken any international regulations ... the HKFA ... would surely not dare to challenge the regulations of FIFA. For those who repeatedly call us to ask for updates, please calm down.'[48]

While the battle between the two Chinese regimes during the Cold War to gain recognition in the international sporting community, including FIFA, is well known,[49] this paper shows that securing membership in international federations was not the only battle fought between these two entities with regard to sports. The attempt of supporters of the PRC in Hong Kong to disrupt Taiwan's plan to send a strong football team comprised of players from Hong Kong to participate in the 1966 Asian Games shows that, even though the PRC decided to focus on the GANEFO movement (before the turmoil of the Cultural Revolution) and withdrew from the Olympic Movement and many other international sporting federations in the 1960s, the PRC and its supporters in Hong Kong were still well aware of the political implications of their rival regime's involvement in the Olympic Movement and the Asian Games. Indeed, the risk of being penalized by the HKFA not only resulted in only 13 (rather than the original 16) players flying to Bangkok to represent the ROC, but also one of the players who defied the HKFA revealed years later that the team drew one match and lost the other two matches because the players wanted to ensure that they would not have to play in the knock out stage, so that they could fly back to Hong Kong to fulfil their league commitment.[50] Thus, none of the players missed any local fixtures because of their participation in the Asian Games. Although the ROC team was not able to try their best to regain the gold medal that they had won in 1954 and 1958, merely flying the ROC flag in the football competition of the Asian Games despite the HKFA's stance was already a victory for the ROC regime, indicating that the pro-PRC forces' attempt to disrupt the ROC's campaign was not successful. The role of FIFA President Stanley Rous was crucial here. Without Rous's approval, it would have been extremely unlikely that the 13 players would have represented the ROC in the Asian Games. Rous's intervention was also instrumental in ensuring that the players did not receive sanctions from the HKFA; otherwise it would have been virtually impossible to find any top players based in Hong Kong to risk their playing careers in order to represent the ROC in the future. As shown by his attitudes towards other thorny political issues, such as the apartheid regime in South Africa, Rous's self-defined neutrality on political issues usually meant that he effectively reinforced the political and sporting status quo.[51] His attitude towards the Hong Kong players' participation in the Asian Games for the ROC was no exception. While Rous may have been influenced by Lee Wai Tong, securing another football team to participate in the Asian Games and ensuring that the players would not be punished for playing in an official international competition can be interpreted as a logical stance for a person who prided himself in putting the interests of football above politics. Because Rous's stance effectively favoured the ROC, the legitimacy of FIFA was reinforced among the pro-ROC forces. However, Rous's stance also disappointed his compatriots in Hong Kong and further alienated the pro-PRC forces from the international sporting community.

## Disclosure statement

No potential conflict of interest was reported by the author.

## Funding

This work was supported by the College of Professional and Continuing Education [grant number 4.8.C.EZ27].

## Notes

1. Lee, 'Politics, Identity and Football during the Cold War'.
2. 'For the reasons why most top Chinese players in Hong Kong chose to present the ROC, see Lee, Football Kingdom.
3. 'H.K.'s Cause a Just One', *South China Morning Post*, February 17, 1967, 3.
4. 'Urgent Appeal Made for Taiwan Team', *South China Morning Post*, December 9, 1966, 2.
5. Henry Fok would later play an instrumental role in bringing the PRC into the international sporting community in the 1970s.
6. 'HKFA Statement', *China Mail*, December 16, 1966, 9. This problem would not have arisen if the HKFA had sent a team to play in the Asian Games, but the HKFA declined to do so, citing financial pressure. The pro-ROC *Hong Kong Times* suggested that the decision were influenced by pro-PRC forces. See Chuanshanja, 'The Decision Not to Participate in the Asian Games is HKFA's Humiliation' [in Chinese], *Hong Kong Times*, 28 October 1966, 8.
7. Xushu, 'Appropriate Action Taken by HKFA' [in Chinese], *Wen Wei Pao*, December 6, 1966, 7.
8. Ibid.; and Wupaifangzhu, 'FIFA President is Offside; HKFA Should Defend its Autonomy' [in Chinese], *Hong Kong Commercial Daily*, December 9, 1966, 2.
9. Guoyoufa, 'Let's see What the HKFA Will Do', *Wen Wei Pao*, December 6, 1966, 7.
10. The term 'Chiang Bandits' comes from the surname of the leader of the ROC regime, Chiang Kai-shek. Xushu, 'Appropriate Action Taken by HKFA' [in Chinese], *Wen Wei Pao*, December 6, 1966, 7.
11. I.M. MacTavish, 'Footballistics', *The China Mail*, December 10, 1966, 14.
12. I.M. MacTavish, 'This Soccer Year', *TheChina Mail*, December 31, 1966, 12.
13. I.M. MacTavish, 'Footballistics', *The China Mail*, December 10, 1966, 14.
14. 'At Last a Blow for Colony Football', *South China Morning Post*, December 9, 1966, 3.
15. Ibid.
16. I.M. MacTavish, 'Footballistics', *The China Mail*, December 10, 1966, 14.
17. Chuanshanja, 'The FA Destroys the FIFA Constitution' [in Chinese], *Hong Kong Times*, December 7, 1966, 8.
18. 'HKFA Dares to Reject China's Notification' [in Chinese], *Kung Sheung Daily News*, December 7, 1966, 8. Both the *Hong Kong Times* and the *Kung Sheung Daily News* argued that the ROC was only notifying the HKFA that they were calling up the Hong Kong league players, rather than seeking approval from the HKFA.
19. 'George Sim Released a Statement Yesterday' [in Chinese], *Hong Kong Times*, December 23, 1966, 8.
20. Lee Fuk Shu was a member of the colonial Legislative Council and Executive Council at that time, meaning that his loyalty to the colony was trustworthy from the perspective of the colonial government.
21. Chuanshanja, 'Who Humiliates the Chinese?' [in Chinese], *Hong Kong Times*, December 10, 1966, 7.
22. 'Questioning the HKFA' [in Chinese], *Kung Sheung Daily News*, December 12, 1966, 2.
23. Saizhongkui, 'Leftist Journalists are Rubbish as They Use Foreigners to Attack Compatriots' [in Chinese], *Hong Kong Times*, December 6, 1966, 8.
24. Suanlatang, 'The Idea that Hong Kong People Should Represent Hong Kong is Ridiculous' [in Chinese], *Hong Kong Times*, December 28, 1966, 8.
25. See Levemore, 'Sport's Role in Constructing "Inter-state" Worldview'.
26. Saizhongkui, 'Bravo! The 13 Fighting Heroes!' [in Chinese], *Hong Kong Times*, December 13, 1966, 8.
27. 'FIFA and AFC Approve Players' Participation' [in Chinese], *Hong Kong Times*, December 14, 1966, 8.
28. 'Commission Drops Charges', *South China Morning Post*, February 8, 1967, 2. Apparently, Stanley Rous and the HKFA Chairman Raleigh Lueng, who was in Bangkok as an official of the Hong Kong Olympic Committee, had a meeting in Bangkok during the Asian Games.

29. 'HKFA Ignores Messages from President Rous and the Asian Games' [in Chinese], *Kung Sheung Daily News*, December 10, 1966, 8.
30. Chuanshanja, 'Who Humiliates the Chinese?' [in Chinese], *Hong Kong Times*, December 10, 1966, 7.
31. 'No Ruling Yet on Rebel 13', *Hong Kong Standard*, February 2, 1967, 17.
32. 'Disobedient Players Will Soon be Put on Trial by the HKFA' [in Chinese], *Wen Wei Pao*, December 28, 1966, 7.
33. 'Taiwanese Figures Use FIFA to Persecute the HKFA, Rous Dares to Ask the HKFA to Release Players for Taiwan' [in Chinese], *Hong Kong Commercial Daily*, December 9, 1966, 2.
34. Wupaifangzhu, 'FIFA President is Offside; HKFA Should Defend its Autonomy' [in Chinese], *Hong Kong Commercial Daily*, December 9, 1966, 2.
35. Guoyoufa, 'Is the Meeting Really Urgent and Special?' [in Chinese], *Wen Wei Pao*, December 9, 1966, 8.
36. Ibid.
37. I.M. MacTavish, 'This FIFA Folly', *The China Mail*, February 18, 1967, 10.
38. 'FIFA Misguided on Taiwan Issues', *South China Morning Post*, December 17, 1966, 3.
39. I.M. MacTavish, 'Footballistics', *The China Mail*, December 10, 1966, 14.
40. Homburg, 'FIFA and the "Chinese Question"'.
41. Lutan and Hong, 'The Politicization of Sport'.
42. Andrews and Wagg, 'Introduction: War Minus the Shotting?'.
43. Just three months after the end of the saga, the pro-PRC forces in Hong Kong would start the 1967 riots which became a serious challenge to British colonial rule in Hong Kong.
44. 'Fans Hail the 13 Fighting Heroes and are Determined to Boycott the HKFA' [in Chinese], *Hong Kong Times*, December 14, 1966, 8.
45. 'The Hong Kong Representative Team to Play the Germany Team Today under Calls for Boycott from all Hong Kong Football Fans; Anger all over the Place, Lots of Tickets Available' [in Chinese], *Hong Kong Times*, December 24, 1966, 8.
46. Wupaifangzhu, 'HKFA Spent $20,000 for a Taiwanese Christmas Dinner' [in Chinese], *Hong Kong Commercial Daily*, December 27, 1966, 2; and Iam Petrie, 'Blitzkrieg', *Hong Kong Standard*, December 28, 1966, 16.
47. Chuanshanja, 'The Issue about the National Team Players Was Not Discussed in Last Night's HKFA Meeting' [in Chinese], *Hong Kong Times*, January 4, 1967, 8.
48. 'The Special Commission Testifies the Asian Games Players' [in Chinese], *Sing Tao Daily*, February 2, 1967, 5.
49. See Brownell, '"Sport and Politics Don't Mix"'; Homburg, 'FIFA and the "Chinese Question"'; and Fan and Xiong, 'Communist China: Sport, Politics and Diplomacy'.
50. Xu and Zhang, 'Famous Football Player: Law Pak'.
51. See Darby, *Africa, Football and FIFA*; Rous, *Football Worlds*; and Sugden and Tomlinson, *Football and the Contest for World Football*.

## References

Andrews, David L., and Stephen Wagg. 'Introduction: War Minus the Shooting'. In *East Plays West: Sport and the Cold War*, ed. Stephen Wagg and David L. Andrews, 1–9. London: Routledge, 2002.

Brownell, Susan. '"Sport and Politics Don't Mix": China's Relationship with the IOC during the Cold War'. In *East Plays West: Sport and the Cold War*, ed. Stephen Wagg and David L. Andrews, 253–71. London: Routledge, 2002.

Darby, Paul. *Africa, Football and FIFA: Politics, Colonialism and Resistance*. London: Frank Cass, 2002.

Fan, Hong, and Xiaozheng Xiong. 'Communist China: Sport, Politics and Diplomacy'. *International Journal of the History of Sport* 19, no. 2 (2002): 319–43.

Homburg, Hiedrun. 'FIFA and the "Chinese Question", 1954–1980: An Exercise of Status'. *Historical Social Research* 31, no. 1 (2006): 69–87.

Lee, Chun Wing. *Football Kingdom: Hong Kong Football in the Early Post-WWII Years* [in Chinese]. Hong Kong: Joint Publishing.

Lee, Chun Wing. 'Politics, Identity and Football during the Cold War: When Hong Kong Played the Republic of China in 1959'. *The International Journal of Sport and Society* 1, no. 4 (2010): 59–70.

Levermore, Roger. 'Sport's Role in Constructing "Inter-state" Worldview'. In *Sport and International Relations: An Emerging Relationship*, ed. Adrian Budd, 16–30. London: Routledge, 2004.

Lutan, Rusli, and Hong Fan. 'The Politicization of Sport: GANEFO – A Case Study'. In *Sport, Nationalism and Orientalism: The Asian Games*, ed. Hong Fan, 22–36. London: Routledge, 2007.

Rous, Stanley. *Football Worlds: A Lifetime in Sport*. Devon: Readers Union, 1979.

Sugden, John, and Alan Tomlinson. *FIFA and the Contest for World Football: Who Rules the People's Game?* Cambridge: Polity Press, 1998.

Xu, Xinxun, and Shengping Zhang. 'Famous Football Player: Law Pak' [in Chinese]. In *Biographies of Figures from 100 Years of Taiwanese Sports: Volume 3*, ed. Body Culture of Society of Taiwan, 98–107. Taipei: Body Culture Society of Taiwan, 2008.

# Devolution of *Les Bleus* as a symbol of a multicultural French future

Lindsay Sarah Krasnoff

When France won the World Cup in 1998, the team's multiethnic composition was feted as a symbol of the nation's new, postcolonial image. Alas, the feel-good story did not last. Wins became scarce, scandals plagued the team and football was politicized as the public deplored the 'Playstation junkies' too individualistic to serve the nation. The infusion of racially charged rhetoric into the discourse of *Les Bleus* led many to believe that French football is rife with racism and that the national team is not well received by the public. On the contrary, the public is generally supportive of *Les Bleus*. The negative discourse is an anti-football backlash against the sport's business climate, one fuelled by traditional disdain for football, and shaded by domestic anxieties. This is the 'second sports crisis', an identity crisis less about racial identity and more about the sociocultural norms of being French.

## Introduction

Four years ago, French football experienced its 'zero hour' when *Les Bleus* spectacularly self-destructed at the 2010 South Africa World Cup. Long-simmering tensions between the players and head coach Raymond Domenech erupted when Nicolas Anelka was sent home from the tournament early. Captain Patrice Evra got into an altercation with Robert Duverne, one of the fitness coaches, during a public practice. In highly French fashion, Anelka's teammates went on strike in protest, just prior to what became their last game in South Africa. Following these incidents, 80% of the 69,000 French polled felt that the team should exit the tournament, regardless of the outcome of their last game.[1]

During the highly publicized, much discussed, toxic aftermath players were called 'caids de collège', 'arrogants' and 'sous-éduqués' while pundits and public alike came to terms with the farce.[2] Sociologist Stéphane Beaud argued that the players' strike was an act of political consciousness, a revolt against the stereotype of them portrayed in the media as young men who were 'Playstation Junkies'.[3] Beaud noted that the 2010 team had many leaders who were born and raised in the rough *banlieues* and that in many ways these players (and thus the team) were still stigmatized by their origins.[4] Press coverage seemed to reaffirm this statement.

The noxious spectacle was a far cry from the height of French football 12 years earlier when France won the World Cup for the first time. The home soil triumph was a victory for the sport in France, and marked the first time that a majority of the public was actively engaged with the national team. Moreover, the players who wore the jersey for *Les Bleus* in 1998 represented the best of France's immigration tradition. Teammates traced their ancestral roots to Europe, North Africa and Sub-Saharan Africa, just as previous generations of *Les Bleus* did. Much was made of the team's multiethnic composition, the *black-blanc-beur* mélange that symbolized the success of the French system of assimilation and the nation's new, postcolonial image. Optimism over the future prevailed, and the winning team radiated a positive message to the national and international press. Despite detractors from the far-right wing *Front National* (FN), who claimed the polyglot team did not represent the 'real' France, most supported the team and players into the new millennium as *Les Bleus* won the 2000 European Championship. Alas, the feel-good story did not last.

A series of lacklustre performances starting with the 2002 World Cup exposed the team's performance to public critique. A new generation of players replaced the ageing gladiators of 1998. Unsportsmanlike actions fuelled criticism, such as Zinédine Zidane's infamous headbutt in the 2006 World Cup final and Thierry Henry's November 2009 'hand ball' goal against Ireland.

Equally detrimental were several high profile off-pitch incidents in which team members were accused of lurid behaviour. Scandalous allegations of underage prostitution tarnished a few players, while escalating intra-squad feuds further strained tensions at the team's encampment at Clairefontaine. Allegations in Spring 2011 that the French Football Federation (FFF) implemented racial quotas for the nation's youth training programmes further sullied football's image. By the early 2010s, it appeared that *Les Bleus* were in decline athletically and symbolically – a direct corollary to the more general sense of the demise of the French state.

Football became politicized as the public deplored 'Playstation junkies' too individualistic to serve the nation. The infusion of racially charged rhetoric into the discourse of *Les Bleus* led many to believe that French football was (and remains) rife with racism. But this is not the full story, as some writers have begun to demonstrate. In June 2014, Beaud argued that the 'violent tone of articles' about the national team during the past decade was rooted in the hyper-mediatization of football, the deterioration of professional relations between players and journalists and the scapegoating of team members, many of who rose from lower sociocultural backgrounds.[5]

Such coverage conveys the notion that the national team is not well received by the public. But is this actually the case? Is the team and all that it stood for in 1998 a mere glimpse in the rear-view mirror? On the contrary, the public is generally supportive of *Les Bleus*, the team itself, which today enjoys an improved and hopeful image. The negative discourse of the past several years is an anti-football backlash, reflective of France's historically poor esteem of the sport and fuelled by frustrations over the growth of the football business. The lack of results on the field has also made *Les Bleus* a target for criticism. Furthermore, dialogue surrounding the team is shaded by the economic downturn, uneasiness about the future and the continued rise of the FN, which seized football as a realm to promote its racist, anti-immigrant platform. Other politicians raced to use football, a widely viewed and consumed sport, for their agendas and thus hijacked the sport.

The politicization of football is not just about racism and the devolved image of *Les Bleus* as the symbol of a positive future. It is a crisis of identity manifested through the athletic realm. This is not the first time that sport serves as a backdrop for a larger *crise de confiance*. The first French 'sports crisis' hinged on the lack of medals and titles at international competitions such as the Olympics in the 1960s. At the time, the image of defeated athletes contrasted sharply with the Fifth Republic's preferred portrait of a resurgent, rejuvenated France that won. The government's quest to rectify the sports crisis was an attempt to change the identity of France from one vanquished by defeat and denuded of empire to a modern, revitalized, youthful leader.

Today, the second 'sports crisis' centres less on what one looks like (i.e. on racial or ethnic identity) and is focused more on the cultural norms of being French. The opinion makers and elite that set such norms have had a difficult relationship with football for much of the past 100 years. They long disdained the sport as a mercenary one. Consequently, many French were not as enamoured by football as were their neighbours in Italy, England or the Netherlands. The 1998 World Cup changed these deeply entrenched attitudes and inaugurated new relationships between the French and their national team. In the process, journalist Joachim Barbier argues, football was kidnapped, its culture forced into the larger value system of French society.[6] It is this intersection of culture and identity that led to the present sports crisis.

## Always a mixing pot

*Les Bleus*, lest anyone forget, is the oldest integrated national football team in Europe. As early as the 1930s, non-Caucasian players represented the nation in international competition. *Les Bleus'* first black footballer, Raoul Diagne, did not cause a stir when he took the field.[7] Similarly, North Africans such as Labri Ben Barek (1st call up: 1938) and Rachid Mekhloufi (October 1956) were also accepted in the pre- and post-1945 as French.

Football has long served as an agent of assimilation. The team that placed third at the 1958 World Cup was led by players whose parents or grandparents immigrated to France decades earlier: Raymond Kopa (Poland), Roger Piatoni (Italy) and Just Fontaine (Spain), who still holds the record for most goals scored at a World Cup. The 'golden generation' of the late 1970s and 1980s boasted players such as Jean Tigana (Mali), Michel Platini (Italy), Marius Trésor (Guadeloupe) and Gérard Janvion (Martinique), whose Frenchness was never questioned. Despite Jean-Marie Le Pen's criticism in the 1990s that *Les Bleus* were not properly French, the nation embraced Lilian Thuram, Thierry Henry, Patrick Viera, Marcel Desailly, Zinédane Zidane and the rest of the 1998 heroes.

Victories helped cement these players as French, and the turn-of-the-century triumphs shone a bright light on the realm of football in new ways. Since the televised diffusion of sports in the 1960s, but most notably after television's liberalization in 1984, the image of what French teams look like reinforces ideas of national identity. Broadcasts of winning athletes were strong symbols of reinventing French identity. By the early 2000s, the image of a victorious, integrated, postcolonial France was viewed through the exploits of Zidane, Thuram and Henry. The prominent attention bestowed upon what it meant to be French by politicians, and the media focused on football, especially the realm of youth development, as an incubator of French citizenship. This is in part why the alleged racial quota issue struck such a nerve as it questioned French football's esteemed tradition of integration and assimilation. As journalist Philippe Auclair wrote in *The Blizzard*, 'there are now tens of thousands of people, at home and abroad, who are convinced that French football is rife with institutional racism and discrimination, when it should be hailed as a model'.[8]

## It's not the team ... it's French society's view of football

It is important to remember that the French historically have not embraced football and its cultural associations. The sport represents the best of republican ideals, such as meritocracy, democracy, fair-play and sportsmanship, and is the most consumed and played in France. However, due to football's social pedigree, or lack thereof, society never truly respected it.

Football was first introduced in France as a sport for the upper and upwardly aspiring middle classes in the latter part of the nineteenth century. It democratized in the 1910s and became a sport of the masses in the 1920s. Its professionalization in 1932, after which sportsmen were paid for their efforts, solidified football's status as working-class sport, one without class.

The mercenary status of professional football pitted it against the ideals of amateur athletics long held by the opinion-making bourgeoisie and educated classes. The emphasis on amateurism was at the root of the first sports crisis. During the 1960s, France had difficulty competing in the new Cold War sports framework where 'amateur' athletes were subsidized in the Eastern Bloc. The Rome 1960 Olympics at which the French placed 25th in the overall medal count demonstrated that in order to win, athletes had to have time, space and freedom from some fiscal responsibilities to train. France's debate over whether or not to subsidize elite athletes endured until the 1975 Mazeaud Law proscribed state support for sport as part of the national culture.

In the context of team sports, rugby, handball and basketball all hold greater prestige within French society than football, despite their more recent professionalization. According to Michel Rat, former basketball player for *Les Bleus* and former director of the National Basketball Center, French esteem for basketball and handball in particular benefitted from their close historic ties to physical education within the school day.[9] For decades, football lacked this association. Another illustration of French prejudice against football was a mid-1950s government suggestion to invest more money in basketball as the team sport best suited to the French cerebral psyche.[10] Football did not receive similar pushes from the Fifth Republic. As the first team sport to professionalize, football was thus stigmatized and long held a low sociocultural status.

Jérôme de Bontin, Chairman of Rush Soccer, former President of AS Monaco FC and former General Manager of the New York Red Bulls, recalled growing up in the French bourgeoisie of the 1960s and 1970s. 'While there were a few kids interested in football', he said, 'we recognized that it was not the proper thing to talk about with our friends' parents'.[11] This sentiment prevailed despite the fact that football began to take its place within popular culture thanks to the winning records of clubs such as Nantes, Sochaux, Bordeaux, Marseille and St. Etienne. For Alexis Gallice, the CEO of the French Soccer Institute, little had changed by the 1980s and 1990s. 'Often in France', Gallice said, 'sport is not a primary focus, and often the intellectual world opposes it'.[12]

The cultural stigma began to change in the 1980s as a generation of dynamic, creative players drove French football to international success. Winning the 1984 Euro and Olympic tournaments and strong performances at the 1982 and 1986

World Cups helped build *Les Bleus'* popularity. De Bontin credited Michel Platini's creativity with generating more interest in football, a phenomenon he believed reoccurred with Zidane, Thuram, and Henry.

The 1998 win helped solidify *Les Bleus'* popularity. Gallice, then 22 years old, believed that it helped change attitudes towards football. The game was 'put on a pedestal', he said.[13] The triumph enabled France to feel good about itself. Yet, for some, such as Laurent Courtois, a professional footballer who played in Europe and the United States, 'winning the World Cup [did not] change the way I see my country'.[14] Despite France's various communities uniting behind the team at the turn-of-the-century, it remained a country with a complicated society.

Hopes were high after *Les Bleus* won the 2000 Euro but there was also now the expectation to win at the highest levels. Starting in 2002, victory did not come as fluidly or frequently. Initial public criticism was muted. According to Daniel Jeandupeux, a former professional player and coach in Switzerland and France, the players of 1998 were untouchable, beyond public critique – until they were eliminated during the first stage of Japan 2002. There, he said, it became clear 'that these idols were only men, with all of their weaknesses and sloppiness'. Importantly, he noted, 'they were forgiven because they also gave'.[15] Yet, wins became scarcer and that translated into lost love for the team.

In contrast to earlier eras, the rapidly changed nature of football after 2000 unnerved the French. The culture of football celebrity permeated the media and, as Jeandupeux noted, 'the personal lives of the players took place in the spotlight', whereas in previous eras, the press did not seek it out.[16] As players for *Les Bleus* played professionally in England, Spain, Italy and Germany, leagues where there was much more money than in Ligue 1, they began to earn tremendous amounts of money. Courtois noted the irony that those who begrudged young footballers the fortunes they earned in professional sport, 'will ask them to perform for and love their country while pointing fingers at them for political reasons'.[17]

French football academies added fuel to the fire, according to Courtois. 'Soccer is so exposed compared to the rest of other professional sports', he said. 'A player can make a living pretty quickly' through the academy system, but 'stop school much too early, and not have the same environment as other athletes in different sports to grow as an individual'. Many young footballers thus do not have the demeanour with which to handle the media scrutiny. The Internet amplified the culture of celebrity and the mishaps of French football's young stars. In France, this is much less tolerated than large salaries.

The sport's rapid commercialization, commodification, celebrity culture and scandals unleashed a backlash. According to de Bontin, these changes 'started refuelling the anti-football sentiment in the country', which was suppressed during the previous periods of *Les Bleus'* successes. 'Seeing uneducated athletes', he said, 'black or white, reach the stardom status that they had, making the money they were making', fuelled public antagonism for a sport so poorly regarded. 'You could be a successful tennis player or successful skier or whatever Olympic discipline you are involved in', he said, 'but football was never fully accepted for what it was'.[18]

Yet, the anti-football backlash is different from a loss of faith or belief in the national team. 'Don't get the wrong idea', de Bontin said. 'The French national team is still very popular'. Despite this, the team suffers from public prejudices and misconceptions.

## The race card

Is the anti-football backlash tied to racism? For de Bontin, the negativity surrounding football in the 1990s could be attributed to racist sentiments. Today, however, 'most French consider French-born blacks French'.[19] This sentiment was aided by the unprecedented popularity of the 1998 team, which muted the issue of race. While it is widely acknowledged that racism exists and is a problem in France, many past and present players emphasize that there is no racism between teammates.[20]

What does one make of racism in the public discourse of football if it is not directly aimed at *Les Bleus* themselves? There is a direct corollary between the public image of *Les Bleus* and their football record. In previous decades, the negative press coverage brutally dissected poor national team performances, even when the team was composed primarily of Caucasian players. For Courtois, recent media vitriol against football expressed 'frustration or jealousy' over results or the players' salaries.[21] Yet, when the team won, criticism was muted. Gallice noted that 'the 1998 final gave to France the sense that all was going well if one won – that the victory meant that one could continue as before'.[22] When things changed, so did that sentiment.

In the years since 1998, France has contended with a multitude of problems, ranging from high youth unemployment and unrest in the *banlieues* to the continued rise of the FN under new party head Marine Le Pen. Moreover, the country continues to confront an economic recession. Historically, when the economy is weak or fragile, the press records the rise of xenophobia within public discourse under the guise of protecting French jobs and culture while scapegoating newer arrivals. This occurred during the economic stagnation of the 1880s/1890s and 1930s when recent immigrant groups, notably Jews from Central and Eastern Europe, but also Poles and Italians, were targets. In previous eras, xenophobia was thus often linked with anti-Semitism. As immigration since decolonization includes large waves of people from north to sub-Saharan Africa with different skin complexions, the more recent xenophobic, anti-immigrant sentiment is tinged with racism.

The rise of racism and xenophobia is not a strictly French phenomenon. As Gallice pointed out, the question of whether immigrants endangered the ideals of a nation as posed today by the far-right-wing occurs in other parts of Europe. 'We see this rise', he said, 'because of a complicated economic situation'.[23] For Jeandupeux, the economic difficulties of France have led to greater rejection of immigration, and this is reflected in racially coded press coverage of the team. 'Players who are not well liked, such as Evra or Anelka, suddenly have different colour skin, while Nasri and Benzema (when he lacks combativeness) are suddenly from another geographic origin', he said. 'When their adopted comportment is less and less like the normal "French" one, such as Ribery and his adaption of Islam in a majority Catholic country', racism rises its head.[24]

Courtois noted that the public image of *Les Bleus* at times suffers from these larger sociopolitical maladies. 'I feel like we want to blame football players for every problem France has', he said.[25] The anti-football backlash has less to do with overt racism than with what it means to be culturally French – a form of discrimination, certainly, but not one necessarily based solely on skin colour. Thus, in this instance, culture is not a code word for racism. There is a long-held, deeply seeded bias against football within French culture. With the exception of rugby, there is very little negative publicity surrounding other national teams, such as basketball, because these teams – as multiethnic as they are – generally win matches. Press and public discourse never question these players' Frenchness. Rugby used to be more immune to negative connotations, but since its professionalization and increased commodification, the sport is increasingly exposed to the problems and critiques experienced by football.

## Conclusions

The players who were named to *Les Bleus* for the two-stage World Cup qualifying matches against Ukraine in November 2013 decided to rewrite history. The quest to qualify for Brazil 2014, dubbed 'Operation Commando' by the players, was an example of team solidarity. It also illuminated national support for the team in a way unprecedented since 2010.[26] As in 1998, the nation came together to stand behind *Les Bleus*.

FFF President Noel Le Graet gave the team a pep talk in the days prior to the derby's second leg, as did comedian Jamel Debbouze. A female television weather reporter bet that, should the team prevail and head to Brazil, she would report the weather live in the buff. Much of Le Graet's talk revolved around feeling together as a team, and mobilizing for love of the French jersey.[27] It was not until the team arrived at the Stade de France a few hours before the final game on 19 November 2013, however, that they understood how much the public supported and cheered for them wholeheartedly. The two-game series helped revive the image of the team, which, Jeandupeux said, 'is once again clean and smooth'.[28] Courtois added that 'we have talent, knowledge, and coaches. We just have an identity-political problem and a lack of passion to accept and promote our athletes'.

The Summer 2014 Brazilian campaign was generally considered a success. The team reached the quarter-finals, and the heart demonstrated on the field won back supporters around the globe. So, too, did the players' conscious efforts to right the perceived wrongs of the previous World Cup crew. *Les Bleus* reached out to fans. To do so, they took to Twitter. By the end of training camp in May 2014, the majority of the squad had Twitter accounts. Those who did not previously have one started an account on their own initiative, without a direct mandate from the federation to do so. Throughout the tournament, their Tweets emphasized team camaraderie, pride to be French and play for the nation, and helped put a new face to *Les Bleus*. Combined with stellar performances on the pitch, the team's popularity at home rose.

Has the image of *Les Bleus* devolved since 1998? On the contrary, Auclair writes, 'like every former imperial power, France is groping for a new sense of national identity. And in this, football is leading the way'.[29] French support for *Les Bleus* remains solid. The negative discourse of the past several years is more a reflection of the growing anti-football (and anti-football establishment) sentiment in France than an actual distaste for the team itself. The ongoing economic crisis, uneasiness over the future and the amplification of provocative *Front National* rhetoric has shaded and politicized football in a way that other sports in France have not yet experienced. This is France's 'second sports crisis', one over identity, not in a racial or ethnic sort of way (i.e. how one looks), but over what is the French way. In some aspects, perhaps the team strike in 2010 demonstrated that *Les Bleus*, even those who rose from the *banlieues*, were indeed thoroughly French.

## Disclosure statement

No potential conflict of interest was reported by the author.

## Notes

1. Haddouche, 'Les Bleus visent une impossible réhabilitation'.
2. Bertrand, *La fabrique des footballeurs*, 8.
3. Bronner, 'Le sociologue, le foot et les banlieues'.
4. Ibid.
5. Beaud, 'Les Bleus seront-ils un jour de "bons Français"?', *Libération*.
6. Barbier, *Ce Pays qui n'aime pas le foot*, 10.
7. Dietschy, 'Histoire des premières migrations de joueurs africains en Europe', 37.
8. Auclair, 'What Makes a Nation?'.
9. Michel Rat, Interview with the Author, 24 October 2014.
10. National Institute of Sport, 'Notes soumises à Monsieur le Directeur Général de la Jeunesse et des Sports à propos de la préparation aux Jeux Olympiques 1960'.
11. Jérome de Bontin, Interview with the Author, 31 January 2014.
12. Alexis Gallice, Interview with the Author, 3 February 2014.
13. Ibid.
14. Laurent Courtois, Email to the Author, 28 March 2014.
15. Daniel Jeandupeux, Email to the Author, 22 March 2014.
16. Ibid.
17. Courtois.
18. De Bontin.
19. Ibid.
20. Courtois.
21. Ibid.
22. Gallice.
23. Ibid.
24. Jeandupeux.
25. Courtois.
26. Laurens, 'Les mots qui ont tout change'.
27. Ibid.
28. Jeandupeux.
29. Auclair, 'What Makes a Nation?'.

## References

Auclair, Philippe. 'What Makes a Nation?' *The Blizzard*, no. 2, September 2011.
Barbier, Joachim. *Ce Pays qui n'aime pas le foot* [The country that does not like football]. Paris: Hugo & Cie, 2012.
Beaud, Stéphane. 'Les Bleus seront-ils un jour de "bons Français [Les Bleus, will they one day be good French']"'. *Libération*, no. 2, June 12, 2014.
Beaud, Stéphane. *Traitres à la nation? Un autre regard sur la grève des Bleus en Afrique du Sud* [Traitors to the nation? Another look at the strike of Les Bleus in South Africa]. Paris: La Découverte, 2011.
Bertrand, Julien. *La fabrique des footballeurs* [Making Footballers]. Paris: La Dispute, 2012.
Bronner, Luc. 'Le sociologue, le foot et les banlieues' [The Sociologist, football, and the banlieues]. *Le Monde*, November 2, 2010.
Dietschy, Paul. 'Histoire des premières migrations de joueurs africains en Europe' [History of the first migrations of African players in Europe]. *Afrique contemporaine* 233 (2010): 35–48.
Dubois, Laurent. *Soccer Empire: France and the 1998 World Cup*. Berkeley: University of California Press, 2010.
Haddouche, Cyrille. 'Les Bleus visent une impossible réhabilitation' [Les Bleus see an impossible rehabilitation]. *Le Figaro*, June 22, 2010.

Lanfranchi, Pierre. 'Mekloufi, un footballeur français dans la guerre d'Algérie' [Mekloufi, a French foobtaller in the Algerian War]. *Actes de la recherche en sciences sociales* 103 (June 1994): 70–4.

Laurens, Julien. 'Les mots qui ont tout change' [The words that changed everything]. *Le Parisien*, November 21, 2013.

National Institute of Sport. 'Notes soumises à Monsieur le Directeur Général de la Jeunesse et des Sports à propos de la préparation aux Jeux Olympiques 1960'. Ministry of Youth and Sports, National Archives of France. *Centre des archives contemporaries* (CAC), 19780586, Article 100 JO Rome.

# Cooper's Block: America's first soccer neighbourhood

Thomas A. McCabe

This essay traces the evolution and influence of Cooper's Block, a previously unknown Kearny, New Jersey soccer neighbourhood. During the late nineteenth and early twentieth centuries, The Block, a tiny soccer-loving hamlet on the banks of the Passaic River, played a pivotal role in nurturing, supporting and growing the game. British immigrants lived, worked and played in what came to be called 'the cradle of American soccer' and, in the process, continued to weave soccer into the fabric of everyday life. Soccer was not on the margins of American sporting space in places like Kearny as the intersection of immigration, labour and leisure established the game in certain urban neighbourhoods. Boys played on sandlots and for junior teams; men competed on weekends in a variety of leagues (amateur, semi-pro and professional) for a plethora of teams; and some players who grew up there went on to represent the United States on foreign tours and in World Cups. Cooper's Block was both a founding and foundational American soccer neighbourhood.

Three hundred people gathered at Kearny's First Ward Republican Club on 15 December 1936, and began the evening's festivities by singing, 'Hail, Hail, the Gang's All Here'! The crowd members sang the popular tune 'loudly and with plenty of feeling' because they had grown up in Cooper's Block, a neighbourhood in lower Kearny, New Jersey. Most had moved on from their humble beginnings, but fondly remembered 'an institution known the world over as The Block'. It was the archetypical working-class neighbourhood where proud people tried to pull themselves up by their own bootstraps. Whether they made it out or not, 'Cooper's Block alumni' came back to toast the memories of what they considered 'a school for life'.

Congressman Fred A. Hartley, dubbed The Block's 'First Citizen', served as toastmaster and chairman of the reunion committee. He read a series of telegrams from the Vice-President of the United States, two senators and the governor of New Jersey. 'Men high in politics, business and industry joined with less fortunate former neighbours' that evening to enjoy the entertainment provided by The Three DeMarco Sisters. Attendees paged through a reunion newsletter that recalled life in the old neighbourhood. Former residents also left with a small wooden square salvaged from tenement clapboards. Imprinted on the souvenir was the saying, 'A Chip Off The Old Block'. 'It was a night of handshaking, backslapping and reminiscing,' noted one attendee. 'The boys got together and recalled their pranks, their happy gatherings and their troubles. They talked about their fights and their romances'. They also talked soccer.

Tom Connell, a sportswriter for the *Newark Evening News*, attended the reunion and wrote about the neighbourhood's sporting importance: 'The Block symbolizes soccer in all its glory, from the time the game was introduced in this country until it reached its peak of popularity [after World War I]'. Reunion attendees, including some of the best players in American soccer history, lauded The Block as the oldest and most important soccer neighbourhood in the country. Like Connell, they appreciated the fact that it raised, nourished and supported players, officials and fans for over five decades.This essay traces the evolution and influence of Cooper's Block, a previously unknown Kearny, New Jersey soccer neighbourhood, during the late nineteenth and early twentieth centuries. The Block, a tiny soccer-loving hamlet on the banks of the Passaic River, was both a founding and foundational American soccer neighbourhood.[1]

John and Fred Cooper were guests of honour at the reunion as it was their parents who built the tenements that had housed generations of soccer-loving immigrants and their descendants. John and Mary Cooper moved to Kearny in the early 1880s and almost immediately noticed a glaring need. There were two monstrous mills, Clark Thread Company of Scotland and Marshall Flax Spinning Company of England, but little housing for its workers. The enterprising couple hired a gang of carpenters, masons and plumbers to build a dozen large wooden tenements and opened up a general store at the neighbourhood's core. A third factory complex sprang up like a brick behemoth north of the Clark and Marshall plants, when Sir Michael Nairn decided to bring his linoleum firm to Kearny in 1886. 'For those families, the first mainland soil they set foot on was [Nairn] property', recalled an employee. A Nairn official 'would collect new arrivals at Ellis Island, take them on a barge through Newark Bay and up the Passaic River, landing right at the company dock by the warehouse'. The same was true for thousands of other newcomers from England, Ireland, and especially Scotland.[2]

The Coopers built additional tenements to accommodate the continual influx of immigrants, and by the turn of the century the 10-block neighbourhood was the centre of working-class life and leisure in Kearny and East Newark, a tiny village that broke away from Kearny in 1895. Bounded by the Passaic River to the west, Belgrove Drive to the north, Kearny Avenue to the east, and the Newark line of the Erie Railroad to the north, The Block was not only shoehorned between three massive mills, its outlines resembled an old-fashioned leather soccer boot. It was altogether fitting because immigrants, often bound to six-year work contracts, brought their love of soccer with them across the Atlantic Ocean. In fact, every conceivable narrative of American soccer occurred within The Block, from the game's pioneer players, teams, leagues and organizations to the confluence of immigration, work and leisure.[3]

It seemed like soccer was everywhere, literally part of The Block's DNA, not on the sporting margins as some scholars have maintained over the years.[4] Children first played soccer on its sandlots before joining youth and school teams. Men played for dozens of teams, ranging from lousy amateur ones to top professional sides, at one of three local fields: Riverside Oval, Washington School Oval, and Clark Field. All three fields were either within the confines of The Block, or within a five-minute walk of its borders, and men and boys flocked there on weekends. Often donning woollen caps and overcoats because soccer was 'the outdoor winter sport', supporters witnessed some of the best soccer the country had to offer. Local semi-professional teams like the West Hudsons and Scottish-Americans succeeded

Clark's ONT as dominant teams by the early 1900s. Young and old watched and talked about the game constantly, whether in local taverns or along the sidelines at matches. It was a cradle-to-grave soccer environment and proof that geography could be sporting destiny.[5]

The Block was an immigrant, working-class district where women waited to buy fish until 6:00 PM, knowing the fishmonger had to give them a good price before it spoiled. It was a place where families shared a common bathtub, and huddled around a wood stove for heat in the wintertime. In the summertime, the kids walked past a foul-smelling slaughterhouse and bathed in the less-than-pristine Passaic River. Each year, it seemed, someone drowned in its murky waters, trying to cool off in the hot summer months. Since there were no indoor bathrooms, one-seat out-houses stood in each backyard. Older members of the family, as well as women, didn't use the 'one-seaters' after dark, and took care of their business inside on a wooden commode lined with a metal bucket. Young boys had to empty it of 'night soil' every morning, and the '6 AM bucket brigade' was described as 'an odoriferous affair'.

The Block was also a place where everyone worked. Family members, male and female and as young as 11, walked to one of the three local mills each morning to work 10 to 12-hour days. And it was a neighbourhood where after work and on weekends, people eagerly sought out recreation. The kids played in the street or vacant lots near their homes, but some even wandered off to play in the Kearny Woods or near the Kearny Castle, the mansion of the town's namesake, Major General Philip Kearny, commander of New Jersey troops in the American Civil War. Men patronized one of the many 'thirst emporiums', including Ford's Bar at the foot of Johnston Avenue, and talked about work, politics, religion and sport. They drank hard, too. And when residents could, they escaped to another world, watching silent films and the first 'talkies' at Grant Theatre.[6]

The Block was a soccer incubator, where, according to local historian and former player George Rogers, 'children are cradled in soccer'.[7] Many clubs had junior teams, which offered teens and young men an opportunity to play before breaking into the first teams. Young kids played the sport, most often in sandlots, but they did not always do so with a ball. 'One of the primary requisites in the business of getting along with the kids on The Block was the ability to kick a tin can with uncanny skill', noted a local newspaperman. That skill transferred over to soccer, and at places like 'Tin Can Oval', a sandlot in the shadow of the mills, soccer players were first made and 'from such a setting came many of the outstanding figures in American soccer'.[8]

In The Block, and in other major 'cradles' of early American soccer like it, soccer was played in both sun and shadow, but also in rain, sleet or snow. Most of the fields had little to no grass, so in the foul weather of mid-winter the ground could be virtually unplayable. Yet, hardy soccer players persisted, playing during a 'disagreeable drizzle', in 'a veritable sea of mud', or 'ankle-deep snow', but such conditions often made for less than desirable soccer. Also, the rough-and-tumble nature of the soccer frequently led to violence, both on the field and in the crowd. 'Fans figured they were entitled to a refund if they were not furnished with a few free-for-all fights', noted one observer. Fans also abused the referee, verbally and physically, and on occasion, spectators charged the field to confront, or even strike, the official. Fuelled by alcohol, 'the saloon element' confirmed soccer's image as a rough, tough, working-class affair. 'Soccer [was] not exactly a gentle pastime', said one commentator on the early game, and therefore, a soccer player 'in those days' was 'one of three things: rough, tough, or both'.[9]

As soccer became more popular, local sportswriters, more attuned to football, basketball and baseball, grudgingly covered the sport in greater detail. They called it 'the soccer bug', like it was some sort of sporting virus brought to American shores as part of the 'immigrant menace'.[10] The historian Stephen Hardy rightly argued that 'the athletic germ that infected the country after the Civil War found its most fertile ground in cities', and in the case of Kearny, and several other surrounding industrial towns, soccer's not-so-visible microbes crept into its various immigrant communities.[11] Marginalized for long periods of time, the game proved to be a resilient strain of the 'sporting craze', and three representative families – the Fishers, Fords and Starks – caught 'the soccer bug' and passed it on to successive generations.

The Fishers are among the first families of American soccer, and they are likely the longest-continually kicking clan in US soccer history. George Fisher lived a mile and one half from central London's Freemasons' Tavern in 1863, where a group of men agreed to the modern rules of association football. While in the English capital young George may well have played the game that would conquer the world, and he most certainly arrived in his adopted country after the global game had splashed ashore. The 24-year-old English immigrant settled in New York City in 1872, and married Margaret McMahon four years later. By 1880, the young couple had three children; a decade later there were ten. Their apartment in Manhattan's Hell's Kitchen was no longer large enough, so the family moved across the Hudson River and Jersey Meadows to Kearny.[12]

The Fishers moved into new worker housing built by Marshall Linen, a block or so from the tenements built by the Coopers, and it must have seemed heavenly to the large family. The house was one of a dozen in a complex called 'The Twelve Apostles' and, fittingly, it was across Watts Street from four homes for the foremen's families that folks referred to as Matthew, Mark, Luke and John.[13] George found work as a brass finisher, an upgrade from his years as a labourer in New York. There was room to play for the children, who played lots of soccer because they now lived in one of the game's hotbeds. The American Football Association (AFA) had been founded in 1884 in a Clark Thread Company building on the Newark side of the river, but the company team played on nearby Clark Field and became the first American soccer dynasty, winning the first three AFA cups from 1885 through 1887. Together, the soccer-centric towns of Kearny, East Newark and Harrison came to be called 'the cradle of American soccer'.[14]

The eldest son George, Jr. listed himself and the family apartment as the contact for a new Under-15 team – Young Kearny Cedars – in 1894, months after the family settled in the area. The Fisher brothers made up the spine of the new team with George, Jr., Leonard and Andrew all playing. Brothers Tommy, Charlie and Frank were all too young for the team, but they would become local legends in due time. The six soccer-playing siblings lived within kicking distance of Riverside Oval, where the Young Cedars played, and a short walk to Clark Field, the mecca of the metropolitan soccer community of New Jersey and New York. Plus, there were several sandlots where neighbourhood boys tested their mettle against one another – a tradition that continued well into the next century. Kurt Rausch, a distant relative of the Fishers, recalled his own father's upbringing in The Block:

My father would see a friend walk out of his house dribbling a soccer ball down the street. He'd whistle and another boy would come out, and then they'd whistle further down the street. Soon, they had enough guys to play.

It was the clarion call that generations answered.[15]

By 1900, most of the Fisher boys and girls worked at local factories: Leonard was a toolmaker; Mary was a winder at the thread mill; Tommy and Charlie worked as tier boys at Nairn Linoleum; and the two youngest, Henry and Frank, still attended school. George, Sr., now 51, still worked as a brass finisher. Several of his sons made their way from the sandlots to the semi-professional squads in the National Association Foot Ball League (NAFBL), the strongest league in the country until the formation of the ASL in 1921. Tommy and Charlie turned out for Clark AA, the reincarnated side of the thread mill, in league and cup games during the 1906–1907 campaign. Wingers in the standard 2-3-5 formation, both brothers scored against West Hudson AA to knock the defending champion out of the AFA Cup. Two seasons later the brothers led Clark AA to the 1909 NAFBL championship, the same year that George, Sr. succumbed to pancreatic cancer. The patriarch of the soccer-loving family died the day after Clark AA beat Fall River, Massachusetts in the cup. Uncharacteristically, Charlie, who old-timers said possessed the deadliest shot 'in the cradle', missed two penalty kicks that day, but the Fisher clan continues to play soccer in New Jersey to this day, an unprecedented run from Cooper's Block to the suburbs of the Garden State.[16]

John and Jim Ford, born in 1889 and 1890, respectively, spent over a third of their lives in the sole of the boot-shaped Cooper's Block. To know their world is to know the roots of much of American soccer because they both made sizable contributions to the local and national soccer scenes. The brothers grew up at 25 Johnston Avenue along with two older sisters, just across the railroad tracks from Clark Thread Mill. Their parents left an English textile town for Kearny in 1886, with James, their father, finding work as a day labourer, and their mother, Rose, raising the young family at home. The boys' uncle also emigrated and he eventually owned a Johnston Avenue tavern called Ford's Bar.[17] Life for many in the predominantly immigrant, working-class community centred on a few simple things – work, religion and leisure – and in the Ford family, the pull of the pulpit, pub and pitch was especially strong.

As Roman Catholics of Irish heritage, the Fords were part of the minority in Kearny, a predominantly Scottish and Presbyterian town. 'The people of Kearny are largely Protestants, while in Harrison, Roman Catholics are in the great majority', wrote Daniel Van Winkle in his 1924 history of Hudson County. Van Winkle insisted 'religious differences or friction, however, do not exist, and never have'.[18] Yet, religious tensions did exist, and when a patron threatened to sing an anti-Catholic song at Ford's bar before Prohibition, another man retorted, 'You'll sing it at your own risk'. On another occasion, two men helped a Block tenant move to a nearby city, and in the process one of them dropped a large framed picture of Pope Leo. 'You Scotch bastard', yelled the other. 'If that was a picture of King William, you'd be more careful'. Religion was a badge, an identifier, so much so that when one resident answered questions on a government form, he wondered if 'occupation' meant 'Catholic or Protestant'?[19] By the early 1900s, Kearny and nearby Harrison had their own version of Glasgow's 'Old Firm', the bitter sectarian rivalry between Protestant Rangers FC and Catholic Celtic FC. Some of the fiercest and best-attended games at Clark's Field were those between the Scottish-Americans and Celtic AC, later the Irish-Americans.[20]

Work mattered, too, and most began work in their teens in order to help supplement the family income. In 1900, the Ford sisters worked as 'doffers' and changed out used spools of thread at the local mill. John and Jim were still in school at St. Cecilia's, a Catholic grammar and high school on Kearny Avenue. But by 1910, after some high school, they also went to work in the mill. Their father no longer worked as a labourer, but tended bar at his brother's tavern, which also sponsored a soccer team. When the Great War broke out in Europe, John worked as an electrician and Jim as a machinist. By the time the brothers registered for the US Army in 1917, John was a labourer at Nairn Linoleum Company, and Jim worked as a machinist at Bethlehem Steel in Pennsylvania, where he also played for their powerhouse company team. Work was always a constant, but so was soccer.

Like the Fishers, soccer helped shape the Fords' worldview, and early on they learned lessons about teamwork, toughness and tenacity in The Block's sandlots. A distant relative saw soccer as a birthright, saying, 'The Fords didn't just feed their children milk, we fed them soccer'.[21] The Ford boys played in pick-up games throughout their childhoods, and when they were old enough they joined junior teams. In their late teens, the brothers finally broke into senior sides. John was a tall, slender striker who played for more than a handful of teams throughout his 17-year-long career, including the Scottish-Americans of Kearny, Jersey AC of Jersey City, the Paterson Rangers, and the Eurekas of Harrison. Jim played even longer, and as a wiry, hard-working outside forward or halfback, he suited up for Brooklyn FC, Bethlehem Steel, Jersey AC, Harrison SC, the New York Giants, and the Newark Skeeters.[22]

Most players of the era saw cup games as the big occasions because they drew the largest crowds and garnered the most publicity from the local sporting press. Soccer in the United States has a long history of cup competition, beginning with the AFA cup in 1884, and then with the National Challenge Cup (NCC) in 1913, which is still played today under a different name – the US Open Cup. Jim Ford scored in the first two NCC winning sides, first for Brooklyn in 1914, and second for Bethlehem Steel in 1915. During the 1915–1916 cup competitions, the brothers played for little-fancied Jersey AC, and managed to shock several top teams.[23]

On 7 November 1915, one thousand spectators watched the Jersey City-based amateurs take on the semi-professional West Hudsons in the first round of the AFA cup. The Jerseys had several players from The Block in their line-up, but it was Jim Ford who made a lasting impression. In the second half he dribbled through the West Hudson defence, and shot with 'lightning speed, straight and true in the net'. That goal stood and the Jerseys knocked out the three-time cup champions. Thomas Adam, the West Hudson coach who lived only blocks from the Fords, filed a protest, accusing Jim of receiving a 10-dollar signing bonus from the Jerseys. As an amateur Jim was not supposed to play for money, but many 'amateurs' did in order to supplement their working-class wages. 'He's sore because I turned [his team] down', said Ford. 'I can prove I am innocent of the charge'. The West Hudsons lost the protest and the Ford brothers moved on to the next round.[24]

Two weeks later, the Jerseys hosted the Scottish-Americans of Kearny in the first round of the other cup, the NCC. The Scots featured the young Stark brothers, Archie and Tommy, who were born in Glasgow, Scotland, but immigrated to Kearny as teenagers. If the Fishers and Fords were among the first families of American soccer, then the Starks would become American soccer royalty. By 1915, at age 17, Archie was already on his way to becoming the most prolific goal-scorer in American soccer history. Tommy, aged 19, was a stalwart defender. The up-and-coming side was a classic blend of youth and experience, and during the 1914–1915 season the Scots challenged the old order, finishing third in the NAFBL and winning the AFA Cup. Archie scored the lone goal in the final while Tommy helped shut down the Brooklyn Celtic attack before 5000 at Newark's Bartell's Park. Both Starks would go on to represent the USA at the international level in 1925, the first official US match on home soil. A quarter century after that historic match, a 6–1 victory over Canada in which Archie scored five, one newspaper poll voted him the best American player in the first half of the twentieth century (25% of the top 12 vote getters were also from The Block).[25]

In the 1916 NCC Cup the underdog Jerseys started poorly, especially since they could not score with gale force winds at their backs during the first half. The Scots scored instead. At the break, several Scots players stood at midfield smoking cigarettes, no doubt thinking that the second half would be a breeze. Yet, the winds of fortune blew in the Jerseys' favour as John won a penalty kick within a minute of the restart. With the game deadlocked, the Scots targeted Jim Ford for rough treatment. At one point, Jim 'was charged so heavily that he was sent flying over the ropes … that lined the field'. Opponents then squared up to give an exhibition of the 'manly art', but the Fords delivered the knockout blow. Jim sent in a cross that his brother smashed home for the winning goal. '[John's] teammates nearly pulled him apart in attempting to shake his hand and hug him and one or two fair rooters insisted upon going on the field and kissing the bashful younger resident of Kearny', noted the local newspaper. Jersey AC had earned another 'sensational victory', and hoped to make a run to the final, which some wanted to stage in Newark's Weequahic Park as part of the city's 250th anniversary celebration.[26]

The Jerseys did not make it to the NCC final (lost in second round to Brooklyn Celtic FC), or to the AFA final either (lost in the quarterfinal to eventual champion Bethlehem Steel FC), but the Ford brothers relished their time together. The two-week stretch in November 1915 was probably the high point for the tandem. Jim, one of the best American wingers, was one of four players from The Block to travel with the first-ever US national team on a tour of Scandinavia that summer. They played together for Jersey AC after Jim's return that fall, but at the end of the 1917 season, the brothers, along with many other players from The Block joined the military and prepared for war.[27]

Stateside soccer struggled during the war as some teams lost the bulk of their players to enlistment. For example, Jersey AC and the West Hudsons lost so many players to the war that the clubs dropped out of the NAFBL before the season started, and the Scots had to take a leave of absence after only five games due to player shortages. While the Fisher brothers played soccer on the home front throughout the war, the Fords and Starks joined the service. John Ford even coached the soldier team for the 309th Infantry of the 78th Division. His efforts were part of the Army's use of sport to ready the troops for combat. Once stationed abroad, American servicemen played against one another, and Uncle Sam's troops even played against French soldiers, beating them 4–0 on one occasion.[28]

War-front soccer boosted morale, noted a YMCA official advising the United States Army in France, because a contest of this kind is not only interesting to the combatants, but provides the officers with an opportunity to thaw out a bit when they also see their subordinates sprawling about in the village street with shins barked, shirts torn, and faces covered with dirt.[29]

Sport allowed men to temporarily escape the horrors of war, but Thomas Cahill, editor of *Spalding's Soccer Guide* and secretary of the United States Football Association (founded in 1913), believed it had restorative powers, too. He said soccer served as 'one of the greatest aides possible to restore the nerves of the soldier, shattered by the crash of tremendous guns, half asphyxiated by poisonous gases, depressed by the sight of shattered comrades'.[30] Some boys from The Block suffered injuries, including George Post, who was shot in battle, and John Ford, who returned home with reduced lung capacity as a victim of mustard gas.[31]

Many of the top soccer players from The Block, including Archie and Tommy Stark, Jim Ford and George Post, played for Erie AA during the 1919–1920 and 1920–1921 seasons. During the war 40 of its 50 members were stationed overseas and still other servicemen joined the Johnston Avenue athletic club upon returning home. The association's soccer team was a truly representative neighbourhood side as they had all grown up together, many on the same streets or just a few blocks away from one another. They had learned the game together, and then figuratively and literally gone to battle with one another on the fields of West Hudson and Western Europe. They had represented their clubs with pride before the war and their country during it, but in a sense, the men of Erie AA possessed a different civic pride in their immediate post-war soccer careers. When they stepped on to the dirty and dusty pitches to face their rivals – Brooklyn Celtic, Bethlehem Steel, Scottish-Americans, Robins Dry Dock of Brooklyn – they went out to play for one another and the neighbourhood that forged them.

Due in part to the soccer talent within its borders and the community pride that the team from The Block had, Erie AA became one of the top teams in the NAFBL, finishing a point behind champion Bethlehem Steel and easily winning the NJ State Cup in 1920. The following season they finished a disappointing fourth in the league, but reached the semi-final of the venerable, yet-soon-to-be defunct AFA cup. The Eries lost to eventual champions Robins Dry Dock, 1–4, in a third replay after two thrilling draws. During the course of those two seasons, the Eries fielded seven past and future US internationals, including Archie and Tommy Stark, Jim Ford, Al Blakey, George Tintle, Davey Brown, and John Hemingsley. All but Blakey, a native Philadelphian, grew up in The Block. Most of The Block's soccer stars became professionals in the newly formed American Soccer League (ASL) beginning in 1921.[32]

Archie Stark, Davey Brown, Jim Ford and John Hemingsley were routinely among the ASL's top goal scorers. Tommy Stark and George Post were top defenders, and George Tintle, a fireman by trade, and Jim Douglas, a 1924 Olympian and 1930 World Cup member, established the long line of top goalkeepers from the area. Men from The Block more than played, though, they passed on the game to those in the neighbourhood and beyond. For example, John Ford coached Paterson FC in the ASL and led them to the NCC cup title in 1922. He also went on to coach soccer at St. Benedict's Prep in Newark, the future school of US national team stars Tab Ramos, Claudio Reyna and Gregg Berhalter. Tintle was a coach at Harrison High School, and another player-turned-coach, Fred Coggin, turned Kearny High into a perennial power. The school's best-ever team with future World Cup veterans John

Harkes and Tony Meola appeared in 1984, 100 years after the AFA was founded in the Clark Thread Mill firehouse.

But long before the beginning of the modern history of American soccer, the gang was all there at Kearny's First Ward Republican Club. They were there to celebrate a truly special place. The Cooper's Block's tenements were torn down in the months after the first reunion in 1936, but The Block's 'alumni' returned for two more gatherings in 1946 and 1955 to remember an era when soccer was birthed and nurtured and raised in the United States. They paid tribute to the country's first and most important soccer neighbourhood.

## Disclosure statement

No potential conflict of interest was reported by the author.

## Notes

1. *The West Hudson Observer*, November 24, 1936; *Newark Evening News*, December 15, 1936; *Newark Star-Eagle*, December 16, 1936; and *Cooper's Block Echo*, April 25, 1946.
2. .*Congoleum News*, May and June 1986; *Newark Sunday Call*, November 17, 1878; *Newark Evening News*, November 20, 1915; Shaw, *A History of Essex and Hudson Counties*, 611–13; van Winkle, ed., *History of Hudson County*, 369–71; and Coats, *Seams Sewn Long Ago*, 125–36.
3. 'Oral History Project, Town of Kearny – George Rogers', December 2005, Tape No. 1.
4. Markovits and Hellerman, *Offside: Soccer & American Exceptionalism*, chap. 1 and 2.
5. *Cooper's Block Echo*, 1936, 1946, and 1955; Shaw, *A History of Essex and Hudson Counties*, 611–13; and van Winkle, ed., *History of Hudson County*, 369–71.
6. *Cooper's Block Echo*, 1936, 1946, and 1955.
7. *Newark Star-Ledger*, June 19, 1990.
8. *Newark Evening News*, November 20, 1915 and December 15, 1936; and *Cooper's Block Echo*, 1936.
9. *Trenton Times*, January 15, 1906; *New York Times*, January 5, 1908; and *Newark Evening News*, December 15, 1936.
10. *New York Times*, January 11, 1903; Kraut, *Silent Travelers*, xx; and Germans called soccer 'the English disease', see Hesse-Lichtenberger, *TOR!*, 25.
11. Hardy, *How Boston Played*, 3.
12. All personal records for Fisher family accessed through www.ancestry.com; Interview with Kurt Rausch, January 14, 2015.
13. *Congoleum News*, May and June 1986.
14. Allaway, *Rangers, Rovers & Spindles*, chap. 1 and 2.
15. Interview with Kurt Rausch, January 14, 2015.
16. Ibid.
17. All personal records for Ford family accessed through www.ancestry.com; Interview with Melanie Ford, February 12, 2012.
18. van Winkle, *History of Hudson County*.
19. *Cooper's Block Echo*, 1936.
20. McCabe, 'Yankee, Cowboy, Fenian Bastard'.
21. Interview with Melanie Ford, February 12, 2012.
22. *Newark Evening News*, February 22, 1964.
23. On early American soccer organizations and cups, see Allaway, *Rangers, Rovers & Spindles*, 35–6, 40–2; Wangerin, *Soccer in a Football World*, 27–8, 30–3; Wangerin, *Distant Corners*, chap. 1 and 2; and McCabe, 'Loose Threads', *Howler*.
24. *Jersey Journal*, November 13, 1915.
25. *Newark Evening News*, February 22, 1915, March 3, 1915, April 14, 1915, March 5, 1950; *Newark Star-Ledger*, March 21, 1978.

26. *Newark Evening News*, November 22, 1915 and January 24, 1916.
27. *Newark Sunday Call*, July 23, 1916; and *Newark Evening News*, September 12, 1916.
28. *Kearny Observer*, December 29, 1917; *New York Times*, October 15, November 12, and December 16, 1917; and Dave Litterer, 'The Year in Soccer – 1919,' http://homepages. sover.net/~spectrum/year/1919.html.
29. *New York Times*, March 31, 1918.
30. Cahill, ed., *Spalding's Official Soccer Football Guide, 1917–18*, 3–4.
31. *Kearny Observer*, November 15, 1918; Interview of Boniface Treanor, September 2, 2011.
32. Jose, *American Soccer League, 1921–1931*.

## References

Allaway, Rangers. *Rovers & Spindles: Soccer, Immigration and Textiles in New England and New Jersey*. Haworth, NJ: St. Johann Press, 2005.
Cahill, Thomas, ed. *Spalding's Official Soccer Football Guide, 1917–18*. New York: American Sports, 1918.
Coats, Brian. *Seams Sewn Long Ago: The Story of Coats Thread makers*. San Diego: Brian Coats, 2013.
*Congoleum News*, May and June, 1986.
*Cooper's Block Echo*, Reunion Newsletters, 1936, 1946 and 1955.
Hardy, Stephen. *How Boston Played: Sport, Recreation, and Community, 1865–1915*. Knoxville: Univ. of Tennessee Press, 2003.
Hesse-Lichtenberger, Ulrich. *TOR! The Story of German Football*. London: When Saturday Comes Books, 2003.
Jose, Colin. *American Soccer League, 1921–1931: The Golden Years of American Soccer*. Lanham, MD: The Scarecrow Press, 1998.
Kraut, Alan M., and Silent Travelers. *Germs, Genes, and The 'Immigrant Menace'*. New York: Basic Books, 1994.
Litterer, Dave. 'The Year in American Soccer – 1919'. http://homepages.sover.net/~spectrum/year/1919.html.
Markovits, Andrei, and Steven L. Hellerman. *Offside: Soccer & American Exceptionalism*. Princeton: Princeton University Press, 2001.
McCabe, Thomas. 'Loose Threads: The Prehistory of U.S. Soccer'. *Howler*, Vol. 3, Summer 2013.
McCabe, Thomas. '"Yankee, Cowboy, Fenian Bastard": An American Catholic at Rangers Football Club'. *XI: A North American Soccer Quarterly*, Vol. 2, December 2012.
'Oral History Project, Town of Kearny – George Rogers'. December 2005, Tape No. 1.
Shaw, William H. *History of Essex and Hudson Counties, New Jersey*. Philadelphia, PA: Everts & Peck, 1884.
Wangerin, David. *Distant Corners: American Soccer's History of Missed Opportunities and Lost Causes*. Philadelphia, PA: Temple University Press, 2011.
Wangerin, David. *Soccer in a Football World: The Story of America's Forgotten Game*. London: When Saturday Comes Books, 2006.
van Winkle, Daniel, ed. *History of the Municipalities of Hudson County New Jersey 1630–1923*. Vol. III. New York: Lewis Historical Publishing, 1924.

# Rethinking 'ethnic' soccer: the National Junior Challenge Cup and the transformation of American soccer's identity (1935–1976)

Kevin Tallec Marston

This paper contends that the way in which the term 'ethnic' is applied to the history of soccer in America needs rethinking. Through a case study of the National Junior Challenge Cup (now know as the JP McGuire Cup), the country's oldest ongoing competition across all youth sports, this paper examines the transformation of American soccer's identity. The tournament began in 1935 and evolved from an initial constituency of ethnic, immigrant and Catholic youth clubs. Following societal demographic trends, the growing national participant base came from more suburban, middle-class neighbourhoods. The 1970s witnessed a paradigm change in youth soccer as the sport began to move closer to mainstream consciousness. The tournament is a window into the complexity of defining the term 'ethnic' and its individuals who straddled both 'ethnic' and 'native' worlds. This article explores the origins of soccer in America, the bridges between ethnic identity, immigration and the foreign-native cultural debate and Soccer Americana.

## Introduction

Soccer in America still maintains an ambivalent place in the national sporting landscape. Long considered the 'foreign' game, it was the one played by immigrants and hyphenated Americans. Over the last 20 years, research has begun to seriously explore the link between soccer and its ethnic roots. However, the use of the term 'ethnic' has not come without some problems. Often used to describe the sport prior to the 1970s, the word 'ethnic' is entangled with other concepts such as 'foreign' or 'immigrant'.

This paper contends that the way in which the term 'ethnic' is applied to the game's past needs rethinking and I argue here for a more cautious and nuanced use. The legacy of the sport's ethnic roots has passed inconspicuously into the literature as an unexamined established story. As such, the term 'ethnic' is in some ways misleading. What do we actually mean when calling soccer's history 'ethnic'? Is this in opposition to other sports in America whose history is 'non-ethnic' or 'native'? Such a contrast ignores some obvious and omnipresent connections between sports such as American football or baseball and the multitude of ethnic, racial and class identities embodied in the Negro Leagues and in players like Jim Thorpe.[1] The 'ethnic-native' dichotomy also restricts the debate to a singular line of enquiry; things are either one or the other.

In his call to rethink the transfer of football from Europe to America, historian Matthew Taylor has noted the lack of empirical studies on the history of stateside soccer.[2] The example of the National Junior Challenge Cup helps to fill this gap. In examining the 'ethnic' question, I ask whether there were clear dividing lines between what was 'ethnic' and what was not; what was of one ethnicity or another? The contention here is that the 'ethnic' soccer prior to the 1970s was more complex than a set of blanket group labels of Italian, Greek, German or Ukrainian team names. Under the surface of the term 'ethnic' lay a world of nuance; for example, players of mixed ethnic heritage playing together as well as the complex identities of second-generation immigrants or what might be termed 'native-born ethnics'.

Through the example of the National Junior Challenge Cup, I also argue that there was a clear shift in the sport's history from the margins to the mainstream. Drawing on the contemporary press, the limited existing institutional records and the US census reports, this paper contends that such a paradigm change was evident in the sport's names and places and how they changed over time. By the 1970s, soccer was not just so-called 'ethnic' clubs or Catholic youth organisations; it had followed demographic trends and had moved towards the suburbs. It became a truly national phenomenon: Soccer Americana.

## Surpassing an 'exceptionalist' fixation and considering the problem of the term 'ethnic'

Other sports in America have benefited from an early and well-oiled historiographical tradition.[3] Research into American soccer's past has in many ways paralleled the growth of the sport in the last quarter of the twentieth century. However, the development of the study of soccer has carried with it some 'exceptionalist' and 'ethnic' baggage.

With the rise of the North American Soccer League (NASL), a budding historiography grew out of the personal experiences of players, coaches, administrators and journalists.[4] But the narrative about the pre-NASL era was generally limited to the notion that soccer was the pastime of many immigrants at least until the arrival of the 'Pelé generation'. The majority of serious scholarship on the sport only started as the league was declining from its big-time Pelé years.[5] Even then, only a handful of studies appeared, and not in history but rather in education and social science departments.[6] This is undoubtedly what prompted Len Oliver in 1986 to bemoan the lack of 'rigorous, analytical studies of soccer in America' and observe that

> ... there is a history of soccer in America, one that is interconnected with the lives of working-class people, but it remains for the most part undocumented. With the new interest in social and working class history, perhaps soccer's link with its ethnic roots will unfold.[7]

It was not history that produced a response to Oliver, but political science. Andrei Markovits' initial question, 'why is there no soccer in the United States?', was the impetus for much of the scholarly interest in soccer in the late 1980s through to the turn of the millennium.[8] Until recently, however, much of this debate about soccer's conspicuous absence had relied heavily on the use of secondary sources (even *Offside*'s key third chapter fails to cite one primary source). As a result, terms such as 'ethnic', 'foreign' and 'immigrant' have not been subject to rigorous empirical analysis. Some of the more recent work has returned to such an empirical approach and has begun to provide a contextual understanding of the game's ebb and flow, its people and organisations, especially in relation to immigrant and ethnic connections and changing perceptions.[9]

Following the lead of eminent sport historian Richard Holt, who reminds us that history is 'incremental rather than oppositional', the core of this paper on the National Junior Challenge Cup seeks to add a new layer to the palimpsest of soccer's past and answer the questions about the assumptions of the frontiers of 'ethnic' soccer.[10]

## From immigrants, ethnics and Catholics to the suburbs of Soccer Americana

A detailed exploration of the country's oldest continuing national junior competition in any sport – the National Junior Challenge Cup – reveals a shifting paradigm of soccer's place in the American sporting landscape. The 1935–1976 timeline is especially relevant because it corresponds precisely to the period commonly labelled as 'ethnic' and which preceded the sport's move into mainstream American consciousness. That youth soccer boomed exponentially from the 1970s onwards is undebatable. However, what does the youth game prior to this demographic shift – precisely during the so-called 'ethnic' years – tell us about the history of the sport, its 'ethnic' nature and cultural identity?

An examination of the identity of the Junior Cup's successful teams, individuals and places challenges the idea that there was a clear singular notion of what was 'Americanized' and what was 'ethnic'. Indeed, it is argued here that 'ethnic' soccer, at least in the case of the junior game, was a more complex phenomenon than the purported clear-cut ethnic divisions along club lines which are often taken as gospel.

To be sure, there are examples of 'ethnic' teams as evidenced by many clubs' and players' names. But the whole picture was more complex. Teams included a mix of ethnicities. Over time, the game moved beyond its historic confines in the bastions of ethnic working-class and immigrant areas. The sport, like society, was in continual flux. Then, as the baby boom generation grew up in the late 1960s and 1970s, its children rushed to the sport and with them, the game migrated to the suburbs.

### 1935–1944 – competition origins and early years

While the National Junior Challenge Cup winner's list starts in 1935, youth soccer had long been a preoccupation of some of the United States Football Association (USFA) leadership well before then.[11] The idea of 'Schoolboys' Challenge Cup Competition' had been floated as early as the 1920s but nothing appears to have materialized.[12] In 1935, the USFA had clarified an established rule that juniors could not be over the age of 18 at the time of registration and were not 'permitted to engage for a senior team or in any competition other than a junior competition'.[13] Hence, by the mid-1930s, the stage was set for a clear and standard approach to national junior or youth competition.

The lack of historical records at the US federation results in a simple list of dates and winners; any further details on the early years of the competition appear to have been lost. As a result the press provides rare information which in some cases even contradicts the 'official' record. It would appear that during the first years of the competition the organizers deliberately held a number of junior finals (and in some cases semi-finals) as curtain raisers for American Soccer League (ASL) or major exhibition games. Not much is known about the first winners in 1935, the Reliable Stores Juniors. Indeed, it is unclear whether they were from New Bedford, Massachusetts – then an industrial and immigrant-filled city – or from farther south in Maryland.[14]

The second and third titles in 1936 and 1937 were won in reliable fashion by a club apparently linked to the Jewish community of Brooklyn, 'Hatikvah Juniors'. Their 1937 semi-final was played as a curtain raiser to an exhibition match at the Polo Grounds featuring the ASL All-stars vs. Charlton Athletic.[15] The players who probably finished their match under 20,000 watchful pairs of eyes included a mix of names. Many appear to be of Jewish or eastern European origin: Zierler, Medjock, Kroll, Berger, Shreshevsky, Wexler, and Shriebman. Others, however, appear to be of Italian (Gioia) or even distinctively English origin (Albert, Harrison). It is impossible to know whether the player with an Italian name was Catholic or if those with apparently English-origin names were Protestants. Hence, while the name of the club was Yiddish-based, Hatikvah is an example of how some clubs may have included other players from the American 'melting pot' of national origins.

The 1938 winners hailed from the Lighthouse Boys' Club in Philadelphia, Pennsylvania; it was a symbolic start for the organization which would establish a reputation over the next 30 years as the most successful individual club.[16] According to Len Oliver, the Philadelphia 'Lighthouse Boys' (where he played as a youth) were rather unique in the sporting landscape.[17]

The Avella Juniors claimed the following two titles in 1939 and 1940, an impressive feat for a small town in western Pennsylvania. The construction of the Wabash railroad was what drew most of the initial immigrants to Avella before the turn of the twentieth century.[18] When the railroad was completed, many immigrants then sought out work in the surrounding coal mines which functioned for nearly two generations until the late 1940s.[19] Avella itself could hardly have been considered a small town and was not even separately listed in the US Government censuses until 1950.[20] Instead, Avella's population was included in two neighbouring townships, Cross Creek and Independence. The population boomed from 1,628 in 1900 to 5,148 in 1930.[21] While some of this was certainly due to waves of early immigrants, the Immigration Act of 1924 resolutely closed the door. By 1940, the foreign-born population of the two townships was just over 19%.[22]

So by 1940 or so, Avella comprised of a large percentage of young second-generation immigrants. In 1930, young people under age 24 made up 54% of the local population; the age group between 5 and 14 made for more than 21%.[23] That latter age group was an important one for present purposes since it probably included some of those youngsters who later played on the 1939 Avella Junior team. The 1939 final against Apache FC from Baltimore was played as a curtain raiser for the US vs. Scotland match at New York's Polo Grounds which drew a crowd of 15,163.[24] The junior eleven, which later received the freshly inaugurated T.W. Cahill cup, included Elonzai, Mambu, Griffon, D'Orio, Campanelli, Ray Donelli, Gabrielli, Beadling, Curtis, Soltesz and Ed Kirschner.[25] Two things stand out here. Firstly, the names ring of such obviously European origin yet are far from the same 'ethnicity'. Secondly, this mix of apparently Anglo, German, Italian and Hungarian youth players were likely to have been native-born. However, not all the starting 11 were originally from Avella as the club probably recruited beyond its town borders. Nick DiOrio, reported 'D'Orio' in the contemporary press, was born in nearby Morgan, PA in 1921, another hotbed of soccer during this period.[26]

## *1945–1955 – mixing ethnicities*

The national competition resumed in 1945 after a three-year hiatus. Several sources list the 'Hornets of Chicago' and 'Baltimore Pompei' [*sic*] as co-champions but the presence of a Chicago team is not corroborated by contemporary press accounts.[27] Reducing the analysis to the club name would suggest that the Baltimore team was from an 'Italian' club, yet another example of 'ethnic' soccer. Indeed, the Pompei club has been described as a team from 'Eastside, Patterson Park all Italian guys'.[28] However, the contemporary press tells a different story, one that presents a more nuanced ethnic picture. The Baltimore papers recount hometown Our Lady of Pompei's loss, not to the Hornets of Chicago but rather, to the Schumacher Juniors of St. Louis. The Pompei club was linked to a Roman Catholic Church built in 1924 by the significant Italian immigrant community of the neighbourhood near Patterson Park.[29] In that 1945 Pompei side, two-thirds of its players had Italian names like Al Massaroni, Trotta, Piccione, Terzi, Isadoro, Di Pasquali, Di Fonzo, and substitute Gabriel Magitti. However, the team also included non-Italian names likes Johnny Meagher, Ed Benzing, Jessi Cox, and Surock.[30] Apparently, this team of mixed ethnic names was awarded the title following an appeal, though no trace of this seems to have been passed down in the competition's records.[31] Thus, the team which played under the auspices of Our Lady of Pompei – with players who were not exclusively Italian – became the competition's first champion in a long tradition of teams linked to Catholic parishes and schools.

By the end of the 1940s, however, the dominant club was Philadelphia's Lighthouse Boys' Club. The team won the 1948 and 1949 titles and Oliver has briefly recounted his first-hand experiences as a player on both of those teams.[32] As noted above, Oliver himself called the club one of the 'few Americanized teams'. However, to divide the soccer scene between the exceptional 'Americanized' clubs like Lighthouse and the rest who were 'ethnic' may be an oversimplification. Oliver's playing career reveals the complexity of defining what 'ethnic' soccer meant. Oliver, the son of a Scottish immigrant father, was born on 3 November 1933 and grew up in northern Philadelphia in the 1930s and 1940s.[33] He began in the 'Americanized' Lighthouse Boys' Club (though the club was coached by retired Scot and English players). At the collegiate level he was a Temple University star in soccer and just missed the cut for the 1952 US Olympic team (but was named an alternate).[34] As an adult in the 1950s and 1960s he played for a variety of clubs over the country, some of which he described in 'ethnic' terms. These included the San Francisco Mercury (a Russian club according to Oliver), the Baltimore Pompei (the 'all Italian guys' as noted above) and the Philadelphia Uhriks (sponsored by the local Uhrik trucking company).[35] So he almost represented the US in the Olympics, but was also fully versed with the 'ethnic' soccer experience. When he played on 'ethnic' teams, was he the token American? Or was he not all that different from other 'ethnics', especially second-generation ones, save that his background offered an easier path for assimilation? As a native Anglophone with roots in the British Isles, he may not have been perceived as 'ethnic' to the same degree as other players with Eastern or Southern European last names, who, like him, were born and grew up in America. In one sense he was both 'ethnic' and 'American', and therefore represents the full complexity of the sport at this time.

In 1952, a new community reached the competition's elite: the Ukrainian-Americans. By no means the largest immigrant group to the United States, the first arrivals came in several waves beginning in the late 1880s up to the Immigration Act of 1924 followed by a second tide from the Second World War into the 1960s.[36] In the wake of the Second World War, a host of 'Displaced Persons', or DPs as they are often referred to, arrived in the United States.[37] The immigrants rejuvenated the Ukrainian sports scene with many of them starting teams in cities across the country. One junior team achieved national acclaim in the 1952 national competition. For that year's Junior Cup it is unclear if they were co-champions with Kollsman of New York or only finalists.[38] The USFA's records in the 1960s simply listed the team as 'Lions' but the Ukrainian-American press proudly reported that it was a team from Chicago's Ukrainian community.[39] The Chicago press reported on the team without characterizing it as a specific ethnic group, only mentioning that the players were from Wells High School – perhaps not a bad thing in the tense climate of McCarthyism. However, two players had clearly Ukrainian names: Julian Kulas (a senior) and Walter Bachir (a sophomore).[40]

Kulas is an interesting case study as he stayed closely involved in the sport but also entered into the political debate about his country of birth. Born in Boratyn, Ukraine, he emigrated in 1950 with his parents to Georgia and then to Chicago.[41] He later earned a law degree from De Paul University, was appointed to Chicago's Commission on Human Relations and later one of President Jimmy Carter's 50 appointees to the Holocaust Memorial Council, and also served as a lieutenant colonel in the US Army Reserves.[42] On the sporting side, he acted as legal counsel for the city's National Soccer League and helped broadcast professional games on local television.[43] A member of the Ukrainian National Association, he even travelled to Washington, D.C. to apprise the US Senate and Congress about human rights violations in Ukraine.[44] If serving as an officer in the US military reserves is any indication, he was undoubtedly attached to America. Yet, he remained closely connected to his Ukrainian culture and roots. Dushnyck and Chirovsky have argued that the Ukrainian community used sports, mainly football and volleyball, to maintain its cultural identity.[45] Kulas, then, is yet another example of the complex boundaries of 'ethnic' soccer.

## *1956–75 – Catholics from St. Louis and the beginnings of suburban migration*

In the 1950s the junior soccer elite moved west to St. Louis. The city has a long history in the game, as recounted by David Lange.[46] From the 1950s on, much of the domination was due to the vast network of Catholic Youth Council (CYC) teams based around Catholic parishes and schools.[47] It would appear that most of these CYC teams required enrolment at a Catholic school. Monsignor Lewis Myer, long-time director of the CYC, even noted that religion classes counted for participating on a team. Not all kids were necessarily Catholic however; Myer's estimates were around 50–60%.[48] The Church and its school system provided the structure for much of the youth scene in St. Louis even if the players themselves were not necessarily all Catholic.

The Midwestern city's hegemonic place in the game's history from 1956 to 1972 is indisputable. Its teams took 13 National Junior Challenge Cup titles in 17 years. In the years it did not win, the city sent two finalists, thus cementing the 'Rome of the West' as the centre of junior soccer. A first examination of team locations reveals an interesting shift during this period. Over the 1960s and 1970s the winning teams progressively came from the growing suburbs, reflecting the moving population trends, as shown in Figure 1.

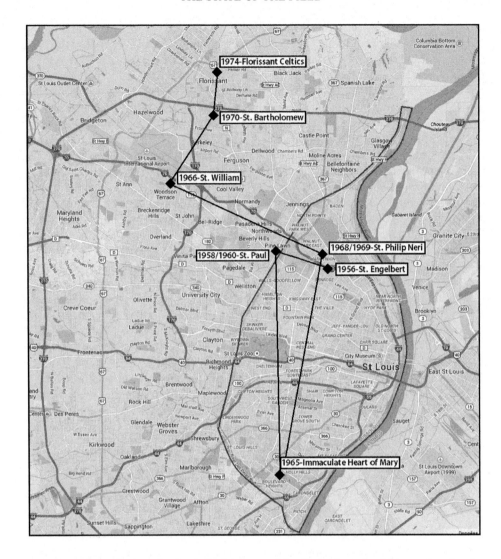

Figure 1. Map of select St. Louis junior teams (city limits in red). (Map produced using Google maps. For all parish and school information, see Archdiocese of St. Louis, 'Closed Parishes'.)

Admittedly, this map does not include the other winning St. Louis teams (Kutis, Schumacher and SECO). However, it is difficult to establish one specific club location for these clubs without full team rosters. In the absence of readily available information, the Catholic parish teams offer, at least in theory, an initial vista on the evolving team locations.

The 1950s victors, St. Engelbert's (1956 winners) and St. Paul's (1958, 1960), were two older churches established in 1891 and 1909, inside the city. Of the subsequent 1960s winning teams, Immaculate Heart of Mary (1965) and St. Philip Neri (1968, 1969, as well as finalists in 1967) were also on or within the St. Louis city limits. St. William (1966) was well beyond the city limits, in newly incorporated Woodson Terrace. The church and school were founded in 1953 to serve a booming young population. Woodson Terrace was not even listed on the 1940 census and 10 years later had only 600 inhabitants; however, by 1960, the population had grown to 6,048.[49] The age breakdown was heavily weighted with the young: 43% of the 1960 population of Woodson Terrace was under age 20, 32% under 15 (the same age bracket which would later cover the 1966 team).[50] This was a fairly well-educated and upper middle-class area with less than 1% of the population foreign-born.[51]

The 1970s saw the winners move even further out into the suburbs. St. Bartholomew, or St. Bart's, (1970) was founded during the heyday of city soccer (1959). The team played in the local CYC's Pepsi League; the corporate sponsorship demonstrated the well-developed nature of the junior game in St. Louis.[52] The Florissant Celtic team (1974) was located even further past the city's highway loop 270. Like Woodson Terrace, Florissant mushroomed from 3,737 inhabitants in 1950 to 65,908 twenty years later.[53] The neighbourhood was also a young one, with 44% of the population under age 18.[54] It was well-off socio-economically, with a median income above the state average and with nearly two-thirds of employed persons in white-collar occupations.[55]

By 1970, the National Junior Challenge Cup had grown significantly over the preceding 40 years and the organizers decided for the first time to hold the semi-finals and finals together over a multiple day tournament.[56] The number of teams increased. In 1938 the press noted a total of 106 entries.[57] In 1974, however, some 220 teams nation-wide had entered the competition.[58] These participating teams represented a wide national constituent base which was much broader than the traditional east coast and select Midwestern cities.

In some ways, St. Louis was a microcosm of what youth soccer was in the process of becoming. While it had its roots in a mix of ethnic communities, Catholic parishes and schools, by the start of the 1970s, the city's top junior teams came from areas with booming young populations, with well-educated, middle to upper-middle-class families who were settling in the suburbs. This was part of a national population trend from a rural and small-town nation in the 1930s to a metropolitan and suburban society by 1970.[59]

## A 1976 revolution as the sport goes national

The 1970s ushered in a new era for the sport. Pelé signed with the New York Cosmos in 1975. Coca-Cola decided to invest $1.2 million in US youth soccer programs the following year.[60] Membership in the United States Youth Soccer Association (USYSA) grew from one-hundred thousand registered youth across 36 states in its 1974 inaugural year to nearly 650,000 youth across 49 states in 1979–1980 – and the missing state, North Dakota, applied that year for membership.[61] The growth in organized high school soccer between 1971 and 1981 followed a similar path. In 1971, among schools that hosted organized basketball – the most widely played sport across the country – only one in 20 had teams for boys' soccer. Within one decade soccer had caught up and was played at almost one-in-four.[62] The number of girls' teams increased by a dramatic factor of 82. In short, this was the decade when soccer found its place on the national sporting map as a recognized activity for young people.

These changes had profound implications for the National Junior Challenge Cup and the bicentennial year 1976 marked the start of a new paradigm in youth soccer. There were a record number of competition entries. The winning side, the

'Annandale Cavaliers', came from the expanding Northern Virginia suburbs of Washington D.C. The representatives from the old 'ethnic' world of youth football, Chicago's Sparta juniors, were soundly beaten 3–0.[63] The Annandale team had not one, but two proverbial feet in that old world; but they also embodied the new youth soccer environment in the 1970s. Budding star, Gary Etherington, had connections to the immigrant world so important to the sport's history but also had spent many of his formative years in his new country.[64] His Annandale club was founded in 1959 by Everett Grant Germain Jr., a Washington, D.C. area native.

Annandale was part of Fairfax County, Virginia, an area which saw enormous demographic growth through suburban migration in the decades following World War Two.[65] It was separately listed for the first time on the 1970 Census. The Annandale area had a native population, largely new to the area, working in white-collar jobs and with significantly higher income and education levels than the rest of the state.[66]

Annandale's victory in 1976 represents the turning point as the game expanded from its traditional bastions of the sport – those with ethnic, immigrant or Catholic ties – to a wider national constituent base. In the previous 41 years of the competition, winners had been limited to the same eight states, all coming from either the eastern seaboard (Lighthouse Boys reaching the final eight times), from historically industrial areas, the Midwest (St. Louis teams owning the lion's share of titles) or (twice) from California.[67] In what was a largely an exclusive group, no less than six clubs had reached the final on at least three occasions. However, the 35 years following 1976 saw champions crowned from 16 different states covering all regions of the country and with only two clubs winning three titles.

## Conclusion – ethnicity and myth

American society has rarely been static and has been defined by its own mythology of a country who opened her arms to Emma Lazarus' 'tired, poor, and huddled masses'. Myth's purpose, of course, is not to craft an accurate account of the past but to serve a didactic or moral role. In the case of America's immigrants, the reality lived by these immigrant masses was often mixed with what Dinnerstein and Reimers, two immigrant historians, refer to as the 'ugly heads of racism and nativism coexisting with our rhetoric of welcome and tolerance'.[68]

Myth is also a powerful force in sport and myths of origin are essential to the construction of a game's identity and the values which are associated to it. Soccer did not have the same kind of creation myths that were carefully developed and preserved for Doubleday's baseball and Camp's gridiron football. Rather, the game in America has endured an ongoing myth: that it was always the 'ethnic', 'immigrant' or 'foreign' game – even as countless immigrants played football, baseball and basketball and many natives played soccer. While there is some truth in the myth, labelling soccer as the 'ethnic' game has tended to veil a complex patchwork of mixed ethnic groups and processes of cultural assimilation.

I have argued here for a more nuanced use of the term 'ethnic' and also for a shifting paradigm in the 1970s as the sport reached out to a national constituency. Soccer forged its history on the cultural margins at least until the 1970s. Its history was intertwined with the stories of immigrants – and their second generation offspring – who straddled the worlds of 'ethnic' and 'American'. Until 1976, the National Junior Challenge Cup was full of teams with these mythological 'ethnic' names. Yet, the individuals involved did not always share that same ethnic background. They did not live 'ethnicity' in a singular and exclusive manner.

The term 'ethnic' encompasses the origin of the sport, its port of entry into society, for example in Len Oliver's Scottish immigrant father. But the term also represents an evolving and permeable mix of worlds where the frontiers of what was deemed 'ethnic' were in continual contact with the world beyond. This is reflected in the mixed names found in youth teams. A strictly bipolar view of 'ethnic' vs. 'native' cultures ignores the fluidity of time. Such a binary perspective is at a loss to understand an immigrant like Julian Kulas who was both 'ethnic' Ukrainian and 'American'. Yet, Kulas personifies the intricacy of what became, through a national revolution of youth and demography, 'Soccer Americana'.

Gary Mormino was one of the rare scholars to articulate the 'complex, often conflicting role' of ethnic soccer in America as it 'fostered acculturation' but also 'promoted ethno-religious identity'.[69] The study of the sport would benefit from more research exploring these crossroads. As the historiography of the period before the 1970s grows, with its city and club specific narratives, the term 'ethnic' may become less of a convenient place-filler and, perhaps, more of a Boorstin-esque 'fertile verge' of history.

## Disclosure statement

No potential conflict of interest was reported by the author.

## Notes

1. See, for example, Riess, 'A Social Profile of the Professional Football Player', 228–9.
2. Taylor, 'Transatlantic Football: Rethinking the Transfer of Football from Europe to the USA, c.1880–c.1930s', 647.
3. By the early 1970s, baseball already had its Society for American Baseball Research (1971), its journal (1972) and the continuation of Harold Seymour's academic study of baseball in a second volume published by Oxford University Press (1971). American football, meanwhile, had its Professional Football Researchers Association (1979) and a decade later had begun to draw serious attention from academics. For more on Seymour see Mills, 'Ghost writing for baseball historian Harold Seymour', 45–58. For American football, see Nauright, 'Writing and Reading American Football: Culture, Identities and Sports Studies', 109–27.
4. See Cascio, *Soccer U.S.A.*; Foulds, and Harris, *America's Soccer Heritage*; Hollander, *American Encyclopedia of Soccer*; and Cirino, *US Soccer Versus the World*.
5. With the exception of Baptista's and Robinson's early doctoral work, little extensive research was published prior to the 1970s. See Baptista, 'A History of Intercollegiate Soccer in the United States of America'; and Robinson, 'The History of Soccer in the City of St. Louis'.
6. Ciccarelli, 'A review of the Historical and Sociological Perspectives Involved in the Acceptance of Soccer as a Professional Sport in the United States'; and Myers, 'The Formation of Organizations: A Case Study of the North American Soccer League'.
7. Oliver, 'Cultural Implications of the Soccer Phenomenon in America', 192–3.
8. Markovits's work inspired a host of responses over the subsequent two decades. For the debate, see Markovits, 'The Other "American Exceptionalism" – Why is There no Soccer in the United States?', 125–50; Sugden, 'USA and the World Cup: American Nativism and the Rejection of the People's Game', 219–52; Abrams, 'Inhibited but not "Crowded Out": The Strange Fate of Soccer in the United States', 1–17; Roderick and Waddington, 'American Exceptionalism: Soccer and American Football', 42–63; Markovits and Hellerman, *Offside: Soccer and American Exceptionalism*; and Pope, 'Rethinking Sport, Empire, and American Exceptionalism', 92–120.

9. Allaway, *Rangers, Rovers and Spindles*; Logan, 'The Rise of Early Chicago Soccer'; Trouille, 'Association Football to fútbol: Ethnic Succession and the History of Chicago-area Soccer since 1920'; Apostolov, 'Everywhere and Nowhere: the Forgotten Past and Clouded Future of American Professional Soccer from the Perspective of Massachusetts'; Bunk, 'The Rise and Fall of Professional Soccer in Holyoke Massachusetts, USA'; and Keyes, 'Making the Mainstream: The Domestication of American Soccer'.

10. Holt, 'Historians and the History of Sport', 3.

11. For a discussion of the lack of a national youth soccer policy and the problem of standardized age categories in the United States, see Tallec Marston, 'An international comparative history of youth football in France and the United States (c.1920–c.2000)', 71–9 and 177–84.

12. Cahill, *Spalding's Official Soccer Foot Ball Guide 1922–23*, 30.

13. United States Football Association, *Rules and Regulations: Season 1935–36*, 25.

14. *The New York Times* listed the team from New Bedford, but interestingly, the Maryland State Soccer Association lists the team among their former national champions. More research could reveal whether they were a junior 'works' team sponsored by a chain of retail stores. The New York Times Stock Exchange listings in the mid-1930s included a company called 'Reliable Stores' which had a stock asking price one-half that of Bloomingdale's. The Massachusetts State corporate records list a company called 'Reliable Stores Corporation' which was first incorporated in the state of Maryland in December 1925 but only registered in MA in 1974. See 'Scots visit stirred interest in soccer', *The New York Times*, 29 December 1935; *New York Times*, 15 May 1938; 'Secretary of the Commonwealth, Corporations Division', http://corp.sec.state.ma.us/corp/corpsearch (accessed June 19, 2011).

15. Effrat, '20,000 see American Soccer League Stars Hold Charlton Squad to a Draw'.

16. In the 27 finals between 1938 and 1967, the Lighthouse juniors won five titles and lost three finals. For the 1938 final, see Fairfield, 'District Soccer Closes most Successful Season'.

17. 'Now there were really exceptions ... There were Americanized clubs like Lighthouse Boys which happened to be an exception because soccer was a low budget sport for wayward kids...Philadelphia was a hotbed, but there were few Americanized teams [elsewhere]'. Len Oliver, interview by the author, Washington DC, January 23, 2006.

18. The area around Avella was settled by significant numbers of Italian and Eastern European immigrants from the end of the nineteenth into the early twentieth century. The railroad was only completed in 1904, the year after the Post-Office was opened and the small town flourished for several decades. The mine was connected to Pittsburgh through the railroad, and once it was completed the immigrant workers began to bring families from Italy. Cerrone, '"Come on to America": Italian Immigrants in Avella, Pennsylvania', 103–4.

19. Muzopappa, 'Tales of Penowa', 115–25.

20. Until then, the townships of Independence and Cross Creek covered the area before they were replaced by Avella. Cerrone has noted the existence of the US manuscript censuses that provide some more detail on the inhabitants of Avella.

21. See 'Table 1-Population of Minor Civil Divisions: 1910, 1900 and 1890', US Census Bureau, *Thirteenth Census of the United States taken in the year 1910*, 551–2. 'Table 21-Population by sex, color, age, etc., for counties by minor civil divisions: 1930', US Census Bureau, *Fifteenth Census of the United States: 1930*, 743.

22. 'Table 28-Race and Age, by Sex, with Rural-farm Population, for Minor Civil Divisions, by Counties: 1940', US Census Bureau, *Sixteenth Census of the United States*, 130–1.

23. 'Table 21', US Census Bureau, *Fifteenth Census of the United States: 1930*, 743.

24. Effrat, 'Scots beat U.S. Soccer Stars'.

25. Fairfield, 'Avella Cops Soccer Title', *The Pittsburgh Press*, June 19, 1939.

26. He graduated high school and won the national title with Avella in the same year. However, his biggest soccer achievement came 11 years later when he made the 1950 US World Cup team, though returned home without playing a match. See 'Obituary: Nicholas DiOrio'; and Blevins, *The Sports Hall of Fame Encyclopedia*, 253.

27. The United States Youth Soccer online records do however concord with the USSFA's annual guides in the 1960s and 1970s.
28. This is how Len Oliver, who played with the Pompei senior pro squad in the early 1960s, recalled the Baltimore team. Len Oliver, interview by the author, Washington DC, January 23, 2006.
29. Scott Calvert, 'An Influx of Hispanic Worshipers Transforms a Traditionally Italian Church, Neighborhood', *The Baltimore Sun*, April 15, 2008.
30. 'St. Louis wins soccer title', *The Sun*, June 25, 1945. The outside left, Surock, was more than likely the same Lawrence Carmen Surock who played with the Pompeii senior side which lost the 1954 US Amateur Cup final (with Al Massaroni) and also appeared on the 1952 US Olympic team in Helsinki. Free, 'E. Baltimore legend Surock just kick from Hall of Fame'.
31. Baltimore appealed based on Schumachers' use of players with senior experience, forbidden under Rule 22 of the competition. The three Schumacher players included one Gino Parianna, who was in fact the same Gino Pariani who later played in the famous 1950 US upset over England. After several months of enquiries, the national committee for the junior tournament 'severely reprimanded' the Schumachers and voted to award the title to Baltimore. See 'Junior soccer protest made' and 'Pompei Soccer Club Awarded Junior U.S.A. Championship'.
32. Oliver, 'American Soccer didn't Start with Pelé: Philadelphia Soccer in the 1940s and 50s', 76.
33. Personal correspondence with the author, April 2, 2012.
34. Temple University's yearbook included Oliver in the 1955 graduating class with a degree in Accounting. He played on the college's soccer team for four years and played baseball for three. He was an All-American player for his sophomore, junior and senior years. *Templar*, 49.
35. Oliver, interview by the author, Washington DC, January 23, 2006.
36. Woroby, 'The Ukrainian Immigrant Left in the United States, 1880–1950', 185–7.
37. Following the 1948 Displaced Persons Act and the 1953 Refugee Relief Act, which extended immigration above the quotas fixed in the 1920s, some 660,000 DP's and refugees arrived on American shores between 1948 and 1960 including over 40,000 directly from the USSR. Ukrainians were not recognized as a separate nationality in the various census reports during this period. Some of them arrived via other countries (Germany and Belgium for example) and so it is difficult to establish exact figures for Ukrainian DP's. See 'Section 3 – Immigration, Emigration, and Naturalization' in US Census Bureau, *Statistical Abstract of the United States 1961*, 88–102.
38. In its year review, the *New York Times* listed Kollsman as victors but later USFA records state co-champions. 'Olympic Triumph by U.S. High Point in Year of Sports', *New York Times*, 21 December 1952.
39. United States Soccer Football Association, *1965–1966 Official Annual Guide*, 44; and Danko, 'Ukrainian Sport Notes'.
40. 'Lions Soccer Squad takes Midwest Title'.
41. 'Kulas meets Brzezinski, Discuss plight of DISSIDENTS'.
42. 'Chicagoan Julian Kulas named to Holocaust Memorial Council'.
43. 'Dr. Kulas Named to Chicago's Human Relations Commission'.
44. 'UNA'ers Meet With Legislators in D.C. Rights Action'.
45. Chirovsky and Dushnyck, *The Ukrainian Heritage in America*, 580–93.
46. Lange, *Soccer Made in St. Louis*.
47. Robinson, 'The History of Soccer', especially chapter 11, 235–51.
48. The author is indebted to Gabe Logan for passing on the transcript of his interview with Monsignor Lewis Meyer, on November 11, 1996.
49. 'Table 7-Population of counties, by minor civil divisions: 1940 to 1960', US Census Bureau, *Eighteenth Decennial Census of the United States: 1960- Part 27: Missouri*, 27–22.
50. 'Table 22-Characteristics of the Population, for Urban Places of 2,500 to 10,000: 1960', ibid., 27–80.
51. The median family income in 1959 was $7,403 and 11.7 median school years completed. The state median family income was $5,127 and 9.6 years of schooling.

'Table 81-Social and Economic Characteristics of the Population, for Urban Places of 2,500 to 10,000: 1960', ibid., 27–260.

52. United States Soccer Football Association, *1971 Official Yearbook*, 93, 201–2.
53. 'Table 7-Population of Incorporated Places of 10,000 or More: 1900 to 1970', US Census Bureau, *Census of the Population: 1970- Part 27: Missouri*, 27–17.
54. 'Table 83-Educational Characteristics for Areas and Places: 1970', ibid., 27–291.
55. 'Table 41-Summary of Economic Characteristics: 1970', ibid., 27–230.
56. United States Soccer Football Association, *1971 Official Yearbook*, 99.
57. Harry Fairfield, 'Soccer Title Battle Set', *The Pittsburgh Press*, 29 May 1938.
58. Yannis, 'Red Army's Soccer Team to Face American Sides'.
59. In 1930 still one-half of the country lived in the countryside or in small towns. By 1970 that figure had shrunk to less than one-third of the population while the suburban population had ballooned from less than 20% to around 40%. Fischer and Hout, *Century of Difference: How America Changed in the Last One Hundred Years*, 172–3.
60. '$1.2 Million given to Soccer in US', *New York Times*, 14 May 1976.
61. United States Youth Soccer Association, *Annual Report 1979–80*, 7.
62. The increase in the number of schools having boys' teams between 1971 and 1981 increased from 2,290 to 4,839. The girls' teams mushroomed from 28 to 2,032. In comparison, boys' basketball was played 19,647 schools in 1971 and 17,922 ten years later. Compiledfrom National Federation of State High School Associations, 'NFHS Participation Figures Search'.
63. 'Virginia Team Captures Junior Soccer Cup, 3–0'.
64. Etherington caused a media stir when he joined the New York Cosmos after Annandale's Cup win in 1976; he represented the United States on a number of occasions and was referred to in the press as a 'native born' player. However, Etherington was actually born in Southampton, England in 1958 and immigrated with his family to the United States at age 12. His father, an amateur player, was said to have started his son at the game 'as soon as [he] could walk'. Etherington really began playing in an organised fashion with the Annandale club. He turned down a scholarship to the University of Virginia and signed a two year pro contract with the Cosmos after his 1976 National Junior title. Of his decision, he said 'I know in America you need a lot of education, but I always wanted to play pro soccer. I guess that was a big decision for an 18-year-old to have to make.' One newspaper noted that he was 'a pleasure to listen to, not only because of his boyish enthusiasm but also because of the slight British accent he still retains.' See 'Gary rests easy with Pele, Cosmos', *Boca Raton News*, 24 August 1977; 'All Cosmos Set to Train Except for a Brazilian', *New York Times*, 16 February 1977; Russell Carter, 'Etherington Flies High With Cosmos; Practice Pays For Etherington', *The Washington Post*, 22 August 1978.
65. Fairfax County's population increased from 1950 to 1960 by 179% (from 98,557 to 275,002) and then again by 65% in 1970 (to 455,021). See 'Table 6 – Area and Population of Counties and Independent Cities, Urban and Rural: 1960 and 1950', US Census Bureau, *Census of the Population: 1961- Part 48: Virginia*, 48–12; and 'Table 9 – Population of Land Area and Counties: 1970 and 1960', US Census Bureau, *Census of the Population: 1970 - Part 48: Virginia*, 48–15.
66. The population of 27,418 in 1970 was almost exclusively native-born (over 96%) and of those employed 78% worked in 'professional', 'managerial', 'clerical' or 'sales' roles. Nearly 60% of the population had just moved to Annandale in the five previous years. The median number of years of schooling for Annandale men and women was 15 and almost 13; the state-wide figures were under 12 years for both sexes. The median state family income was $9,000. In Annandale the median was $15,504 and more than 50% of the population actually earned more. See 'Table 40-Summary of social characteristics: 1970', US Census Bureau, *Census of the Population: 1973- Part 48: Virginia*, 48–201; 'Table 41-Summary of economic characteristics: 1970', ibid., 48–202; 'Table 68-Income in 1969 of families, unrelated individuals, and persons by size of place: 1970', ibid., 48–241, 'Table 62-Educational characteristics by size of place: 1970', ibid., 48–235; 'Table 102-Social characteristics for places of 10,000 to 50,000: 1970', ibid., 48–359; and 'Table 103-Educational and family characteristics for places of 10,000 to 50,000': 1970', ibid., 48–362.

67. The runners-up were not much more representative of the nation. They came from seven of the same eight states.
68. Dinnerstein and Reimers, *Ethnic Americans: A history of immigration*, 2.
69. Mormino, 'The Playing Fields of St. Louis – Italian Immigrants and Sports, 1925–1941', 15–16.

## References

Abrams, Nathan D. "Inhibited but Not "Crowded out"": The Strange Fate of Soccer in the United States'. *The International Journal of the History of Sport* 12, no. 3 (1995): 1–17.

Allaway, Roger. *Rangers, Rovers and Spindles: Soccer, Immigration, and Textiles in New England and New Jersey*. Haworth: St. Johann Press, 2005.

Apostolov, Steven. 'Everywhere and Nowhere: The Forgotten past and Clouded Future of American Professional Soccer from the Perspective of Massachusetts'. *Soccer & Society* 13, no. 4 (2012): 510–35.

Archdiocese of St. Louis. 'Closed Parishes'. http://archstl.org/archives/page/closed-parishes.

Baptista, Robert. 'A History of Intercollegiate Soccer in the United States of America'. PhD diss., Indiana University, 1962.

Blevins, Dave. *The Sports Hall of Fame Encyclopedia: Baseball, Basketball, Football, Hockey, Soccer*. Lanham, MD: Scarecrow Press, 2011.

Bunk, Brian. 'The Rise and Fall of Professional Soccer in Holyoke Massachusetts, USA'. *Sport in History* 31, no. 3 (2011): 283–306.

Cahill, Tom, ed. *Spalding's Official Soccer Foot Ball Guide 1922–23*. New York: Spalding, 1923.

Calvert, Scott. 'An Influx of Hispanic Worshipers Transforms a Traditionally Italian Church, Neighborhood'. *The Baltimore Sun*, April 15, 2008.

Cascio, Chuck. *Soccer U.S.A.* Washington, DC: Robert B. Luce, 1975.

Cerrone, Catherine. '"Come on to America": Italian Immigrants in Avella, Pennsylvania'. *Pittsburgh History* 78, no. 3 (1995): 100–14.

'Chicagoan Julian Kulas Named to Holocaust Memorial Council'. *The Ukrainian Weekly*, May 11, 1980.

Chirovsky, Nicholas L., and Walter Dushnyck. *The Ukrainian Heritage in America*. New York: Ukrainian Congress Committee of America, 1991.

Ciccarelli, Daniel L. 'A Review of the Historical and Sociological Perspectives Involved in the Acceptance of Soccer as a Professional Sport in the United States'. PhD diss., Temple University, 1983.

Cirino, Tony. *US Soccer Versus the World*. Leonia: Damon Press, 1983.

Danko, Walter. 'Ukrainian Sport Notes'. *Ukrainian Weekly*, June 9, 1952.

Dinnerstein, Leonard, and David M. Reimers. *Ethnic Americans: A History of Immigration*. 5th ed. New York: Columbia University Press, 2009.

'Dr. Kulas Named to Chicago's Human Relations Commission'. *The Ukrainian Weekly*, April 30, 1978.

Effrat, Louis. 'Scots Beat U.S. Soccer Stars'. *New York Times*, June 19, 1939.

Effrat, Louis. '20,000 See American Soccer League Stars Hold Charlton Squad to a Draw'. *New York Times*, May 31, 1937.

Fairfield, Harry. 'Avella Cops Soccer Title'. *The Pittsburgh Press*, June 19, 1939.

Fairfield, Harry. 'District Soccer Closes Most Successful Season'. *The Pittsburgh Press*, June 5, 1938.

Fairfield, Harry. 'Soccer Title Battle Set'. *The Pittsburgh Press*, May 29, 1938.

Fischer, Claude S., and Michael Hout. *Century of Difference: How America Changed in the Last One Hundred Years*. New York: Russell Sage Foundation, 2006.

Foulds, Sam, and Paul Harris. *America's Soccer Heritage*. Manhattan Beach: Soccer for Americans, 1979.

Free, Bill. 'E. Baltimore Legend Surock Just Kick from Hall of Fame'. *The Baltimore Sun.*, May 6, 1992.

Hollander, Zander. *American Encyclopedia of Soccer*. New York: Everest House, 1980.

Holt, Richard. 'Historians and the History of Sport'. *Sport in History* 34, no. 1 (2014): 1–33.

'Junior Soccer Protest Made'. *The Sun*, July 6, 1945.

Keyes, David. 'Making the Mainstream: The Domestication of American Soccer'. In *Soccer Culture in America: Essays on the World's Sport in Red, White and Blue*, ed. Yuya Kiuchi, 9–24. Jefferson, NC: McFarland, 2014.

'Kulas Meets Brzezinski, Discuss Plight of Dissidents'. *The Ukrainian Weekly*, April 6, 1980.

Lange, David. *Soccer Made in St. Louis: A History of the Game in America's First Soccer Capital*. St. Louis: Reedy Press, 2011.

'Lions Soccer Squad Takes Midwest Title'. *Chicago Daily Tribune*, May 26, 1952.

Logan, Gabe. 'The Rise of Early Chicago Soccer'. In *Sports in Chicago*, ed. Elliot J. Gorn, 19–42. Chicago: University of Illinois Press, 2008.

Markovits, Andrei S. 'The Other American Exceptionalism' – Why is There No Soccer in the United States?' *Praxis International* 8, no. 2 (1988): 125–50.

Markovits, Andrei S., and Steven L. Hellerman. *Offside: Soccer and American Exceptionalism*. Princeton: Princeton University Press, 2001.

Mills, Dorthy Jane. 'Ghost Writing for Baseball Historian Harold Seymour'. *NINE: A Journal of Baseball History and Culture* 11, no. 1 (2002): 45–58.

Mormino, Gary. 'The Playing Fields of St. Louis – Italian Immigrants and Sports, 1925–1941'. *Journal of Sport History* 9, no. 2 (1982): 5–19.

Muzopappa, Anthony. 'Tales of Penowa'. *Pittsburgh History* 78, no. 3 (1995): 115–25.

Myers, Phyllis Marie Goudy. 'The Formation of Organizations: A Case Study of the North American Soccer League'. PhD diss., Purdue University, 1984.

National Federation of State High School Associations. 'NFHS Participation Figures Search'. http://www.nfhs.org/custom/participation_figures (accessed June 3, 2009).

Nauright, John. 'Writing and Reading American Football: Culture, Identities and Sports Studies'. *Sporting Traditions* 13, no. 1 (1996): 109–27.

'Obituary: Nicholas DiOrio'. *Pittsburgh Post-Gazette*, September 14, 2003.

Oliver, Len. 'American Soccer Didn't Start with Pelé: Philadelphia Soccer in the 1940s and 50s'. *Journal of Ethno-Development*, no. 1 (1992): 72–81.

Oliver, Len. 'Cultural Implications of the Soccer Phenomenon in America'. In *Cultural Dimensions of Play, Games and Sport*, ed. Bernard Mergen, 191–208. Champaign, IL: Human Kinetics, 1986.

'Olympic Triumph by U.S. High Point in Year of Sports'. *New York Times*, December 21, 1952.

'Pompei Soccer Club Awarded Junior U.S.A. Championship'. *The Sun*, October 21, 1945.

Pope, Steven W. 'Rethinking Sport, Empire, and American Exceptionalism'. *Sport History Review* 38 (2007): 92–120.

Riess, Steven. 'A Social Profile of the Professional Football Player'. In *The Business of Professional Sports*, ed. Paul D. Staudohar, and J.A. Mangan, 222–46. Chicago: University of Illinois Press, 1991.

Robinson, James. 'The History of Soccer in the City of St. Louis'. PhD diss., St. Louis University, 1966.

Roderick, Martin, and Ivan Waddington. 'American Exceptionalism: Soccer and American Football'. *The Sports Historian* 16 (1996): 42–63.

'St. Louis Wins Soccer Title'. *The Sun*, June 25, 1945.

Sugden, John. 'USA and the World Cup: American Nativism and the Rejection of the People's Game'. In *Hosts and Champions – Soccer Cultures, National Identities and the USA World Cup*, ed. John Sugden, and Alan Tomlinson. London: Ashgate, 1994.

Tallec Marston, Kevin. 'An International Comparative History of Youth Football in France and the United States (C.1920–C.2000): The Age Paradigm and the Demarcation of the Youth Game as a Separate Sector of the Sport'. PhD diss., De Montfort University, 2012.

Taylor, Matthew. 'Transatlantic Football: Rethinking the Transfer of Football from Europe to the USA, C.1880–C.1930s'. *Ethnologie française* 41, no. 4 (2011): 645–54.

*Templar*. Philadelphia: Temple University, 1955.

Trouille, David. 'Association Football to Fútbol: Ethnic Succession and the History of Chicago-Area Soccer since 1920'. *Soccer & Society* 10, no. 6 (2009): 455–76.

'UNA'ers Meet with Legislators in D.C. Rights Action'. *The Ukrainian Weekly*, June 5, 1977.

United States Census Bureau. *Census of the Population: 1970 – Volume I – Characteristics of the Population – Part 27: Missouri*. Washington, DC: Government Printing Office, 1973.

United States Census Bureau. *Census of the Population: 1970 – Volume I – Characteristics of the Population – Part 48: Virginia*. Washington, DC: Government Printing Office, 1973.

United States Census Bureau. *Eighteenth Decennial Census of the United States: 1960 – Population – Volume I – Characteristics of the Population – Part 27: Missouri*. Washington, DC: Government Printing Office, 1961.

United States Census Bureau. *Eighteenth Decennial Census of the United States: 1960 – Population – Volume I – Characteristics of the Population – Part 48: Virginia*. Washington, DC: Government Printing Office, 1961.

United States Census Bureau. *Fifteenth Census of the United States: 1930 – Population, Volume III – Reports by States, Showing the Composition and Characteristics of the Population for Counties, Cities, and Townships or Other Minor Civil Divisions – Part 2 – Pennsylvania*. Washington, DC: Government Printing Office, 1932.

United States Census Bureau. *Sixteenth Census of the United States: 1940 – Population – Volume II – Characteristics of the Population – Sex, Age, Race, Nativity, Citizenship, Country of Birth of Foreign-Born White, School Attendance, Education, Employment Status, Class of Worker, Major Occupation Group, and Industry Group – Part 6: Pennsylvania-Texas*. Washington, DC: Government Printing Office, 1943.

United States Census Bureau. *Statistical Abstract of the United States 1961*. Washington, DC: Government Printing Office, 1961.

United States Census Bureau. *Thirteenth Census of the United States Taken in the Year 1910 – Volume III – Population: Reports by States, with Statistics for Counties, Cities and Other Civil Divisions – Pennsylvania*. Washington, DC: Government Printing Office, 1913.

United States Football Association. *Rules and Regulations: Season 1935–36*. United States Football Association.

United States Soccer Football Association. *1965–1966 Official Annual Guide*. New York: United States Soccer Football Association.

United States Soccer Football Association. *1971 Official Yearbook*. New York: United States Soccer Football Association.

United States Youth Soccer Association. *Annual Report 1979–80*. United States Youth Soccer Association.

'Virginia Team Captures Junior Soccer Cup, 3-0'. *New York Times*, June 21, 1976.

Woroby, Maria. 'The Ukrainian Immigrant Left in the United States, 1880–1950'. In *The Immigrant Left in the United States*, ed. Paul Buhle and Dan Georgakas, 185–207. Albany: State University of New York Press, 1996.

Yannis, Alex. 'Red Army's Soccer Team to Face American Sides'. *New York Times*, February 3, 1974.

'$1.2 Million given to Soccer in US'. *New York Times*, May 14, 1976.

**Appendix 1. Table of winners and runners-up, National Junior Challenge Cup 1935–1976***

| Year | Winner | City | State | Runner-Up | State | Score | Date | City | State | Location of Final |
|---|---|---|---|---|---|---|---|---|---|---|
| 1935 | Reliable Stores Juniors | New Bedford | MA | Greenock West of Scotland | | | | Brooklyn, NYC | NY | |
| 1936 | Hatikvah Juniors | Brooklyn, NYC | NY | Bethlehem Midgets | NY | | | | | |
| 1937 | Hatikvah Juniors | Brooklyn, NYC | NY | Belloise FC or Beloise FC? | NY | | 27.06.1937 | Pittsburgh | PA | |
| 1938 | Lighthouse Boys' Club | Philadelphia | PA | Beadling | PA | 1-0 | | Beadling | PA | Bridgeville Park (Bridgeville, PA) |
| 1939 | Avella Juniors | Avella | PA | Apache FC | PA | 3-1 | 19.06.1939 | Baltimore | MD | Polo Grounds (New York City, NY) |
| 1940 | Avella Juniors | Avella | PA | Yorkville Athletic Club Juniors | PA | 1-0 | 19.05.1940 | Manhattan? | NY | Celtic Park (Brooklyn, NYC) |
| 1941 | Mercerville Juniors | Trenton | NJ | Kensington Rec. | NJ | | | E. Penn | PA | |
| 1942 | No Competition | | | | | | | | | |
| 1943 | No Competition | | | | | | | | | |
| 1944 | No Competition | | | | | | | | | |
| **1945 | Baltimore Pompeii | Baltimore | MD | Schumacher Juniors | MD | | | St. Louis | MO | |
| 1946 | Schumacher Juniors | St. Louis | MO | Prague A.C. | MO | 2-0 | 23.06.1946 | NYC? | NY | (New York City, NY) |
| 1947 | Heidelberg Juniors | Heidelberg | PA | Baldwin Hill | PA | | | Trenton | NJ | |
| 1948 | Lighthouse Boys' Club | Philadelphia | PA | Schumacher Juniors | PA | 1-0 | | St. Louis | MO | (Philadelphia, PA) |
| 1949 | Lighthouse Boys' Club | Philadelphia | PA | Windsor Athletic Club | PA | 2-1 | | St. Louis | MO | (St. Louis, MO) |
| 1950 | Harrison (Boys Club?) Juniors | Harrison | NJ | SECO (Southern Equipment Company) Juniors | NJ | | | St. Louis | MO | |
| 1951 | SECO (Southern Equipment Company) Juniors | St. Louis | MO | Midway (Boys' Club) | MO | 5-1 | 02.06.1951 | Philadelphia | PA | (St. Louis, MO) |
| **1952 | Kollsman S.C. | Brooklyn, NYC | NY | Lions (Ukrainian Sports Club) | NY | | | Chicago | IL | |
| **1953 | Newark Boys Club | Newark | NJ | Hansa | NJ | | | Chicago | IL | |
| 1954 | Hansa S.C. | Chicago | IL | Heidelberg | IL | | | Heidelberg | PA | |
| **1955 | Schwaben | Chicago | IL | Blau Weiss Gottschee | IL | | | Queens, NYC | NY | |
| 1956 | St. Engelbert | St. Louis | MO | Heidelberg | MO | 1-0 | 25.06.1956 | Heidelberg | PA | (St. Louis, MO) |

**Appendix 1.** (*Continued*).

| Year | Winner | City | State | Runner-Up | City | State | Score | Date | Location of Final |
|---|---|---|---|---|---|---|---|---|---|
| 1957 | Lighthouse Boys' Club | Philadelphia | PA | Kregshower or Kriegshauser? | St. Louis | MO | | | |
| 1958 | St. Paul the Apostle | St. Louis | MO | Blau Weiss Gottschee | Queens, NYC | NY | | | Winnemac stadium (Chicago, IL) |
| 1959 | Ukrainian American Sport Club of NY | New York | NY | Fitchte Rams | Chicago | IL | | 21.06.1959 | (New York City, NY) |
| 1960 | St. Paul the Apostle | St. Louis | MO | Elizabeth | Elizabeth | NJ | | | |
| 1961 | Hakoah | San Francisco | CA | Lighthouse Boys' Club | Philadelphia | PA | 3-2 | 23.07.1961 | (Philadelphia, PA) |
| 1962 | Schumacher Juniors | St. Louis | MO | Good Counsel | Baltimore | MD | | | |
| 1963 | Kutis | St. Louis | MO | Eintracht | Queens, NYC | NY | | | |
| 1964 | Kutis | St. Louis | MO | Lighthouse Boys Celtics | Philadelphia | PA | | | |
| 1965 | Immaculate Heart of Mary | St. Louis | MO | Lighthouse Boys Celtics | Philadelphia | PA | 2-0 | 27.06.1965 | (Philadelphia, PA) |
| 1966 | St. William | St. Louis | MO | German–Hungarian Sports Club / The Knitters | Brooklyn, NYC | NY | 1-0 | 02.07.1966 | (St. Louis, MO) |
| 1967 | Lighthouse Boys' Club '49ers | Philadelphia | PA | St. Phillip Neri | St. Louis | MO | 2-1 | | |
| 1968 | St. Phillip Neri | St. Louis | MO | Hammsetts or Harmnetts or Hammetts? | Trenton | NJ | 8-1 | | (St. Louis, MO) |
| 1969 | St. Phillip Neri | St. Louis | MO | Tom's Produce or Tom-Boy Market Club? | Baltimore | MD | on PKs | | |
| 1970 | St. Bartholomew | St. Louis | MO | Blau Weiss Gottschee | Queens, NYC | NY | 5-2 | 07.06.1970 | (St. Louis, MO) |
| 1971 | SECO (Southern Equipment Company) | St. Louis | MO | Italia-Casa Bianca | Baltimore | MD | 2-0 | 30.05.1971 | Winnemac stadium (Chicago, IL) |
| 1972 | SECO (Southern Equipment Company) Jets | St. Louis | MO | Italia-Casa Bianca | Baltimore | MD | 2-1 | 28.05.1972 | (Trenton, NJ) |
| 1973 | St. Elizabeth S.C. | Baltimore | MD | Sparta | San Diego | CA | 3-2 | | Cotton Bowl (Dallas, TX) |
| 1974 | Florissant Celtics | St. Louis | MO | | | | | | |
| 1975 | Imo's Pizza | St. Louis | MO | | | | | | (Milwaukee, WI) |
| 1976 | Annandale Boys Club (Cavaliers) | Annandale | VA | Sparta | Chicago | IL | 3-0 | | Adelphi Field (Long Island, NY) |

*Consolidated from contemporary press, USSFA annual guides and current USYS records.
**Both old USSFA and current USYS records list both teams as co-champions.

# Soccer, politics and the American public: still 'exceptional'?

Christian Collet ⓘ

In 1988, Andrei Markovits first published the argument that soccer in the United States encounters an 'exceptional' experience because America's 'hegemonic sports culture' has 'crowded out' the sport by virtue of historically determined factors, including popular acceptance. Twenty years after USA '94, it seems appropriate to revisit this idea. In this paper, I utilize survey data from multiple sources to make three arguments. First, interest in soccer among the public has been generally stable over time; second, relative to other countries, American fans are not discernibly exceptional; third, what discerns fans are characteristics that appear to be a function of the sport's diversity. This makes the ongoing 'exceptional' characterization ironic, as the binary continues to serve those who deride soccer as 'un-American'. While Markovits has identified a critical period in soccer's past, moving beyond the deterministic exceptionalist model is imperative for future research on the American game.

## Introduction

On 4 June 2010, a week before the US Men's National Team (MNT) kicked off in the first Group C match of the World Cup in Rustenberg, South Africa, a story ran on *The Onion* under the headline 'Nation's Soccer Fan Becoming Insufferable'. The farce described the growing frustration that was surrounding Brad Janovich, 'the United States' lone soccer fan'. A photo showing a serious Brad at his work cubicle sporting a crisp navy USA track jacket overlaid the following 'report':

> Wilmington, DE – As the 2010 World Cup approaches, friends, family and coworkers of 32-year old Brad Janovich are growing less tolerant of the exuberant behavior of the United States' lone soccer fan.
>
> 'Who's got World Cup fever?' Janovich asked his officemates at Credit Solutions Friday, failing to notice their silent stares as he reported for work clad in the sole Team USA jersey sold this year. 'I do! I've got World Cup fever!' …
>
> According to sources only peripherally aware of the World Cup, Janovich's infuriating behavior first became apparent during a Super Bowl viewing party last February when he repeatedly used the phrase 'American football' to describe the action on the field …
>
> Last week he was talking about how 'footy' is really heating up and asked me to come over for the 'friendly' against Turkey', said Janovich's friend Beth Gleason, who has known the only projected viewer of this year's World Cup broadcast since college …
> 'I was like "Brad, don't talk like that. People don't talk like that"'.

Layering irony upon irony, real news would reveal that more than eight million American households tuned in to watch the draw with England, a record that was broken two weeks later when Ghana ended the MNT's hopes of advancing. This would not be the first time that stereotype and empiricism would collide: American soccer, like American politics, has almost always been more comfortable with myth than reality – and the fact that there are likely to be millions of Brad Janovichs does little to dispel the prevailing belief that the US is an exceptional society and monolithic culture in which soccer does not play a part. Whether sports or politics, there has long alleged to be an 'American Way' of practices and preferences that is singularly – if not, proudly – at odds with those that prevail in the rest of the world. Soccer, it has been said, is the socialism of American sports: it simply doesn't fit in, conform to tastes and, as Brad's friend Beth says, its 'people don't talk like that'.

The purpose of this paper is to address this allegation as it has manifested in academic forms, with specific regard to the appropriateness of exceptionalism as a premise or label for describing soccer's place in the culture of the United States. Since Andrei Markovits published the first of several papers around this idea in 1988, and then notably developed the exceptionalist framework in book form,[1] the notion of a unique national character for the United States has come under severe scrutiny. The turning point was the incursions into Afghanistan and Iraq following the attacks of 11 September 2001 – actions that not only transformed world opinion, but led disciples of neo-conservative thought to reconsider the America Alone premise.[2] Even Charles Murray, in a fawning tribute to exceptionalism, concedes that 'just about everything that was exceptional about America's setting has changed'.[3]

Yet, when it comes to sports, exceptionalism remains trenchant. While *Offside* offered one of the first, and most direct, applications of exceptionalism to sports in the United States (cited over 200 times, as of this writing, according to Google Scholar), it is not difficult to find the same Americans vs. the World binary elsewhere when soccer is discussed:

- 'You can buy a McDonald's Big Mac on the Champs-Elysées and anything from anywhere in the world on Fifth Avenue, but American sporting culture and the world soccer culture do not mix'[4];
- 'America is the exception to the rule that soccer is the global spectator sport. Soccer is certainly played in the United States, but despite several attempts and millions of dollars, it is a sport that only a relatively few follow and those few are generally either immigrants or highly paid and educated elites ... it is the "Africa" of soccer globalization'[5];
- 'America is a sports "island" ... America's sports culture is exceptional partly because interest in soccer is so anemic. This American exception has deep historical roots ... Far from shaping the global game, America has stood "offside"'.[6]

Although an initial wave of criticism pointed out oversights in Markovits' historicization and conceptualization – soccer 'did not just disappear' in the early twentieth century, Abrams argues, but is an '"indigenous" sport' whose resistance to elite 'manipulation' has been overlooked – recent papers have continued to accept tenets of exceptionalism even as they have sought to move towards a more complex portrait of the American game.[7] One author, recognizing that *Offside* 'should have further explored [the] concepts of exceptionalism ... [for] there is no model which defines America as unique vis-a-vis the world', contends nonetheless that the thesis 'bears much weight upon understanding the historical and contemporary failure of soccer in the United States ... there is validity in the self-proclaimed provincialism and exceptionalism of American culture'.[8] Another 'resists any simplistic notions of exceptionalism and national identity being conveniently imposed upon soccer in America' and argues for understanding it 'as a site of cultural negotiation'. But the essay then goes on to point out how 'soccer is also un-American in many ways too' – its 'tribal, almost religious fanaticism' or its 'sense of compromise' in tied outcomes that are 'so alien to so much of the American civic culture'.[9]

Others have begun to chip away at the idea, noting how the model presented in *Offside* 'is denuded of the type of cultural analysis capable of exposing American exceptionalism as part of national myth'.[10] Glen Duerr goes a step further, putting the notion in the past tense, by explaining that 'over the course of the 2000s, soccer went from being part of American "exceptionalism" to a more natural part of the national sporting scene'.[11] David Keyes makes the critical linkage between soccer's suburban rise and its changing multicultural population, showing how the American Youth Soccer Association (AYSO) has facilitated the game's rise towards 'mainstream' institutionalization.[12]

My argument builds on this movement, but proceeds on a different methodological front and endeavours to take the discussion back to the basics. By looking directly at the views of the American public towards soccer since the early 1970s, I assess the central claims in *Offside* and its precursors about domestic sporting culture: namely, whether exceptionalism continues to be an empirically sound premise for describing the game at the popular level. While there can be little doubt that men's professional soccer has yet to achieve a status that is anywhere comparable to the National Football League, Major League Baseball or the National Basketball Association, arrogating what Markovits and Hellerman call the 'organizational-institutional' weakness of the American Soccer League, North American Soccer League (NASL) or Major League Soccer (MLS) to the level of a cultural trait, 'deeply rooted' and unique to the world, is a different question altogether – one that is perpetually challenged by the other alleged 'exceptions' pointed out elsewhere in Markovits' work[13]: the popularity of the sport at the youth level, as well as the enthusiasm that has crystallized around the MNT and women's national teams (WNT). It seems reasonable to posit, at this juncture in soccer's development trajectory, whether America's allegedly exceptional traits have been more a reflection of a narrowed conceptual and methodological focus on an elite-driven, corporate marketplace (and, as Abrams argues, a dearth of available history) than of a grounded, holistic assessment of US society and culture.

Do the conventional views that have been asserted and repeated within an exceptionalist-infused literature align with the way Americans have seen and treated the game? Using available survey data dating back to the 1970s, I pose four questions:

(1) Is it true that soccer is faddish and appeals only to the margins of the American public?
(2) Are soccer fans and watchers isolated within an alleged American 'sports space'?
(3) Do soccer fans and watchers possess unique social characteristics – and a distinct political ideology?
(4) Do these characteristics and orientations make American soccer fans unique from others around the world?

## American exceptionalism and sporting culture: the asserted linkage

The crux of *Offside* is to provide an overarching scholarly narrative for the development of sports in the United States that links it to other 'clearly *sui generis*' components of American society, its socio-economic history, its political system and its education and religiosity.[14] The primary reference point is political; 'American exceptionalism', as the authors specify, 'refers to the curious situation in which the United States was the only major industrial country of the twentieth century without the presence of a significant socialist/social democratic and/or communist party in its polity'. They contend 'the single most pervasive underlying variable for an understanding of American politics and society' is the 'quintessentially bourgeois nature of America's objective development and subjective self-legitimation from its very inception to the present'. This 'bourgeoisification', chronicled famously by Tocqueville, 'created certain structures and an accompanying atmosphere that differentiated the United States from all other countries'. At its 'core' is 'the free individual who was to attain his fulfilment by being an independent, autonomous, sovereign and rational actor in a free market unfettered by any oppressive collectivities'. American 'sports exceptionalism', therefore, 'is deeply rooted in [these] other exceptionalisms that constitute essential features of modern American life'.[15]

The critical concept is a nationally demarcated, economically inspired 'sports space', which derives from the authors' definition of 'sports culture' – 'what people follow as opposed to what people do'. For Markovits and Hellerman, 'space', so defined, is intrinsically the domain of elite influence; it is nationalistic, restrictive ('a finite entity of entrants') and subject to monopolization, such that a 'hegemonic sports culture' emerges in such a peculiar way that it 'dominates a country's emotional attachments rather than its calisthenic activities'.[16] With hegemony the vantage point through which American opinions and discourses towards sports are viewed, sports space becomes 'less about the world of athletes than ... that of couch potatoes' and 'what we mean by hegemonic sports culture [occurs] with greater frequency on sports radio call-in programs than on sports fields'.[17] Representations flow and are self-evident in the 'mainstream': from Hollywood films to mass media coverage, soccer has been virtually invisible relative to other American pastimes. Overwhelmed by the 'Big Three and a Half' – gridiron football, baseball, basketball and ice hockey – soccer was 'crowded out' during industrialization and has since failed to be accepted as an element of domestic culture.

The important point is that the model is deterministic: soccer is, and will likely remain, marginal in the United States for the simple reason that 'sports culture' is 'path dependent'. Due to the game's inability to gain a foothold in the industrialization period between 1870 and 1930, it suffers chronically from 'the liability of newness' as well as being 'identified as a non-American sport with foreign origins'.[18] To put things more colloquially, soccer had a chance at goal, squandered it and history has determined the rest – in a model of path dependency, only an unlikely shock to the system will alter the conditions to such an extent that a 'new' sport can enter the field.[19] Sports spaces, in this way, are likened to Lipset and Rokkan's once influential theory of party systems: once class-driven cleavages formed and institutionalized with parties that are the object of individual attachments, they 'froze': discouraging challengers and perpetuating the status quo of the oligarchs.[20]

Class, thus, is the critical independent variable accounting for soccer's popularity.[21] Because soccer is seen worldwide as a 'proletarian' sport, claim

Markovits and Hellerman, its image in the US is akin to a Socialist Party candidate seeking votes for the presidency: it struggles to be heard or taken seriously because the 'bourgeoisified' political culture is built exclusively around the Republicans and Democrats in a venue where the rhetoric of class warfare falls on deaf ears. Rather, owing to soccer's establishment as Ivy League recreation, it can, à la Ralph Nader, only attract a sporadic niche following among intellectuals who harbour sympathies for the oppressed underclass. This, *Offside* argues, explains soccer's uneven trajectory. While it can attain a fashion and cult following among the Hollywood and campus sets, its impact is ephemeral, as the (first) North American Soccer League (NASL) demonstrated. This is because soccer's 'outsider' image cannot penetrate 'mainstream' affinities and align itself broadly with the American national identity – a force that prospers, again uniquely, in isolation to others and with pastimes that explicitly reject 'internationalism ... [and] remain confined to a world all their own'.[22]

### The 20–30%: what polls tell us about soccer's place in America

Public opinion is an appropriate domain for examining Markovits' thesis, for at least two reasons: insofar as culture may be defined as 'a system of inherited conceptions expressed in symbolic forms by means of which men communicate, perpetuate and develop their knowledge about and their attitudes toward life',[23] probability surveys can cast a reasonably wide and representative light on such meanings; two, polls of Americans on individualism and the role of government are often cited as among the more powerful evidence in exceptionalism's defense.[24] The problem is that there appear to be no publicly usable, nationally representative survey data devoted solely to soccer and few related at all to sports. What one is left with are questions embedded within the context of wide-ranging interviews on social, political and lifestyle topics. While this poses limitations, the argument for their analysis is that they may better represent soccer's 'true' position within American society since it seems possible that any sports-specific survey would confront particularities in non-response bias (e.g. gender) and, given its timing, may be inclined to overstate (or understate) the sport's salience and intensity.

That American interest in soccer has overwhelmingly been gauged by stadium attendances and television ratings – the latter, in Markovits and Hellerman's terms, being 'all important', the ultimate arbiter that will determine the 'success or failure of soccer to attain the level of culture in the United States'[25] speaks to the bias given in *Offside* to the commercial aspects of the sport. Yet, where such a focus on crowds and coverage may offer insight into Americans as consumers, it indicates little in terms of soccer's place in the broader social fabric. National polls and academic surveys, with all their potential sources of error, are at least as worthy of an implement for measuring a country's 'level of sports culture' as Nielsen ratings (a near-monopolistic indicator that faces little transparent scrutiny), gate receipts or who is on the Jim Rome Show.

A search of 'soccer' in the online iPoll archives of the Roper Center for Public Opinion Research at the University of Connecticut yielded 135 questions as of this writing asked at different intervals. The earliest – *Have you ever gone to a soccer game?* – appears in a Gallup Poll conducted in early February 1950. For the record, 16% from an approximate random sample of 1500 said that they had – roughly the same proportion who told interviewers they had written their member of Congress recently and opposed US efforts to build a hydrogen bomb.

The next questions do not appear until a generation later. In 1974, a year before Pelé's arrival with the New York Cosmos, 8% of Americans said they were 'more interested' in soccer than 'a couple of years ago'; 12% said their interest was unchanged (Figure 1).

By September of 1975, the proportions were 9 and 13%, respectively. Thereafter, and until 1984, the Roper Organization repeated their *interest* question but replaced the retrospective phrasing of *more ... than* with an ordinal scale in the present tense: *Now here is a list of some spectator sports. Would you go down that list, and for each one tell me whether it is something you're very interested in following, or moderately interested in following, or something you're not interested in following ... soccer.* Coinciding with the life cycle of the first NASL, the question picked up a similar dynamic among the broader public: in March of 1977, 14% told Harris they were 'very' or 'moderately' interested in the game; five years later, this increased substantially to 27%, before falling down again to 19% in the league's final season.

The lack of consistent questions, fielded at consistent intervals, complicates any ability to discern trends. At the same time, we can get a reasonable handle on public sentiment by stringing together those that are closely worded. The Gallup Organization, starting in 1990, began to ask Americans about their interest in the game, modifying Roper's question from *interested in following* to simply asking whether one is *very, somewhat, not too or not at all interested in soccer.* More than a fifth said they were 'very' or 'somewhat' interested, reaching a peak of 35% in mid-June 2002,

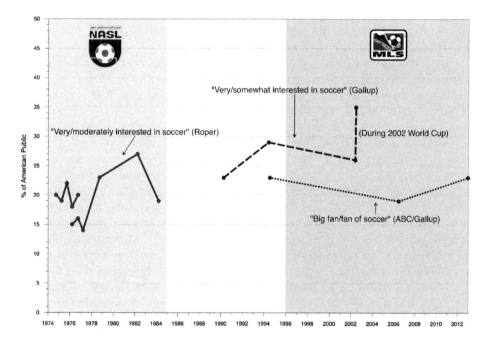

Figure 1.   Trends in American interest in soccer and the World Cup, 1974–2012.
Source: Compiled from The Roper Center for Public Opinion Research (iPoll Database), the University of Connecticut (www.ropercenter.uconn.edu).

when the question was last asked in the build-up to the men's World Cup quarterfinal against Germany in Ulsan. Several different questions have been asked about Americans' intention to watch, or their reactions to, the World Cup on television. Louis Harris and Associates, who tracked soccer attitudes closely in the months leading up to, and following, USA '94, found the highest proportion of potential watchers in the 44–47% range between October 1993 and May 1994. By contrast, Gallup found 38% saying, during the same interval, that they planned to watch 'some' of the matches or 'as much as possible'. Gallup repeated the question in both 2002 and 2006, finding 27 and 31%, respectively, falling into the same categories. In 2006, they picked up on an earlier question from a 1994 ABC News survey about whether Americans considered themselves 'fans' of soccer. The percentage identifying as such remained virtually unchanged through 2012, when 23% told Gallup that they were either 'a fan' or 'somewhat of a fan'.

The convergence of USA '94 and the home triumph of the WNT inspired a watershed for soccer polling in the 1990s. Three themes have since been apparent. The first is that hosting the World Cup appears to have lifted soccer's visibility among the public. Harris found the proportion of Americans who had 'read or heard' about the tournament grow from 53% in October of 1993 to 73% in May 1994; a similar proportion in the 'read/heard' category (74%) held until the next tournament in France four years later. Moreover, Harris found just 13% in 1993 who knew that the US was hosting the event. When Pew asked a similar question in 2010, asking Americans whether they knew if the World Cup was being held in one of the four given countries, 63% correctly chose 'South Africa' from the list of responses. In 1998 and 2002, Pew found 38 and 31% of Americans, respectively, correctly identifying the team that had won the tournament. In 2007, Pew asked if Americans could identify the 'the most popular sport worldwide'; 65% chose 'soccer', higher than the proportion who could identify Nancy Pelosi as the then-current Speaker of the House (59%).

The second theme is that the WNT has, at least to date, generated spikes in public attention. The best evidence is provided by Pew's News Interest Index which, at five intervals between 1999 and 2011, asked about the World Cup. As the brown line in Figure 1 demonstrates, the crests appear in 1999 and 2011, during the women's tournament. The enthusiasm for the WNT was also captured at a high-water mark by a series of questions on a July 1999 Fox News/Opinion Dynamics poll which found, among other things, that: women's soccer was preferred over men's soccer by a 3-to-1 margin; that 70% of Americans would support a proposed women's soccer league; and that 63% had seen Brandi Chastain tear her jersey off in Pasadena following the historic triumph over China. This compares to 61% who agreed after the Brazil–Italy men's final in 1994 that 'there should be a professional soccer league in the United States' and 47% saying they would be 'very' or 'somewhat' likely to watch its matches on television. Harris instead asked *Would you like there to be a professional soccer league in the US shown on TV, or don't you care?* and found 29% saying they 'would like' such a league. A month into the inaugural season of MLS, *US News and World Report* found 26% of Americans saying their interest in professional soccer 'increased a lot' or 'somewhat increased' over the last five years.

As the *or don't you care* appended to the Harris question suggests, the final theme is the ambivalence of pollsters. Consider a question asked by ABC News in July 1994: *Which of these four phrases best describes your view of soccer?* 'Interesting' was the plurality choice of 35%; another 22% selected 'exciting'.

Thirty-five per cent, on the other hand, chose one of the two remaining options: 'big bore' or 'on the dull side'. Out of the 135 soccer questions retrieved from the Roper database, 34 contained a variant on the term 'interest' – about one-fourth of all items. By comparison, the term 'interest' appears in just 11% of the questions about golf, 9% of those about gridiron, 8% of the baseball questions and less than 1% of those about auto racing.

The data, in sum, leave us with two conclusions about soccer's place among the American public. First, since the early days of the original NASL, anywhere from 20 to 30% of Americans have consistently showed interest in soccer or identified as 'fans'. Second, at critical junctures like a World Cup, interest may exceed 30%, sometimes significantly. The narrative of soccer's precarious position in American society has been so dominant that it has led, in some instances, to poll questions that have sought to do little other than reinforce that narrative. This overshadows the empirical evidence that, at least across similarly worded, closed-ended questions, soccer has held, for at least three decades, a consistent position among a significant proportion of the American public.

## American 'Sports Space': How real is it?

The pessimist might see the 20–30% as confirmation of soccer's inability to break-through to a majority; the optimist might ask whether anything that consistently compels the interest of one in five Americans – and, depending on the quality of the national teams, as many as one in three – is really so marginal. But the overall sta-bility of soccer's place among the public, over time, leads naturally to the core ques-tions raised in Markovits' work about its alleged ephemerality and exclusion from the 'mainstream'. Although the idea of a uniquely American terrain dominated by a 'Big Three and One-Half' is, as Waddington and Roderick write, 'superficially attractive',[26] the critical test is whether it has any empirical validity. Are soccer fans indeed an exceptional, transient and isolated fan community?

The General Social Survey (GSS) in 2008 and the 2012 *USA Today*/Gallup Poll offer a chance to look at this in detail, from different perspectives: of Americans who indicate that a particular sport is the one they *watch on TV most frequently* and of those who consider themselves *a fan of the sport or not*. The combination of defi-nitions is useful in that TV watching, a self-reported behavioural measure, offers the purest test of the exceptionalism thesis, as Markovits and Hellerman render it, and declaring oneself a 'fan' is a measure of group attachment. The GSS format forces respondents to prioritize the sport of greatest viewing interest; Gallup's format allows fans of multiple sports to crossover as they wish. Both surveys include a variety of sports to which soccer interest can be compared; for simplicity's sake, the GSS analysis includes six – gridiron, baseball, basketball, hockey, auto racing (labelled 'nascartv')[27] and golf; the Gallup analysis includes five (each of the above minus golf).

To address the question of soccer's alleged isolation, a two-step process was taken for analysing the data: first, matrices were constructed based on tetrachoric correlations between the variables in the two surveys; second, a factor analysis was performed on each matrix, respectively. The factor analysis is particularly useful for assessing the 'sports space' hypothesis, in that the results can lend themselves to a simple visualization of how closely individual sports relate to one another in terms of their underlying social and attitudinal structures. Therefore, if the exceptionalist framework has validity, the results should reveal two things: (1) gridiron, baseball, basketball and hockey should load heavily on the same dimension and be clustered near one another in the same quadrant of 'space'; (2) soccer should be distant from this cluster.

Considering the correlations first, what we find is that the evidence for soccer's isolation – whether as TV spectacle or fan nation – is weak. Watching soccer correlates ($p < .05$) with watching basketball (.41), hockey (.31) and baseball (.26). The correlation between watching soccer and gridiron, however, is negative (−.15). Similarly, soccer fandom correlates with hockey (.43) and basketball (.36) fandom. The correlation between soccer and baseball fans is weaker (.22), but still positive. Put another way, being a viewer or 'fan' of soccer does not appear to preclude being a 'fan' of other major American sports.

The results of the factor analysis (constrained to two factors and rotated using orthogonal varimax criteria) appear in Figure 2. The results underscore the point about TV watching: soccer is proximal both to basketball and hockey and loads on the same factor as baseball and gridiron. Rather, it is the two individual sports – auto racing and golf – that appear distinct in television land among the 'couch potato' set. Where soccer appears to be more distinct is as a *fan community*. As displayed on the right-sided graph in Figure 2, gridiron, baseball and basketball cluster near one another in first factor 'space', in a fashion that would be consistent with *Off-side's* rendering. But, contrary to exceptionalist expectations, both soccer and hockey load substantially on the second factor, suggesting that the two, at least on this measure, have claim to being the 'One-Half'. More importantly, if any sport can stake a credible claim for 'exceptionalism' in the US cultural atmosphere, it is not soccer, but auto racing. It not only fails to load on either factor as a fan community, but appears to be almost diametrically opposite of soccer and basketball as a television spectacle.

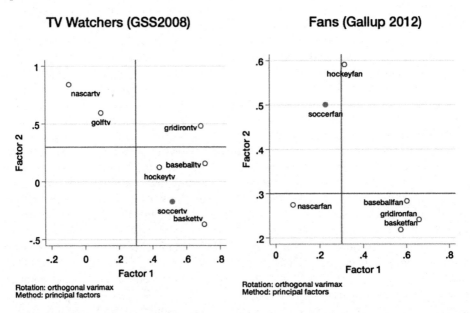

Figure 2.   Assessing American 'Sports Space' in two-factor dimensions: TV watchers and fans compared.

Thus, the cultural dynamics of American sports not only appear to be different from what the exceptionalist framework has suggested, but that any 'sports space' should be taken as complex and sensitive to potential change. Soccer may be more distinct as a 'fan' culture than as a 'couch potato' culture, a point *Offside* misses, but in neither case does the sport appear as marginal as Markovits' work implies. In terms of TV, it is auto racing and golf that are the outliers; watching soccer is akin to watching basketball and other team sports. In terms of self-identification, being an American 'soccer fan' is no more 'unique' than being a 'hockey fan': distinct from a 'Big Three', perhaps, but more attached to the 'mainstream' than a clearly distinctive fan community like those who follow auto racing.

## Are American soccer fans 'Mostly Mozart' goers?

In *Offside*, the authors write:

America's 'soccer constituency' *excepting those of specific ethnic or immigrant groups*, tends to be mostly suburban, white, fairly well educated and relatively affluent ... the typical member of this 'constituency' ... finds a supposed antithesis to the Big Three and One Half in soccer: less emphasis on competition ... non-violence, co-educational participation ... and little partisanship ... soccer provides provides identification with a quasi-elitist notion of sophistication by way of internationalism, multiculturalism, and iconoclastic nonconformity ... hence, as opposed to the stereotypical American male sports fans who supposedly argue, beers in hand, about the NFL or baseball from their bar stools, stereotypical American soccer fans ... supposedly segue from a discussion of Mozart to one on Maradona over cappuccino at the cafe or smoothies at the health club.[28]

Table 1 summarizes the results of several binary regression models that were run from the GSS and *USA Today*/Gallup Poll predicting the viewers and fans of different sports. What distinguishes those who follow soccer is Hispanic identification, living in a mid-Atlantic state and being foreign born. Like those of most other sports, soccer fans are more likely to be male; like hockey fans, they appear to be younger. Gridiron fans are disproportionately male and its viewers are US born; baseball fans older, whiter and also domestic. Basketball fans are disproportionately black, Asian, urban and mid-Western. Fans of hockey are also regionally concentrated, often in Eastern urban centres, and are marginally whiter. Auto racing fans are disproportionately found in rural areas.

The findings dispel two things: the notion that the American soccer community is elitist and that class is a significant predictor. Neither education nor income have any discernible linear effect on being either a viewer of fan of soccer – and, it is important to note, this finding holds when the same model is run with a subset of white non-Hispanics (WNH). Rather, class is the variable that divides two of the 'mainstream' sports – gridiron and baseball – from auto racing; the remaining sports appear to be defined more by race, ethnicity and urbanity. There also appears to be a nativist/acculturative line that divides gridiron/baseball from soccer in which race/ethnicity could be playing an indirect role. One gathers that if Mozart or smoothies is to be had over any sports-related conversation in the United States, chances are that conversation is going to be about baseball or gridiron, respectively.

What is important to underscore is that, as the factor analysis suggested, soccer viewers/fans share a number of characteristics with other 'typical' Americans. Like baseball fans, soccer supporters attend church more frequently than non-fans. Like

Table 1. Social characteristics of American sports viewers and fans.

| | Soccer viewers | Soccer 'fans' | Gridiron 'fans' | Baseball 'fans' | Basketball 'fans' | Hockey 'fans' | Auto racing 'fans' |
|---|---|---|---|---|---|---|---|
| Significant social characteristics | Hispanic, male, mid-Atlantic and east South Central state, less likely to be 50–64 | Hispanic, male, more urban, East, less likely to be 50–64, Midwest or South | Male, marginally Black or 'Other' race | White, East, Mid-west, Male, marginally 65 and older, less likely to be non-Hispanic Black | Black, Asian, marginally 'Other' race, urban, male and Midwestern | East, more urban, male, marginally White, less likely to be above 50, South or West | Male, more rural |
| Effect of education* | Non-linear. Marginally more likely to have 12–14 years of education | Non-linear. Marginally less likely to be HS graduate | Positive | Positive | Non-linear. Marginally less likely to be HS graduate | None | None |
| Effect of income* | None | Non-linear. Strongest in middle (30–75 k) income groups. | Positive. Higher in all income categories above 30 k | Positive. Highest in 100 k and above categories | None | Non-linear. Strongest in higher (100–150 k) income group | Negative. Lower in all income groups above 30 k |
| Effect of church attendance* | Positive | Positive | Non-linear. More likely to attend monthly | Positive | None | None | Non-linear. More likely to attend monthly |
| Effect of being married* | Positive | Positive | Positive | None | None | None | None |
| Effect of having school-age kids* | None | None | None | None | None | None | None |
| Effect of being US born (viewers only) | Negative | – | Viewers only: Positive* | Viewers only: Positive* | None | None | None |

*Controlled effect, meaning the variable was tested in the presence of other factors, including age, race, Hispanic, male, urban density and region. All effects noted as 'positive' or 'negative' met $p < 0.05$ threshold for significance tests; those noted as 'marginally' met $p < 0.10$ threshold.

gridiron fans, they're more likely to be married. And like those who follow all other sports, having children appears to have no impact on their interests; one can presume that, for those who do have children, their ventures into the sport preceded their ventures into parenthood. This calls into question the Soccer Mom/Dad image, at least insofar as youth participation and professional sports fandom are conflated into any 'soccer constituency' monolith. The tendency to conflate leads to one of the bigger specification errors in writing about soccer in America, for if the 'specific ethnic and immigrant groups' are treated as the exception, rather than an integral element of the 'mainstream', one is likely to presume that the white mom in the black SUV (or *the Onion's* Brad Janovich) *is* the 'soccer constituency'.

## 'Smug, Liberal Elites'?

The broader implication of the 'soccer constituency' myth is that whiteness and class produce a certain set of attitudes: an effete leftist worldview that favours multiculturalism and multilateralism – and is otherwise disdainful of patriotic expressions and 'mainstream' culture. We can evaluate this by regressing soccer fandom/interest on ideology in various surveys to determine the extent to which soccer is favoured by, as one conservative commentator put it during the 2014 World Cup, 'smug, liberal elites'.[29]

The results indicate that, regardless of whether ideology is regressed alone or in conjunction with the other socio-economic variables in the previous models, it has an expected negative effect. Yet, as Figure 3 demonstrates, the impact is not always linear nor, statistically speaking, powerful enough to eliminate the possibility, in some instances, of the effect being a function of chance or random error. Put another way, self-identified liberalism is a weak and inconsistent predictor of whether or not one identifies as a soccer watcher or fan, which makes it difficult to ascertain what impact, if any, it is having on the popular culture of the sport.

For example, in the Harris Poll from 1994, 'liberal' has a marginally greater impact on being more interested in the World Cup than being 'conservative'; in the GSS, in fact, the ideological category that has the largest influence on soccer watching is 'slightly conservative' (although difference between it and the other groups is minor.) The 2002 Gallup Poll, which asks about 'interest' in soccer, demonstrates the strongest, most consistent evidence of an ideology effect (upper left graph in Figure 3). In the 2012 USA Today/Gallup Poll, it is instead the 'very' liberal category that has the demonstrable impact on being a 'fan'. The important contrast, from a statistical perspective, is between those who are 'very' liberal and those who are 'very' conservative. If a common theme emerges across all four surveys, and across time, it is not that soccer has a consistently left-wing bent, but that those farthest to the right consistently have the lowest likelihood of interest, watching or fandom.

It should be noted further that the differences between left and right are more apparent than the differences between Democrats and Republicans. When partisanship is tested in place of ideology in each of the four surveys, only in one instance – again, the 2002 Gallup Poll – do noteworthy effects appear (in the direction of the Democrats.) The reason may boil down to timing or the question wording; not only is the 2002 Gallup Poll the only one of the four to measure 'interest' in soccer, but it is also the only one to accommodate a full valence range of positive ('very') and negative ('not at all') response categories. One can hypothesize, therefore, that the extreme response categories tapped into the popular debate over whether the sport is

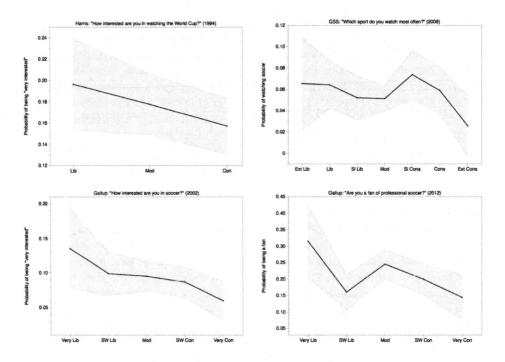

Figure 3. The marginal effects of ideology on American soccer interest/fandom, 1994–2012.

'exciting' or 'boring' – and it is this faultline, perhaps more than any other, that teases out ideological and partisan differences.

The oftentimes inconclusive relationship that we see between ideology, partisanship and soccer is likely due to the influence of independents and moderates. While this lends weight to the notion of soccer fans as feeling 'little partisanship', it is worth noting that the independent label is common across all American sports fans – and Americans generally. Independents constitute a higher proportion of hockey fans than soccer fans (43–38%); the differences between soccer and baseball (36%), auto racing (36%) and gridiron (35%) are slight. When 'leaners' (labelled as such because they tell pollsters that they are 'independent', but then, after probing, 'lean' towards one of the parties) are allocated to party bins, auto racing fans emerge as the most Republican (47%). But the only fan communities that appear to be consistent partisans are those Americans who watch, and consider themselves fans of, basketball. All things being equal, basketball watchers and fans manifest the most clearly partisan affiliations in American sports culture – towards the Democrats.

### Are the Americans unique?

Although the enthusiasm for soccer/football in Western Europe is often assumed from across the Atlantic, getting a handle on the degree to which the sport penetrates contemporary European society poses a similar data challenge as in the United States. A rough gauge is offered in Figure 4, which juxtaposes the responses to two comparably written questions asked in 1990 and 2013 by the Eurobarometer project and YouGov, respectively.

In both instances, respondents are asked whether they are 'interested' in the game: the Eurobarometer *whether you are personally interested in football*, and YouGov asking *How interested, if at all, are you in football?* What is apparent is that the 'world's game' is hardly a universal passion: only in Spain, Italy and Germany can it be said that football followers constitute a majority of the general population. What is also apparent is that football following may be declining in parts of the continent, most notably in the Netherlands, the UK and France, where roughly a third of the public express interest in the game. The French case is curious when juxtaposed to the 20–30% in the US, given that *le foot* is considered to be the nation's most popular pastime in a presumably less crowded 'sports space'. As in the US, available trend data in France suggest that World Cup performances produce fluctuations in popular interest, leaving us to ask, again, whether the alleged fickleness of the American supporter is anything that should be deemed unique.[30]

What is also curious is that, for whatever habits and orientations that may distinguish American soccer fans at the domestic level, such orientations appear undistinguished at the global level. The International Social Survey Programme included a 'Sports and Leisure' module in 2007, in which publics from 36 countries (yielding a total of 49,729 respondents) were asked about their use of free time, involvement in game-related activities as well as their social and political participation. Soccer enthusiasts could be distinguished in two ways: one, by identifying soccer as the sport they *watch on TV most frequently*; two, by saying it was *the sport or physical*

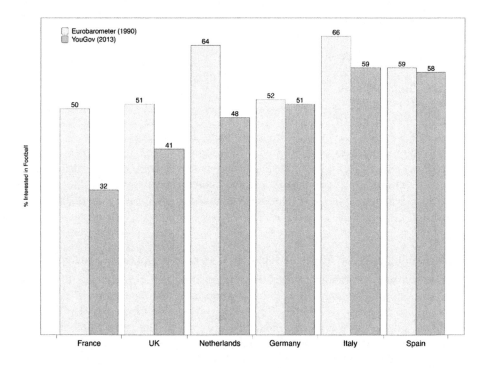

Figure 4. Percentage of European publics 'Very' or 'Fairly Interested' in Football, 1990–2013.

*activity [they] take part in most frequently.* Because the number of players in the survey is relatively small – and because the crux of the argument rests on the spectator sport – the focus here is on the watchers.

What the ISSP reveals (regression results summarized in Table 2) is that only one of these variables – suburban living – clearly matters in explaining soccer watching in the United States. And even on that measure, Americans are not alone: soccer fandom is also found disproportionately in Australian, British, Japanese, Korean and Swedish suburbs, among others. On all other measures, the American fan shows no discernible characteristics: neither highly religious or secular,[31] neither rich nor poor. Whereas in Australia, Cyprus, Finland, Mexico and several Asian countries, football watching can be linked with higher status and educational attainment, and in France and South Africa with the 'proletarian' status that *Offside* claims is evident 'elsewhere in the world';[32] it is unaffected by either variable in the American case. Class does not shape American soccer fandom. Nor does it shape the fans in 17 other countries in the study.

On an international scale, soccer watchers in the United States are also among the less politicized. Again, this is not unique. Of the 34 countries in the ISSP, the publics of 25 revealed statistically significant positive relationships between soccer watching and interest in politics; the United States, along with Australia, Japan and the Dominican Republic, were among the few for whom there was no relationship. Further, another 12 publics revealed significant positive relationships between activism in a political organization or party and soccer watching. The Americans were not among them. Thus, relative to Israelis, Bulgarians, Austrians, Koreans and British fans – where soccer watching and politics appear to be intertwined – those in the United States appear benign.

When Americans are compared to others in terms of their self-placement on a left–right ideological scale, one sees that the fans of 13 other countries also hew to the left of their publics. In this context, the American fan appears similar to the British fan, occupying a position that is to the left of an already left-leaning public (Figure 5). Both are in the same relative company as those in countries where soccer would be considered dominant (as indicated by the larger markers, whose size reflects the proportion of the public who say soccer is the sport they watch 'most frequently') – South Korea and Uruguay – and appear less conservative than the average supporter in Mexico or Germany. Through this lens, as well as the demonstrable direct effect of religiosity on fandom, it is the Australians and Austrians that appear 'exceptional', at least on the left and right, respectively, with the Japanese, Belgians, Croatians, Swiss and Dominicans making their own claims for unique designation.

## Mainstreaming and the future of soccer in a stratified, polarizing society

While *Offside* and its attendant papers have been important contributions to the literature, promoting discussion about the US game and helping identify the historical factors in its struggles, continuing to position American soccer in the binary of exceptionalism flies in the face of contemporary reality. The central problem is that soccer's place, particularly in the US, cannot be attributable to a single, 'silver bullet', deterministic variable (class), but is instead the product of a confluence of social, generational, economic and attitudinal factors. Like the Lipset/Rokkan thesis upon which it is modelled, and the Toquevillean mythology upon which it is based,

Table 2. Soccer watchers in the United States in comparative perspective.

| | Urbanization | Living in a sub-urb | Self-perceived status or income* | Education | Religiosity | Politicization (interest and activism) |
|---|---|---|---|---|---|---|
| Where effect increases the likelihood of watching football | Australia, Finland, Great Britain, Ireland, Israel, Japan, New Zealand, Norway, Philippines, South Korea, Sweden and Taiwan | Australia, Cyprus, Great Britain, Japan, South Africa, South Korea, Sweden, Taiwan and United States | Argentina, Australia, Croatia, Cyprus, Dominican Republic, Finland, Israel, Great Britain*, Latvia, Mexico, Philippines, South Korea and Taiwan | Australia, Cyprus, Dominican Republic, Finland, Hungary, Japan, Mexico, Philippines, South Korea and Taiwan | Australia, Austria | Argentina, Belgium-Flanders, Bulgaria, Croatia, Cyprus, Great Britain, Israel, Latvia, Slovak, South Africa, South Korea and Sweden |
| Where effect decreases the likelihood of watching football | Argentina, Austria, Belgium-Flanders, Croatia and Slovak | Belgium-Flanders | South Africa | France | Argentina, Bulgaria, Cyprus, Czech, Finland, Ireland, Latvia, Poland, Russia, Slovak, Switzerland and Uruguay | None |
| Where the variable has no direct effect on watching football | United States and 17 others | 25 others | United States* and 17 others | United States and 24 others | United States and 21 others | Australia, Dominican Republic, Japan, Philippines and United States |

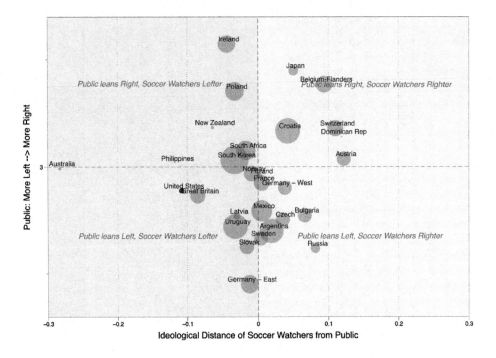

Figure 5.   Left–right ideological distance between soccer watchers and general publics.

an exceptionalist approach to American sports may have had traction at a time when the US was less diverse, had less technology and more cultural homogeneity; without more history, we can never been certain. What we do know is that framing the American experience as culturally unique at a time when the game is both expanding and intertwining itself with foreign observers and global institutions is a challenge to credibility. In soccer, as in politics, it has become clear: American exceptionalism has run its course.

   Ultimately, the failure of the idea – putting aside the simple fact that there are few indications that soccer watchers in the US are different in any significant way from many others around the world – lies in its obsession with outliers: anything that is 'exceptional', by definition, cannot accommodate normal. This is how, throughout modern history, the notion has served odd political bedfellows. For foreign critics, from Stalin to Putin, American exceptionalism has been a vehicle for questioning Western capitalist hegemony; for domestic politicians, from Reagan to Romney, it has been a call-to-cultural-arms – a reaffirmation of identity in a complex, changing and insecure world. More pertinent to the argument here is that exceptionalism, in politically minded soccer discourses, has come around to offer an ideological foundation for harbouring suspicions about the 'world's game' and its alleged 'liberal' agenda. As one conservative blogger writes:

> The liberal media have always been uncomfortable with 'American exceptionalism' – the belief that the United States is unique among nations, a leader and a force for good. And they are no happier with America's rejection of soccer than with its rejection of socialism.

Hence Americans are 'xenophobic,' 'isolated' and lacking in understanding for other nations and their passion for 'the planetary pastime,' as Time magazine put it. But, they are confident, as America becomes more Hispanic, the nation will have to give in and adopt the immigrants' game. On the other hand, the media assure the public that soccer is already 'America's Game,' and Americans are enthusiastically anticipating the World Cup, even though the numbers don't bear that contention out.

So, every four years they return with renewed determination to force soccer's square peg in the round hole of American culture.[33]

Exceptionalism, thus, provides a reductive, ready-to-wear label that perpetuates the myth of a homogeneous, contained, sovereign-and-defiant-in-the-face-of-globalization culture. This, one can argue, is why the narrative of soccer's 'failure', whether sarcastically in *The Onion* or literally in *Offside*, has become so intransigent: only when the American game does something 'extraordinary' – winning the World Cup, for example, or displacing a made-for-TV corporate hegemon like gridiron – will it ever 'arrive'. Exceptionalism has not only created an intellectual paradox and conceptual confusion for soccer's observers; it has imposed a virtually impregnable barrier for the game's practitioners.

In the end, exceptionalism runs head-on not just into empirical reality, but into the sport's immigrant and multicultural legacy at the grassroots – and the global variables that then, as now, have had the greater influence on its trajectory.[34] To adhere to such an approach in American soccer is to paper over these variables; the racial and ethnic stratification and nativist exclusion that continue to define it, and all US sports, must come to the forefront of research. For scholarship to reveal the game's rich past and reach towards its organic truths, it must reflect – much as Rogers Smith has done with Tocqueville – American soccer not as 'unique' (or at least any more 'unique' than, say, the Japanese or Australian versions), but as a cultural venue in which multiple traditions, groups and ideas collide.[35] As recent authors have begun to argue, it is this lens that offers greater promise because the median point where soccer's WASPish, collegiate and immigrant/Latino histories converge is precisely what is making it a 'mainstream' cultural practice in the US – and why it is now, and has for many and for some time, been a part of everyday civic life.

## Disclosure statement

No potential conflict of interest was reported by the author.

## Notes

1. Markovits, 'The Other "American Exceptionalism"'; and Markovits and Hellerman, *Offside.*
2. Kohut and Stokes, *America Against the World*; and Fukuyama, *America at the Crossroads.*
3. Murray, *American Exceptionalism*, 40.
4. Szymanski and Zimbalist, *National Pastime*, 1.
5. Veseth, *Globaloney 2.0*, 102, 112.c.
6. Lechner, *Globalization*, 46–8.
7. Abrams, 'Inhibited but not "Crowded Out"'; and Waddington and Roderick, 'American Exceptionalism'.
8. Collins, 'National Sports and Other Myths', 359–60.
9. Scott, 'From NASL to MLS', 833–6.

10. Buffington, 'Us and Them', 149.
11. Duerr, 'Becoming Apple Pie', 143.
12. Keyes, 'Making the Mainstream'.
13. e.g. Markovits and Hellerman, 'Women's Soccer in the United States'.
14. Markovits and Hellerman, *Offside*, 7, 46.
15. Ibid., 8–9.
16. Ibid., 10.
17. Ibid., 10.
18. Ibid., 15, 53.
19. Ibid., 15–16.
20. Lispet and Rokkan, *Party Systems and Voter Alignments*; and Mair, 'Myths of Electoral Change'.
21. Markovits and Hellerman, Offside, 28–33.
22. Ibid., 49.
23. Geertz, *The Interpretation of Cultures,* 89.
24. See Citrin, 'Political Culture', although Kohut and Stokes arrive at different conclusions.
25. Markovits and Hellerman, *Offside*, 131.
26. Waddington and Roderick, 'American Exceptionalism', 33.
27. NASCAR refers to the National Association for Stock Car Auto Racing.
28. Markovits and Hellerman, *Offside*, 204. Emphasis added.
29. Goldberg, 'The Anti-American Pastime'.
30. See the August 2012 study of trends by l'Institut Français d'Opinion Publique (IFOP) (2012), in which the authors ask 'La France, pays de football?' and find, since 2003, that French interest in the game has typically sat at around a third of the population.
31. This, at first glance, appears to be in contradiction with the findings from the GSS above, which administers the US portion of the ISSP. The reason why the effect is present in one and not the other boils down to sample size: the domestic GSS contains more than twice as many respondents ($N = 3559$) and the ISSP ($N = 1536$). The direction of religiosity in the ISSP is, as in the GSS, positive, but with fewer respondents, the effect is insufficiently strong so as to prevent one from being certain it is not attributable to error or chance.
32. Markovits and Hellerman, *Offside,* 28.
33. Philbin, 'Media Make Selling Soccer a Goal'.
34. Giulianotti and Robertson, 'Sport and Globalization'; and Giulianotti and Robertson, 'Mapping the Global Football Field'.
35. Smith, 'Beyond Tocqueville, Myrdal and Hartz'.

## ORCID

*Christian Collet* ⓘ http://orcid.org/0000-0003-1611-1007

## References

Abrams, Nathan D. "Inhibited but Not "Crowded out"': The Strange Fate of Soccer in the United States'. *The International Journal of the History of Sport* 12, no. 3 (1995): 1–17.
Buffington, Daniel Taylor. 'Us and Them: U.S. Ambivalence toward the World Cup and American Nationalism'. *Journal of Sport & Social Issues* 36, no. 2 (2012): 135–54.
Citrin, Jack. 'Political Culture'. In *Understanding America: The Anatomy of an Exceptional Nation*, ed. Peter Schuck and James Q. Wilson, 147–80. New York: PublicAffairs, 2008.
Collins, Sandra. 'National Sports and Other Myths: The Failure of US Soccer'. *Soccer and Society* 7, nos. 2–3 (2006): 353–63.
Département Opinion et Stratégies d'Entreprises. *Les français et le football.* [The French and Football]. Technical Report 68, l'Institut Français d'Opinion Publique, August 2012.
Duerr, Glen M. 'Becoming Apple Pie: Soccer as the Fifth Major Team Sport in the United States?' In *Soccer Culture in America: Essays on the World Sport in Red, White and Blue*, ed. Yuya Kiuchi, 121–42. Jefferson, NC: McFarland, 2014.

Fukuyama, Francis. *America at the Crossroads: Democracy, Power, and the Neoconservative Legacy*. New Haven, CT: Yale University Press, 2007.

Geertz, Clifford. *The Interpretation of Cultures: Selected Essays*. New York: Basic Books, 1973.

Giulianotti, Richard, and Roland Robertson. 'Mapping the Global Football Field: A Sociological Model of Transnational Forces within the World Game'. *The British Journal of Sociology* 63, no. 2 (2012): 216–40.

Giulianotti, Richard, and Roland Robertson. 'Sport and Globalization: Transnational Dimensions'. *Global Networks* 7, no. 2 (2007): 107–12.

Goldberg, Bernard. 'The Anti-American Pastime'. *National Review Online*, July 8, 2014. http://www.nationalreview.com/article/382153/anti-american-pastime-bernard-goldberg.

Keyes, David. 'Making the Mainstream: The Domestication of American Soccer'. In *Soccer Culture in America: Essays on the World Sport in Red, White and Blue*, ed. Yuya Kiuchi, 9–24. Jefferson, NC: McFarland, 2014.

Kohut, Andrew, and Bruce Stokes. *America against the World: How We Are Different and Why We Are Disliked*. New York: Times Books, 2006.

Lechner, Frank J. *Globalization: The Making of World Society*. West Sussex: Wiley, 2009.

Lipset, Seymour Martin, and Stein Rokkan. *Party Systems and Voter Alignments: Cross-national Perspectives*. Toronto: The Free Press, 1967.

Mair, Peter. 'Myths of Electoral Change and the Survival of Traditional Parties'. *European Journal of Political Research* 24, no. 2 (1993): 121–33.

Markovits, Andrei S. 'The Other "American Exceptionalism" – Why is There No Soccer in the United States?'. *Praxis International* 2 (1988): 125–50.

Markovits, Andrei S., and Steven L. Hellerman. *Offside: Soccer and American Exceptionalism*. Princeton: Princeton University Press, 2001.

Markovits, Andrei S., and Steven L. Hellerman. 'Women's Soccer in the United States: Yet Another American "Exceptionalism"'. *Soccer and Society* 4, no. 2–3 (2003): 14–29.

Murray, Charles. *American Exceptionalism: An Experiment in History*. Washington, DC: AEI Press, 2013.

Philbin, Matthew. 'Media Make Selling Soccer a Goal.' *Newsbusters.Org*, June 9, 2010. http://newsbusters.org/blogs/matthew-philbin/2010/06/09/media-make-selling-soccer-goal.

Scott, Ian. 'From NASL to MLS: Transnational Culture, Exceptionalism and Britain's Part in American Soccer's Coming of Age'. *The Journal of Popular Culture* 44, no. 4 (2011): 831–53.

Smith, Rogers. 'Beyond Tocqueville, Myrdal and Hartz: The Multiple Traditions in America'. *The American Political Science Review* 87, no. 3 (1993): 549–66.

Szymanski, Stefan, and Andrew S. Zimbalist. *National Pastime: How Americans Play Baseball and the Rest of the World Plays Soccer*. Washington, DC: Brookings Institution Press, 2006.

Veseth, Michael. *Globaloney 2.0: The Crash of 2008 and the Future of Globalization*. Lanham: Rowman & Littlefield, 2010.

Waddington, Ivan, and Martin Roderick. 'American Exceptionalism: Soccer and American Football'. *The Sports Historian* 16, no. 1 (1996): 42–63.

# Transforming soccer to achieve solidarity: 'Golombiao' in Colombia

Ricardo Duarte Bajaña

This essay takes as a case study 'the Golombiao': a government strategy of the Colombian state (South America), which aims to transform the practice of recreational soccer to promote coexistence, social participation and gender equity in armed conflict zones. The practice of 'Golombiao' is similar to soccer but some of its rules are formulated by the people who play it. Winning depends on several factors, among them, the respect for the collective rules. I propose to compare this government strategy with the conceptual apparatus of bioethics. Bioethics is a bridge between the sciences and other disciplines used to understand and propose alternatives to specific cases where life is threatened. Bioethics has some relations with the objectives proposed by the Golombiao. This government strategy defines life as a process of reflection and of collective action, and also seeks the construction of community solidarity using the transformation of sport as a tool.

## Golombiao in armed conflict zones in Colombia

Colombia is located in the North Western tip of South America. This is a country of countless assets; however, her citizens have endured several decades of violence. Trying to assess the actual scope of the violence brought on by the armed conflicts with the participation of the guerrilla, paramilitarism, drug trafficking and the army will be an arduous task. According to the Informe General del Grupo de Memoria Histórica (General Report of the Historical Memory Group) published in 2013, the collection and processing of the information pertaining to this armed conflict started out late in time. There are many factors to this delay: in essence, the armed conflict was underestimated, and there was no political will to acknowledge and deal with the issue. The armed conflict in Colombia accounts for approximately 220.000 casualties. 81.5% of the dead were civilians and 18.5% soldiers; this means that nearly eight out of ten victims were civilians.

'Golombiao' is a national strategy, as it is part of the Presidential Programme entitled Colombia Joven (Youth Colombia). This strategy was launched in 2003. It is based on the use of sports, play and recreation, aimed at 'bolstering protective environments for girls, boys, teenagers and young adults, to secure their development through the promotion of coexistence, social participation and gender equity' (Golombiao official website). This programme has been supported both technically and financially by UNICEF, the German Society for International Cooperation (GIZ), the Canadian International Development Agency (ACDI) and the Swedish

International Development Cooperation Agency (SIDA), in addition to other Colombian entities and organizations which have joined in as partners.

Golombiao is played like soccer, although there are some variables. The Golombiao game is divided into four periods[1]:

Period 1: two mixed teams and the game advisors meet in a large venue. They set the rules of the game. The rules of the game comprise technical agreements and coexistence agreements, such as: 'Every time a player from one team scores a goal, all the players from the opposing team will praise him/her'.[2]

Period 2: Both teams play the game, seeking to put into practice the rules agreed on in Period 1. The first goal scored by each team at every period must be scored by a girl[3]; after that, all goals must be scored by taking turns: boy–girl–boy and all the players in both teams play; there is no Game Referee, but rather a Game Advisor. Since there is no referee, the players themselves must oversee that the rules are observed. In case a conflict arises, the advisors intervene. Meanwhile, one of the advisors writes a report detailing every event, inside and outside the field.

Period 3: When the game is over, the players from both teams get together with the advisors, in order to evaluate both their performance in the field, and the interaction with their supporters. The coexistence agreements are evaluated, since the rating process is a collective exercise, based on self-evaluation. Having complied with the established rules a score will be given to each team; the most outstanding team will then be recognized. There are no winners, no losers; only teams with an outstanding coexistence and social participation score.

Period 4: When the game is over, the participants lead complementary activities to deepen the dialogue and the reflection regarding the possible issues that convened the game, such as workshops, movie forums, training and encounter seminars on coexistence, social participation and gender equity.

## Conceptual apparatus of bioethics

My idea is to analyse the Golombiao through the conceptual apparatus of bioethics. Bioethics is a bridge between the sciences and other disciplines used to understand and propose alternatives to specific cases where life is threatened.

Bioethics takes into account the fact that every bioethical dilemma is unique and reacts to a particular context, or characteristics, needs and specific issues, which differ from the context of other population groups. Along the same lines, the theoretical constitution and the practice of Bioethics are viewed as an interdisciplinary field, meaning that multiple dilemmas are dealt with from the perspective of different disciplines, when life and the quality of life are at risk. The scope of Bioethics surpasses all particular professional barriers.[4]

Pluralism is yet another Bioethics watershed, where issues and alternatives are not intended to be framed within any specific tradition; instead, it formulates problems and answers in an open-ended manner, to be rationally analysed by individuals with divergent viewpoints about reality, and the different value systems.[5] From this stance, it is possible to acknowledge the different conflicting perspectives and present several alternatives to the same dilemma.

In the Bioethics context, the deliberation process empowers individuals to bring forth their proposals, and build the tools to open communication channels which will facilitate both the negotiation and the dialogue, in the understanding that this communication channel is a dialectical synthesis of the ideas and criteria which will derive into joint proposals, enabling the production of coexistence and social participation elements.

Furthermore, Bioethics takes root in the principle of the autonomy[6] of human beings, their decision-making abilities, and their skills to become organized and take action. In this regard and although individuals become organized with a sense of solidarity, they still are greatly responsible for building the freedoms and opportunities to improve their quality of life. Quality of life cannot be narrowed down to a mere evaluation of economic conditions; on the other hand, it enhances the possibilities human beings have to work, improve and develop their capacities according to their needs, within a framework of freedom,[7] opportunities and participation.[8,9]

## Explaining Golombiao from the conceptual apparatus of bioethics

Bioethics as a conceptual device to explain the community sport has been used in previous papers.[10] The explanation of Bioethics suggests that soccer played as Golombiao promotes a process of social development that dovetails from the philosophy of modern sports. Modern sports focus on performance, production and achievement[11,12]; in fact, some social sports projects turn into championships and sports competitions, and we see time and again the high-performance sports scheme, though at a smaller scale. While Golombiao defines life as a process of reflection and collective action, it also aims at building community solidarity, using the transformation power of sports as a tool.

Unlike modern sports, Golombiao is not a standardized sports activity in the venues where it is practised. In bioethical terms, it is contextual for it recognizes the problems that beset many population groups. Golombiao targets specific issues which threaten coexistence, social participation and gender equity in armed conflict zones in Colombia.

Golombiao is an interdisciplinary process whose development depends on its relations with institutions such as UNICEF, the German Society for International Cooperation (GIZ), the Canadian International Development Agency (ACDI), and the Swedish International Development Cooperation Agency (SIDA). Colombian Professionals from different disciplines (social sciences, pedagogy and management, among others) share their expertise so that Golombiao may become a strategy to achieve long-lasting and rewarding community progress and transformations, in some areas where life and the quality of life are at risk.

The players agree to the rules by which Golombiao will be played. These rules must comprise technical and coexistence agreements. In this regard, Golombiao operates within the context of pluralism as defined by Bioethics, and takes diversity into account.[13] It is a strategy which understands that the participants are not all alike, and that their individual moral values may differ. It recognizes that there are conflicting opinions within a community and it is mindful of the differences and similarities brought about by these conflicts, in order to have an understanding and consequently help bring the players closer together.

Golombiao can be understood as an inclusion venue,[14] where differences should be included instead of being integrated, in the understanding that integration requires the ongoing adaptation of the participants to a set of beliefs, norms, values or hegemonic principles,[15] whereas inclusion fosters pluralism in the context of a common social project which keeps changing, shaped by the needs of the population.[16]

The players are responsible for overseeing the respect of Golombiao standards; the players from both teams meet with the advisors, in order to evaluate the events in the field and among the team supporters. Hence, the dialogue understood as a bioethical tool is a fundamental learning curve in Golombiao. The players set the rules and agreements to be the guidelines of the sports game; this entails a negotiation process where their value systems will be put into play, as well as some of the expectations and social concerns of the participants. These deliberative processes open the path towards coexistence, overriding isolation and submissiveness.[17]

Based on the bioethical principle of autonomy, Golombiao participants develop their decision-making capacity, and their skills to become organized and take action. In addition to establishing collectively certain technical rules and coexistence agreements in the game, they promote activities such as workshops and movie forums, to empower them to reflect on their social issues. Along these lines, sports are an additional tool to the set of community processes seeking to reinforce coexistence, social participation and gender equity.

## In conclusion

Golombiao works on the grounds of a value system which differs from modern sports. The main goal is no longer trying to beat the opposing team; the goals are geared at building community solidarity driven by the transforming power of sports as a tool.

Golombiao is practised in communities which have been overwhelmed by the armed conflict in Colombia. The practice of the game drives the participants to 'acquire the tools for coexistence, for peaceful dispute settlements, social participation, gender equity-based relations, respect and dialogue. The goal is that the players become key coexistence actors in the neighborhood, in their families and among their friends, and that they are able to settle any conflict, through the use of dialogue and reflection'.[18]

According to the information disclosed by the presidential programme 'Youth Colombia' ('Colombia Joven'), the Golombiao promoting institution,

> over 60,000 girls, boys, teenagers and young adults have learnt, practiced and promoted Golombiao since it was created. Golombiao has been recognized and included in departmental and municipal development plans for the promotion of coexistence and social participation of children and young adults in different territorial entities. 631 strategic partnerships with departmental and municipal social actors have been created.[19]

Golombiao can be considered a sports tool aiming at promoting social organization processes to empower the population to learn through reflection and awareness how to tackle their issues, while striving to build their community solidarity.

In this reference framework, it is possible to weave the ties between the community and the sports world, unlike the axiological principles of modern sports. From a bioethical stance, Golombiao can be seen as an interdisciplinary and plural environment to be used as a tool to help communities create their own deliberation and reflection processes. From this bioethical perspective, Golombiao could become a learning process to enable the participants to reflect over their life and their cultural context. Furthermore, Golombiao can put into play the value system of the participants, as well as their goals, their expectations, their standards and concerns, thus strengthening contextual transformation processes such as coexistence, social participation and gender equity, in the specific case of zones ravaged by the violence of armed conflicts in Colombia.

However, it is necessary to advance ethnographic field work and anthropological analyses to understand in depth the social bonds created during the practice of Golombiao, as well as the medium and long-term impact of this government strategy.

## Disclosure statement

No potential conflict of interest was reported by the author.

## Notes

1. The information on the Golombiao game presented in this paper was extracted from the following sources: official webpage: http://www.golombiao.com, O. Mena, *El Golombiao: El juego de la paz* [Golombiao: the game of peace] (2006). Practice Manual Bogotá: Programa Presidencial Colombia Joven (Bogotá: Presidential Programme Youth Colombia), Deutsche Gesellschaft für Technische Zusammenarbeit (GTZ), 'Programa Participación Ciudadana para la Paz PACIPAZ' [Citizen participation programme for peace PACIPAZ.] http://www.unicef.org/lac/Manual_de_practica.pdf.
2. Mena, *El Golombiao*, 20.
3. Ibid., 16.
4. Engelhardt, *Los fundamentos de la bioética.*
5. Ibid.
6. Beauchamp and Childress, *Principios de Ética Biomédica.*
7. Amartya Sen, *Libertad y desarrollo.*
8. Bañez Tello, *Ciudadanía y Participación.*
9. Chávez Carapia, *La participación social.*
10. Duarte, 'Fundamentación del deporte social comunitario'.
11. Brohm, *Sociología política del deporte.*
12. Velázquez Buendía, 'El deporte moderno'.
13. Gell-Mann, *El quark y el jaguar.*
14. Lleixà, 'Actividad física, deporte y ciudadanía intercultural'.
15. Rubio-Carracedo, 'Pluralismo, multiculturalismo y ciudadanía'.
16. Durán and Giné, 'Index for Inclusión'.
17. López Forero, 'La comunicación en la comunidad'.
18. Golombiao website.
19. Ibid.

## References

Ander-Egg, E. *Metodología y práctica de la animación sociocultural* [Methodology and practice of sociocultural animation]. Madrid: Instituto de Ciencias Sociales Aplicadas, 2001.

Bañez Tello, T. 'Ciudadanía y Participación' [Citizenship and Participation]. In *Ciudadanía: dinámicas de pertenencia y exclusión* [Citizenship: dynamics of belonging and exclusion], ed. M. Benruz Beneites and B. Susin, 97–112. Logroño: Universidad de la Rioja, publicaciones, 2003.

Beauchamp, T., and J. Childress. *Principios de Ética Biomédica* [Principles of Biomedical Ethics]. Barcelona: Editorial Masson, 1999.

Brohm, J. *Sociología política del deporte* [Political sociology of sport]. México: Fondo de cultura económica, 1982.

Chavez Carapia, J. *La participación social: retos y perspectivas* [Social participation: challenges and prospects]. México: UNAM, Escuela Nacional de Trabajo Social, 2003.

Duarte Bajana, R. 'Fundamentación del deporte social comunitario a partir de las categorías bioéticas: una opción hacia el mejoramiento de la calidad de vida que trasciende el deporte moderno' [Foundation of the communitarian sport from bioethics categories: an option towards the improvement of the quality of life that extends the modern sport]. *Lúdica pedagógica* 2, no. 16 (2011): 13–21.

Duran, D., C. Giné Giné. 'Index for Inclusión: Una guía para la evaluación y mejora de la educación inclusiva' [A guide for the evaluation and improvement of inclusive education]. *Contextos educativos: Revista de educación* 5 (2002): 227–38.

Engelhardt, T. *Los fundamentos de la bioética* [The Foundations of Bioethics]. Barcelona: Paidós, 1995.

Gell-Mann, M. *El quark y el jaguar, aventuras de lo simple a lo complejo* [The Quark and the Jaguar: Adventures in the Simple and the Complex] Barcelona: Tusquets, 1995.

Grupo de Memoria Histórica. *¡basta ya! Colombia: Memorias de guerra y dignidad* [stop it! Colombia: Memories of war and dignity]. Bogotá: Imprenta Nacional, 2013.

Lleixia, T. 'Actividad física, deporte y ciudadanía intercultural' [physical activity, sport and intercultural citizenship]. In *Actividad física y deporte en sociedades multiculturales. ¿integración o segregación?* [Physical activity and sport in multicultural societies. Integration or segregation?], ed. Teresa Lleixa and Susana Soler, 97–112. Barcelona: Horsori, 2004.

Lopez Forero, L. 'La comunicación en la comunidad' [Communication in the community]. In *Organización y promoción de la comunidad* [Organization and promotion of community], ed. L. Gonzalez G. Vargas, D. Betancourt, T. Houghton, M. Barreto, V. Crespo, G. Fandiño, et al., 127–54. Bogotá: El búho, 1999.

Mandell, R. *Historia Cultural del deporte* [Cultural history of sport]. Barcelona: Bellaterra, 1986.

Mena, O. *El Golombiao: El juego de la paz. Manual de práctica* [The Golombiao: The game of peace. Practice Manual]. Bogotá: Programa Presidencial Colombia Joven, Deutsche Gesellschaft für Technische, 2006.

O'Farrell, P. *Pluralismo, tolerancia, multiculturalismo: reflexiones para un mundo plural* [Pluralism, tolerance, multiculturalism: Exploring a pluralistic world], 173–94. España: Akal. 2003.

Rubio-Carracedo, J. 'Pluralismo, multiculturalismo y ciudadanía' [Pluralism, multiculturalism and citizenship]. In *Pluralismo, tolerancia, multiculturalismo: reflexiones para un mundo plural* [Pluralism, tolerance, multiculturalism: Exploring a pluralistic world], ed. P. O'Farrell, 173–94. España: Akal, 2003.

Sen, A. *Libertad y desarrollo* [Development as Freedom]. México: Fondo de cultura económica, 2010.

Velazquez Buendia, R. 'El deporte moderno. Consideraciones acerca de su génesis y de la evolución de su significado y funciones sociales' [The modern sport. Considerations about its genesis and the evolution of its meaning and social functions]. *Revista Educación Física y deportes* 36 (2001). Buenos Aires. [July 7, 2011]. http://www.efdeportes.com/efd36/deporte.htm.

Zusammenarbeit (GTZ). 'Programa Participación Ciudadana para la Paz Pacipaz' [Citizen Participation for Peace program - Pacipaz]. http://www.unicef.org/lac/Manual_de_practica.pdf.

# Innovation in soccer clubs – the case of Sweden

Magnus Forslund

This essay gathers what we know about innovation in soccer clubs but also reports from an ongoing study on innovation in Swedish elite soccer clubs. The research could be described as an ethnographic endeavour into the world of Swedish elite soccer. By picking up pieces here and there at meetings, games, interviews and so on, I gradually build knowledge on 'what is going on' and 'what do they think they are up to?', The empirical material is presented in relation to four innovation options identified in the literature: adding new products/services, changes in the business model, new ways to manage the team and organize the team around the team and rethinking what the business is all about. The study shows that there are many innovations going on in Swedish soccer but also that there are several ways to improve both what is being done and how.

## Introduction

The soccer world is commonly described as affected by two major trends: increased commercialization and professionalization.[1] Soccer is increasingly seen as any other business. This paper departures from the basic question: how could or should a soccer club deal with these trends?

When environmental changes occur in the general business sector, usually there are major calls for innovation. While innovation can mean many things, it is here understood as the generation, acceptance, and implementation of new ideas, processes, products or services, new to the relevant unit of adoption.[2] Innovation thus does not only concern new products or services, but organizational processes, routines, etc.

Calls for innovation are followed by research in attempts to contribute to knowledge and further innovation activities. Hence we can find numerous studies in the world of general business. However, currently it seems as if 'soccer business' does not follow the same pattern. However, since little research is made on innovation in soccer clubs the state-of-the-art is unclear. This paper gathers what we know but also reflects upon current state-of-the-art and reports from an ongoing study on innovation in Swedish elite soccer clubs.

The paper is structured as follows. Firstly there is a general section on soccer as business. This is followed by a general section on innovation. Previous research on innovation in soccer clubs is then reviewed. Methods for conducting the empirical study then follow. The empirical part starts with short notes on Swedish soccer before innovation in Swedish soccer clubs is presented and discussed. This includes remarks concerning 'who' is doing business in Swedish soccer clubs and how the innovation process could be described and understood. The paper concludes with a discussion and suggestions for further research.

## On soccer as business

Texts on soccer as business often have as their starting point that the sport has become more commercialized and professionalized.[3] A central discussion concerns the new media age[4] in which more money is paid for TV rights. This has stimulated texts on soccer, globalization and television[5] but also critical texts that take the stand point that soccer no longer is a beautiful game.[6] There are also texts discussing the development of soccer from the perspectives of politics, economics, law, spectators and actual playing.[7]

Many texts focus on soccer as a sport. General questions dominate, such as competitive balance[8] and financial status of elite clubs in a country.[9] Clubs seem to have a hard time generating profits[10] and several clubs have been suffering such big problems that they have been put under administration.

There are several reasons for financial problems. One is that focus is on pitch performance, not financial performance.[11] Fans demand sporting success. Since both practical experience and research show strong support for the thesis that the more money is spent on players, the better the performance on pitch,[12] this drives a club to spend more and more on players. Even if success on the pitch leads to higher revenue, profits do not seem to increase since additional revenue usually is spent on players.[13] Another cause of problems is the league structure. Relegation from a higher division means strongly reduced revenues, while a large portion of costs are fixed.[14] Often these clubs attempt to return to the higher division, which however requires further costs. They gamble hoping that this extra investment will be paid back the following season in the higher division. Another explanation is that there are not enough incentives for achieving healthy finances. In Spain, scholars claim that the government and banks help clubs with financial difficulties, since they want to avoid clubs going bankrupt.[15] Another factor reducing incentives is the existence of different kinds of patrons or 'sugar daddies'.[16] Rich people bring new capital to the clubs in order to cover losses. According to Storm[17] this explains why there is a need for regulation.

## On innovation

Organizations need to strike a balance between the exploitation of old certainties and the exploration of new possibilities.[18] The former concerns doing what we are doing, while the latter concerns searching for and discovering new things, i.e. innovation.[19] This has led to an understanding that innovation only concerns radical new products. However there is a large body of literature arguing that firstly, innovation could also concern organizational and other social processes and secondly, that it might not necessarily be considered as very radical to be considered an innovation.[20] The notion of creative imitation[21] is one way to express this widening of how innovation is understood.

Innovation is not the only concept dealing with 'doing new things'. I have chosen to use the innovation concept since there are established distinctions that are useful in organizing our discussion of innovation in soccer clubs. One is between product/service innovation and organizational innovations. In previous research most interest seems to have been on the former, while the latter has been left more or less unattended. Examples of this will be shown later in the article. A second distinction concerns the difference between incremental and radical innovation. Another argument is that interesting subconcepts have emerged. One such concept is open innovation,[22] proposed as an alternative to closed innovation. This means involving many actors in- and outside of the organization in the innovation process. Since soccer clubs usually are described as having close and loyal fans,[23] open innovation as a concept appears interesting and relevant. Another subconcept is innovation networks[24] where organizations collaborate in order to innovate.

The innovation process is sometimes described as a process that should be systematic, very well-planned and controlled.[25] Innovation follows natural phases concerning identifying opportunity, defining the business concept, estimating resource requirements and so on.[26] On the other hand, we have scholars arguing that innovation is something irrational, spontaneous, undisciplined and uncontrollable.[27] The idea that innovation follows discrete phases is criticized.[28] In practice, it is very difficult to separate different phases. On a general level we might differentiate between periods of initiation, development and implementation.[29] Mostly it is argued that innovation follows non-linear paths.[30]

## Previous research on innovation in soccer clubs

Gilmore and Gilson[31] claim that (people in) soccer are notorious for being suspicious of ideas generated outside their own experience base. If this is true, we would expect little innovation in soccer clubs. Williams[32] notes that there are few studies on general soccer club management. Thus, it is not surprising that it is rather difficult to find studies focusing on innovation, understanding this as a dimension of club management. Searching the science database ONESEARCH for keywords: innovation soccer club, resulted in 28 matches. Out of these, only a few articles could be said to explicitly deal with innovation in soccer clubs. One rare example investigates attitudes toward the adoption of 3G technology.[33]

Widening our search however, we can find studies on how clubs have responded to changing circumstances. Mainly these revolve around the change from focusing solely on the soccer game event and attracting as many spectators as possible to the introduction of a variety of products and services. This includes building new or improving existing stadiums in order to enable a number of game-related offerings,[34] creating strategic alliances in order to multiply the number of merchandise products branded with the club logo,[35] creating museums with guided tours and creating a TV channel (for example, LFC TV or MUTV). Popular examples are Manchester United,[36] Arsenal FC,[37] Liverpool FC,[38] Real Madrid,[39] Barcelona.[40] A recurring theme is the internationalization of the club brand.[41] Big clubs now operate on a global market, with fans all over the world.

Adding products/services is however only one way to innovate. Another is to change what scholars label 'the business model'.[42] Such model is the result of choices concerning two dimensions.[43] The first concerns buying expensive or cheap players. The other concerns creating an experienced or an inexperienced team. A not so surprising result is that buying expensive players and creating an experienced team result in the best performance, measured in points during a season. More interesting is that a change in strategy is risky since it is likely to result in performance decline. This encourages retaining 'as is' and prevents innovation.

Related to this is the question whether it is possible to combine success on and off the pitch or not. Previous research (see earlier this article) implies that the answer is no. There are a few exceptions. Gerrard[44] finds that Manchester United differs from many other clubs in their successful combination of sport and financial performance. The reason for this is sought in the history of the club but also in the development of unique capabilities regarding organization and leadership.[45]

Clubs search for ways to find less expensive players, either by internal talent development or by finding talent in less developed countries. Some clubs create strategic alliances or joint ventures to set up soccer academies for example in Africa.[46] Another business model is to combine the recruitment of international superstars with high media attention and the recruitment of cheap junior players, like Real Madrid once did.[47] The idea was to generate increased revenues and success on the pitch.

A third option is to explore new ways to manage and organize the team itself, for example, regarding tactics[48] or leadership[49] and the team around the team. By creating a network of doctors, professors and experts in helping developing a new soccer/physio/medicine philosophy clubs attempt to get ahead of competitors. In Sweden this has meant the use of sport psychology consulting.[50] For Bolton Wanderers, this meant that they could attract older star players in the twilight of their career, helping these players to prolong their careers.[51]

A fourth option is to go beyond a focus on either products or soccer team strategy to rethink what the business is all about. Instead of retaining the idea that the core product is the soccer match, we could imagine that the core product is the experience created within the customer. Van Uden describes the transformation of the Dutch club Vitesse from being a soccer club to being an experience entertainment company.[52] They wanted to reduce the importance of the performance on the pitch and create a more robust business model. This means creating a relation between the club and members that extends beyond the soccer game. Even if the soccer game still is important, the focus is to offer an expression of identity. Put differently, soccer is not the end but the means to build an image for oneself.[53] This means connecting different parts to each other in new ways and as Van Uden puts it, to control everything that affects the experience of the members. Players have to personify the values that the club links to the desired experience. What goes on outside and inside the stadium is equally important.

The development of FC Copenhagen in Denmark followed a similar path.[54] An arena takeover was followed by a number of activities founded in the entertainment sector. Soccer became a medium for other activities. This success however paved the way for success on the playing field, which yet again stimulated the profit-orientated business

An area of development that could be linked to either the first or the fourth 'innovation option' concerns what in England is termed 'soccer in the community'.[55] Sometimes set up as a trust, it is charity work designated to provide soccer-related activities for schools and groups around the club and strengthen the bond between the club and the community. In some cases, the soccer is used as a tool to improve personal and social skills or to promote healthful behaviour changes.[56]

The emergence in England of the supporters trust model of ownership[57] represents yet another way to discuss what a soccer club is all about: is it about organizing activities for its members, for generating profit to owners or delivering experiences for spectators?

Continuing this line of reasoning Thrassou et al. argue for a redefinition of the soccer core product.[58] Soccer has a 'plastic' quality enabling it to fit the needs and wants of very different market segments. The value created can be of many sorts. This opens up for many innovation possibilities.

Summarizing, we have four innovation options: adding new products/services, changes in business model, new ways to manage the team and organize the team around the team and rethinking what the business is all about. These innovation options contain both product/service and organizational innovations. Few scholars however make an explicit link to the innovation concept. Mostly radical innovation is focused, while everyday incremental innovation is largely absent. We can note that there are few detailed descriptions on the innovation process. It remains a black box. Occasionally glimpses in articles reveal that there are a lot of challenges:

> We struggled, I think, when we first got to the Reebok to understand just how enormous the stadium was to run in terms of going from Burnden Park with two boxes and probably feeding 200 people to going to the Reebok with 42 boxes and feeding 2 1/2 thousand people on match day. It's a steep learning curve … You can't necessarily do it and you certainly can't do it overnight. So I think the whole organization had to become a lot more professional. (Vice Chairman, Brett Warburton)[59]

The everyday challenges of becoming more professional, setting up joint ventures to explore player talents in Africa, managing new approaches to merchandise and so on, are largely unknown, even if for example Shaw[60] demonstrates the complexity of the partner network of Manchester United. To what extent soccer clubs have joined the overall business trend when it comes to open innovation or innovation networks is unclear. Studies of innovation involving higher management levels of soccer clubs are difficult to find. To what extent they engage in organizational or product innovation is unclear.

Research largely fails to discuss obstacles and resistance to innovation. One exception is a study of Ajax, where supporters and former club celebrities like Johan Cruyff acted to block what they experienced as a professionalization going too far.[61]

Resistance could also be innovation. Instead of just accepting the global trends and following the competitors, clubs have been observed to exhibit resistance of different degrees. Liverpool FC is one example of a club that has not responded to the challenges the same way as Chelsea or Manchester United. There have been resisting forces in- and outside the club.[62] Spanish elite club Athletic de Bilbao only hires local players, accepts only local sponsors and plays in an old stadium where fans bring their own sandwiches.[63]

## Method

This article is a result of an ongoing research project concerning soccer club management in Sweden. The research approach could be described as an ethnographic endeavour. For several years, I have explored the world of Swedish male elite soccer. By picking up pieces I gradually build knowledge on 'what is going on' and 'what do they think they are up to?'[64] The last should be understood as a genuine search for cultural meanings. Why are things happening the way they do? How do they make sense of actions, events, incidents and so on? Even if I have a few experiences of elite soccer as junior player and as volunteer, I consider myself as a professional stranger.[65]

A mix of different methods is used, ranging from interviews to participant observation and action research. The basis for this article is empirical material concerning AIK, Djurgårdens IF (DIF), Malmö FF (MFF), Östers IF (ÖIF), and Kalmar FF (KFF). During the time of the study they were all in the first division (Allsvenskan). They represent different parts of Sweden and different city sizes. All clubs have a long history in elite soccer but they have also experienced difficulties, with periods of time in divisions below the top division. Currently ÖIF is the club with weakest results during the last five years (only one year in Allsvenskan). Since 2013 all clubs have new stadiums. In addition, I also have material from IF Elfsborg (IFE).

The depth and scope of material varies. For two years I was part of ÖIF as a board member of women's soccer. From this position I had the possibility to observe and discuss the development of the whole club, including men's soccer. Currently I am a coach for a youth team. I have had no other formal position for three years. When it comes to the other clubs, I have conducted interviews but also informal talks with representatives, document studies, observations and participant observations during match day events.

The respondents include CEO, Club Manager, Marketing/Sales Manager, Head Scout, Sport Managers, Head of Soccer Academy, fans and more. I have observed discussions on supporter forums to some of the clubs. I have interviewed two representatives of SEF (Swedish Elite Soccer): Chairman (President) Lars-Christer Olsson and General Secretary (CEO) Mats Enquist. In different forums I have also listened to presentations by the latter. I have participated in two conferences in which representatives from clubs, media, sport management consultants and more, meet to discuss current status of Swedish soccer. During 2013, I participated in strategic discussions concerning the future of Swedish soccer during a workshop in Växjö. This workshop was chaired by Karl-Erik Nilsson, the chairman of Swedish Soccer Association.

Participant observations were conducted at four games as a VIP/Business guest. These were made without anyone knowing my role as a researcher. I paid the tickets by myself and experienced the event as any other customer. On two occasions I brought with me corporate people who were not club customers, to explore the experienced value of the event. The event included access to a lounge with the possibility to buy beer, wine and other kinds of liquid, food, premium seats (with easy access to comfortable chairs), a visit by a coach, former player or sport manager. Half-time activities could include coffee and more presentations by club celebrities.

## Swedish soccer

Scandinavian sport has been described as an amalgam of voluntarism and commercialism with roots in the development of the Welfare State.[66] Sport clubs have partly been seen as a tool for government. In clubs children should learn democracy and receive social and moral guidance. Historically there has been close links between soccer clubs and the local community. In several small towns and villages, the club was run by or at least very closely related to the local foundry or iron works.[67]

Swedish soccer was directed by amateur rules up until 1967. On a broad scale, players however did not become professional until well into the 1990s. Soccer clubs were and still are organized as voluntary organizations in which each member has a vote. The employment of people 'at the club office' is of a rather late date. According to scholars this means that Swedish soccer has been dominated by the spirit of play.[68] Nowadays we could argue that elite clubs exist in a tension between being a voluntary organization run by its members and a professional organization with employed professionals.

The SvFF (Swedish Soccer Association) is the top governing organization of soccer in Sweden. It was formed in 1904 and is the largest national sport organization in Sweden with over 3200 clubs and 1 million members. In 1928, SEF (Association Swedish Elite Soccer) was formed as a counterpart to SvFF. It is a league association for the 32 clubs in Allsvenskan and Superettan (second Division). Their mission is to lead the development of Swedish soccer when it comes to sport, finance and administration.

A goal is that in 2017 Allsvenskan will be the best league in the Nordic countries. They have identified five strategic areas. One is to increase revenue from selling broadcasting rights. Another is that clubs need to develop their own revenue generating capabilities. This also means that SEF has changed their role, from being solely a service organization for their member organizations, to being a driver for change. Currently they are working with new information technology platforms, rebranding the league and planning for a unified CRM-system. A goal is to double the turnover of clubs in Allsvenskan. This means an increase from roughly 130 million euros to 260 million euros. The fiscal year 2012 MFF generated 17 million euros in revenue, including player sales. This was more than anyone else. The club with lowest level of revenue was Syrianska FC, generating only 2.5 million euros. Table 1 shows clubs included in this study.

Compared to other leagues in Europe revenues are low. Among several reasons one suggested reason is that a Swedish club cannot be owned by a private actor by more than 49%. This means that no individual can step in and take control over the club as is the case in England.

## Innovation in Swedish soccer clubs

In my quest for innovation in Swedish soccer clubs, I begin by linking to previous research describing the transformation of soccer to a business and more specifically show business. Do these descriptions apply to Swedish clubs? If so, this is an expression of innovation but also constitutes context for other kinds of innovation.

Club representatives do state that soccer now is like any other business and that soccer nowadays is entertainment. However, it is difficult to understand what is meant by such statements. One thing seems clear: it does not mean that they should

Table 1. Revenue in 2013.

|  | Rev | Profit |
| --- | --- | --- |
| Malmö FF | 17 | −1.4 |
| AIK | 13 | −0.45 |
| IFE | 12 | 0.23 |
| Kalmar FF | 8.2 | −0.08 |
| Djurgården IF | 8.0 | −0.53 |
| Östers IF | 5.5 | 0.03 (this season in second division) |

make a profit. The aim still is to excel on the pitch, regardless of whether they have created limited companies or not. The reason AIK Fotboll AB is noted on the Swedish stock exchange is more about giving fans an option to own stock in the club and raising money than maximizing profit.

One interpretation of 'soccer as business' is that running a soccer club nowadays is experienced by many as being much more about money than before. As club manager Peo Jönsson (ÖIF) put it, 'we are always hunting money'. This is also evident in the Twitter hashtag #amf – against modern soccer (in Swedish: #mdmf – mot den moderna fotbollen) where fans criticize this emphasis on money.

Another interpretation is that 'business' means 'professional' and 'serious'. All respondents say that you need to be more professional nowadays. They describe it as 'you need to know what you are doing', especially when it concerns sponsors. You have to be able 'to deliver value'. The whole game day event must be taken seriously, including anything from ticket handling, to security, selling beer and broadcasting issues. You cannot 'mess around', implying that is what Swedish soccer clubs used to do. KFF club manager Svante Samuelsson comments that before it was as though the accounting was kept 'in a bag' and issues like tax and insurance were not that important.

This process has spurred different kinds of changes. Some of these emanate from within the clubs, while others emanate from outside the club. Regarding the latter, SvFF in 2002 introduced a professional club license concerning economic capacity. At the end of a fiscal year a soccer club must not have negative shareholder equity. If they do they must present a trustworthy plan for restoring this the year after. If they fail to do this they might be relegated, as was Örebro in 2004. The license also includes stadia requirements concerning floodlight and underground heating, security issues and the level of head coach education. SEF has added different regulations and guidelines. Of special interest is a certification process regarding youth academies, where clubs are measured on several dimensions, including organizational.

Together these form pressures on the club regarding organization and competence. At the same time, clubs on their own have felt a need to employ people to handle the increasing number of tasks that must be managed. This has not necessarily meant an increase in competence. Sometimes old players, coaches or former volunteers are employed. Occasionally we can find managers with relevant academic business education. Svante Samuelsson, club manager in KFF is one example having studied business administration. In ÖIF people studying Coaching and Sport Management have assumed positions in sales and event. In 2013, a rather unique move was made by DIF when they employed a political scientist to work with corporate social responsibility. Exact information regarding the number of full-time employees and their education is missing. Mainly the administrative staff is made up of few people, where former knowledge of the club is valued. Clubs seem reluctant to employ people not working directly with soccer. IFE club manager Stefan Andreasson said 'it takes time', adding that clubs have just recently come to terms with the idea that they need to employ professional people in all positions. Raising revenue enough to fill these positions will take time. This and statements made by other club representatives, reinforce the observation made in other countries. It is difficult for clubs to break with the tradition that soccer performance on the pitch in the short term matters most.

Looking back 10 years, there is however no doubt that a lot has happened in Swedish soccer clubs. Let us look closer at what the clubs have done and are doing regarding the four innovation options reviewed in previous sections. Naturally this is not an exhaustive review. I have chosen a few things that stand out.

### Innovation option 1: adding new products/services

One of the most striking changes over the last 10 years has been that several clubs have built new soccer stadiums. Stadiums were built for the world championship in Sweden 1958. For many years after that not much development took place. There is no doubt that the old ones did not live up to the needs of modern clubs. In 2005 IFE took the lead by finalizing a new stadium. Early reports were positive and revenues seemed to increase. Other clubs followed shortly: MFF 2009, KFF 2011, ÖIF 2012, AIK 2012 and DIF 2013.

All clubs have developed new or updated offerings in relation to match day, predominately targeted at business customers. Mostly these are fairly conventional and in some cases merely comprise 'freshening up' old offerings. There are more boxes and the seats are more comfortable, while the food and drink are not necessarily of higher quality than before. There are lounge areas which are available for you to sit down with your friends and the whole atmosphere is somewhat more 'modern'. In ÖIF's stadium, you can see large photographs of famous players, while DIF's stadium has a lounge named after a famous player.

When studying offers we can note that free Wi-fi and high-definition screens are highlighted as two key features when you pay for a private box of 10 seats (DIF). Such a box costs 21,000 euro per year (i.e. 2100 euro/person). There is no doubt that the business customers I talked to appreciate the more modern facilities. When I participated in their typical VIP event I cannot deny a feeling of luxury, even if paying over 100 euro in itself might convince you to think that this is luxurious. A product manager for Ericsson who joined me at an AIK-match was really happy when he could take a photo together with Daniel Tjärnström, a legendary AIK player. To him, such a photo was worth at least 30–40 euros. Another business customer was positively surprised by the seating comfort and the sound system at the MFF stadium. A third business customer enjoyed the close distance between premium seats and the warm restaurant with beer already served at half-time at the ÖIF stadium. Several people have given positive comments regarding the aesthetics of the DIF stadium.

However, there is also no doubt that we can find questionable aspects concerning these match events and that further innovation is possible. At a MFF match we were so many people that we could not hear the celebrity on the stage talking and the seating during dinner was very crowded. This did not create a feeling of comfort and luxury. Leaving the arena we walked downstairs through a very grey and rather sad area. No photographs, no 'thank you' or 'welcome back'. Should Wi-Fi be something the customer should pay very much extra for or should it be granted free to all visitors? Would not a club want many photos and messages sent during 'a world class experience'?

Niklas Nestlander, Head of commercial sales in AIK, warns against having too high expectations at an early stage. A new stadium requires a lot of work and much learning. The technical problems experienced by new stadiums will naturally affect the spectator experience negatively. Thomas Perslund, CEO at Sweden arena, the company running Friends arena, home of both AIK and the Swedish national soccer team, confirmed this at a meeting in August 2013. He said that it usually takes three years before everything is running as desired, while acknowledging also that the design of the stadium had not been optimal from the beginning.

Generally the innovation process regarding stadiums seems to have been and still is a bumpy ride. It seems as if most clubs follow a rather standardized innovation path lacking an overarching strategy. Sometimes it seems as if they are offering products that are rather unclear. Let me take 'networking' as an example.

An often used sales argument is that being a sponsor to the club means good opportunities for networking. Participating in a VIP event on match day is highlighted as such an opportunity. However, after participating in four such events, my conclusion is that they mainly stimulate networking with those you bring with you or already know. These events are not designed to let you meet new business contacts. The general feeling is that there are small groups of people that have fun within their groups. As an outsider there is no easy way to start a conversation.

AIK presents 'The Network' (nätverket) as a platform to make new contacts and do business. It costs 8000 euro to participate in 'The Network'. In addition to the usual package: having VIP access to the stadium, food before game, opportunity to buy alcohol, newsletters and so on, the following are included:

- Four seats
- Opportunity to mingle with VIP customers and club profiles
- Four network meetings
- Two tickets to an away game with AIK
- The opportunity to send mail to AIK B2B-network

Assuming from previous observations that it is difficult to make new contacts during games, this leaves us with four network meetings and a trip to an away game to make new contacts. There is no information on how these meetings are designed or how they help the customer make new contacts.

Summing this up, the question is if 'The Network' is about meeting new people that I find 'inside' AIK activities or having meetings at AIK activities with new people I bring in from outside? Is AIK just a context or is it also content?

Focusing on the regular spectator we can conclude that they also seem to appreciate new, modern facilities. Besides that however, it is difficult to ascertain if and how the total experience has changed. Clubs are struggling with the identity of events. Niklas Nestlander (AIK) says:

> we will never become USA, putting up a SHOW. There are strong forces against 'modern soccer'. They do not want a show. They are very sensitive to this. If we make too much fun out of it, it will not be appreciated. We have to go step-by-step. Doing things in a smooth, nice way, adding value to the event. Helping people get closer to the sport.

There are occasionally pre-game activities, mostly targeted at kids. Twice a year AIK arranges 'Gnagisland' before a game. This includes speed shooting, face painting, balloons and more. Kids could be dubbed to become a knight. The club has created a story about AIK knights who protect the holy AIK. ÖIF has created a Kids club offering activities before some games. However, on the whole, there seems to be a lack of systematic work. Different activities are not very well integrated. One example is that key words used regarding AIK knights do not perfectly match key words in 'The AIK Style' (AIK-stilen), an attempt to describe values important to

AIK. The reason for the choice of a dog as a mascot in Östers IF is unclear. It is also difficult to find a clear connection to the values expressed in their Strategic plan 2010–2014.

### Innovation option 2: changes in the business model

There is a trend for Swedish clubs to invest in cheap, preferably local players and to develop a cohesive team. ÖIF state in their Strategic plan 2010–2014 that there should be a 'wholehearted investment in local players'. Similar statements can be found regarding AIK, DIF, KFF and MFF even though they all accept exceptions. KFF stands out most since for a number of years it scouted lower ranked Brazilian players and successfully developed them. AIK has turned to the suburbs of Stockholm in order to find and develop talented players. Sport Manager Björn Wesström says that the identity of AIK has changed. Nowadays AIK should express diversity in order to better reflect society. The reason behind this is of course that this enables the club to avoid buying expensive players. Björn however notes that learning how to manage a more diverse squad is challenging.

Clubs are constantly exploring how to develop their academies so that more players can be promoted into the first team. MFF head scout, Vito Stavljanin, says that they currently know too little about the quality of the academy. They need to track down where players leaving the academy end up. Another question is how long a talent should remain in the A-team. Remaining as a substitute in the club thus might be detrimental. Perhaps there are innovations to be made here. There are signs of a growing trend for players to move to lower class clubs on loan in order to gain playing time.

### Innovation option 3: new ways to manage the team and the team around the team

This study does not have extensive empirical material regarding the detailed ways teams are managed. What could be noted however, are changes in approaches to head coaches and their coaching style. KFF head coach, Nanne Bergstrand, was employed between 2002 and 2013, an unusually long time period. AIK, DIF and ÖIF also espouse a desire to have a long-term relationship with a head coach. The head coach of AIK now enters his fourth season, while DIF and ÖIF recently recruited new coaches. In the case of DIF, they have recruited an experienced coach used to build cohesive teams with small resources and that formerly was employed for nine seasons by elite club Gefle. Club representatives support the idea that the ideal is long-term employment. They mention Manchester United and Arsenal as role models.

When it comes to coaching styles, former head coach of KFF, Nanne Bergstrand, stands out. He has been inspired by Kaizen: a concept on everyday continuous improvements originating from Japanese car manufacturers.[69]Nanne talks about wanting his player to understand that life is a mystery and that they should explore it with an open mind. This leads to a natural desire for everyday improvement. Kaizen has also helped them in moving focus from the result of the game to develop the players and their play. The Kaizen approach reasons well with the development of KFF as a whole. Since the 1990s, the club has taken small steps and with small resources explored new ways of running the club.

Gradually, the team around the team is growing in the clubs that have been studied. Besides employing people, they try to create networks of experts in areas of medicine, physical training, etc. ÖIF highlights the possibility of collaborating with Linnaeus University regarding training and test facilities.

### Innovation option 4: rethinking what the business is all about

In this section, I explore innovation in relation to what is perceived as being 'the business'. Are there any more profound innovative activities going on in clubs or not? Are clubs transforming into entertainment companies, staging experiences as the Dutch club Vitesse[70] has done?

Key here is the meaning of 'entertainment' and 'experience'. Following Pine II and Gilmore[71] an experience is more than entertainment. It is about engaging with customers in a personal and memorable way. Put this way, any soccer game has the potential to be an experience. A game could also be very surprising, which enhances the possibility to be remembered. However, an organization staging an experience usually wants to control the surprise. From this follows that a game perhaps is not a good thing to design as an experience. This is also why the club Vitesse wants to add other things that could absorb negative soccer performances. Delivering experiences is also about the whole process: before, during and after the actual event. This article is not the place for a thorough analysis. An initial and general interpretation is that the clubs still have a long way to go before they could be said to deliver experiences in a systematic way. A few examples may suffice. Being a member of AIK and ÖIF, I can conclude that they do not communicate directly with their members other than sparsely. It is difficult to identify any benefits from being a member. I have been a VIP customer at four clubs. No club has contacted me afterwards to check my experience. Only two have offered me a similar kind of experience. During the event, nothing was presented to me as a memorable gift. DIF claims that they offer 'a fantastic stadium experience in a world class arena'. The arena might be world class, but according to theory the experience must be staged, in order to be 'fantastic'.

Another line of development is soccer in the community. In Sweden this represents a somewhat paradoxical development. On the one hand, the very roots of Swedish soccer are in the community. Historically there has been a close relation between the club, local politicians in the municipality and local media.[72] This should not be anything new to the clubs. On the other hand, it is possible to argue that Swedish elite clubs at least partially did lose the local connection. One example is that for several years it was not natural for ÖIF to have players visiting local schools or to show up at charity events. Now, clubs are doing more and more things. For many years 'MFF in the community' has been a central feature in rhetoric and action. On their web page we can read that 'MFF is not and should not be only a soccer club but also a positive force in society'. In 2014, MFF set up a career academy that will help young people get a job. This will be enabled through collaboration with companies.

In 2006 DIF and two trusts set up 'The Spirit of DIF'. This gathers community activities in the club. There are three areas: active community engagement, value work and positive supporter culture. The most famous project is drive-in soccer in the suburbs. Young kids are invited to indoor arenas for pick-up soccer. By doing this, kids are lured away from the streets. Another activity is 'The Job Opportunity', an integration project where kids in trouble are offered education and internships in companies. By the end of the process, 70% of the kids are expected to have become employed. DIF is also the first club to have issued a complete CSR-report.

AIK also arranges pick-up soccer in the suburbs and hosts a summer tournament called 'Who owns the suburb?' for local friendly teams. A supporter commented on this on a forum: 'This tournament is good PR for AIK – and for the suburbs!'

Clubs report that sponsors appreciate the work they are doing when it comes to the community. In some cases they have been surprised that this has led to increased revenues from sponsors. It is however not always an easy process. DIF analyst Filip Lundberg says that he has put a lot of effort into finding ways to motivate these investments not only to fans, but people working in DIF.

While soccer in the community could be seen as a new way to look good in the eyes of the sponsors or a way to find talented players there are also reasons to interpret this as a crack in the established image of what 'the business' is all about. Even if club representatives exhibit a will to win on the pitch and an appreciation of good games, there is a slight tiredness to be noticed regarding 'modern soccer'. Club officials are tired of young players demanding too high salaries and expecting to be picked for the A-team too early. MFF CEO Per Nilsson commented that 'some young players lose ground contact' and that the club needs to counteract this. Clubs are tired of 'buying foreign players only interested in furthering their own career'. There is no point anymore on having players with no heart or soul for the club. This could partly be interpreted that if investing in local players with such heart and soul means reduced pitch performance, then clubs are becoming increasingly ready to accept it. Following this means a change in the idea of what 'the business' is all about.

### Who is doing business?

A slightly different approach to the discussion on what the business is all about is to explore how the clubs themselves define 'business development' and which actors they consider as involved in business development. MFF CEO Per Nilsson says that 'everything we do is our business: talent development, developing the squad, coaching, attracting spectators, running the stadium and so on. Business development thus concerns everything we do in order to develop our club'. AIK sales manager Niklas Nestlander gives a more narrow answer in that he emphasizes how the club can capitalize on the brand. It is about 'packaging the brand in different ways'. In that sense it is important to what extent AIK players are locals or globals. However, the very act of developing players is not seen as business development in AIK. Thus the head coach is not 'doing' business, the sales people are. This stands in contrast to MFF in which the head coach is to a greater extent involved in 'doing' business.

### Innovation: how?

The research projects have only begun to scratch the surface regarding how innovation happens in the clubs studied. So far, what has surfaced is an image of unstructured, non-systematic and random processes. It is difficult to find a strategic direction which is clearly expressed in operational activities. This is not to say that the clubs do not have strategies. New stadiums did not emerge spontaneously. When looking deeper into the stadium processes however, we can find some degree of chaos and randomness. Things are forgotten at the planning phase and planned things are not implemented.[73] The final object is to some extent a surprise. In one case, key actors revealed that things happened very fast and decisions were made without formal documents in order.

Judging from what is visible from the outside, actions, events and things seem only occasionally linked to each other. KFF club manager Svante Samuelsson says that they are not working with strategy in the textbook sense. However, every year key actors in the club go on a trip to discuss the future. The outcome of this trip however is not a written plan but more a 'soft' input to the running of the club. Some respondents claim that they know what they should do, but they do not have enough resources to do it. One step on the road has been internal work to clarify what the club actually stands for, i.e. the club values. In theory, these values should permeate everything in the clubs. However, it is not easy to find expressions of these values, for example on club websites. On a page 'about AIK soccer', we are only given numbers and factual information. Nothing is said about key values. On ÖIF's website we are asked to be become a member, but no reason is given as to why. MFF website is different in the sense that they have a page describing vision, mission and objectives where we also learn about MFF club values. Similar information is possible to find on the other club websites, but is more difficult.

SEF general secretary Mats Enquist claims that the clubs have a long way to go. One problem is the lack of continuity. Mats reports that during his two-year-long employment at SEF, 11 out of 12 key actors have been replaced in the 3 elite soccer clubs in Stockholm town. This includes sport manager, club manager, head coach and chairman of the board. The new actors that enter the discussion do not always have the same opinions as their predecessors. The innovation process is slowed down. According to Mats there is also resistance. Partly this is linked to a self-image that the clubs know best themselves when it comes to club management, he claims. According to sport management consultants, clubs are sceptical regarding competencies of consultants and possible effects. Mats believes that the clubs need to open up for more radical changes.

Talking to club representatives there is no evident resistance among those responsible for developing the club. Everybody speaks about the need for change and development. They do acknowledge that there is a lot of resistance in different 'corners' of the club including the fans. Clubs still rely on volunteers to do important tasks. It is difficult to balance the need for professional performance and volunteer retention. Putting too much pressure on volunteers could make them leave.

However, there is also a kind of subtle resistance even among club representatives that is somewhat difficult to pinpoint. One expression of this is the lack of strategic systematic cooperation with universities. Students do occasional course assignments at the clubs. There is however no systematic interaction regarding soccer club management. Even if there is a positive attitude there is also a scepticism regarding possible contributions from the university. So far there is only one club representative that strongly deviates from the other in the study. He himself has approached academics around the country in search for knowledge that could be used to further his work with CSR related issues.

## Discussion

There is no doubt that there is a lot of innovation going on in soccer clubs. We can find examples of most of what the innovation literature is dealing with. All clubs have experienced radical innovation when it comes to the building of stadiums. While the very stadium itself is an innovation that has spawned or better put, demanded innovation in related areas as logistics, VIP offers and food sales, it has also hampered innovation in other areas.

It is fairly evident that there is a lot of creative imitation going on.[74] The clubs are mainly doing similar things to other clubs in Sweden, even though there are variations. Swedish clubs follow the same paths as clubs in England and Germany. From the standpoint of institutional theory, especially considering isomorphism,[75] this is no surprise. It seems also as if this has been regarded as the fastest way to innovation.

However if Swedish soccer clubs are to close the gaps between themselves and clubs from countries like Italy, Germany, the Netherlands and so on, too much imitation might not suffice. Instead they need to find innovative ways to speed up the innovation process.

Since Swedish clubs are governed by the 51%-rule no single person can take control over the club. It has been argued that this slows down the innovation process. Even if 'sugar daddies' do exist in Swedish soccer clubs, there is less incentive to go 'all-in' since they cannot assume full control over the club. The history of amateur voluntary sport clubs also plays a part in hampering innovation. Since members have votes, they can exercise their right to vote at annual meetings. While the debate regarding changing this rule currently seems to be put on hold, it still remains as an interesting option. Changing this rule would certainly represent a radical move. This is however not to claim that this is the only or most important move.

So far we might say that the innovation processes at the clubs reinforce those scholars arguing that innovation in practice is a chaotic non-linear process.[76] However, it should not be impossible for clubs to create a more coherent strategic framework for innovation and a more elaborated management model designed to work with such chaotic processes.[77] A question is how such a change could be accomplished. The somewhat hesitating attitude towards external partners like universities does not contribute positively. The attitude could be interpreted as lack of knowledge as how to collaborate. Research from other industries reports a general scepticism towards the academic world.[78] Mistrust dominates until actors have learned how to collaborate. The only question is how to take these first steps. While this is a question we cannot answer in this paper, a suggestion to soccer clubs is to consider taking initiative to develop such collaborations, not only regarding physiology and soccer tactics, but the whole issue of managing soccer clubs.

Further research on product/service innovation in soccer clubs would be very interesting. Here, innovation networks[79] and open innovation[80] are concepts that seem fruitful since it deals with how organizations can use external resources in innovation. That is, it would represent a viable option for organizations that claim that they have too few internal resources. So why not open up and use external resources?

## Disclosure statement

No potential conflict of interest was reported by the author.

## Funding

This work was supported by Centrum för Idrottsforskning.

## Notes

1. Enjolras, 'The Commercialization of Voluntary Sport Organizations in Norway'; and Slack, *The Commercialisation of Sport*.
2. Aiken and Hage, 'The Organic Organization and Innovation'; Thompson, 'Bureaucracy and Innovation'; and West and Farr, 'Innovation at Work'.
3. Williams, 'The Local and the Global in English Soccer and the Rise of Satellite Television'
4. Boyle and Haynes, *Football in the New Media Age*.
5. Baimbridge and Cameron, 'Satellite Television and the Demand for Football: A Whole New Ball Game?'; and Sandvoss, *A Game of Two Halves: Football, Television and Globalization*.
6. Bower, *Broken Dreams: Vanity, Greed and the Souring of British Football*.
7. Andersson and Carlsson, 'Football in Scandinavia: A Fusion of Welfare Policy and the Market'; and Garland et al., *The Future of Football: Challenges for the Twenty-first Century*.
8. Cairns et al., 'The Economics of Professional Team Sports: A Survey of Theory and Evidence'; Forrest and Simmons, 'Outcome Uncertainty and Attendance Demand in Sport: The Case of English Soccer'; Kesenne, 'Competetive Balance in Team Sports and the Impact of Revenue Sharing'; and Szymanski, 'Income Inequality, Competitive Balance and the Attractiveness of Team Sports: Some Evidence and a Natural Experiment from English Soccer'.
9. Baroncelli and Lago, 'Italian Football'; and Lago et al., 'The Financial Crisis in European Football: An Introduction'.
10. Babatunde et al., 'English Football'; Barros, 'Portuguese Football'; Beech et al., 'Insolvency Events among English Football Clubs'; Hamil and Walters, 'Financial Performance in English Professional Football: "An Inconvenient Truth"'; and Dejonghe and Vandeweghe, 'Belgian Football'.
11. Arnold and Benveniste, 'Wealth and Poverty in the English Football League'; Garcia-del-Barrio and Szymanski, 'Goal! Profit Maximization Versus Win Maximization in Soccer'; and Kuper and Szymanski, *Why England Lose: & Other Curious Football Phenomena Explained*.
12. Mnzava, 'Do Intangible Investments Matter? Evidence from Soccer Corporations'; and Szymanski, 'Why is Manchester United so Successful?'.
13. Lago et al., 'The Financial Crisis in European Football: An Introduction'.
14. Buraimo et al., 'English Football'.
15. Ascari and Gagnepain, 'Spanish Football'.
16. Franck and Lang, *A Theoretical Analysis of the Influence of Money Injections on Risk Taking in Football Clubs*; and Szymanski and Smith, 'The English Football Industry: Profit, Performance and ...'.
17. Storm, 'The Need for Regulating Professional Soccer in Europe. A Soft Budget Constraint Approach Argument'.
18. Schumpeter, *The Theory of Economic Development*.
19. March, 'Exploration and Exploitation in Organizational Learning'.
20. Brooks, 'Social and Technological Innovation'; Damanpour and Evan, 'Organizational Innovation and Performance: The Problem of "Organizational Lag"'; and King et al., 'Organizational Innovation in the UK: A Case Study of Perceptions and Processes'.
21. Johansson and Lindberg, 'Making a Case for Gender-inclusive Innovation through the Concept of Creative Imitation'.
22. Chesbrough, *Open Innovation: The New Imperative for Creating and Profiting from Technology*.
23. Hamil and Chadwick, 'Introduction and Market Overview'.
24. den Hertog et al., 'Capabilities for Managing Service Innovation: Towards a Conceptual Framework'.

25. Drucker, *Innovation and Entrepreneurship*; Schuler, 'Fostering and Facilitating Entrepreneurship in Organizations: Implications for Organization Structure and Human Resource Management Practices'; and Stevenson and Jarillo, 'A Paradigm of Entrepreneurship: Entrepreneurial Management'.
26. Morris et al., *Corporate Entrepreneurship and Innovation: Entrepreneurial Development within Organizations*.
27. Quinn, 'Technological Innovation, Entrepreneurship, and Strategy'.
28. King and Anderson, *Managing Innovation and Change: A Critical Guide for Organizations*.
29. Van de Ven, *The Innovation Journey*.
30. Pinchot and Pellman, *Intrapreneuring in Action: A Handbook for Business Innovation*.
31. Gilmore and Gilson, 'Finding Form: Elite Sports and the Business of Change'.
32. Williams, 'The Fall of Liverpool FC and the English Football "Revolution"'.
33. Henderson, 'Football Broadcasting: Tipping Point or Bleeding Edge?'.
34. Paramio et al., 'From Modern to Postmodern: The Development of Football Stadia in Europe'.
35. Gammelsæter, 'The Organization of Professional Football in Scandinavia'; and Rosca, 'Strategic Development of the Manchester United Football Club'.
36. Gerrard, 'Why do Manchester United Keep Winning on and off the Field?'; Shaw, 'Manchester United Football Club: Developing a Network Orchestration Model'; and Szymanski, 'Why is Manchester United so Successful?'.
37. Demil and Lecocq, 'Business Model Evolution: In Search of Dynamic Consistency'; and Grundy, 'Managing Strategic Breakthroughs-lessons from the Football Industry 1997–98'.
38. Williams et al., *Passing Rhythms. Liverpool FC and the Transformation of Football*.
39. Callejo and Forcadell, 'Real Madrid Football Club: A New Model of Business Organization for Sports Clubs in Spain'; and Garcia and Rodrigues, 'From Sports Clubs to Stock Companies: The Financial Structure of Football in Spain, 1992–2001'.
40. Hamil et al., 'The Model of Governance at FC Barcelona: Balancing Member Democracy, Commercial Strategy, Corporate Social Responsibility and Sporting Performance'; and Richelieu et al., 'The Internationalisation of a Sports Team Brand: The Case of European Soccer Teams'.
41. Chadwick and Clowes, 'The Use of Extension Strategies by Clubs in the English Football Premier League'.
42. Baden-Fuller et al., 'Editorial'.
43. McNamara et al., 'Competing Business Models, Value Creation and Appropriation in English Football'.
44. Gerrard, 'Why do Manchester United keep Winning on and off the field?'.
45. Ibid., 85.
46. Darby et al., 'Football Academies and the Migration of African Football Labor to Europe'; and De Heij et al., 'Strategic Actions in European Soccer: Do They Matter?'.
47. Hoyos, 'Media Sport Stars and Junior Players: The Design and Analysis of the Recruiting Methods of Players in Real Madrid'.
48. Wilson, *Inverting the Pyramid*.
49. Kelly and Waddington, 'Abuse, Intimidation and Violence as Aspects of Managerial Control in Professional Soccer in Britain and Ireland'; and Wilders, 'The Football Club Manager – A Precarious Occupation?'
50. Johnson et al., 'Sport Psychology Consulting among Swedish Premier Soccer Coaches'.
51. Gilmore and Gilson, 'Finding Form: Elite Sports and the Business of Change'.
52. Van Uden, 'Transforming a Football Club into a "Total Experience" Entertainment Company: Implications for Management'.
53. Thrassou et al., 'Contemporary Marketing Communications Framework for Football Clubs'.
54. Storm, 'The Rational Emotions of FC København: A Lesson on Generating Profit in Professional Soccer'.
55. McGuire, 'Football in the Community: Still "the Game's Best Kept Secret"?'; and Watson, 'Football in the Community: "What's the Score?"'.

56. Parnell et al., 'Football in the Community Schemes: Exploring the Effectiveness of an Intervention in Promoting Healthful Behaviour Change'.
57. Walters and Hamil, 'Ownership and Governance'.
58. Thrassou et al., 'Contemporary Marketing Communications Framework for Football Clubs'.
59. Gilmore and Gilson, 'Finding Form: Elite Sports and the Business of Change'.
60. Shaw, 'Manchester United Football Club: Developing a Network Orchestration Model'.
61. Stokvis, 'Ajax isn't Ajax Anymore: On Power, Rhetoric and Identity'.
62. Sondaal, 'Football's Grobalization or Globalization? The Lessons of Liverpool Football Club's Evolution in the Premier League Era'.
63. Castillo, 'The Other Basque Subversives: Athletic de Bilbao vs. the New Age of Soccer'.
64. Geertz, *The Interpretation of Cultures*.
65. Agar, *The Professional Stranger: An Informal Introduction to Ethnography*.
66. Andersson and Carlsson, 'Football in Scandinavia: A Fusion of Welfare Policy and the Market'.
67. Ericsson, 'Football, Foundry Communities and the Swedish Model'.
68. Billing et al., 'Paradoxes of Football Professionalization in Sweden: A Club Approach'.
69. Imai, Kaizen: The Key to Japan's Competitive Success.
70. Van Uden, 'Transforming a Football Club into a "Total Experience" Entertainment Company: Implications for Management'.
71. Pine II and Gilmore, 'Welcome to the Experience Economy'.
72. Andersson, "Spela fotboll bondjävlar!" : en studie av svensk klubbkultur och local identitet från 1950 till 2000-talets början [Play Soccer You Peasants!: A Study of Swedish Clubculture and Local Identity 1950 to 2000].
73. A Whole Section of the Stadium was "Forgotten", MFF CEO Per Nilsson said.
74. Compare Johansson and Lindberg, 'Making a Case for Gender-inclusive Innovation through the Concept of Creative Imitation'.
75. DiMaggio and Powell, 'The Iron Cage Revisited: Institutional Isomorphism and Collective Rationality in Organizational Fields'.
76. Quinn, 'Managing Innovation: Controlled Chaos'.
77. Stacey, *Managing Chaos. Dynamic Business Strategies in an Unpredictable World.*
78. Flores et al., 'Universities as Key Enablers to Develop New Collaborative Environments for Innovation: Successful Experiences from Switzerland and India'.
79. den Hertog et al., 'Capabilities for Managing Service Innovation: Towards a Conceptual Framework'.
80. Chesbrough, *Open Innovation: The New Imperative for Creating and Profiting from Technology.*

## References

Agar, M. *The Professional Stranger: An Informal Introduction to Ethnography.* 2nd ed. San Diego, CA: Academic Press, 1996.

Aiken, M., and J. Hage. 'The Organic Organization and Innovation'. *Sociology* 5, no. 1 (1971): 63–82. doi:10.1177/003803857100500105.

Andersson, T. *"Spela fotboll bondjävlar!" : en studie av svensk klubbkultur och lokal identitet från 1950 till 2000-talets början. Del 1* [Play Soccer You Peasants!: A Study of Swedish Clubculture and Local Identity 1950 to 2000]. Eslöv: Brutus Östlings bokförlag Symposion, 2011.

Andersson, T., and B. Carlsson. 'Football in Scandinavia: A Fusion of Welfare Policy and the Market'. *Soccer & Society* 10, no. 3–4 (2009): 299–305. doi:10.1080/14660970902771365.

Arnold, A.J., and I. Benveniste. 'Wealth and Poverty in the English Football League'. *Accounting & Business Research (Wolters Kluwer UK)* 17, no. 67 (1987): 195–203. doi:10.1080/00014788.1987.9729800.

Ascari, G., and P. Gagnepain. 'Spanish Football'. *Journal of Sports Economics* 7, no. 1 (2006): 76–89. doi:10.1177/1527002505282869.

Babatunde, B., R. Simmons, and S. Szymanski. 'English Football'. *Journal of Sports Economics* 7, no. 1 (2006): 29–46. doi:10.1177/1527002505282911.

Baden-Fuller, C., B. Demil, X. Lecoq, and I. MacMillan. 'Editorial'. *Long Range Planning* 43 (2010): 143–5. doi:10.1016/j.lrp.2010.03.002.

Baimbridge, M., and S. Cameron. 'Satellite Television and the Demand for Football: A Whole New Ball Game?' *Scottish Journal of Political Economy* 43, no. 3 (1996): 317–33. doi:10.1111/j.1467-9485.1996.tb00848.x.

Baroncelli, A., and U. Lago. 'Italian Football'. *Journal of Sports Economics* 7, no. 1 (2006): 13–28. doi:10.1177/1527002505282863.

Barros, C.P. 'Portuguese Football'. *Journal of Sports Economics* 7, no. 1 (2006): 96–104. doi:10.1177/1527002505282870.

Beech, J., S. Horsman, and J. Magraw. 'Insolvency Events among English Football Clubs'. *International Journal of Sports Marketing & Sponsorship* 11, no. 3 (2010): 236–49. doi:50321071.

Billing, P., M. Franzén, and T. Peterson. 'Paradoxes of Football Professionalization in Sweden: A Club Approach'. *Soccer and Society* 5, no. 1 (2004): 82–99. doi:10.1080/14660970512331391014.

Bower, T. *Broken Dreams: Vanity, Greed and the Souring of British Football*. London: Simon & Schuster, 2003.

Boyle, R., and R. Haynes. *Football in the New Media Age*. London: Routledge, 2004.

Brooks, H. 'Social and Technological Innovation'. In *Managing Innovation*, ed. S.B. Lundstedt and E.W. Colglazier Jr., 1–30. New York: Pergamon, 1982.

Buraimo, B., R. Simmons, and S. Szymanski. 'English Football'. *Journal of Sports Economics* 7, no. 1 (2006): 29–46.

Cairns, J.A., N. Jennett, and P.J. Sloane. 'The Economics of Professional Team Sports: A Survey of Theory and Evidence'. *Journal of Economic Studies* 13 (1986): 1–80. doi:10.1108/eb002618.

Callejo, M.B., and F.J. Forcadell. 'Real Madrid Football Club: A New Model of Business Organization for Sports Clubs in Spain'. *Global Business and Organizational Excellence* 26, no. 1 (2006): 51–64. doi:10.1002/joe.20121.

Castillo, J.C. 'The Other Basque Subversives: Athletic De Bilbao Vs. the New Age of Soccer'. *Sport in Society* 11, no. 6 (2008): 711–21. doi:10.1080/17430430802283997.

Chadwick, S., and J. Clowes 'The Use of Extension Strategies by Clubs in the English Football Premier League'. *Managing Leisure* 3, no. 4 (1998): 194–203. doi:10.1080/136067198375978.

Chesbrough, H.W. *Open Innovation: The New Imperative for Creating and Profiting from Technology*. Boston, MA: Harvard Business School Press, 2003.

Damanpour, F., and W.M. Evan. 'Organizational Innovation and Performance: The Problem of "Organizational Lag"'. *Administrative Science Quarterly* 29, no. 3 (1984): 392–409. doi:10.2307/2393031.

Darby, P., G. Akindes, and M. Kirwin. 'Football Academies and the Migration of African Football Labor to Europe'. *Journal of Sport and Social Issues* 31, no. 2 (2007): 143–61. doi:10.1177/0193723507300481.

De Heij, R., P. Vermeulen, and L. Teunter. 'Strategic Actions in European Soccer: Do They Matter?' *The Service Industries Journal* 26, no. 6 (2006): 615–32. doi:10.1080/02642060600850659.

Dejonghe, T., and H. Vandeweghe. 'Belgian Football'. *Journal of Sports Economics* 7, no. 1 (2006): 105–13. doi:10.1177/1527002505283022.

Demil, B., and X. Lecocq. 'Business Model Evolution. in Search of Dynamic Consistency'. *Long Range Planning* 43, no. 2–3 (2010): 227–46. doi:10.1016/j.lrp.2010.02.004.

DiMaggio, P.J., and W.W. Powell. 'The Iron Cage Revisited: Institutional Isomorphism and Collective Rationality in Organizational Fields'. *American Sociological Review* 48, no. 2 (April 1983): 147–60. doi:10.1016/S0742-3322(00)17011-1.

Drucker, P.F. *Innovation and Entrepreneurship*. London: Heinemann, 1985.

Enjolras, B. 'The Commercialization of Voluntary Sport Organizations in Norway'. *Nonprofit and Voluntary Sector Quarterly* 31, no. 3 (2002): 352–76. doi:10.1177/0899764002313003.

Ericsson, C. 'Football, Foundry Communities and the Swedish Model'. *Soccer and Society* 4, no. 1 (2003): 20–40. doi:10.1080/14660970512331390713.

Flores, M., C. Boër, C. Huber, A. Plüss, R. Schoch, and M. Pouly. 'Universities as Key Enablers to Develop New Collaborative Environments for Innovation: Successful Experiences from Switzerland and India'. *International Journal of Production Research* 47, no. 17 (2009): 4935–53. doi:10.1080/00207540902847454.

Forrest, D., and R. Simmons. 'Outcome Uncertainty and Attendance Demand in Sport: The Case of English Soccer'. *The Statistician* 51, no. 2 (2002): 229–41.

Franck, E., and M. Lang. 'A Theoretical Analysis of the Influence of Money Injections on Risk Taking in Football Clubs'. *Scottish Journal of Political Economy* 61, no. 4 (2012): 430–54. doi:10.1111/sjpe.12052

Gammelsæter, H. 'The Organization of Professional Football in Scandinavia'. *Soccer and Society* 10, no. 3-4 (2009): 305–23. doi:10.1080/14660970902771373.

García, J., and P. Rodríguez. 'From Sports Clubs to Stock Companies: The Financial Structure of Football in Spain, 1992–2001'. *European Sport Management Quarterly* 3, no. 4 (2003): 253–69. doi:10.1080/16184740308721955.

Garcia-del-Barrio, P., and S. Szymanski. 'Goal! Profit Maximization versus Win Maximization in Soccer'. *Review of Industrial Organization* 34, no. 1 (2009): 45–68. doi:10.1007/s11151-009-9203-6.

Garland, J., D. Malcolm, and M. Rowe. *The Future of Football: Challenges for the Twenty-First Century, Sport in the Global Society, 17,* London: F. Cass, 2000.

Geertz, C. *The Interpretation of Cultures.* New York: Basic Books, 1973.

Gerrard, B. 'Why Do Manchester United Keep Winning on and off the Field?'. In *Manchester United*, ed. D.L. Andrews, 65–86. London: Routledge, 2004.

Gilmore, S., and C. Gilson. 'Finding Form: Elite Sports and the Business of Change'. *Journal of Organizational Change Management* 20, no. 3 (2007): 409–28. doi:10.1108/09534810710740218.

Grundy, T. 'Managing Strategic Breakthroughs-Lessons from the Football Industry 1997–98'. *Strategic Change* 8, no. 8 (1999): 435–44. doi:10.1002/(SICI)1099-1697(199912)8:8<435:AID-JSC469>3.0.CO;2-4.

Hamil, S., and S. Chadwick. 'Introduction and Market Overview'. In *Managing Football. an International Perspective*, ed. S. Hamil and S. Chadwick, 3–16. London: Elsevier, 2009.

Hamil, S., and G. Walters 'Financial Performance in English Professional Football: 'an Inconvenient Truth''. *Soccer & Society* 11, no. 4 (2010): 354–72. doi:10.1080/14660971003780214.

Hamil, S., G. Walters, and L. Watson 'The Model of Governance at FC Barcelona: Balancing Member Democracy, Commercial Strategy, Corporate Social Responsibility and Sporting Performance'. *Soccer & Society* 11, no. 4 (2010): 475–504. doi:10.1080/14660971003780446.

Henderson, S. 'Football Broadcasting: Tipping Point or Bleeding Edge?' *Soccer & Society* 11, no. 5 (2010): 614–26. doi:10.1080/14660970.2010.497361.

den Hertog, P., W. van der Aa, and M.W. de Jong. 'Capabilities for Managing Service Innovation: Towards a Conceptual Framework'. *Journal of Service Management* 21, no. 4 (2010): 490–514. doi:10.1108/09564231011066123.

Hoyos, I.U.d. 'Media Sport Stars and Junior Players: The Design and Analysis of the Recruiting Methods of Players in Real Madrid'. *Soccer & Society* 9, no. 4 (2008): 551–63. doi:10.1080/14660970802257614.

Imai, M. *Kaizen: The Key to Japan's Competitive Success.* New York: Random House Business Division, 1986.

Johansson, A.W., and M. Lindberg. 'Making a Case for Gender-Inclusive Innovation through the Concept of Creative Imitation'. *Annals of Innovation & Entrepreneurship* 2, no. 2 (2011): 1–13. doi:10.3402/aie.v2i2.8440.

Johnson, U., K. Andersson, and J. Fallby. 'Sport Psychology Consulting among Swedish Premier Soccer Coaches'. *International Journal of Sport and Exercise Psychology* 9, no. 4 (2011): 308–22. doi:10.1080/1612197x.2011.623455.

Kelly, S., and I. Waddington. 'Abuse, Intimidation and Violence as Aspects of Managerial Control in Professional Soccer in Britain and Ireland'. *International Review for the Sociology of Sport* 41, no. 2 (2006): 147–64. doi:10.1177/1012690206075417.

Kesenne, S. 'Competetive Balance in Team Sports and the Impact of Revenue Sharing'. *Journal of Sport Management* 20, no. 1 (2006): 39–51. doi:10.1177/152700250000100105.

King, N., and N. Anderson. *Managing Innovation and Change: A Critical Guide for Organizations*. 2nd ed. *Psychology at Work*. London: Thomson Learning, 2002.

King, N., N. Anderson, and M.A. West. 'Organizational Innovation in the UK: A Case Study of Perceptions and Processes'. *Work & Stress* 5, no. 4 (1991): 331–9. doi:10.1080/02678379108257031.

Kuper, S., and S. Szymanski. *Why England Lose: & Other Curious Football Phenomena Explained*. London: HarperCollins, 2009.

Lago, U., R. Simmons, and S. Szymanski. 'The Financial Crisis in European Football: An Introduction'. *Journal of Sports Economics* 7, no. 1 (2006): 3–12. doi:10.1177/1527002505282871.

March, J.G. 'Exploration and Exploitation in Organizational Learning'. *Organization Science* 2, no. 1 (1991): 71–87. doi:10.2307/2634940.

McGuire, B. 'Football in the Community: Still 'the Game's Best Kept Secret'?' *Soccer and Society* 9, no. 4 (2008): 439–54. doi:10.1080/14660970802257481.

McNamara, P., S.I. Peck, and A. Sasson. 'Competing Business Models, Value Creation and Appropriation in English Football'. *Long Range Planning* 46 (2013): 475–87. doi:10.1016/j.lrp.2011.10.002.

Mnzava, B. 'Do Intangible Investments Matter? Evidence from Soccer Corporations'. *Sport, Business & Management* 3, no. 2 (2013): 158–68. doi:10.1108/20426781311325087.

Morris, M.H., J.G. Covin, and D.F. Kuratko. *Corporate Entrepreneurship and Innovation: Entrepreneurial Development within Organizations*. 2nd ed. Mason, OH: Thomson/South-Western, 2008.

Paramio, Juan Luis, B. Buraimo, and C. Campos. 'From Modern to Postmodern: The Development of Football Stadia in Europe'. *Sport in Society* 11, no. 5 (2008): 517–34.

Parnell, D., G. Stratton, B. Drust, and D. Richardson. 'Football in the Community Schemes: Exploring the Effectiveness of an Intervention in Promoting Healthful Behaviour Change'. *Soccer & Society* 14, no. 1 (2013): 35–51. doi:10.1080/14660970.2012.692678.

Pinchot, G., and R. Pellman. *Intrapreneuring in Action: A Handbook for Business Innovation*. San Francisco, CA: Berrett-Koehler, 1999.

Pine II, B.J., and J.H. Gilmore. 'Welcome to the Experience Economy'. *Harvard Business Review* 76. (July–August 1998): 97–105.

Quinn, J.B. 'Managing Innovation: Controlled Chaos'. *McKinsey Quarterly* 22, no. 2 (1986): 2–21.

Quinn, J.B. 'Technological Innovation, Entrepreneurship, and Strategy'. *Sloan Management Review* 20 (Spring 1979): 19–30.

Richelieu, A., S. Lopez, and M. Desbordes. 'The Internationalisation of a Sports Team Brand: The Case of European Soccer Teams'. *International Journal of Sports Marketing & Sponsorship* 10, no. 1 (2008): 29–44.

Rosca, V. 'Strategic Development of the Manchester United Football Club'. *Economia: Seria Management* 13, no. 2 (2010): 478–84.

Sandvoss, C. *A Game of Two Halves: Football, Television and Globalization*. London: Routledge, 2003.

Schuler, R.S. 'Fostering and Facilitating Entrepreneurship in Organizations: Implications for Organization Structure and Human Resource Management Practices'. *Human Resource Management* 25 (Winter 1986): 607–29. doi:10.1002/hrm.3930250408.

Schumpeter, J.A. *The Theory of Economic Development*. Transaction ed. London: Transaction, 1934.

Shaw, D.R.D.S. 'Manchester United Football Club: Developing a Network Orchestration Model'. *European Journal of Information Systems* 16, no. 5 (2007): 628–42. doi:10.1057/palgrave.ejis.3000702.

Slack, T. *The Commercialisation of Sport, Sport in the Global Society*. London: Routledge, 2004.

Sondaal, T. 'Football's Grobalization or Globalization? The Lessons of Liverpool Football Club's Evolution in the Premier League Era'. *Soccer & Society* 14, no. 4 (2013): 485–501. doi:10.1080/14660970.2013.810432.

Stacey, R.D. *Managing Chaos. Dynamic Business Strategies in an Unpredictable World.* London: Kogan Page, 1992.

Stevenson, H.H., and J.C. Jarillo. 'A Paradigm of Entrepreneurship: Entrepreneurial Management'. *Strategic Management Journal* 11 (1990): 17–27. doi:10.1007/978-3-540-48543-8_7.

Stokvis, R. 'Ajax Isn't Ajax Anymore: On Power, Rhetoric and Identity'. *Soccer and Society* 9, no. 4 (2008): 497–508. doi:10.1080/14660970802257564.

Storm, R.K. 'The Need for Regulating Professional Soccer in Europe. a Soft Budget Constraint Approach Argument'. *Sport, Business & Management* 2, no. 1 (2012): 21–38. doi:10.1108/20426781211207647.

Storm, R.K. 'The Rational Emotions of FC København: A Lesson on Generating Profit in Professional Soccer'. *Soccer and Society* 10, no. 3–4 (2009): 459–76. doi:10.1080/14660970902771506.

Szymanski, S. 'Income Inequality, Competitive Balance and the Attractiveness of Team Sports: Some Evidence and a Natural Experiment from English Soccer'. *Economic Journal* 111, no. 469 (2001): 69–84. doi:10.1111/1468-0297.00599

Szymanski, S. 'Why is Manchester United So Successful?'. *Business Strategy Review* 9, no. 4 (1998): 47–54.

Szymanski, S., and R. Smith. 'The English Football Industry: Profit, Performance and Industrial Structure'. *International Review of Applied Economics* 11, no. 1 (1997): 135–53. doi:10.1080/02692179700000008.

Thompson, V.A. 'Bureaucracy and Innovation'. *Administrative Science Quarterly* 10, no. 1 (1965): 1–20.

Thrassou, A., D. Vrontis, N.L. Kartakoullis, and T. Kriemadis 'Contemporary Marketing Communications Framework for Football Clubs'. *Journal of Promotion Management* 18, no. 3 (2012): 278–305. doi:10.1080/10496491.2012.696454.

Van de Ven, A.H. *The Innovation Journey.* New York: Oxford University Press, 1999.

Van Uden, J. 'Transforming a Football Club into a 'Total Experience' Entertainment Company: Implications for Management'. *Managing Leisure* 10, no. 3 (2005): 184–98. doi:10.1080/13606710500239087.

Walters, G., and S. Hamil. 'Ownership and Governance'. In *Managing Football. an International Perspective*, ed. S. Hamil and S. Chadwick, 17–36. Oxford: Butterworth-Heineman, 2009.

Watson, N. 'Football in the Community: "What's the Score?"'. *Soccer and Society* 1, no. 1 (2000): 114–25. doi:10.1080/14660970008721253.

West, M.A., and J.L. Farr. 'Innovation at Work'. In *Innovation at Work. Psychological and Organizational Strategies*, ed. M.A. West and J.L. Farr, 3–14. Chichester: Wiley, 1990.

Wilders, M.G. 'The Football Club Manager? A Precarious Occupation?' *Journal of Management Studies* 13, no. 2 (1976): 152–63. doi:10.1111/j.1467-6486.1976.tb00530.x.

Williams, J. 'The Fall of Liverpool FC and the English Football "Revolution"'. In *Passing Rhythms. Liverpool FC and the Transformation of Football*, ed. J. Williams, S. Hopkins, and C. Long, 147–72. Oxford: Berg, 2001.

Williams, A.M. 'The Local and the Global in English Soccer and the Rise of Satellite Television'. *Sociology of Sport Journal* 11, no. 4 (1994): 376–97.

Williams, J., S. Hopkins, and C. Long, eds. *Passing Rhythms. Liverpool FC and the Transformation of Football.* Oxford: Berg, 2001.

Wilson, J. *Inverting the Pyramid: A History of Football Tactics.* London: Orion, 2008.

# Sustainability initiatives in professional soccer

Taiyo Francis, Joanne Norris and Robert Brinkmann

Professional soccer, as an important driver of popular culture, has the potential to transform how we view and practice sustainability. Since the 1980s, the field of sustainability has focused on trying to reduce the impact of human activity on the planet by measuring and assessing the behaviour of organizations. While much progress has been made in a number of areas such as recycling and pollution, much more needs to be done to ensure that future generations are not harmed by today's consumptive society. It is worth examining what all major institutions, including professional soccer, are doing to reduce their impacts. This study focuses on an analysis of the 19 professional soccer teams in the US by assessing sustainability initiatives highlighted on team Websites and on the Websites of their home stadium. The results demonstrate that most teams are doing something to advance sustainability goals. However, the most active teams on sustainability initiatives are found in the Western Conference where the Timbers, Sounders, Whitecaps, Galaxy and Chivas USA are setting high standards for organizational sustainability.

## Soccer as a driver of social change

Soccer is the world's sport. The Fédération Internationale de Football Association (FIFA) conducted a survey in 2006 to account for the impact and significance of soccer around the world. They surveyed FIFA soccer associations in the 207 member nations to assess the number of registered players (professional players, amateur players over 18 and amateur players under 18) and referees. They found that there were over 265 million players. Just in 2000, six years prior, there were 242 million players – a growth rate of about 10%.[1] This is a stunning trend, which reflects the growing influence of soccer as a cultural factor worldwide.

An even larger growth trend in soccer is seen in North America. The United States and Canada account for 10% of the world's soccer participants.[2] Major League Soccer, since its foundation in 1993, has nearly doubled in size from 10 to 19 teams. By the year 2017, the league will have 22 teams in some of the country's top sporting markets.[3] The league has seen a steady rise in attendance since its opening years. It recently became the third largest sport by attendance only behind the National Football League and Major League Baseball.[4]

As with any new franchise, revenue gain was slow at first for MLS. The increase in capital throughout the years provided an opportunity to build stadiums specifically for soccer teams, rather than using stadiums shared with other sports. The Columbus Crew was the first of the MLS teams to build a soccer-specific stadium in 1999. Currently, 13 of the 19 teams in the league play in soccer-specific stadiums. The three new expansion teams, as well as three current teams, are seeking to build soccer-specific stadiums, or have plans to build one.[5] As we will see, some soccer teams are moving heavily into sustainability initiatives, particularly those that have their own stadiums.

## Modern sustainability movement

The modern sustainability movement in America started about a century after association football (soccer) was created in 1863, but environmentalism and sustainable practices have existed for longer. There have been three waves of the modern environmental movement in the United States. Theodore Roosevelt began the first wave by initiating land conservation in the period between the late-1800s to the 1920s.[6] He signed legislation establishing National Parks across the nation and went on to create the Antiquities Act in 1906. Roosevelt utilized this executive order to preserve and conserve nature and landscapes across the United States. The second wave of environmentalism, in the 1930s through the 1960s, came under the helm of biologist Rachel Carson and author Aldo Leopold.[7] Carson's book *Silent Spring* brought environmental awareness to the forefront of politics and policy.[8] During this era, much of the regulation we rely on to protect the environment was born. Carson brought attention to the overuse of pesticides and chemicals such as DDT, and as a result, we continue to see increasing regulation of harmful products (lead, mercury, greenhouse gases, etc.). The third and current wave, ranging from the 1970s to the present, focuses more broadly on social and economic issues within the context of environmental sustainability. Today, many governments, businesses and industries are investing in renewable energy, green building certification and other sustainable initiatives. This form of sustainability is what we see many sports franchises attempting.

The world's modern sustainability movement, or the third wave of US environmentalism, took stage beginning in 1972 when the United Nations held its Conference on the Human Environment. This is when the world saw an intergovernmental, global focus on sustainability and sustainable development. The Conference on the Human Environment resulted in the creation of the UN Environmental Programme, in reaction to the rapid industrialization of countries, globalization of the world and destruction of ecosystems.[9] A decade later, the World Commission on Environment and Development (WCED) was established. This group (often called the Brundtland Commission) took a deeper look into environmental problems and their causes. *Our Common Future: The World Commission on Environment and Development,* often referred to as the Brundtland Report, proposed long-term environmental strategies and policies to attain sustainable development by the end of the century and beyond.[10] The report outlined ways in which governments could work closely together to pursue economic and social development without environmental degradation. The idea was to enhance the environment by preserving and protecting it. This is when the three E's of sustainability were envisioned to link the ideas of Environment, Economics and Social Equity as keys to long-term survivability of our planet in a technological age.

The sustainability movement is still progressing. There is most notably an increasing amount of interest in sustainable development, climate change and environmental protection. The United Nations, for instance, created the Millennium

Development Goals, Sustainable Development Goals and carbon emission standards for entire nations (Rio + 20).[11] The United Nations continues to promote what sustainability stands for: environmental sustainability, social equity and thriving economics. However, the key to understanding sustainability is that it focuses heavily on measuring and assessing current practices in order to plan how to make improvements. These meticulous and measurable practices, referred to as 'benchmarking' in the sustainability community, break apart all actions of organizations in order to examine the environmental, economic and social impacts they have on the planet and society. Adaptations then come from the development of new aspirations which are optimistic, yet achievable enough for an organization to carry out in a reasonable amount of time.

Part of the drive to become green in professional sports comes from the growing trend in business to embrace sustainability. Most Fortune 500 firms now have distinct sustainability initiatives that are widely publicized. Wal-Mart, for example, is often, surprisingly, thought of as one of the leading corporate voices on green initiative.[12] At the same time, corporate leaders like Ray Anderson made a strong case for the role of ethics in promoting sustainability within a modern business culture.[13] This paper explores the benchmarking techniques of Major League Soccer teams in regard to sustainability in their facilities.

**Green stadiums**

Environmentally friendly stadiums are a new movement in the field of architecture and sports franchises. Teams in the National Football League, National Basketball Association, National Hockey League, Major League Baseball and Major League Soccer have begun to discover the environmental and economic benefits of green stadiums. These stadiums have a number of features that include energy and water efficiency, waste management and mass transit accessibility. Some organizations are certifying their buildings using a rating system called LEED accreditation. LEED, or Leadership in Energy and Environmental Design, is a rating system that takes into account the design, construction and functionality of an environmentally friendly structure.[14] There are four certification levels: certified, silver, gold and platinum; certified being the lowest and platinum being the highest rating. These levels are based on points that are gained from categories such as: energy performance, water performance, indoor environmental quality, sustainable sites, materials and resources and innovation in design. There are two types of LEED certified buildings; the first is a LEED certified existing building, the second is a LEED certified new construction. A few sports stadiums that are LEED certified are: National's Park in Washington DC (LEED certified silver new construction), Marlins Park in Miami (LEED certified gold new construction), Providence Park in Portland (LEED certified silver existing building) and Soldier Field in Chicago (LEED certified new construction).

The LEED programme was introduced by the United States Green Building Council (USGBC) which also works with an organization called the Green Sports Alliance (GSA). The GSA has made its mission to reduce the environmental impact of sports. Working with the USGBC, the GSA promotes LEED accredited new buildings and LEED renovations. The GSA has more than 180 members that are professional and collegiate sports teams and venues. The GSA was started in 2011 in the Pacific Northwest by the Seattle Mariners of Major League Baseball, the Seattle Seahawks of the National Football League, the Portland Trailblazers of the National

Basketball Association, the Vancouver Canucks of the National Hockey League, the Seattle Storm of the Women's National Basketball Association and the Seattle Sounders of Major League Soccer. The GSA does not work exclusively with the USGBC, but also works with the EPA, Natural Resources Defense Council and other environmental organizations. The GSA has worked with schools and sports organizations to bring environmental awareness and action to their communities. Recently, the GSA has collaborated with the San Francisco 49ers to begin construction on the first zero-energy stadium in California.[15]

## Methodology

This paper summarizes sustainability initiatives of Major League Soccer franchises. The paper delves into the forces and inspirations that have driven Major League Soccer and its teams to become a bigger role in the sustainability movement. To do this, Websites of the 19 Major League Soccer teams and their individual stadium Websites were examined to determine their efforts toward sustainability. A spreadsheet of their sustainable initiatives was created that included stadium design, efficiency and functionality; waste reduction, recycling and composting; sustainable food options; community outreach; and various other elements of sustainability. The Websites were also examined to ascertain if the teams acknowledged the awareness of environmental issues in the community and beyond as reasoning for their commitment. Like most professional sports leagues, Major League Soccer has designated a root template for their Websites. Some teams included sustainable initiatives, others do not.

The effectiveness of each franchise on sustainability initiatives was based on 13 standards: total attendance (2013), average attendance per game (2013), green building (LEED), construction, water conservation or reuse, green grounds management; local, organic and vegetarian food initiatives; waste management, community outreach, supporting local businesses, energy use and carbon credits, parking and transit and travel. We chose to include attendance numbers to provide us with an understanding of how many people these initiatives are affecting, and the impact being made by teams during a game and over the course of a season. There are a few franchises that have something in place for nearly every category, and others that have nothing.

The methodology does not provide us with information beyond the publicly accessible information on Websites. Nevertheless, it is a sound way to assess the significance of sustainability to the organization.

## Results

### Green building (LEED certification and construction)

Currently, there is only one LEED Certified stadium in Major League Soccer and it belongs to the Portland Timbers and Providence Park. According to the Timbers' Website, the stadium opened in 1926 and needed a thorough renovation. The club received a LEED Silver Certification for an existing building after renovations in 2011 improved its efficiency and sustainability. The construction materials from the renovation of Providence Park were donated to Habitat for Humanity. The Portland Timbers embarked on a mission, in partnership with Office Depot and the GSA, to create a green office space. There is a possibility that two new LEED stadiums may come on the scene in the near future. The San Jose Earthquakes are in the process of building their new stadium which could become a LEED certified new construction and should open in 2015. DC United has been looking to build a new stadium for the past several years. Like National's Park, also in Washington DC for the Washington Nationals of Major League Baseball, United is looking to build a LEED certified new structure.

A common theme for newer stadiums or stadiums that have been renovated is using reusable and repurposed materials for the construction of the structure. BBVA Compass Stadium, home of the Houston Dynamo, states on their Website that they had 98.42% of the wood-based building materials sourced from a Forest Stewardship Council certified forest.[16] The Forest Stewardship Council helps manage forests and set standards to make sure companies are environmentally, economically and socially responsible. They also reportedly diverted 86.85% of the generated construction waste from landfills. When it was decided that the Kingdome in Seattle was to be demolished, the city chose to recycle 97% of the concrete. After the demolition and cleanup of the Kingdome site, 35% of the recycled concrete was used to build CenturyLink Field which replaced the Kingdome. BC Place, home of the Vancouver Whitecaps, was refitted with a retractable roof in 2007. This new roof replaced a dome that was inflated and kept up by air pressure. The steel that was used in the dome roofing was shipped to a local steel recycler. The dome had begun to deteriorate, but instead of rebuilding a new stadium which could have generated up to 120,000 tons of greenhouse gas emissions, it was decided to renovate the roof. The majority of the old roof was recycled and made into tarps, handbags, movie screens, water runoff lining and tents. During the renovation process, the old plastic seats and their metal constraints were removed and recycled. More and more stadiums and buildings are repurposing and recycling old materials to build new structures in a more sustainable fashion.

### Water conservation and reuse

The StubHub Center, which houses the Los Angeles Galaxy and Chivas USA, is making strides in water conservation and reuse. StubHub Center collects grey water from surrounding areas and it is treated by the municipality to reuse for landscaping and industrial uses. The Center is part of an extensive existing grey water reclamation system that is controlled by the local municipality. In 2009, the stadium replaced traditional one flush gallon urinals with zero-gallon urinals. The urinals are manufactured by Falcon Water free Technologies, which save money on water and conserve the liquid as well. StubHub Center has been outfitted with sink aerators to reduce the flow of water dispensed through sinks in the stadium. Bathrooms are an important part of sustainable stadiums because thousands of fans each game are using those facilities; and that is where a lot of water is wasted. The stadium has had smaller, efficient washing machines that reduce water usage installed. Precision nozzles were installed on 1400 sprinklers in decorative flower beds around the stadium. These sprinklers save around 1.5 million gallons of water a year by using 30% less than the old nozzles. The pavement design outside of the stadium helps to control water usage from the sprinklers. The walkways surrounding StubHub Center reduce the area that needs to be watered.

CenturyLink Field is much like StubHub Center, they place a heavy importance on water conservation and reuse. The stadium has retrofitted all of their urinals with ultra-low-flow technology that saves 1.3 million gallons of water a year. In 2012,

CenturyLink Field used 15% less water than their previous year; which was enough water for 21,533 people for a year. Approximately 94% of the cleaning and soap products used in restrooms are Green Seal certified.

According to this research, several teams are embracing water conservation and reuse. The Houston Dynamo and BBVA Compass Stadium are reducing water use by 41% through high-efficiency low-flush toilets and non-water urinals. Gillette Stadium, home of the New England Revolution, uses its own on-site wastewater treatment plant and irrigation well. This way they can treat their own water on site and reuse it; also with their own irrigation well they are providing water for themselves. Providence Park in Portland has adopted low-flow urinals and toilets, and switched to foam soap dispensers; all part of their design to become LEED certified. Some teams may not list their practices on their website or their stadium's Website, but it is safe to make the assumption that they are embracing some of these water conservation and restroom techniques to save water and money.

### Green grounds and facilities management

Green grounds management, a measurement of the sustainability of the operations and maintenance of the stadium, takes into account management and cleaning of the grounds. Two teams reported on this section, the Vancouver Whitecaps and Portland Timbers. However, we can assume that the LA Galaxy and Chivas USA both have excellent standards for ground management because StubHub Center was the first stadium in the US to achieve ISO 14001 certification for their Environmental Management System. This means they have expressed written goals for the venue to exceed in environmental performance. Some of these goals or initiatives are: reduced cost of waste management, lower energy consumption, lower water consumption, lower material consumption and a lower cost for distribution.

The Vancouver Whitecaps and BC Place have committed to sourcing biodegradable cleaning products. These are products that, should they be disposed of in a landfill will break down over time. The Portland Timbers have committed to a change over from traditional janitorial supplies to green products where it would be practical and applicable. This includes: green floor scrubbers, green ice melt and all cleaning products are 100% green. Green ice melt is placed on pavement to help melt the snow and ice and clear pathways.

### Local, organic and vegetarian food initiatives and support for local businesses

Many professional sports venues are continuing to search for local, organic and vegetarian food options not only to become more sustainable, but to provide services to customers who are requesting these sustainable options. Venders are now composting and recycling food, as well as recycling kitchen materials. StubHub Center is now partnering with their food service provider Levy Restaurants to compost food waste in their kitchens. This is similar to the Portland Timbers, who at Providence Park, compost throughout stadium kitchens and donate left-over food products to St. Vincent DePaul. The Timbers also donate their glass bottles to charity and recycle their cooking oil.

CenturyLink Field and BC Place are both deeply invested into buying locally and purchasing organic foods. CenturyLink Field partnered with their concessions and vendors in 2010 to implement a sustainability programme to focus on using organic fruits and vegetables. They did not stop there as they also sought out sustainably harvested seafood, meats from humanely raised livestock and local products where applicable. Excess food at CenturyLink field donated to programmes in Seattle such as Food Lifeline and Operation Sack Lunch. In 2011, nearly 4600 meals were donated, roughly 11,000 lb of food. BC Place is partner with and supports SOLE foods which is an urban farm located only a few hundred yards away from the stadium. It is an initiative that cultivates organic food. The head Chef Ryan Stone sources fresh vegetables and fruit from the 2-acre farm. The initiative also provides agricultural training and employment for local residents.

BC Place and their partnership with SOLE food farm also supports local business by giving construction materials such as tarps, steel, metals, wood and other reusable products to local recycling agencies. The Portland Timbers utilize the same concept by donating all of their old electronics to Free Geek which takes those electronics and recycles them for reuse.

### Community outreach

Professional sports teams, because of their notoriety and famous athletes, excel in community outreach. They have the money and draw to spread awareness and promote change within communities. With the increasing interest in Major League Soccer, the base for larger community outreach is being created, especially in terms of environmental awareness and sustainability. The Chicago Fire hosted a 'Fire Goes Green' match against the Houston Dynamo in 2010. Before the game, the staff and team planted 40 trees around Toyota Park. When fans entered for the game, they were handed reusable bags and recycling was added throughout the stadium. These are the opportunities that franchises can create to educate the public and make strides in the sustainability movement. MLS WORKS, which is a community outreach programme for Major League Soccer, partnered with the Columbus Crew to redesign and makeover the Linden Village Green Space Community Garden. BC Place donated a portion of their old inflated roof to Celista, BC to line their community ice rink.

The Portland Timbers have embarked on a variety of community outreach programmes that help the environment. Providence Park takes old banners and partners with Relan to re-purpose them as bags. They made investments in environmentally focused nonprofits through the Community Fund of the Timbers. The Timbers have teamed up with local municipalities to help build soccer fields in the Portland Metro area to encourage kids to be healthy and active, as well as plant thousands of trees. In addition to building soccer fields and areas of activity for kids, the Timbers worked on an Earth Day project with MLS WORKS at Hosford Middle School outside of Portland. Unclaimed 'Lost & Found' clothing at Providence Park is donated to Goodwill and The Lions Club, and unclaimed cell phones are donated to the Cell Phones for Soldiers programme.

### Waste management and energy use

Waste management and energy usage are arguably the most important facets of a sports venue's sustainability. Fans come and they consume food, materials, water and energy; so it is important for stadiums to be efficient with energy and waste disposal if they want to maximize their sustainability. Many of the teams outlined their plans for sustainable waste disposal and energy on either their team website or their stadium's website. Some of the league's teams are only making small changes. The New England Revolution, for example, added solar trash compactors to their site and developed policies to reduce packaging waste from vendors. Other teams are making strong investments to save money on waste disposal. Teams like: the LA Galaxy, Chivas USA, Portland Timbers, Seattle Sounders and the Vancouver White-caps are some of the biggest investors in sustainable waste disposal.

Teams that are making strides in energy use reduction and efficiency are: the Houston Dynamo, New England Revolution, Philadelphia Union and Sporting Kansas City. The Houston Dynamo were able to reduce their energy use by 20.41% in 2007 by changing their standards to fit that of the American Society of Heating, Refrigerating, and Air Conditioning. The New England Revolution utilizes solar energy to provide 30% of the power used in the Patriot Place shopping center out-side of the stadium. Gillette Stadium also features white roofs on all its building, which give off a high Solar Reflectance Index; this helps facilitate heat island reduc-tion. The Philadelphia Union use PPL Energy, the company that owns the stadium rights, to explore alternative energy options and efficiency in its facilities. Sporting Kansas City sports a solar-friendly stadium.

The Los Angeles Galaxy and Chivas USA, at the StubHub Center, have imple-mented a public recycling programme to capture the bottles, cans and paper waste generated on the main levels of the stadium. Stadium Operations recycles card-boards, metals, glass and plastics. Together the two teams work with companies to divert batteries, light bulbs, kitchen grease, electronic waste and hazardous materials from landfills. Both teams also partner with Long Beach Conservation Corps, to sep-arate and divert additional recyclables from their waste system. This way non-biodegradable products and hazardous materials remain out of the environment and are disposed of properly. The StubHub Center participates in the Southern California Edison's Demand Response programmes which enable reduction of usage at the facility when statewide energy demand peak. Using a Building Management System to link both the HVAC and lighting systems to motion sensors, throughout the facil-ity energy efficiency is increased by only powering rooms that are in use and occu-pied. This coincides with a field lighting policy which limits tenant lighting use before and after field or court usage. Underneath the seating and the field they have installed high-efficiency boilers and invested 100,000 power outlets in the facility to reduce the need for event based, gasoline consuming power generators.

In Portland, the Timbers recycle and donate glass, plastics, paper, cardboard, food, cooking oil, pallets, unclaimed 'lost and found' clothes, glasses and cell phones. Their First Bowl clean-up programme identifies the possible recyclable goods. Packed around the stadium are commingled disposal stations that feature recycling and trash. Recycle stations are on the concourse and in suites to promote recycling across the stadium on different levels. For a reduction and conscious approach to energy usage, lights and heaters are turned off when not in use, restrooms have automated lights and automatic paper towel dispensers and compact energy-efficient fluorescent bulbs are used where practical.

CenturyLink Field and its Event Center divert 94% of the waste from landfills; which is up 47% from just four years ago. According to the 'sustainability' section of their website, CenturyLink Field produced five million gallons of biodiesel fuel from recycling used cooking oil in 2012; in 2013 they expect to have increased that number. Approximately 614 recycle and compost bins are located throughout the facilities, all the containers are compostable, and all plastic bottles sold at the stadium are recyclable. CenturyLink Field makes substantial efforts to become more energy efficient. Arch lighting in the stadium was replaced by LEDs, which has resulted in energy savings for the stadium. Solar panels atop the CenturyLink Field Event Center cover an area of approximately 12,000 square feet and generate more than 800,000 kW h of electricity annually. Roughly 30% of CenturyLink Field's facility's energy needs are powered by solar energy. This led to 3.8 million pounds of $CO_2$ being diverted from the atmosphere last year, which equates to 260 cars removed from Seattle roadways. Overall, these changes led to a reduction in energy consumption by 12% despite an increase in fans during 2012.

BC Place strategically separates its entire receptacle facility into four categories: papers, plastics, metals and waste products which are recycled or disposed of accordingly. Hazardous chemicals, carpets and ballast (gravel or coarse stone used for stabilization) are handled and disposed of appropriately. The renovations and reconstruction of the roofing of BC Place avoided on-site pollution from extraction, manufacturing and transportation of hazardous materials that also could have ended up in landfills. The renovation of BC Place's roof eliminated 1.7 GW of energy usage that provides $350,000 per year in energy savings (BC Place website). New integrated LED lighting fixtures are 40% more efficient than the previous lighting system. Dark exterior windows were replaced with energy-efficient glass to increase natural light, therefore, reduce a reliance on energy-supplied lighting. These upgrades to BC Place have reduced environmental impact of the stadium by saving natural resources, recycling raw materials, reducing energy usage and conserving water resources. Building an entirely new stadium would have created a much larger environmental impact than the renovations.

### Parking, transit and travel

All teams had information about transit sustainability on their websites. Each stadium is built in a location that is accessible by multimodal transportation. On each Website, there are detailed instructions on how to get to the stadium via public transportation, car, bike, walking, etc. This is such a vital part of sustainability for sports venues because tens of thousands of fans driving individually would add to the greenhouse emissions and atmospheric burden. With each team giving out precise directives on transportation options and accessibility, more fans are going to utilize public transportation, carpooling and sustainable transportation options. However, there was little information on whether or not the teams utilized green transit options for team travel.

### Conclusion

Major League Soccer is continually growing in fan base and popularity each year. After a thorough examination of MLS team Websites and stadium Websites, each team is embracing some form of sustainable initiative. There are a few select teams consistently mentioned in this paper that are making obvious efforts to contribute to the sustainability movement. Other teams are doing the minimum to provide a sustainability spin to their stadium or franchise. Some teams' numbers are skewed because they share stadiums with football teams or other sports franchises and teams. However, that does not take away from the initiatives that happen at each game played at the stadium.

The location and environment that these franchises are in tell a bit of the reason why some of the teams are making contributions to the sustainability movement. The Western Conference of the MLS, mainly in the Pacific Northwest and California, are taking the biggest steps, investing in new technology and retrofits, and embracing recycling and sustainable waste management. The Timbers, Sounders, Whitecaps, Galaxy and Chivas USA are all pushing to make their teams and stadiums more sustainable. These teams are also the most invested in supporting local businesses, local produce and food production, and waste diversion. In the coming years, with more attention on the MLS, more soccer-specific stadiums being built, more expansion teams, and more influence, we expect the MLS to have a larger impact on sustainability in professional sports and in the movement as a whole.

## Disclosure statement

No potential conflict of interest was reported by the authors.

## Notes

1. Kuntz, '265 Million Playing Football'.
2. Ibid.
3. MLSSoccer.com.
4. Statista, 'Major U.S. Sports Leagues: Average Attendance'.
5. Smith, 'Major League Soccer's Stadium Revolution'.
6. Brinkley, *The Wilderness Warrier: Theodore Roosevelt and the Crusade for America*.
7. Leopold, *A Sand County Almanac*.
8. Carson, *Silent Spring*.
9. United Nations, *Report of the United Nations Conference on the Human Environment*.
10. World Commission on Environment and Development, *Our Common Future*.
11. http://www.un.org/millenniumgoals/.
12. Freidberg, 'It's Complicated: Corporate Sustainability and the Uneasiness of Life Cycle Assessment'.
13. Anderson, *Mid-Course Correction: Toward a Sustainable Enterprise: The Interface Model*.
14. www.usgbc.org.
15. www.greensportsalliance.org.
16. https://us.fsc.org.

## References

Brinkley, D. *The Wilderness Warrier: Theodore Roosevelt and the Campaign for America*. New York: Harper Collins, 2009.
Carson, R. *Silent Spring*. New York: Houghton Mifflin, 1962.
Freidberg, S. 2014. 'It's Complicated: Corporate Sustainability and the Uneasiness of Life Cycle Assessment'. *Science and Culture* 42 (2014). http://www.tandfonline.com/doi/abs/10.1080/09505431.2014.942622#.VNZbkBY0pUQ.
Kunz, M. '265 Million Playing Football'. *FIFA Magazine*, n.d. http://www.fifa.com/mm/docu ment/fifafacts/bcoffsurv/emaga_9384_10704.pdf.
Leopold, A. *A Sand County Almanac*. Oxford: Oxford University Press, 1949.
Smith, Chris. 'Major League Soccer's Stadium Revolution'. *Forbes Magazine*, 20, November 2013.
Statista. 'Major U.S. Sports Leagues: Average Attendance 2013–2014'. *Statista*, n.d. http://www.statista.com/statistics/207458/per-game-attendance-of-major-us-sports-leagues/.

United Nations. *Report of the United Nations Conference on the Human Environment: Stockholm, 5–6 June 1972*. New York: United Nations, 1973.
World Commission on Environment and Development. *Our Common Future*. Oxford: Oxford University Press, 1987.

# Teaching history and political economy through soccer

Nigel Boyle

The author draws lessons from having taught 'soccer courses' on eight occasions in a wide variety of settings: a Californian liberal arts college; a German university; and Californian and Ugandan prisons. In outlining this experience he makes four arguments. First, it is not difficult to craft academically rigorous courses focused on the game. Second, soccer courses lend themselves to experimental pedagogies, particularly with regard to community engagement. Third, the immense popular appeal soccer classes have can make getting students to think critically about the game difficult. Finally, anyone thinking about teaching a soccer course should do it; it could be the best teaching experience of your life.

## Introduction

In this essay, I draw some lessons from having taught eight academic 'soccer classes' in a wide variety of settings. At Pitzer College, a small liberal arts college near Los Angeles, I have twice co-taught a 'History and Political Economy of World Soccer' as a lecture course with an historian, Andre Wakefield, and I also taught a modified version of this course as a community-engaged first-year seminar 'Soccer and Social Change'. I taught 'History and Political Economy of World Soccer' as a seminar at the University of Koblenz-Landau, a large public university in Germany while on a Fulbright there in 2008–2009. I led a teacher professional development institute for California high school teachers, 'The Global Game, Women's Soccer and Germany' in which I taught a version of my Pitzer course and then led a group of schoolteachers and Pitzer students on a study tour of Germany for the 2011 Women's World Cup. I have taught 'History and Politics of World Soccer/Futbol' twice at CRC Prison in Norco, California, a medium-security men's prison. In summer 2014 I co-taught 'History & Politics of Football and the World Cup' at Upper Prison, Luzira, Uganda's maximum security men's prison.[1]

The essay is divided into five sections. First I review my experience teaching soccer classes at Pitzer College in 2006 and 2010. It is out of this teaching experience at my home institution that I developed the core content for what I have taught at other institutions. In the second part of the chapter I present an outline of the academic content: what I teach through soccer. I next review teaching a soccer class at a German university in 2009, and the 2011 teaching and study abroad initiative that resulted from this German experience. I then report on my experiences explicitly connecting teaching about soccer with community engagement, a 2011 first-year seminar at Pitzer on 'soccer and social change' and then using soccer to teach in prison education, and classes I have taught at prisons in California and Uganda. In the last part of the chapter I draw out lessons regarding course content and pedagogy, and I make some recommendations for colleagues who are interested in teaching similar courses.

## Teaching soccer classes at a liberal arts college, seriously?

I am not a soccer scholar. I am a political scientist, a comparativist, an historical institutionalist and a Europeanist whose research is focused on European welfare state politics. At a small, west-coast liberal arts college I have had both the require-ment and the liberty to teach a wide variety of courses. One of my original motives in teaching through soccer was to establish the curricular relevance of European political-economy and European integration. I readily acknowledge that the loss of the privileged status European Studies enjoyed during the cold war, and the larger intellectual Eurocentrism that this institutional privilege perpetuated, is not to be mourned. But I was keen to refudiate the notions that there is little 'demand' for European-related courses and that Europe is no longer theoretically interesting in the globalized twenty-first century. That the political economy of world soccer provides an interesting counter to those who conflate globalization with Americanization has always been striking. For sport as commodified mass culture it is the 'American' games that have remained somewhat parochial by comparison. But even within field of European and EU studies the dominant school of thought[2] stresses the unexcep-tional nature of European integration: Europe may have been the first to undergo the selective bargaining away of areas of sovereignty in order to attain other desired nation state goals, but there was nothing unique to the circumstances which gener-ated this. My own analytic approach emphasizes both the specifically European determinants of European integration, and the importance of distinct and variable national-level factors: the varieties of European states and capitalist economies and the different ways in which these shape events. This approach stresses the need for historically rooted knowledge of European societies, not mere 'area studies' but an approach focused on path-dependent development.

I had long used soccer examples in other courses to explain 'varieties of capital-ism' and 'varieties of national identity' in Europe. The idea of a soccer-specific course arose in conversation (I confess, over beers) with my colleague Andre Wake-field, an historian of early modern Germany. We taught 'History and Political Econ-omy of World Soccer' the semester before the 2006 World Cup in Germany, assuming, correctly, that there would be a high level of student interest. We capped the course at 50 (in a college where average class size is 15), and were besieged by students trying to get in. In 2006 we held the line in enrollment because it was an experimental course and, frankly, we were not too confident about the quality of much of the literature available. There weren't appropriate books to assign as course texts but we cobbled together a topic-by-topic reader that proved sufficient. Happily the academic literature on soccer has improved exponentially since 2005–2006. Andre Wakefield and I ruefully read David Goldblatt's *The Ball is Round* a couple of months after the spring 2006 course, but at least we knew that next time we taught it we would have a superb core historical text.

Teaching the course the first time was very rewarding. The huge interest in soc-cer at the Claremont colleges was not a surprise Anecdotally it has been clear to us, and to many other college and high school teachers, that soccer enjoys a certain cache among American youth. It's easy to underestimate the level of interest in soccer in the United States. While Major League Soccer has developed into a strong and stable platform for men's professional soccer, *most* US soccer fans follow European clubs rather than US soccer teams, hence 'American soccer is alive and well and lying on the sofa watching Manchester United on the Fox Soccer Channel'.[3] Pitzer and its sister colleges in the Claremont consortium were perhaps sociologically precocious in 2006 in having unusually high proportions of both (a) upper middle-class students raised on suburban youth soccer and (b) students from immigrant communities with strong soccer cultures (including, but not limited to, Latin American soccer cultures).

Generationally, we had tapped into the passions of the 'cosmopolitan millennials'.[4] The full extent of this became apparent when we taught the class again the semester before the 2010 World Cup in South Africa. Confident in the now robust soccer literature we could assign (Goldblatt, Galeano, Kuper and Szymanski, Wilson) but still thinking that the course would follow the quadrennial cycle of soccer's mega event, we decided to teach the class as a large lecture class with related enrichment programming – a film series, field trips and pick-up games (the syllabus is appended). This time, the class was the most popular course in the history of the Claremont colleges, a belated cap (which meant that only seniors and juniors could register) managed to hold the number to 160, plus a couple of dozen 'auditors'. We even gained some local and international media attention.[5] But popular appeal posed the pedagogical challenge: how to help a predominantly US student audience understand the predominantly European contexts which have shaped the contemporary world game. A secondary challenge was to combat the Anglo-centric bias evident in US soccer culture, and to some extent in the soccer literature, much of which is written by English authors.

### Teaching *what* through soccer? A political economy of globalization 1863–2014

The narrative frame to be used for the 2006 and 2010 'History and Political Economy of World Soccer' courses occasioned interesting differences between the political scientist and the historian co-teaching them. My version of the history of the game, is more 'developmental' in its orientation than an historian like Andre Wakefield may be comfortable with.[6] The history of soccer has reflected wider European history. The legacy of *Pax Britannica*'s long nineteenth century, soccer was shaped by capitalist economic development, the emergence of proletarian subcultures, the First World War, fascism, communism, the holocaust, the dislocated history of cold war Europe, the *Trente Glorieuses*, western European integration, xenophobias, neoliberalism and globalization. But, I also develop a specific thesis: that the modern global game, manifest at its peak levels in the European Champions League and the men's World Cup, has, for better or worse, a *European* character. Only by understanding European history can one understand modern soccer: the way it is organized, the way it is played and the way it is watched. This is not to say that there has been European intelligent design at work. *Au contraire* neither Victoria's governments nor the contemporary EU sought to propagate the game. Rather, the forces that have shaped wider European history have also shaped what has become the irrepressible global game. This narrative frame consisted of four eras, a periodization representing my distillation of what I see as the best of soccer literature[7]: (1) 1863–1925: the English game emanates around the world; (2)

1925–1970: soccer's metastasis and developmental divergence; (3) 1970–1992: Europeanized rapid, collectivized soccer; (4) 1992–present: the global plutocratic game.

## Teaching Fußball & the Weltmeisterschaft der Frauen 2011

A year spent on a Fulbright at the University of Koblenz-Landau gave me the opportunity to teach a version of my soccer class in a Germany basking in the afterglow of hosting the 2006 men's World Cup and in a somewhat quizzical run-up to the 2011 women's World Cup. The relationship between the academy and the game is rather different than in the United States. On the one hand I had no difficulty explaining that a course focused on soccer was entirely serious: German academics take the game as a social phenomenon very seriously. On the other hand a high proportion of German academics express personal disdain for the game, I was surprised how many *Luftmenschen* boasted of never having attended a Bundesliga game.

My students in Landau, who mostly cleaved between the historically important Kaiserslautern and Karlsruhe clubs (with a smattering of St. Pauli leftists and some much-despised Bayern fans) were easy to engage, especially on fan culture. The generation born at *Die Wende*, they were especially animated on the subject of German nationalism and the flag-waving carnival of 2006. Seventy-five per cent male and most deeply engaged in the game at a local level, I was surprised by how parochial and ahistorical their knowledge was (none knew Walther Bensemann – the Jewish founder of the DFB, Kicker magazine, the DFB, and many south German clubs, including Karlsruhe). The contrast to my California 'cosmopolitan millennials' was striking: soccer fandom represented a localist not a cosmopolitan identity. I had anticipated the ignorance that most Europeans have about US soccer culture (AYSO, collegiate soccer, women's soccer, women's professional and semi-professional soccer, grassroots soccer, as well as the MLS tip of the iceberg) and I devoted energies to enlightening them. The 'aha' moment came in a class in which a student noted that soccer was Obama's America at play: women, Latinos, soccer moms, techies, and the suburban upper middle class. German infatuation with Obama knew few bounds in 2008–2009. The most interesting assignment I gave my students was to have them interview grandparents or other elderly people about their memories of the 1954 Miracle of Bern. That this West German team was built around a Pfalzisch core, including the iconic Fritz Walter, evoked an especially strong response, including many stories that were completely new to the students themselves.

Although the research component of my Fulbright in Germany was on Hartz IV welfare reform not soccer, being close to the Hessian heart of German soccer did allow me to conduct interviews with two rather different German organizations: the *Deutscher Fussball-Bund* and *Ballance Hessen*. The DFB's overhaul of youth soccer after the Euro 2000 debacle had not yet yielded the results now widely celebrated, and it was in full reactionary mode in seeing the upcoming women's World Cup as a PR exercise in which the goal was to minimize inevitable financial losses by keeping the tournament small scale. But the politically progressive aspect of the post 2000 overhaul was evident in the development of the *Ballance Hessen* organization. Originally founded as an effort to counter racism and xenophobia in soccer in the state of Hesse, *Ballance Hessen Fussball für Integration, Toleranz und Fair Play* had developed into a national initiative, *Ballance 2006 – Integration und Toleranz für eine friedliche Fußball-Weltmeisterschaft*, sponsored by the DFB to inoculate soccer from the taint of xenophobic German nationalism in the run-up to 2006. Widely judged a success in associating the game with 'multikulti' definitions of German identity, it had greatly expanded the idea of soccer as a vehicle for social inclusion, becoming deeply involved in what I knew as 'homeless soccer' in the US, *Straßenfußball* in Germany, as well as focusing on the integration of both women and ethnic minorities into soccer clubs right down to local levels. The DFB had extended and expanded its support of *Ballance Hessen* through the 2011 World Cup. I was able to get some of the leadership of *Ballance Hessen* to speak to my class, which made for some absorbing sessions. That this 'Californicated' course scored the highest evaluation ratings of any taught in the political science department that year suggested that I had struck a nerve.

A protracted, and mostly behind-the-scenes, fight within the DFB about the 2011 women's World Cup occurred in 2008–2009. The old guard (such as Gerhard Mayer-Vorfelder) was convinced of the unattractiveness of women's soccer as a spectator sport and sought to minimize the budget for the event and confine it to small stadia. The progressives, led by Steffi Jones, President of the Organizing Committee of the 2011 World Cup (often identified with the back-handed moniker of 'the female Beckenbauer') campaigned for aggressive marketing of the tournament and a maximalist approach to attendance expectations. The progressives prevailed, allegedly after the intercession of Chancellor Merkel (not on the grounds of gender equality but those of national prestige). By the time I left Germany, it was clear that the organizers of the 2011 women's World Cup saw it as an opportunity to do for women's soccer in Europe what the 1999 women's World Cup had done for women's soccer in the US, an event and a process I had witnessed in southern California.

I had been the founder and academic advisor of a local branch of a state-supported, California-wide education project, the California International Studies Project, which provided refresher courses and professional development for California public school social studies teachers. With the soccerphile project director, Michelle Dymerski, I hatched a plot to run a 2010–2011 teacher institute with the theme of 'Europe through a Soccer Lens' with academic content from southern California scholars and a study tour to Germany during the 2011 World Cup. Anticipating a group of mostly white, female teachers wondering how they could motivate all their Chicharito shirt-wearing students, we in fact drew a very high-calibre group of teachers of all genders and ethnicities, over half of whom doubled as social studies teachers and high school soccer coaches. Never did a group so avidly devour *Inverting the Triangle*. The lecture-based component of the course allowed me to draw in faculty speakers from various disciplines, the most provocative of whom was Jennifer Doyle, who writes on feminist and queer theory and who maintained the late, lamented *From a Left Wing* soccer blog. Jennifer Doyle subsequently agreed to serve as co-organizer of the 2011 study tour.

We were able to integrate 14 Pitzer students and 20 high school social studies teachers into the taught institute in 2010–2011. From these, a subset of 2 students and 13 teachers participated in the 4-week study tour. The tour included non-soccer programming and visits to German schools, the European Parliament, the European Central Bank, concentration camps, and other sites of historical interest that are in the all-important California Social Studies Standards. The soccer portion included visits to FIFA HQ in Zurich, meetings with FIFA and DFB officials in Frankfurt, programming with Ballance Hessen, including the national (homeless) streetfootball tournament, and planned and impromptu pick-up games. It also included attending eight World Cup games, including the Japan–US final, and watching most of the rest in large public fanzones. While the soccer was enthralling (especially the global convergence in technical skill and tactical sophistication, and the ultimate triumph of Japanese tiki-taka) and the crowds were huge, it is the opportunities for sociological observation afforded by a tournament that are still on a more intimate scale than is true for the men's World Cup that were especially profound. We were able to meet with players (and players' families) from several teams, including the US and Japan. And camaraderie among the fans of competing teams (we even found Equatorial Guinea fans) led to many conversations about women's soccer. The omnipresent marketing and sponsorship, slick, with high production values, resulted in a level of public interest that was impressive. We never had to explain why the study tour was there and the record crowds and German viewing figures (higher in 2011 for the first round Germany games than they were for the 2006 men's tournament) vindicated the DFB maximalists. The tournament's substantial profit came as a shock to FIFA, as a FIFA official interrogated by Jennifer Doyle acknowledged to the group. Acknowledging that most of the FIFA executive committee had never watched a full women's game before, and that the sexual violence suffered by South African and Nigerian soccer players was something FIFA was powerless to address were equally candid (jaw-dropping?) admissions which gave the group a good sense of FIFA's masculinist and corporate mindset.

The teachers and students brought back lesson plans and modules which were implemented into high school social studies classes in 2011–2012. That so many teachers found their own ways to 'teach history and politics thru soccer', with particularly strong emphases on gender, global mega-events and sport-for-social-change impressed me greatly.

### Community-engaged courses and soccer courses in US and Ugandan prisons

Inspired by the study tour of teachers and students, I decided to try an experimental first-year seminar in the fall semester 2011, 'Soccer and Social Change', at Pitzer college. Essentially, I combined a condensed version of my standard course with community-engaged projects. Students studied cases where soccer had been used for social or political mobilization (including the evocative *Kicking It* documentary about the Homeless World Cup), and then also got involved with local groups doing the same, including day labourers soccer teams/leagues (through which significant union/community organization has been done) and the LA homeless soccer team. Students became involved in founding and coaching the LA women's homeless team. The course culminated with the students organizing a fundraising tournament featuring 12 teams from community organizations and students/faculty, with funds raised to send the LA homeless men's and women's teams to the national homeless tournament in New York. As a course, as a way of engaging students with local communities, and as a team-building exercise unleashing entrepreneurial skills which astonished me, the seminar worked remarkably well. This group has remained involved in soccer-related social action, and one, Lilli Barrett-O'Keefe, made 'Global/Local Community Organizing through Soccer' her major, to my knowledge the first-ever soccer major.

I initially became interested in prison education through the involvement of some of my students in the volunteer Prison Education Project, founded by Cal Poly

Pomona political scientist Renford Reese. He persuaded me to try teaching a version of my soccer class at a local medium-security state prison, the California Rehabilitation Center (CRC) at Norco, suggesting that with a 2/3rds Latino inmate population it had a natural constituency for this class. I taught it in fall semester 2013 in the prison's 'Sensitive Needs Yard' (inmates unsafe on the General Population yard – primarily those who have fallen foul of gang politics, but also those convicted of sex crimes, and gay and transsexual inmates). The class of 19 was ethnically mixed (three African-Americans, one Native American, four white, three Mexican-born, four bilingual Mexican-Americans, one Guatemalan-born and three non-Spanish speaking Chicanos). All these students were already involved in educational programming at the prison. With my limited access to visual aids, it was helpful that inmates could share their Chivas and Club America tattoos with the class. Student knowledge about the history of the game in the US, Mexico and globally was very patchy, but I was delighted with the enthusiasm with which they read assigned material, and some exceptional essays that they generated. One interesting theme which developed concerned Mexican-American identity, the notion of soccer as a 'Latino' game, and whether US-born 'pocho' Chicanos were 'real Latinos' if they did not play soccer. I was able to have the film-maker Pablo Miralles show his *Gringos at the Gate* film about US–Mexico soccer rivalry, which generated a lot of discussion about symbols of national identity. The class really took off once my (female) student TA and I realized that the scheduling would allow us to play a short pick-up game after the end of classes. We would play games between four 5-a-side teams, including me and 'the girl', with an enthusiastic crowd of 100+ cheering. Having Gwen Oxenham come as a guest speaker talking about her film *Pelada* was a great way to connect the playing of the game with class-based content. The games were fun, but they also served to change the atmosphere in the class, where the participants became super-engaged with the material and uninhibited in both class discussion and written work. It was a great teaching experience I was sad to see end.

In spring 2014 I taught the class again at CRC, this time on the General Population Yard, in which gangs are very active. This was a larger group of 35–45; few were involved in educational programming. There were eight African-American participants, the rest were Latino, some monolingual Spanish speakers, some monolingual English, most bilingual Mexican-Americans. Irregular participation and lack of enthusiasm for completing reading made this group a much more challenging one to teach. They were happy enough to listen to me (and on one occasion guest speaker David Goldblatt) talk, but discussion was inhibited. I belatedly realized that this group was most interested in soccer as recreation, so I attempted to organize a 9-a-side pick-up tournament in an indoor gym. But, I ran into gang politics when I was informed by Latino participants that games involving African-American and Latino players on the field at the same time contravened violently enforced gang proscription. Flummoxed, I eventually allowed separate African-American and Latino games, on condition that they wrote essays about the proscription and what they thought of it. All essays I received conveyed that the writers bore no personal animosity to the 'other' group, but that this was just 'gang law on the lower yard'. This argument was consistent with my observations of body language. The staff person present noted his surprise at interested spectating of the 'other' game by those sidelined, and some hand-shaking across the divide that took place at the end of games.

For the last day of the class, I planned an afternoon-long 2-court tournament for which I brought in a Pitzer student team, and programming around a film I knew from previous use to be a great pedagogical tool. I had both my 'inside' students and my Pitzer students watch Gwen Oxenham's film *Pelada* (about pick-up soccer in the unlikeliest settings around the world) earlier in the week, and I was able to invite her in to talk about the film, and then participate in a CRC prison 'Pelada'. Gwen Oxenham led a fantastic discussion in which we were able to get the 'inside' and 'outside' students to mix and discuss the film and the universal appeal of playing soccer. The segments featuring a Bolivian prison league and the Israeli–Palestinian pick up drew the most animated discussion, CRC students noting that although Israelis and Palestinians could play on the same field (unlike the CRC groups) the evident malice and spite in the game showed sport cannot overcome hate. In the tournament which followed, the African-American and 3 Latino teams never shared the same court. The (multiethnic and co-ed) student team, deemed 'neutral', could play everyone and stayed on a court continuously and were utterly wiped out, as well as exhilarated, by the end. This second experience at CRC enlightened me about prison politics, but as an exercise in teaching the soccer class it was chastening.

Renford Reese's Prison Education Project in California has forged a connection with a prison education project in Kampala, Uganda led by Arthur Sserwanga at Makerere University and focused on Uganda's top maximum security prison, the Upper Prison, Luzira. A colonial prison (complete with art deco entrance gate) of notorious harshness, in post-colonial Uganda until the mid-1990s, it was best known for incarcerating political prisoners from whatever constituted the opposition at a given juncture. Starting in the mid-1990s, as the inmate population became predominantly non-political criminal, a more progressive regime emerged out of: (a) human rights campaigns led by an Italian Catholic priest Fr. Agostini (initially against the death penalty – now in moratorium – later for the right to education); (b) a professionalization of the prison service as university-educated staff replaced earlier colonial hold-overs; (c) the Museveni government applying a model of army-supervised education programming for soldiers who had helped bring him to power but had missed out on an education; (d) self-organization by inmates who pressed for greater educational programming (e) the involvement of university-based faculty from Makerere University. This has led to a system of education in the prison which runs from basic literacy to degree-level.

The most remarkable feature of this progressive system is the extent to which inmates are allowed to run their own affairs. Inmates conduct much of the education (there is an inmate co-principal of the school and many inmate teachers), as well as much of the prison's security, healthcare and cultural organizations. I was aware that there was a 10-team soccer league in UP Luzira, but I was not aware just how important the soccer clubs were in the history of the prison. Soccer had been played in the main courtyard in the entire post-colonial period, but organized soccer had been prison-organized, based on 'wards' (the chronically overcrowded dormitories in which inmates sleep). But starting in the late 1980s, independent inmate-organized soccer clubs developed, sometimes reflecting cleavages among the inmates (ex-army teams for example). By the late 1990s, these congealed into 10 clubs competing in the Upper Prison Football Association (UPFA): Manchester United, Liverpool, Aston Villa, Leeds, Chelsea, Arsenal, Barcelona, Juventus, Newcastle and Everton. Soccer became the primary associational activity undertaken by inmates and one that was in a position to negotiate with prison leadership on narrow soccer issues such as the use of the field, but also larger ones such as the right to contact outside organizations for sponsorship and for greater leniency in allowing families to bring food and other items to inmates.

I went to Luzira to co-teach a version of my soccer class with my colleague Lako Tongun, a specialist on East African politics. We taught the course for four hours per day (2 h in the morning, 2 after lunch) over the two-week period immediately prior to the World Cup in Brazil. We had over 60 students, who ranged from some who were in university-level programmes to some illiterate, non-English-speaking ex-Kony soldiers. The class contained most of the leadership of the 10 clubs and UPFA. In terms of soccer knowledge, the vast popularity and viewership of the Premiership in Uganda meant that our students were very knowledgeable about current Premiership soccer, as well as African international soccer and Ugandan professional soccer. However, knowledge about the history of the game (including in Africa) before the 1990s was thin, even figures like Maradona, Eusebio and Pelé were only dimly known. In the light of our educationally mixed student population, we dispensed with much of the planned syllabus. In particular, we decided to ditch the plan to have students write individual short essays and instead formed them into 10 groups charged with writing the histories of the 10 clubs at Luzira. This occasioned an enormous effort to gather, collate and then consensually arrive at a narrative for each club history. During class time, Lako Tongun and I responded to student questions regarding the history and political economy of the game (with a strong focus on Africa and the history of soccer leagues in carceral settings such as English private schools, Robben Island, and the Terezin concentration camp), and the groups of students talked about their club histories and soccer at Luzira.

Lako Tongun and I used the large amount of unmediated access to inmates afforded by the laissez-faire prison administration to interview inmates about where the history of soccer 'association' intersected with the history of the prison. The UPFA constitution, and the constitutions of the constituent clubs, are astonishingly sophisticated documents in which everything from player and fan behaviour is tightly self-regulated, from a ban on tribally oriented soccer clubs to an elaborate player transfer system modelled explicitly on the Premiership (complete with transfer windows, fair play financial rules, etc.). The units of currency are a bar of laundry soap or kilos of sugar. The clubs are able to extract resources from their supporters such that UPFA is now wrestling with the problem of asymmetric competition: rich clubs (Liverpool, Manchester United and Aston Villa) vs. poor clubs (Chelsea and Barcelona). Some clubs (Newcastle and Everton) function as feeder teams for the rich clubs via loaning systems. We were also able to interview both the custodial and educational staff at the prison. This unanticipated opportunity to conduct ethnography has resulted in a wealth of research material.

We watched several games at the prison including a tournament between the 10 clubs, a game between the select prison team and another prison team (Murcheson Bay Prison), and one between the a prison team (Arsenal) and the prison staff team. All games were competitive but free of any ungentlemanly conduct and spectated by the vast majority of the 3500 inmates. Games are the primary entertainment at the prison. I managed to put together a team of US students and students from Makerere University (on which I played) in a game against the Arsenal B team. I scored and finally had the thrill of a 3000 crowd roar at something I did on a soccer field, for the first and, almost certainly, last time in my life. As this narrative indicates, this was an extraordinary teaching and learning experience.

### Lessons from teaching soccer classes

As I embark on my 20th year as a college professor, I can say that teaching soccer classes has been among the most fulfilling work I have done. It has also been among the best teaching I have done. The near universal appeal of the game can lend itself to a wide variety of teaching opportunities, both as 'straight' academic courses and as courses modified for different types of community-engagement, in which the instructor can build from the lived experience of students with the game. In the US setting, that European soccer has replaced British rock as American youth culture's most commercially significant cultural import is a guarantee of student demand, and the increasing breadth and quality of the academic literature means that crafting rigorous courses is not difficult: syllabi will pass muster with the fussiest Curriculum Committees. Courses quite different from the disciplinary and theoretical focus shown in mine are possible across the humanities and social sciences.

I have noted that academic classes that also involve playing the game in some form have been particularly successful. The levelling equality of the field is a factor here: it informalizes the teacher–student relationship, and also creates opportunities for students to interact with others as players, as humans. In a huge variety of cultural and social settings, the ability to 'play' opens up chances to learn and to teach (my experience at Luzira has convinced me that human rights must be inclusive of the ludic). My experience suggests that soccer courses lend themselves to experimental pedagogies, particularly with regard to community engagement. Studying homelessness is important for students; playing with homeless person and getting to know your teammate, as a player and as human can take understanding to another level.

One problem in teaching soccer classes is that they tend to draw soccer 'fans'; the immense popular appeal soccer classes have can make getting students to think critically about the game difficult. Student fans may be quite tribal in their loyalty to a team (as was true for many of my students in Germany) or they may be among the global 'brand consumers' for whom the Premiership shirt is a fashion statement. Disabusing students of the idea that a soccer class is just 'fun' is not too difficult (100 pages of David Goldblatt usually does the trick). Reading and assignments can be devised which induce students to use the game as a way of understanding colonialism or homophobia. But, a more subtle problem exists in the idea that the game is a 'good thing'. Students may perceive the soccer communities to which they belong as a social movement. This is not unique to soccer, since fields from Women's Studies to Business Studies are populated by scholars and students who are ideologically committed to the phenomena being studied. But the perception among US millennial cosmopolitans that soccer and its culture is more enlightened than the American sports, or among German students that contemporary German soccer nationalism is a healthy sign of the 'normalization' of German national identity, or among CRC prison students that soccer is the rising game of a rising, Latino people, or even in Luzira the idea that soccer is a liberating activity and form of association exposes the instructor to the risk of being an advocate instead of a teacher, a dilemma I have wrestled with repeatedly. But with this proviso, I unhesitatingly urge colleagues to devise and teach their own soccer courses. Galeano has reprimanded intellectuals for not taking the global game seriously. I urge teachers not to make the same mistake.

## Disclosure statement

No potential conflict of interest was reported by the author.

## Notes

1. Syllabi for all of these courses are available from the author.
2. The rational choice analytic framework most fully articulated by Moravcik, *The Choice for Europe*. Moravcik's parsimonious thesis is that EU integration was driven by rational national economic preferences and interstate bargaining (and not by EU institutions, as neo-functionalists such as Haas had asserted).
3. Kuper and Szymanski, *Soccernomics*, 178.
4. Strauss and Howe, *Millennials Rising*.
5. Coverage by BBC TV, BBC Radio 4, Canadian CBC Radio, as well as local radio and newspaper coverage. We even drew Nike's attention.
6. Academics teaching soccer courses might well use other disciplinary lenses and pedagogical approaches. Laurent Dubois's soccer courses at Duke in 2009 and 2013 are great examples of courses taught (a) by an historian of the Francophone world and (b) as research seminars rather than lecture courses. Having Lilian Thuram in a residency attached to the course is staggeringly impressive.
7. Goldblatt, *The Ball is Round*; Kuper and Szymanski, *Soccernomics*; and Wilson, *Inverting the Pyramid*.

## References

Dubois, Laurent. *Soccer Politics*. http://sites.duke.edu/wcwp/research-projects/.
Goldblatt, David. *The Ball is Round: A Global History of World Soccer*. New York: Penguin, 2006.
Kuper, Simon, and Stefan Szymanski. *Soccernomics*. New York: Nation, 2009.
Moravcik, Andrew. *The Choice for Europe: Social Purpose and State Power from Messina to Maastricht*. Ithaca, NY: Cornell University Press, 1998.
Strauss, William, and Neil Howe. *Millennials Rising: The Next Great Generation*. Toronto: Vintage, 2000.
Wilson, Jonathan. *Inverting the Pyramid: The History of Football Tactics*. London: Orient, 2009.

# Soccer changes lives: from learned helplessness to self-directed learners

Judith Gates and Brian Suskiewicz

Coaches Across Continents uses a three-year Hat-Trick Initiative to work alongside partners in developing communities globally. This paper examines their Chance to Choice curriculum, and shows how they use this to guide local community coaches, teachers, and leaders from learned helplessness towards self-directed learning. Program participants learn applicable life skills in parallel to football skills on the field. They become self-directed learners with growing ability to challenge the existing order and thus to change their lives, their communities, and their countries.

## Introduction

Traditional methods of teaching have failed countless numbers of individuals, cultures and societies. It has been said that insanity is defined as doing the same thing over and over again while expecting different results. With this in mind, Coaches Across Continents (CAC) has attempted a bold new strategy, bringing the goal of higher level education, namely creating self-directed learners, into a new venue – the soccer field. Education has been taken out of the classroom and placed squarely into an arena that is beloved globally, changing the dynamic of how to best educate and create free thinkers in the twenty-first century.

## Background

CAC is a registered charity in both the United States and the United Kingdom. Founded in 2008, CAC has a unique approach in using sport for social impact through their Hat-Trick Initiative. Partnering with like-minded organizations all over the world, CAC has revolutionized the sport for development (SFD) landscape through their ability to create self-directed learners utilizing a unique curriculum based on Dr. Judith Gates' 'From Chance to Choice' philosophy. This paper investigates CACs' philosophy and methodology of creating self-directed learners. The success of their work has led to a demand in their services, allowing CAC to grow from one partnership in 2008 to working with 89 communities in 29 countries in 2015.[1]

## Sport for development

Sport is one of a number of alternative approaches to development aid that has received increasing attention since the United Nations' Millennium Declaration outlined eight Millennium Development Goals (MDGs).[2] It is important to understand how certain 'engines' of development have historically contributed, both positively and negatively, to developing communities. For example, an emphasis upon financial aid, without proper governance, has led to developing countries remaining in a perpetual state of dependency and poverty.[3] Nobel Prize winning economist, Amartya Sen focused upon the development of individual 'capabilities' rather than macroeconomic policy as a means of addressing poverty.[4] More focused development approaches have now been established that move away from economic-based government partnerships towards private foundations and NGOs which aim to provide a direct and real impact on the lives of recipients.[5]

Sport has been included in the quest to accomplish the MDGs and has been applied to development efforts in diverse contexts.[6] Sport can be applied as a means or an end of development[7]; sport can be utilized as a gateway through which development initiatives can be introduced[8]; and sport can be a distinct genre of development practice with its own successes, critiques and case studies.[9] The identification of sport as a viable tool of development from international agencies such as the UN has provided credibility to the field. In 2003, the UN published a report entitled 'Sport for Development and Peace: Towards Achieving the Millennium Development Goals' that clearly supported the use of sport within development.

It is important to make the distinction between applying development concepts to sport studies and the infusion of sport into development. CAC uses sport as the vehicle to educate, and is not simply looking to improve sport. Soccer is merely the tool that allows for greater social impact than would apply simply by teaching sport in and of itself. Simon Darnell and David Black outlined an argument in favour of 'mainstreaming sport into international development studies'.[10] Further, Bruce Kidd identified SFD as a 'new social movement' and acknowledged the difference between programmes supporting the development of sport (coach, athlete and officials) and development through sport (the process of addressing development objectives with sport).[11] Supporting this distinction, Hartmann and Kwauk claim that for sport to be an effective tool of development, it needs to be implemented purposively, methodically, and through a coordinated and organized process of community engagement.[12] CAC is an organization that aims for development through sport.[13]

Constructive organization and implementation of SFD should address individual growth by developing characteristics like self-efficacy, which can then influence the broader community.[14] Community development is defined as the process and outcome of developing community resources that focus on benefitting both the community as a whole as well as the individuals that make up the community.[15] Sport can be utilized to inform community development goals through the development of local leadership.[16]

With these perspectives in mind, CAC has developed a unique approach to the SFD discourse. CAC has based their programme of development through sport in terms of a strongly structured educational theorem, with the end goal of creating self-directed learners (SDLs) who, following on from CAC programmes, are subsequently able to continue development practices and have a social impact in their own communities. CAC looks to leave a permanent sustainable legacy through this formula.

**Self-directed learning (SDL)**

Before delving into the methodology of CAC, it is important to define self-directed learners (SDLs) and why it is important to create them. SDLs possess attitudes such as independence of mind, confidence in their own judgement, a sense of self-esteem leading to self-actualization and the ability to cooperate and collaborate with others. They are independent thinkers who can define and solve problems, reason logically, engage in the imaginative projection of their own ideas and set goals and strategies to achieve them. They reflect upon experience and learn from it. Creating SDLs is a staple benchmark of secondary and university educations in the western world, sometimes under the phrase 'developing critical thinkers'.

Understanding that 'west is not best', CAC recognizes that locally based SDLs are essential for community development. Only they have the insider knowledge and understanding that enables them to identify local issues and become effective problem-solvers within their local communities. CAC initially aims to create SDLs on the soccer field, knowing that the problem solving skill set developed On-Field are transferable to all areas of community life. In order to address the myriad of social challenges in any community, and in order to constructively consider and address the prevailing culture, traditions and religions, local SDLs are necessary. By developing locally based capacity to identify and address social issues within their communities, the potential for sustainable development is optimized.

**Mission**

The mission of CAC is based on the philosophy that communities can create lasting social change through sport. CAC believes in:

- The capacity of communities to change.
- The need to question tradition, religion and culture.
- The opportunity for women to be treated as equals in sport and society.
- The unifying nature of soccer.
- The ability for individuals, groups and communities to choose their future.

This paper illustrates how CACs' Hat-Trick Curriculum uses sport to guide community partners through three stages of learning, namely from learned helplessness through a Self-Organized Learning (SOL) stage, and ultimately to self-directed learning (SDL). Programme participants learn applicable life skills in tandem with football skills On-Field. They become SDLs with growing ability to challenge the existing order and thus to change their lives, their communities and their countries.

**From chance to choice**

CAC has adopted an innovative curriculum development programme based upon their own 'From Chance to Choice' philosophy first identified and described by Dr. Judith Gates, a member of their Coach Advisory Board.[17] This philosophy postulates that young people throughout the world go through similar stages of development:

- Chance of birth – the inheritance of country, culture, religion, family norms and traditions determine lifestyle.

- Conformity of childhood – unquestioning acceptance, fitting in to inherited culture, unawareness of alternatives lead to cultural acquiescence.
- Conflict of adolescence – ritual rebellion, self-assertion, questioning of the taken–for-granted contributes to the emerging individual.
- Certainty of post-adolescence – need for peer approval, for similarity, for acceptance, for the avoidance of doubt, leads to culturally created complacency.
- Contradictions – awareness of ambiguities, recognition of complexity, acceptance that no one answer is sufficient, deepen uncertainty and doubt supporting rejection of that which was previously taken for granted.
- Challenge – widening horizons, gaining insights, glimpsing alternative ways of thinking, considering options, imagining a different future, open up previously unrecognized possibilities for new ways of living.
- Choice – growing in confidence, taking personal responsibility, owning your life, creating oneself, choosing a future, empower and liberate from the constraints of the past.

'From Chance to Choice' focuses upon the principles of moving from the chance and conformity of an unquestioned lifestyle, through deepening insight, to the recognition of potential choices.[18] Personal life skills are required to make and act upon these choices.

CAC has adopted this philosophy and implemented it strictly using sport to support the progress of learners from 'Chance' all the way to 'Choice'. This educational model, based on soccer, develops learners with a high level of critical thinking skills encompassing the abilities to identify problems, postulate a variety of solutions to that problem, select an appropriate solution and implement this solution. In short, by reaching the 'Choice' stage of learning, they are demonstrating self-directed learning.

## Historical traditions in the educational model

The historical context of education with its colonial heritage has relied on didactic teaching.[19] The learner is seen as an empty vessel, and the teacher simply gives information to 'fill up' the learner with knowledge. This factually based didactic teaching method provides learners with absolutes and truths, not to be questioned because of the didactic nature of the teaching. This will progress the learner to a level of 'Certainty' on the 'From Chance to Choice' spectrum, but no further. Such teaching methods have created generations of dependent learners who are told facts and then tested on their ability to regurgitate information without necessarily having the ability to process its relevance or relationship to other issues. More importantly, this method of learning has stifled the ability for learners to develop the creative and crucial life skills that enable them to gain the confidence and critical thinking abilities required to solve problems. Such learned helplessness has resulted in a vast culture of dependency and continuously created and recreated a cycle of need in developing countries. This type of didactic teaching develops learners to a specific point, most notably 'Certainty'. It reinforces the certainty of their current state of personal and community development and ensures the unlikelihood of change. It fails to create the higher level thinking skills associated with SDLs which is quintessential for change (Figure 1).

## Creating self-directed learners

One of the major goals of education should be to create SDLs who are able to function and flourish in a complex and rapidly changing world. Experiential learning has been championed by the likes of Dewey, Lewin and Piaget among others. For them, learning is best perceived as a process, not in terms of outcomes.[20] The concept of learning is considerably broader than that commonly associated with the school classroom. It occurs in all human settings, and it encompasses all stages of life. It therefore, includes adaptive concepts such as creativity, problem-solving, decision-making and attitude change that focus heavily on the basic aspects of adaptation.[21]

For this to occur, the teacher has to move away from didactic teaching, adopting the methods of a problem poser and subsequently taking on the role of an active facilitator. The teaching style becomes experiential, encourages reflection, facilitates collaboration and communication, and incorporates learner-driven problem-solving. It maintains a factual base for its curriculum content and learning objectives, and, in turn, the learner grows in independence, self-esteem and confidence. Their thinking skills involve setting goals, utilizing problem-solving techniques, arriving at conclusions through logical reasoning based on factual evidence, developing the ability to locate their own answers, and critical thinking. Communication, cooperation and collaboration are stressed throughout the process. The learner has developed from the stage of learned helplessness, of being an empty vessel in which teachers deposit information into a critical thinking, problem-solving, Self-Directed Learner (Figure 2).

## Creating self-directed learners through sport

CAC's curriculum aims to use the 'From Chance to Choice' philosophy to create an educational learning environment conducive to the development of SDLs on the soccer field. The classroom is the soccer pitch rather than the traditional schoolroom. The series of games and the three-year process of the Hat-Trick Initiative guide learners from a state of learned helplessness associated with educator-controlled

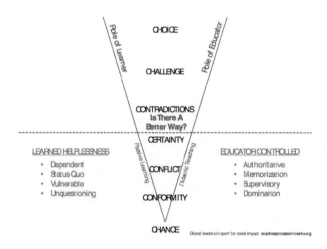

Figure 1.   The 'Chance to Choice' philosophy.

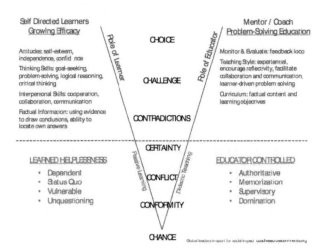

Figure 2.    Creating self-directed learners.

content into learners who have the ability to make their own evidence-based decisions. These SDLs then have the capacity to identify and solve their own community-based social problems. In short, they are proactive and positive agents of change for their local as well as the global society.

Soccer was chosen because of its simplicity, its existing global appreciation and its ability to transcend cultural, religious and linguistic boundaries. Sport is a powerful educational tool. One of the key reasons for the success of CAC is its background in competitive soccer development that immediately engages people at all levels of ability. At CAC, there is a belief that they can simultaneously develop soccer skills as well as have a social impact. Soccer is a universal language and most of all – it is fun.

Creating SDLs through sport also implies an experiential learning model. Sport allows for a safe space in which to learn, and creates a strong learning environment. Recent studies have shown that first-hand activities, emotional response to experiences, human interactions, amount of self-efficacy and intensity of experiences, all contribute to an experiential learning environment that fosters behavioural change.[22]

Experiential learning is a pedagogy that actively engages the student in the phenomena that they are studying through activity-based learning. When students develop their own agenda, engage in critical thinking and test their interpersonal skills, they come face-to-face with an alternative world view, learning through both action and reflection, including the consequences of the larger social and ethical implications of this knowledge. This type of learning engages students in a deliberate process of hands-on problem-solving and critical thinking. It often evolves with a minimum of the usual institutional structure dictated to the student in advance of the learning experience. Students in an experiential learning context are not memorizing and feeding back information: they are generating their own ideas and working through possible solutions to complex problems. This integration of concrete action and reflective thought makes possible the evaluation of learning through intentional, measurable learning goals and objectives.[23]

## The Hat-Trick Initiative

CAC has a carefully structured approach by which local communities request partnership. This essential step ensures that partnerships are only established with organizations that are aligned with the educational values of CAC and want to continue their educational process towards 'Choice' utilizing the non-traditional medium of soccer. Such communities have already begun to question previously taken-for-granted cultural certainties and started to ask themselves the vital question, 'Is there a better way?' They are somewhere on the 'From Chance to Choice' spectrum between 'Certainty' and 'Contradictions'.

The Hat-Trick Initiative is a three-year partnership, constituting both On-Field and Off-Field progression. On-Field at least 33 unique games are taught to coaches annually in the primary modules of Soccer Skills for Life, Conflict Prevention including social inclusion, Female Empowerment including gender equity, Child Rights, and Health and Wellness including HIV behavioural change, and fun. Besides teaching factual information through these games, they are also designed each year to progress the learners towards becoming SDLs. This happens through a systematic progression with important benchmarks that are continuously monitored by CAC.

Off-Field CAC encourages and monitors coaches as they implement the games they have learned into their community practices, allowing them to find their own coaching style in teaching these games over the course of the next year. Support is provided through online resources such as an online games database, and a framework to follow for the first 24 weeks of their trainings. Further support is given with the opportunity to Skype with a senior staff member to gauge their progress and provide coaching assistance as they work towards adapting and creating new games in a crucial step towards achieving self-directed learning.

## Example of the CAC curriculum creating self-directed learners

Until the CAC curriculum is experienced On-Field, it is difficult to rationalize how sport can be used to create SDLs. Understanding that the role of the Coach Practitioner is to mimic that of a professor in the teaching model, the curriculum and coach practitioner must work in concert in order to create circumstances that allow participants, both local coaches and children alike, to 'solve their problem'. Many of the CAC games throughout all three years of the curriculum create these circumstances.

One simple and primary example is a CAC conflict resolution game that involves passing. There are five lines for players, with two to three players per line. Starting with one ball at one line, the person at the front of the line must pass the ball to any line, and then run to the end of a different line. Problems occur when any single line becomes empty, or when a player does not follow the rules and goes to the end of the same line of their pass (Figure 3).

It is important to note that as SFD practitioners, the CAC staff does not step in to solve any problems for the participants. They are there to encourage the players and ensure that the rules are being followed. Initially problems can occur frequently as the participants struggle to come up with solutions to make sure that play continues while observing the rules of the game.

The learning during this simple activity is remarkable. First, the group must recognize and understand why problems are occurring, and later on anticipating and

Figure 3.   On-field example of creating self-directed learners through sport.

predicting when problems are going to occur. Then, either individually or collectively, they must come up with a solution on how to solve the problems, oftentimes before they arise. Finally, the group must engage in collaboration, communication and cooperation to implement their solutions. Sometimes their solutions do not work effectively and require practice, or potentially their solutions may not directly solve the problem. A trial-and-error period often occurs where they continue to display and develop the skill set that become the hallmark of SDLs.

As with any game, after a period of time, a level of success is achieved, reinforcing confidence and self-esteem. The CAC practitioner is able to add to the difficulty of the game in a number of ways, but the most prominent way is to add a second ball to the activity while mandating that the rules still be followed. The cycle of learning continues as the game becomes more challenging, the participants are learning and practising both football skills (passing and receiving) as well as the skills necessary to develop along the 'From Chance to Choice' spectrum.

This single game is just one of hundreds that CAC can select over the course of a partnership. Three years of games with similar learning outcomes, selected in a progressive manner, allow CAC to create SDLs over the course of their partnerships.

## Benchmarks for the Hat-Trick Initiative

Through years of systematic and structured monitoring and evaluation, CAC has discovered that many practitioners who claim to be using sport for social development do not fully understand the concept of SFD. CAC's research shows that only 11% of local coaches at the implementation level understand and have implemented games of sport for social development prior to the first year of partnership with CAC.[24] Although partner organizations may have executives who understand the theory of SFD, at the ground level, the local implementing coaches have a limited capacity in their understanding of how to use SFD. These partner organizations approach CAC for a partnership, demonstrating their mindset of 'Is There a Better

Way', but not necessarily knowing how to progress from their current state of 'Certainty/Contradictions' to that of 'Choice'. By the end of the Hat-Trick Initiative, CAC looks to progress these learners through various stages designed to bring them into the realm of self-directed learners.

During the Hat-Trick Initiative CAC monitors its partner participants and uses valuable annual benchmarks to ascertain the progress from learned helplessness to SDL. From Year 1 to Year 3 of the Hat-Trick Initiative, the role of the educator evolves from its initial style of didactic teaching to that of a problem poser, and finally to that of an active facilitator. This mirrors the learner progressing from a role of a disempowered learner through the stage of SOL to that of a Self-Directed Learner (Figure 4).

### Year 1: educate

Through the first year of partnership, CAC educates each partner coach in the best practices of using sport for social impact. This correlates to the 'Contradictions' stage in the 'From Chance to Choice' process. The unique quality of the CAC curriculum is that the games themselves teach factual information about social issues. Each activity has an analogy associated with it so that it is not just a soccer activity, but rather a soccer activity where there is a clear social message tied to the behaviours elicited by the game. This differs greatly from many NGOs who simply use sport as a hook to get children to attend sessions and then discuss or lecture them before, during or after training. With CAC's curriculum, the learning is directly linked to the physical activities and experiential learning occurs.

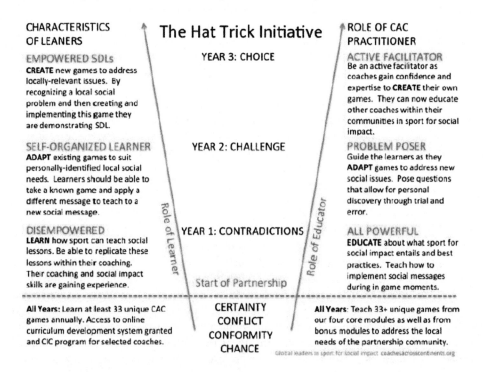

Figure 4.   Creating self-directed learners through sport.

At this stage of the training, CAC is educating partners on best sport for social impact practices. Through On-Field experiential training, the participants are both learning factual information and gaining an understanding of how sport can be used as a teaching tool. The level of the learner is progressing to just above that of 'Certainty'.

'I hear and I forget, I see and I remember, I do and I understand'. This powerful quotation from Confucius demonstrates that it is only by experiencing something fully that a person really understands it. Experiential learning is participative and interactive. It involves the whole person and thus becomes incorporated into the future actions of the learner. CAC has embraced this philosophy through their On-Field participatory activities.

## Year 2: adapt

By the second year of On-Field training, CAC focuses upon creating Self-Organized Learners. Stating that 'education is a self-organizing system, where learning is an emergent phenomenon', Sugata Mitra seeks to develop a curriculum driven by questions, not answers.[25] A Self-Organized Learner is someone who benefits from questions posed by educators, but who is then encouraged to undergo a journey of personal discovery. CAC subscribes to this concept. In terms of On-Field with CAC, this translates to partner coaches developing the ability to adapt known games to address new social issues by slightly changing the rules of games to suit their particular objective. At this stage, partner coaches are growing in confidence and ability and increasingly demonstrating their independence from reliance on a set curriculum. CAC provides a further 33 unique games to expand knowledge, but also encourages adaptation through a series of coach-backs where local partners are able to adapt games that they know to address their own chosen social issues. Off-Field assistance is still in effect, similar to the first year.

During the second year of the partnership, local coaches can also be selected to participate in CAC's Community Impact Coach programme. At its essence, this CIC programme is an exchange of local coaches to other communities within CAC's network. This exchange of coaches allows for continued On-Field learning alongside CAC senior staff as well as sharing of ideas, cooperation, collaboration and communication, which are all steps in growing efficacy in creating SDLs.

At this stage of development, CAC acts as a problem poser, guiding the partners through their continued development. Although they continue to teach new games from the curriculum, a significant effort is made towards allowing the partners to adapt existing games and to experiment with their own coaching styles through the coach-backs as well as the Community Impact Coach programme. The partner programme has reached the level of 'Challenge' on the 'From Chance to Choice' philosophy.

## Year 3: create

This is the final step in achieving 'Choice' through the SDL process. During Year 3 of working with CAC, participants are able to create their own games to address a locally relevant social issue and teach this game to other individuals. This process requires participants to recognize a locally situated social issue, consider multiple solutions on how to teach a game regarding this issue, create a game in order to address said issue, and then ultimately implement this game with their team, students or peers. By definition they are now self-directed learners through applied demonstration. Programme participants reach a level of professional proficiency where they are able to educate others in their community using the 'From Chance to Choice' curriculum and take new participants through three years of training themselves to create more SDLs. The cycle is therefore set to continue and the potential for sustainable development is maximized.

In the final year of the CAC partnership, the relationship between that of educator and learner is significantly changed. The role of active facilitator is embraced, allowing the learner to reach the stage of 'Choice'. At this stage, SDL is evident as described above.

## Role of the CAC practitioner

CAC utilizes several dimensions to develop self-directed learners.

Primarily, CAC employs and develops highly skilled 'sport for development' (SFD) practitioners who avoid didactic coaching methods and instead are problem posers and facilitators who initiate and allow learning opportunities. They are expert at recognizing 'teachable moments' throughout each module of the CAC curriculum. These SFD practitioners engage participants in experiential learning, observe thoughtfully, do not interfere with the process of trial and error, and allow participants to solve their own problems in a safe space thus supporting the development of the SDLs. As learners become more comfortable with this SDL process, they progress towards 'Choice' in their coaching and in their lives.

Secondly, CAC concedes more and more power to participants throughout the three years of the Hat-Trick Initiative, guiding participants from learned helplessness through SOL and ultimately to self-directed learning through the benchmarks of Educate, Adapt and Create.

Finally, the carefully constructed curriculum, activities and games provide integrated learning opportunities within the game itself. This is a sharp distinction from other discussion-based programmes where the game is merely an activity instead of a teaching opportunity.

## Application of skill set beyond the soccer field

The skill set learned by local coaches and youth participants reaches far beyond the soccer field.

In the terms of the Hat-Trick Initiative, CAC teaches activities with factually based messages which educate participants on the issues, allowing them to make their own evidence-based decisions. CAC encourages them to adapt existing games. Participants are ultimately empowered to create their own games, demonstrating that they have the abilities of an SDL. They then reflect on their experience, both through formal and informal monitoring and evaluation, and the cycle continues and extends into all arenas of their lives – not just sports.

Self-directed learning is essential for people to question and change their lives and their communities. Learned helplessness is oppressive, and erects a ceiling on an individual and a community's development. CAC educates according to an overarching philosophy, namely 'man's ontological vocation is to be a Subject who acts upon and transforms his world, and in doing so moves toward ever new possibilities of fuller and richer life individually and collectively'.[26]

## Conclusion

Through CAC three-year Hat-Trick Initiative, they are providing an educational model on the soccer field instead of inside the traditional classroom. Based on the 'From Chance to Choice' philosophy, CAC uses systematic benchmarks and a unique curriculum that focuses on creating self-directed learners. CAC provides local coaches with factual knowledge as well as the skill set necessary for them to make evidence-based choices in their lives, determine their own destiny and have the power to solve their own problems. CAC reaches thousands of coaches who themselves reach hundreds of thousands of children annually. These self-directed learners of the future will be able to make their own choices in order to solve social problems and impact their own lives, their communities, their countries and beyond.

## Disclosure statement

No potential conflict of interest was reported by the authors.

## Notes

1. Coaches Across Continents, homepage.
2. United Nations, 'Sport for Development and Peace'.
3. Moyo, *Dead Aid*, 22.
4. Sen, *Development as Freedom*, 87.
5. Develtere and De Bruyn, 'The Emergence of a Fourth Pillar in Development Aid', 913.
6. Beutler, 'Sport Serving Development and Peace', 359–69.
7. Pedlar, *Community Development*, 255.
8. Willis, 'Sport and Development', 841–2.
9. Kidd, 'Peace, Sport, and Development', 186.
10. Darnell and Black, 'Mainstreaming Sport into Development', 367.
11. Kidd, 'A New Social Movement', 371.
12. Hartmann and Kwuak, 'Sport and Development', 280.
13. Josh Budish, 'Who Holds the Whistle?', 8–36, 38.
14. Willis, 'Sport and Development', 842; Dyck, 'Football and Post-War', 395; and Colucci, 'Sport as a Tool', 345.
15. Kozlow, 'Developing Community Leadership Skills', 120.
16. Nichols, 'On the Backs of Peer Educators', 156; and Willis, 'Sport and Development', 830.
17. Gates, 'From Chance to Choice'.
18. Ibid.
19. Mitra, 'Beyond the Hole in the Wall', *TED Talk*.
20. Kolb, *Experiential Learning*, 26.
21. Ibid., 32.
22. PhysOrg, 'Experiential Learning Teaches Change', chap. 4.
23. Montrose, 'International Study and Experiential Learning', chap. 5.
24. Coaches Across Continents, *Annual Report: 2013*, 23.
25. Mitra, 'Beyond the Hole in the Wall', *TED Talk*.
26. Friere, *Pedagogy of the Oppressed*, 32.

## References

Beutler, Ingrid. 'Sport Serving Development and Peace: Achieving the Goals of the United Nations through Sport'. *Sport in Society* 11, no. 4 (2008): 359–69.
Budish, Joshua. 'Who Holds the Whistle?' Masters Thesis Proposal, Acadia University, Forthcoming.
Coaches Across Continents. www.coachesacrosscontinents.org (accessed February 12, 2015).

Coaches Across Continents. *Annual Report: 2013*. Coaches Across Continents. http://coach esacrosscontinents.org/wp-content/uploads/2014/04/CAC_AR_010_LR.pdf (accessed June 13, 2014).

Colucci, Emma. 'Sport as a Tool for Participatory Education: Exploring the Grassroots Soccer Methodology'. In *Sport, Peace and Development*, ed. Keith Gilbert and Will Bennett, 341–54. Champaign, IL: Common Ground Publishing LLC, 2012.

Darnell, Simon, and David Black. 'Mainstreaming Sport into International Development Studies'. *Third World Quarterly* 32, no. 3 (2011): 367–78.

Develtere, Patrick, and Tom De Bruyn. 'The Emergence of a Fourth Pillar in Development Aid'. *Development in Practice* 19, no. 7 (2009): 912–22.

Dyck, Christopher. 'Football and Post-War Reintegration: Exploring the Role of Sport in DDR Processes in Sierra Leone'. *Third World Quarterly* 32, no. 3 (2011): 395–415.

Freire, Paulo. *Pedagogy of the Oppressed*. New York: Bloomsbury Academic, 1968.

Gates, Judith M. 'From Chance to Choice: The Development of Teachers in a Postmodern World'. PhD diss., University of Durham, UK, 1995.

Hartmann, Douglas, and Christina Kwauk. 'Sport and Development: An Overview, Critique, and Reconstruction'. *Journal of Sport & Social Issues* 35, no. 3 (2011): 284–305.

Kidd, Bruce. 'Cautions, Questions and Opportunities in Sport for Development and Peace'. *Third World Quarterly* 32, no. 3 (2011): 603–9.

Kidd, Bruce. 'A New Social Movement: Sport for Development and Peace'. *Sport in Society* 11, no. 4 (2008): 370–80.

Kidd, Bruce. 'Peace, Sport and Development'. In *Sport for Development and Peace International Working Group on Sport for Development and Peace (SDP IWG) Secretariat (Commissioned) Literature Reviews on Sport for Development and Peace*, ed. Maggie MacDonnell, 158–94. Toronto: University of Toronto, 2007.

Kolzow, David R. 'Developing Community Leadership Skills'. In *An Introduction to Community Development*, edited by Rhonda Phillips and Robert H. Pittman, 119–32. New York: Routledge, 2009.

Kolb, David A. *Experiential Learning: Experience as the Source of Learning and Development*. Englewood Cliffs, NJ: Prentice-Hall, 1984.

Mitra, Sugata. 'Beyond the Hole in the Wall: Discover the Power of Self-Organised Learning'. TED Talk, Recorded at the Lift Conference, Geneva, Switzerland (February, 2007). https://www.youtube.com/watch?v=xRb7_ffl2D0.

Montrose, Lynn. 'International Study and Experiential Learning: The Academic Context'. *Frontiers Journal* 8, no. 8 (2008). http://www.frontiersjournal.com/issues/vol8/vol8-08_montrose.htm.

Moyo, Dambisa. *Dead Aid*. Vancouver: D&M Publishers, 2009.

Narayan, Uma. 'Working Together across Differences'. In *Social Work Processes*, ed. B. Compton and B. Galway, 317–28. Belmont: Wadsworth, 1989.

Nichols, Sara. 'On the Backs of Peer Educators: Using Theory to Interrogate the Role of Young People in the Field of Sport for Development'. In *Sport and International Development*, ed. Roger Levermore and Aaron Beacom, 156–75. New York: Palgrave Macmillan, 2012.

Pedlar, Alison. 'Community Development'. In *Leisure for Canadians*, ed. Ron McCarville and Kelly MacKay, 253–62. State College, PA: Venture Publishing, 2007.

PhysOrg. 'Experiential Learning Teaches Change and Adaptation'. PhysOrg. http://phys.org/news180104344.html (accessed December 15, 2009).

Sen, Amartya. *Development as Freedom*. New York: Anchor Books, 1999.

Shank, Gary D. *Qualitative Research a Personal Skills Approach*. Columbus, OH: Merill Prentice Hall, 2002.

United Nations. 'Sport for Development and Peace: Towards Achieving the Millennium Development Goals'. *Report from the United Nations Inter-Agency Task Force on Sport for Development and Peace*. United Nations, 2003. http://www.un.org/wcm/webdav/site/sport/shared/sport/pdfs/Repor/2003_interagency_report_ENGLISH.pdf

Willis, Owen. 'Sport and Development: The Significance of Mathare Youth Sports Association'. *Canadian Journal of International Development Studies* 21, no. 3 (2000): 825–49.

# Index

Note: Page numbers in *italic* type refer to figures
Page numbers in **bold** type refer to tables
Page numbers followed by 'n' refer to notes

ABC News 192
Abrams, N. 187
acculturation 177
administrators 169, 219
aesthetics (creation/visual devices) 19–24
Afanas'ev, I. 127
Africa 9–12, 215–16
Ageevets, V. 126
Agostini, Fr. 252
agricultural industry 84
Ajax, supporters and celebrities 216
Albania 7
Aldao, R.C. 117
Alga (Frunze-Kyrgyzstan) 125
Algeria 7, 31; National Liberal Front (FLN) 31
All Blacks (New Zealand) 65
Allison, L. 69–70
Althusser, L. 37n16
Alves, D. 35
amateur clubs 32, 112–13; Danish 85; Glasgow
93–4; and players 76
amateurism 57, 60–2, 66, 85, 152
American Football Association (AFA) 161–6
American soccer 158–67; Cooper's Block (1st
neighborhood) 158–66; cradle-to-grave
environment 160–6; enthusiasm and Europe
comparison 198–200, *199*; First Ward
Republican Club reunion (1936) 158–9, 166;
historiography 169–70, 177–8nn3–9; identity
(1935–76) and the ethnic years 168–77;
Kearny (New Jersey) as cradle 158–67;
mainstreaming and soccer watchers 199–203,
**201**, *202*; Major League (MLS) 33, 78, 192,
234–7, 240, 247; Men's National Team
(MNT) 186–7; Mom and Dad 26, 197; and
National Association Foot Ball League
(NAFBL) 162–5, 188; National Challenge
Cup (NCC) 163–4; National Junior
Challenge Cup 168–77; public opinion,
image and exceptionalism 186–204, *191*;

representative families (Fishers/Fords/Starks)
161–5; semi-professional teams 159–63;
war-front and morale 164–5; Women's
National Team (WNT) 188, 192
American Soccer League (ASL) 165, 170, 188;
All-stars vs. Charlton Athletic 171
American Society of Heating, Refrigerating and
Air Conditioning 241
Anderson, B. 43
Anderson, C., and Sally, D. 12–13, 15n44
Anderson, R. 236
Anderssen, H.C. 100
Andreasson, S. 219
Anelka, N. 149, 154
Angola 30
Annan, K. 5, 29–30
Annandale Cavaliers (Fairfax County) 176,
180nn64–6
antagonism, public 153
anti-Semitism 27–8, 35, 154
apartheid 33, 36
Apollonian notion 21–2
Argentina 2, 13, 69, 73; *Asociación de Football*
114; Automovil Club 117; clientelism and
patronage-orientation 108–18; Conservative
Party 113, 116; dictatorship and democracy
109–10; football and politics 113–14; and
immigration 108–9; Independent Socialist
Party 116; places to play and members 112;
population 108; Progressive Democrat Party
116–18; and public service deficiencies
108–9; Radical and Anti-Personalist Party
109–10, 113–17; soccer clubs and civic
associations 108–18; Socialist Party 109–15;
and *sociedades de fomento* 114–18; year of
professionalization (1931) 112, *see also*
Buenos Aires
Arias, F. 116–17
aristocracy 109
Armenia 125

Arnold, Thomas 60
Arsenal 22
Arsenal FC 9–10, 15n45, 77–8, 214, 222; and
    Emirates Stadium 78
AS Monaco FC 152
Asia 9; Football Confederation (AFC) 136;
    Games (1954–66) 134–45
assimilation 151
association football *see* soccer
*Association Game, The* (Taylor) 58
Aston Villa 9, 57, 61, 78
athletics 85
Atlanta Silverbacks 2
Atlético Madrid 14, 49
Auclair, P. 151–2, 155
Australia 65, 200
Austria 200
authoritarianism 28–9, 32
auto racing 193–5, 198
autonomy 208–9
*Avanti!* 30
Avella Juniors (Pennsylvania) 171, 178nn18–
    26; Final vs. Apache FC (Baltimore) 171;
    Independence and Cross Creek 171, 178n20;
    population and US Census 171, 178n21;
    team ethnic origins 171
Azerbaijan 125

Bachir, W. 173
Bajaňa, R.D. 2, 206–11
*Ball is Round, The* (Goldblatt) 246
Balotelli, M. 34
Baltimore Pompeii 172, 179nn30–1; Italian
    origins 172, 179n28
*El Baluarte* 116
Bandera, S. 34
bankruptcy 213
Baptista, R. 177n5
Bar-On, T. 2, 26–41
Barbier, J. 151
Barcelona 7, 10, 14, 16n45, 75, 214; and Camp
    Nou 75; and Espanyol 7
Barclays Premier League (BPL) 42
Barek, L.B. 151
Barrett-O'Keefe, L. 250
Bartell Park (Newark) 164
baseball 78, 161, 189, 193–5; Major League
    188, 234–7; Research Society 177n3
basketball 152, 155, 161, 175, 180n62, 189,
    193–5; National Association 188, 236–7
Basque players 49
Bayern Munich 9–10, 75
BBC Radio 5 Live 68
Beaud, S. 149–50
Beautiful Game 7, 19–21, 32, 36, 213
Beck, P. 70–1
Beckenbauer, F. 19
Beckham, D. 11, 29

Belarus 125
Belgium 68, 85, 200
Belgrade 75
*Bell's Life in London and Sporting Chronicle*
    61
Benzema, K. 154
Benzing, E. 172
Bergstrand, N. 222
Berhalter, G. 165
Berlusconi, S. 31–2
Best, G. 69
Bethlehem Steel 163–5
bias 73–4
Bidegain, P. 114
Big Four 15n45
Big Three and a Half 189, 193–5
bioethics 207–9
Birley, D. 70
Black, D., and Darnell, S. 257
Blackburn Olympic 56–66; and Old Etonians
    F.A. Cup Final (1883) 56–66; victory
    narrative 65
Blackburn Rovers 57, 61
Blakey, A. 165
Blatter, S. 5
*Les Bleus* (French national team) 149–56;
    *banlieues* raised players 149, 154–5; and
    French society's view of football 152–3; as
    multicultural mixing pot 150–5; public image
    154–5; racism and anti-immigrant platform
    149–55; and republican ideals 152; self-
    destruction (2010) 149; strikes and scandals
    149–50, 153; Summer (2014) Brazilian
    campaign 155
*Blizzard, The* (Auclair) 151–2
boastfulness 28
Bohemia 71, 74, 92
Bolivia 6
Bolton Wanderers 61, 215
bonding capital 34
bourgeoisification 189–90
bowling 65
boycotts 36
Boyle, N. 2, 245–55
Boyle, R., and Monteiro, C. 86
branding 10–11, 78, 214
Brazil 1, 6, 12–14, 16n67, 31–3, 36, 68, 73,
    155, 192; and club football 42, 46, 49, 113;
    Confederations Cup 32, 36; Corinthians 33;
    and World Cups 1, 24–6, 31–3, 155, 192
Breton, R. 52
bribery 24
Brinkmann, R., Francis, T. and Norris, J. 2,
    234–44
British Commonwealth 65, 76
British Olympic Association (BOA) 72, 93
Brooklyn, Celtic and FC 164–5
Brown, D. 165

Brown, M. 86
Bruschtein, S. 113
Buenos Aires 109–11; All Boys club 112;
    *Amigos de la Ciudad* 116; Argentinos, Boca
    and Chacarita Juniors clubs 111–14;
    *Asociación de Fomento de Villa Pueyrredón
    Norte* 114; *Asociación de Fomento of Villa
    Devoto* 115; *Asociación General Alvear de
    Fomento Edilico* 116; *Asociación Manuel
    Belgrano* 115–17; barrios and councillors
    110, 115–17; civic associations and
    membership 110–18; Club Floresta 112–13;
    club foundings and sponsorship roles
    111–14, 119n20; *Estudiantes* club 111;
    *Facultad de Agronomia* (School of
    Agriculture) 115; *Gimnesia y Esgrima*
    sporting club 117; Mataderos 110–11;
    mayors (*intendente*) 115–17; *Nueva Chicago*
    football club and bocce court 110–13, 117;
    River Plate club 111–12; San Lorenzo de
    Almagro 111–14, 119–20n18, n35; *Sociedad
    de Fomento de Versailles* 114, 117, 120n54;
    *Sociedad de Fomento Tte. General Luis
    María Campos* 117; *Sociedad de Fomento of
    Villa Lugano* 115; *Universidad Popular
    Florentino Ameghino* 117–18; *Vélez Sarsfield*
    112
Buffon, G. 34
Bulgaria 200
Burnley 63–4
Busby, M. 74–5
businessmen 9, 49–51, 60, 69, 78

Cahill, T.W. 165, 171
Cairo clubs 7–8, 32
Cal Poly Pomona 250–1
California International Studies Project 3, 249
Calvert, S. 179n29
Cameroon 33
Campbell, C. 100
Canada 45, 52
Canadian International Development Agency
    (ACDI) 206–8
*canillitas* (newspaper vendors) 113
Cantilo, J.L. 115
capitalism 29–32, 143, 246–7
Cardiff 9
Cardoso, F.H. 36
Carson, R. 235
Carter, Pres. J. 173
Castellanos, A. 26
*catenaccio* 13
Catholicism 7, 11, 154, 172; and American
    soccer families 162; St. Louis and suburban
    migration 173–5; Youth Council (CYC)
    173–5
celebrity 153
Celtic AC 163

Charles, J. 76
Charlton, B. 69, 75
Chastain, B. 192
Chávez, O. 33
Chelsea FC 9–10, 15n45, 33, 72–4, 77, 216
Chicago Fire 240
Chicago Sparta Juniors 176
Chiellini, G. 24
Chile 32
China *see* People's Republic of China (PRC);
    Republic of China (ROC)
*China Mail* 138
Chinese Nationalist Party (KMT) 134
Chirovsky, N., and Dushnyck, W. 173
Chivas USA 44, 47, 51, 238–43
*Choice for Europe* (Moravcik) 255n2
Christiania (Norway) *see* Oslo
citizenship 45
civic associations 109–18; leadership and
    reciprocal obligation 110
civic nationalisms 1–2, 42–53
Civil Service FC 89, *96*
civil society 27, 31–2
Claisse, J. 117
Clapton FC 85
Claremont Colleges 246–7
Clark Thread Company of Scotland 159–62,
    166; Clark AA and ONT teams 159–62
class 6, 31; and American soccer fan
    characteristics 189–90, 195–200, **196**;
    conflict 28–9; middle 83–6, 90, 93–4, 116;
    representation and divides 56–66;
    transnational capitalist 9, 69; upper 62–4;
    working 4–6, 32, 56–66, 69–70, 90, 159–66,
    169–70
clientelism 118; and patronage-orientation
    108–18
Club Deportivo Chivas Guadalajara 44, 47
club football 42–52; ethnic and civic
    nationalism 42–52; *Nacional* (Latin America)
    46; public school vs. working class 56–66;
    role 43
coaches 2–3, 11, 95, 153, 169, 219; as
    disciplinarians 129–30; fitness 149; head
    126–9, 149; migration 42, 69, 75–6, 85; role
    75
Coaches Across Continents (CAC) 3, 256–67;
    Advisory Board 258; Chance to Choice
    curriculum 256–67, *260*; Community Impact
    Coach programme 265; educational model
    historical traditions 259; Hat-Trick Initiative
    and benchmarks 262; mission and SOL 258,
    265–6; On/Off-Field skills and modules 258,
    262–5, *263*; and SDLs 257–67, *261–4*; and
    SFD 256–7, 263, 266
Coggin, F. 165
cognition 20–1
Cold War 86, 144, 247; sports framework 152

Collet, C. 2, 186–205
Colombia 2, 46; armed conflict zones 206–7; and *Golombiao* 206–10; *Informe General del Grupo de Memoria Histórica* 206
colonialism 46, 65, 77; British in Hong Kong 134, 138–43; influence and game spread 68–80
Columbia 76
Columbus Crew 234–5, 240
commercialization 30–2, 153, 212–13
commodification 24, 153–5
common sense, and understanding distinction 20, 30
communicability 20–1
Communism 2, 28, 32
community 6; development 257; imagined 43; spirit 22
competition 6, 21, 30, 69; in Argentina 112; County championships 62; disinterested 60–2; first England–Scotland (1872) 43; high level 49, 66; intercity matches 62–4; international 43, 70–1; pre-qualifying 72; regulation 59
conflict 7–8, 30; class 28–9; ethnic 45
Connecticut University 190
Connell, T. 159
Cooper, J., and Cooper, F. 159–61
cooperation 5–7
Cooper's Block 158–67; as cradle of American soccer 158–67; famous families and teams 161–5; new worker's tenements and mills 159–61, 166; sandlots and fields 159–63; tin cans and violence 160–1; Twelve Apostles and Ford's Bar 161–2
*Copa América* titles 33
Copenhagen 83–5; Carlsberg Brewery 102; Danish Royal Library 86; Football Club 215; Idrædsplads ground at Fælledparken 89–90; middle-class clubs 83; *Politiken* 88-91, *90–9*; sights and excursions 100–1; State Archives 86
Corinthian Casuals and London 62, 85
corruption 24, 32, 35–6, 73
Corsica 34
cosmopolitanism 12–14, 26, 69, 75
Costa Rica 49; Deportivo Saprissa 49
Coubertin, P. de 70
Courtois, L. 153–5
creation 21–3
cricket 65, 70, 84
*Critica* (Argentina) 110
Croatia 200
Cruyff, J. 13, 216
Crystal Palace 63–4
culinary traditions 12
Cullen, T.R. 117
culture 2–5, 11–14, 77; American sporting 187–90; and class representations and change

56–66; fan 24; reconciliation 65; schoolyard sporting 60; transnational activity 11–12; wars 2
Cup Winners Cup 75
Currie, J., and Currie, D. 85
Cyprus 200

Dagnino Pastore, L. 116, 120n51
*Daily Mail* 73, 77
Darnell, S., and Black, D. 257
Daugava (Riga-Latvia) 125
DC United 238
De Bontin, J. 152–4
Debbouze, J. 155
Debord, G. 23–4
decolonization 154
Del Burgo, M.B. 32
Deloitte Football Money League 10
democracy 36, 109–10; and voter fraud 109
*Democracy in America* (de Tocqueville) 109
Denmark 83–105; Akademisk Boldklub (AB) 85–9; amateur clubs 85; Boldklubben (B93) 86–9; Football Association (DBU) and select teams 83–6, 89, *90*, 93; football origins 84–5; Frem 86–9; holiday sights and tourism 98–102; Københavens Boldklub (KB) 84–9; royalty and football match visits 91, *99*; and Skotsborg 100–1; Søro Akademi (Zealand) 84; Sports Federation (DIF) 85; and United Kingdom relationship (1898–1914) 83–105, *see also* Copenhagen
Desailly, M. 151
Dewey, J. 260
Diagne, R. 151
Díaz, F. 111
dictatorships 31–2, 35, 48–9, 109
Dinnerstein, L., and Reimers, D. 176
Dionysian notion 21–2
DiOrio, N. 171, 178n26
*Dios es redondo* (Villoro) 27
discourses 26–39; Gramscian 26, 30–4; Nobel Prize 26, 29–30, 34; Soccer War 26–30, 34
discrimination 33, 42–4, 46–7, 50–2, 152
disenfranchisement 66
disinterestedness 20, 60–2
Displaced Persons Act (US, 1948) 179n37
dissemination 69
dissent 36
diversionary war 28
divisiveness 24
Dole, B. 26
Domenech, R. 149
Dominican Republic 200
Dorsey, J. 32
Douglas, J. 165
Doyle, J. 249–50
Dubois, L. 15n22, 30, 255n6
Duckworth, J. 89

Duerr, G.M.E. 2, 42–55, 188
Dundee 84
Durham, W. 27
Dushnyck, W., and Chirovsky, N. 173
Duverne, R. 149
Dyke, G. 68
Dymerski, M. 249

Eagleton, T. 28–9
Eastern Europe 13
economics 4–5, 8–11, 14, 77, 150, 155; and
   professionalism 58–9; success or failure
   10–11
Ecuador 46; Club Deportivo El Nacional
   46–7
Edinburgh 48; *Evening News* and Diogenes 89,
   92, 99; Hearts FC 48, 86, 89–92, 99, 102;
   Hibernian FC 48, 74; National Library of
   Scotland 86
Edison's Demand Response programs
   (Southern California) 241
education 33, 35, 86, 176, 179n51, 189
Egypt 6–7, 32, 74; Al Zamalek SC 32; Premier
   League 46
El Salvador 7, 15n22, 26–9; FC Alianza 32;
   San Salvador 27
Ellis Island 159
Elsey, B. 32; and Pugliese, S. 1
embassies, British 91, 96
empiricism 187
England 6, 12, 151, 226; and Argentina (1951)
   73; class representation and divides 56–66;
   defeated by US and Hungary (1953) 73; first
   clubs 31; and first international (1872) 70;
   Football Association 56–66, 93; and
   Germany with Nazi salute (1938) 73;
   Hackney Laces 32, 35; Highbury vs. Rest of
   Europe (1938) 72; and international
   friendlies 72; military and public schools 57;
   and racism 35–6; and Scotland 70–2; soccer
   in the community 215; Victorian sporting
   culture 57, 61–4; and Wembley Stadium 73;
   and World Cups 72–3
English Premier League (EPL) 9, 13, 75–9; and
   foreign player statistics 68–9; international
   games 68–9; player status 76–7; television
   rights 68
Enquist, M. 217, 225
entrenchment 7–9
environmentalism 2, 235; Linden Village Green
   Space Community Garden 240; and soccer
   stadiums 236–43
*L'Equipe* 74
Erdoğan, R.T. 32
Ericsson ICT Services 220
Erie AA 165
Etherington, G. 176, 180n64
ethics 63

ethnicities 1–2, 29, 195; and American soccer
   168–77; and civic nationalism 42–53;
   distinction 46; and French football team
   149–55; minority protection 48–9; national
   33–4; prisoner 251–2
Eto'o, S. 33
Eurekas (Harrison) 163
Euro 2016 qualifiers 7
Eurobarometer project 199
Eurocentrism 246
European Championships 150–3, 247
European Club League and championships
   74–5; English team place denial 74–5
European Court of Justice (ECJ) 9; *Bosman*
   ruling 9, 77
European Economic Community (EEC) 77
European Union (EU) 51, 246
Eusebio 253
Evra, P. 149, 154
exceptionalism 169–70, 194, 202; and
   American sporting culture 187–90
exclusionism 29, 46, 74
exhibitions 10
expansionism 8
exploitation 62
expulsion 28

Falcon Water-free Technologies 238
Fall River football team 162
fans 7, 10, 14, 31–4, 50, 225; and American
   public opinion 186–204; and class 189–90,
   195–200, **196**; as club owners 32;
   community 194; culture 24; and game
   discussions 66nn4&5; Hungarian 28;
   international 69; Mexican-American 47; and
   popularity expansion 59–61; recognition 63;
   and referee abuse 160; success demand 213;
   travel and game attendance 63
Fascism 31, 34
Fédération Internationale de Football
   Association (FIFA) 1, 5–11, 26, 73–6, 249;
   British representation and absence 68, 71–4;
   China and Hong Kong players 134–6, 141–5,
   146n28; corruption scandals 35–6; Fair Play
   prize 32; and geographical spread 11; impact
   and significance survey (2006) 234;
   legitimacy 142; *Magazine* 8; and
   opportunistic nationalism 35; original eight
   countries 71–2, 92; Say No to Racism
   campaign 51–2; Scotland's relationship 83;
   standardization and practice convergence 8,
   13
Ferguson, Sir A. 78
*Fever Pitch* (Hornby) 4
Figueroa, M. 33
financial viability 2
fines 75
Finland 200

first-aid 114
Fisher, G. 161–2; and footballing brothers 161–4
fitness 62
flat world 12
flooding 115
floodlight installations 74
Foer, F. 4, 7, 13
Fok, H. 136, 146n5
following the money theory 77–8
Fontaine, J. 151
Football Association (F.A.) 56–66, 68, 72; authority challenges 60; Final (Blackburn Olympic vs. Old Etonians 1883) 56–66; influence and impact 59–63; match discussion and significance 58, 65, 66nn4&5; modern development (sociocultural) 56–66; origination as amateur body 60, 69–70; professionalism motivation and adoption 58–66; public interest 60–1; representation 56–66
Football Association of Wales (FAW) 92
*Football in England* (Szymanski) 59
footballization 5, 15n10
Ford, Jim 162–5
Ford, John 162–5
foreign players 9, 15nn42&43; and owners 9
Forslund, M. 2, 212–33
Fortune Global 500 list 10, 14, 16n52, 236
*Forza Italy* 31
Foucault, M. 23
Foudy, J. 33
Foulkes, W. 75
Fox News/Opinion Dynamics poll 192
Fox Soccer Channel 247
France 2, 6, 13, 68, 72, 151, 200; club winning records 152; Football Federation (FFF) 150, 155; and *Front National* (FN) 150, 154; and *Les Bleus* 149–56; Mazeaud Law (1975) 152; National Basketball Center 152; National Team 2, 29–30; and opinion polls 199, 204n30; racism and anti-football backlash 149–54; Soccer Institute 152; sports crises, cultural stigma and identity 149–55; *Trente Glorieuses* 247; and World Cups 31, 35, 72–3, 149–51, 199
Francis, T., Norris, J. and Brinkmann, R. 2, 234–44
Franco, F. 48–9
Franco-Prussian War (1870–1) 44
Franklin, N. 76
fraud 24
Frederick VIII, King of Denmark 91, 99, 102
Free Geek 240
freedom, enframed/cultic 22
Friedman, T. 8, 12
friendship 5
Frondizi, A. 114

Fulham 9
*Fussballsport als Ideologie* (Vinnai) 31
*futebol* 12, 16n67
Fyodorov, V. 127

Galeano, E. 12–13, 33
Gallice, A. 152–4
Gallup Polls 190–7
Games of the New Emerging Forces (GANEFO) 143–5
Gates, J., and Suskiewicz, B. 3, 256–68
Gazprom Company 125
General Social Survey (GSS) 193–5, 204n31
genocide 28
gentlemanly code 62
gentlemen's clubs 69
geography 57, 77; and class divides 58
geopolitics 2, 92; discourses 26–39
German Society for International Cooperation (GIZ) 206–8
Germany 3, 6, 11–13, 16n45, 29, 49, 68, 199, 226; *Ballance Hessen* 248–9; Bundesliga 42, 248; *Deutscher Fussball-Bund* (DFB) 248–50; Eintracht Frankfurt 144; and England 73, 97; FC St. Pauli 32; Kaiserslauten and Karlsruhe clubs 248; Miracle of Bern (1954) 248; nationalism and football classes 248–50; Nazi 44; and *Straßenfußball* 249; and World Cups 29, 72
Gerrard, B. 215
Ghana 6, 29, 187
Ghio, F. 110–11
Gibralter 35
Gilmore, S. 223; and Gilson, C. 214
Giulianotti, R., and Robertson, R. 5, 9, 13, 15n10
Glasgow (Scotland) 7, 48, 101, 162; amateur clubs 93–4; Celtic (Catholic) 7, 44, 48, 51, 75, 86, 89–92, *91–3*, 96, *97–8* 101–2, 162; *Evening Times* 86–8; International Exhibition (1901) 86; Mitchell Library 86; *News* 88, 95–6, 101; *Observer* and Man in the Know 88, 96, 101; Queen's Park FC 84–90, *89*, 93–4, *94*, 97, *99*, 101–2; Rangers (Protestant) 7, 44, 48, 51, 85–90, *95*, *98*, 162; Scottish Football Museum 86
Gleason, B. 186–7
globalization 2–17, 42, 45, 51, 69, 78, 187, 213, 246; of culture 11–12; definition and language 11–12; economic activity 9–11, 247–8; imaginary 4, 14; politics and consequences 5–11
*glocalization* 13
Goldblatt, D. 5, 10–11, 14, 246
golf 193–5
*Golombiao* (Colombia) 2, 206–10; and armed conflict zones 206–7; and bioethics 207–9; as inclusion venue 208; periods and rule setting

207–9; target issues 207–10; and Youth
Colombia (Colombia Joven) Programme
206, 209
governance 69–71, 84, 92
*El Gráfico* (sports magazine) 113
Gramsci, A. 26; discourse 30–4
Grant Germain Jr., E. 176
Great Britain 6–8; clubs ban 75; Empire and
game spread 8, 68–80; foreign player
statistics 68–9; as game originators 69–70;
Home International Championships 68,
71–2; National Archives (Kew) 91; national
players abroad 75–6
Great Lever 61
Greaves, J. 76
Green, G. 58
greenhouse gas emissions 238
gridiron football 176, 189, 193–8, 203
*Gringos at the Gate* (2012) 251
Grønkjær, A., and Olsen, D. 84
*Guardian, The* 28
Guerrico, J. 117
Gustafsson, L. 29
gymnastics 85

*Haaretz* 28
Habitat for Humanity 237
hacking 61
Hall, S. 31
Hamilton, A. 84
handball 152
Hanot, G. 74
Hardaker, A. 74
Hardy, S. 161
Harkes, J. 165–6
Harland and Wolff shipyards 90
Hartley, F.A. 158
Hartman, D., and Kwauk, C. 257
*Hatikvah* 28
Hatikvah Juniors (Brooklyn) 171; team ethnic
origins 171
hatred 28
Hayes, V. 95
HBO Real Sports 47
Hellerman, S., and Markovits, A. 189–90, 193
Helsinki Accords (1975) 51
Hemingsley, J. 165
Henry, T. 150–3
Herrera, H. 13
heterogeneity 42, 46
Heysel Stadium disaster 75
Hezbollah 28
hierarchies 11
Hill, J. 63–4, 69–71
*History of the Football Association* (Green) 58
Hobsbawm, E. 43
Hofstra (New York) 1–3; Shuart Stadium 2;
University 1

Holland 12, 68
Holocaust Memorial Council 173
Holt, R. 62, 70, 170
Holzmeister, J.R. 2, 56–67
homelessness 28
homogeneity 13, 45, 47
homophobia 254
Honduras 7, 15n22, 26–9; Black 33; land
reform law 28; Tegucigalpa 27
Hong Kong 134–47; Army Sports Board 136;
Chinese Amateur Athletic Federation
(CAAF) 135–6, 139; Chinese Football
Association (CFA) 135–6; Chinese players
and China representation 135–45, 147n45;
Cold War and politics 143–5; FIFA role
134–6, 141–5; First Division and ex-pat
clubs 136, 139; Football Association (HKFA)
and boycotts 134–45; media representation
club vs. country conflict 138–44, 146n6;
16-player rejection and defiance 135–45,
**137**, 146n18
*Hong Kong Commercial Daily* 138, 142
*Hong Kong Times* 139–44
hooliganism 24, 28–9, 35
Hornby, N. 4
Hornets of Chicago 172
Horowitz, J. 2, 108–23
housing lots 114
Houston Dynamo 238–41
Huggins, M. 99
Hughes, T. 60
Hull 84–5
Hungary 71; Honved 74
Hutchison, P. 31
hybridity 12–14, 64

ice hockey 189, 193–5, 198; National League
236–7
iconoclastic nonconformity 195
identities 1–2, 23, 195, 202, 246; American
soccer transformation (1935–76) 168–77;
entrenchment 7–8; ethnic and civic 42–53,
149–55; formation 2; global 4; national 1–2,
6, 34; negotiation 2; socio-cultural 63–4; and
vision of the self 64
ideologies 2, 30–1, 198; effects 197–8, *198,
202*; state apparatus 27
imagery 22
imagination 20–1, 43; globalization 4, 14
immigrants 28, 108–11, 154–5; and American
soccer's ethnic years (1935–76) 168–77;
anti- 29, 35; associations 114; British and
Cooper's Block (New Jersey) 158–67;
French tradition 150; Italian 172; Ukrainian
172–3, 177, 179n37
Immigration Act: UK (1948) 77; USA (1924)
171
imperialism 85

income 175–6, 179n51
individualism 190
industrialization 189
inequality 66
innovation 212–29; business model changes 214–15, 222; business re-think 215–16, 223–4; new products and services addition 214, 220–2; open 214; options 214–16, 218–25; previous research 214–16; soccer as business 213; study method and teams 216–17; Swedish research project 216–26; team management 215, 222–3; who and how 224–5
l'Institute Français d'Opinion Publique (IFOP) 204n30
Institute of Physical Education (USSR) 131
integration 4, 78, 151; economic 9–10; European 246, 255n2
intermarriages 46
International F.A. Board (IFAB) 71–4
International Festival of Sports and Gymnastics 85
International Olympic Committee (IOC) 70–1, 135
International Social Survey Programme (ISSP) 200, 204n31
internationalization 69–70, 195, 214; early years 84; Hungary–Bohemia (1st non-British) 71
investment 59
Iran 6, 68
Ireland 70, 85, 150; Football Association (IFA) 92; and Gaelic games 70; potato famine (1840s) 7
Iriondo, R. 117–18
Islamic Republic of Iran 28
isolation 10–11, 74–5, 78; and America Alone premise 187, 193–4, 203
isomorphism 226
Israel 6, 28, 48, 200; Arabs 34, 48; Beitar Jerusalem 48; and Jewish symbols 48
Italy 6, 11–13, 24, 31, 35, 49, 68–70, 76, 151, 199, 226; A.S. Livorno Calcio 32; Serie A 15n45, 42; and World Cups 31, 72, 192
Ivanov, L. 127
Ivory Coast 36

Janovich, B. 186–7
Janvion, G. 151
Japan 6, 13, 153, 200, 250
jealousy 28, 154
Jeandupeux, D. 153–5
Jersey AC 164
Jews 48, 154
Jill, J. 63
Jim Rome Show 190
jingoism 27
Johnston Avenue Athletic Club 165

Jones, G. 35
Jones, S. 249
Jönsson, P. 219
journalists 7, 169
JP McGuire Cup 168
juntas 27
Juventus 75, 76

Kalev (Tallinn-Estonia) 125
Kant, I. 2, 20; moments of judgement of taste 20–1; sublime concept 21–2
Kapuściński, R. 27, 31
Karon, A. 10
Karpaty (Lvov USSR) 125
Kazakhstan 125; Kairat 125
Kearny, Maj. Gen. P. 160
Kenya 6
Keyes, D. 188
Khrushchev 129
Kidd, B. 257
Kilmarnock 85
Kilpatrick, D. 1–3, 19, 22–3
Kitching, G. 69
Koblenz-Landau University 245, 248
Kohn, H. 33
Kopa, R. 151
Kosovo 35
Kowalski, R., and Porter, D. 86
Krasnoff, L.S. 2, 149–57
Kuchinsky, E. 127
Kulas, J. 173, 177
Kung Sheung Daily News 139–41, 144
Kuper, S. 4, 7; and Szymanski, S. 10, 35
Kwauk, C., and Hartman, D. 257

La Plata (Argentina) 111
Lancashire Cup 59
Lanfranchi, P., and Taylor, M. 70, 75–8
Lange, D. 173
Lange, S.L. de 35
language 45, 86; historiography 83–4, 100; of sport (English) 70
Lasin, G. 131
Latin America 9, 26, 31, 46
Law, D. 76
laws 31; employment 77; immigration 77, 171; land reform 28
Le Graet, N. 155
Le Pen, J.-M. 151
Le Pen, M. 154
Leadership in Energy and Environmental Design (LEED) 236–9; certification levels and types 236
leadership skills 32–3, 70
league structure 213
Lebanon 48
Lee, C.W. 2, 134–48
Lee Fuk Shu 140, 146n20

Lee Wai Tong 142–3
Leith, Hull and Hamburg Steam Packet
    Company 85, 100
Leningrad 125–6; Council of the Union 127;
    optical-mechanical plant (Association
    LOMO) 126–7, 132; Regional Council of
    voluntary sport society (Trud) 126–7;
    Regional Party Committee 126; Zenit Soccer
    Club 124–32
Leninism 129
Leopold, A. 235
Lever, J. 113
Levy Restaurants 239
Lewin, K. 260
liberalism 31
libraries 86, 109–11
lifestyles 76–8
Lighthouse Boys' Club (Philadelphia) 171–2,
    178nn16&17
Lippe, G. von der, and MacLean, M. 86
Lipset/Rokkan thesis 200
Liverpool F.C. 9–10, 15n45, 27, 75, 78, 86,
    214–16
Long Beach Conservation Corps 241
Los Angeles Galaxy 33, 238–43
Louis Harris and Associates (polls) 191–2, 197
Lundberg, F. 224

McCabe, T.A. 2, 158–67
McCarthyism 173
McDonaldization 8, 12–14
McDonnell Douglas 8
McDowell, M.L. 2, 83–107
McGovern, P. 69
McKenna, J. 76
MacLean, M., and von der Lippe, G. 86
MacTavish, I.M. 138–9, 142
Mafeking, relief of 88
Maguire, J. 77
Makana Football Association 33
Maley, W. 102
management 77, 222–3; and Kaizen concept
    222
managers 9, 78, 102
Manchester 9
Manchester City 9, 36
Manchester United 9–10, 15n45, 69, 74–8, 95,
    214–16, 222, 247
Mangan, J.A. 65
manifesto, club 32
Maradona, D. 195, 253
Mariona, S. 32
Markovits, A. 169, 177n8, 186–90, 195; and
    Hellerman, S. 189–90, 193; and Rensmann,
    L. 4, 29–31
Marshall Flax Spinning Company (Linen)
    159–61
Marston, K. 2, 168–85

Marxism 29–30, 37n16, 129
Mason, A. 71
Massa, L. 111, 119n18
masses 23–4; and mentality 23; soccer and
    crack cocaine 29; support of 31
masseuse 127
match-fixing 24
Materazzi, M. 24
Meagher, J. 172
media 23, 34, 153, *see also* newspapers
Mekhloufi, R. 151
Melchior, C. 100
mentality 23–4; *laissez-faire* 24
Meola, T. 166
merchandizing 10
Merdeka Cup 134
Messi, L. 19
Mexico 46–7, 200; and World Cups 27
Michels, R. 13
Middleboe, N. 84
Middlesbrough 86, 89, *90*
migration 44, 52, 69, 75–7, 85
Milan 10; AC 10, 31, 70; Inter 10, 75
Milanovic, B. 9, 15–16nn43&45
military regimes 27, 31–3
Milla, R. 33
Miralles, P. 251
Miramón, G.G. 112
misconception 153
Mitchell, D. 85
Mitra, S. 265
Mitten, C. 76
modality 20
Montague, J. 7
Monteiro, C., and Boyle, R. 86
morality 20–1
Moravcik, A. 246n2
Mormino, G. 177
Morris, D. 27
Mozart, W.A. 195
Mubarak, H. 7–8, 32
Muhren, A. 77
multiculturalism 195
Murray, C. 187
Muscular Christianity 60
Mussolini, B. 31
mutual-aid societies 114
Myer, Monsignor L. 173, 179n48

*Nacional* (*puros curollos*) clubs 46
Nadel, J.H. 33
Nader, R. 190
Nairn Linoleum Company 162–3
Nairn, Sir M. 159
Nasri, S. 154
National Junior Challenge Cup 168–77;
    ethnicity and identity 169–73, 176–7; origins
    and early years 170–1; revolution (1976)

175–6; St. Louis Catholics, teams and suburban migration 173–5, *174*; teams, winners and runners-up 171–6, **184–5**; and youth soccer policy lack 170, 178n11

nationalism 1–2, 6, 27–30; cases 43, **50**; civic 34, 42–53; club football impacts 50–1; competing models 44–5; ethnic 33–4, 42–53; extreme 27–9, 32, 35; military connection 46–7; minority protection 48–9; opportunistic 35; and sectarianism 47–8; selling the team 47; transitions 51–2; and unity 28, 33; youth system building 49–50

nativism 176

Negro Leagues 168

neo-fascism 28

neo-Marxism 32

neo-Nazism 28, 34

Nestlander, N. 220–1, 224

Netherlands 151, 199, 226; Vitesse 215, 223

networking 9, 221–3; AIK style 221–2

New England Revolution 239–41

New York City 161; Cosmos 2, 175, 180n64, 191; Hell's Kitchen (Manhattan) 161; Kollsman 173, 179n38; Polo Grounds 171; Red Bulls 152; Stock Exchange 78; Yankees Baseball 78

*New York Times* 178n14, 179n38

*Newark Evening News* 159

Newcastle United 85–6

newspapers 86–95; Chinese and HKFA players 135–44; and Denmark–Scotland pre-war tours 86–96, *86–99*; and French national team 149–50; German 88; legation and coverage 88

Nielsen, K. 45

Nietzsche, F. 2, 21–4

Nigeria 36

nihilism 23–4

Nike 10

Nilsson, K.-E. 217

Nilsson, P. 224

Nistru (Kishnev) 125

Nobel Prize discourse 26, 29–30, 34; Norwegian Committee 29

Norris, J., Brinkmann, R. and Francis, T. 2, 234–44

North American Soccer League (NASL) 2, 169, 190–3

North End 61

Northern Ireland 48, 73

Norway 90, 95–6; Football Association (NFF) 95

Notts County 61

*Numbers Game, The* (Anderson and Sally) 12–13, 15n44

Núñez, D.B. 116

*Offside* 169, 187–90, 195, 200, 203

Old Etonians 56, 62; and Blackburn Olympic F.A. Cup Final (1883) 56–66

Old Firm rivalry 7–8

Oliva, J.R. 116

Oliver, L. 169-172, 177, 179nn28, 34&35

Olsen, D., and Grønkjær, A. 84

Olsson, L.-C. 217

Olympic Games 5, 74, 143–5, 151–2, 172; Athens (1896) 70; Berlin (1936) 6, 74; and British values 74; excessive spending 32; jealousy and performance 96–7; London (1908&2012) 72, 84; Los Angeles (1932) 74; Paris (1900) 70; Rome (1960) 134, 152; Stockholm (1912) 84, 93, 96–7

ONESEARCH science database 214

*Onion, The* 186, 203

Operation Commando 155

opinion polls 190–200, *191, 199*

Ortiz de Zárate, M. 113

Orwell, G. 28

Oslo 90–1; St Olav's Cathedral 90

*Outcasts United* (St. John) 6; and Luma Mufleh 6

Ovsepyan, K. 2, 124–33

ownership 9, 49–51, 78–9, 215

Oxenham, G. 6, 251–2

Oxford University Press 177n3

Palacios, W. 33

Pamir (Dushanbe,Tajikistan) 125

Panfilov, M. 126

Paraguay 74

Pariani, G. 179n31

Paris International Convention (1894) 70

Paris St. Germain 9

partisanship 61–3, 195, 198

Paterson Rangers and FC teams 163–5

patriotism 43

paving 114–17

peace 5–6, 14

pedagogies 2; experimental 2

*pelada* 2

*Pelada* (Oxenham) 6, 251–2

Pelé 1, 14, 17n84, 19, 36, 169, 191, 253

pelota 113

Penelón, J. 115

People's Republic of China (PRC) 134–45, 192; establishment (1949) 134; and riots in Hong Kong 147n43

Perslund, N. 220

Peru 6

Pew Research Center 192; News Interest Index 192

Philadelphia Uhriks 172

Philadelphia Union 241

Philippines 68

philosophy 19–25; Active vs. Passive 23; aesthetics 19–24; Affects 23–4; ecstatics 21–3; and nihilism 23–4; problems 23–4; Quality vs. Quantity 23

Piaget, J. 260
Piatoni, R. 151
pick-up games 2, 6, 163, 250
Pinochet, A. 32
Pitzer College 245; Soccer and Social Change
   250
Platini, M. 151–3
play 2, 12–14; fair 28–34; meaningful 4; and
   playful mode 20; quality 61, 74; sign of 4,
   14, *see also* styles
players 9–11, 19, 22, 42, 50–2, 169, 219;
   across class and culture 56–66; Arab and
   Chechen 48; Basque 49; Black 33–6;
   foreign statistics (national clubs) 68–9; gay
   33; great/high-profile 19, 21–3, 33, 76; and
   lucrative deals 77; markets and costs 9,
   15nn42&43, 214–16; mentality 60;
   Mexican and Mexican-American 46–7;
   migration (transfers) 69, 75–7, 153, 224;
   Muslim 48; performance 213–15; role 75;
   uneducated 153; Witty brothers 75; young
   English 68
Playstation junkies 149–50
pluralism 207–8
politics 4–9, 14, 31–2, 77; and civic
   associations 115–18; and conflict 7–8;
   consequences 8–9; and football 108, 113–14,
   150–1; globalization economy 247–8; as
   motivation 50; news and sports (USSR)
   128–9; right-wing 35; and social change
   28–32
polo 69
popularity expansion 59–60, 66n4; and
   organization 62
populations 28, 173–5, 180n59; and US Census
   171, 176, 178n21, 180nn64-6
Port Said 7; Al Masry club 7
Porter, D., and Kowalski, R. 86
Portland Timbers (MLS) 237–43; Community
   Fund and outreach projects 240
Portland Trailblazers 236–7
Post, G. 165
poverty 26, 33, 257
PPL Energy 241
Prandelli, C. 35
pre-war summer tours (U.K. and Scandinavia
   1898–1914) 83–107; club interactions **87–8**;
   jealousy and performance 96–7; match prices
   89, *97–8*; and politics 91–8; press accounts
   and sketches 83, 86–97, *89–99*; purposes 83;
   royalty and crowd exclusivity 89–91, *99*; and
   their sources 85–91; tourism and toasts 83–4,
   98–102
prejudice 7, 152–3
pride 29, 43
prisoners-of-war 76
prisons 3, 6, 33, 245–6, 250–3; California
   Rehabilitation Center (CRC) 251–2;

Education Project 250–2; inmate ethnicities
   251–2; Upper (Luzira Uganda) and Football
   Association (UPFA) 252–4
Privitello, L. de 115
Professional Football Researchers Association
   (PFRA) 177n3
Professional Footballers Association (PFA) 77
professionalism 56–66, 112, 131, 155;
   acceptance by F.A. 61–3; accusations 61,
   66n9; aversion to 59; fan and supporter
   recognition 63; and influence within working
   class teams 61; and mercenary status 152;
   transitions to 58–66
professionalization 212–13, 216
profits 213
Prohibition 162
Protestantism 7, 90; and American soccer
   families 162
protests 32
provincialism 188
public schools 57, 69; sporting tradition 60
public services 108–9
Pugliese, S., and Elsey, B. 1
Putin, V. 202
Putnam, R. 34, 108–9

Qatar World Cup bid 35–6, 73

race 6, 42–4, 195; mixed 44
racism 27–8, 35–6, 51–2, 176, 248; anti- and
   initiatives 33–6; French national team and
   anti-football backlash 149–55; *Kick It Out*
   33; *Show Racism the Red Card* 33
Ramos, T. 165
Rat, M. 152
rationality 34
rationing 73
Rausch, K. 161–2
Ravignani, E. 117
Razori, A. 115
Reagan, R. 202
Real Madrid 7, 10, 16n45, 74, 214–15
recycling 238, 241
Reese, R. 251–2
referees 68, 160; bias 74; British ban 72;
   standards 68
Refugee Relief Act (US, 1953) 179n37
Regatta Cup 85
regime theory 8
regulations 59–63; behavior and ethics 63;
   interpretation 74, *see also* rules
Reimers, D., and Dinnerstein, L. 176
relegation 213, 219
Reliable Stores Juniors 171, 178n14
religion 6, 90, 189, 204n31; pagan ritual 27;
   rivalry 48
Renan, E. 44
Rensmann, L., and Markovits, A. 4, 29–31

representations 56–66; socio-cultural 56–66; working class and F.A. Final (1883) 56–66
Republic of China (ROC) 2, 134–45; Chiang Bandits 138–9; Civil War and two regimes 134–5, 138; Football Commission 135–6; and HKFA rejection 135–9, **137**; and Hong Kong player selection 138–9; player ban 135–6; and PRC establishment (1949) 134
resistance 216, 225
revenues 10, 16n52
Reyna, C. 165
Ribery 154
rights, equal 31, 34; and minority 48–9
Rígola, L. 113
Riley, J. 44, 47
Ritzer, G. 12
Roberts, N. 111
Robertson, R. 13; and Giulianotti, R. 5, 9, 13, 15n10
Robins Dry Dock of Brooklyn 165
Robinson, J. 177n5
Robinson, R. 97, 100
Robirosa, E., and Robirosa, J. 116
Rocco, N. 13
Roderick, M., and Waddington, I. 193
Rogers, G. 160
Rogers, R. 33
Roma 10, 76
Romney, M. 202
Ronaldo, C. 11
Roosevelt, T. 235
Roper Center for Public Opinion Research 190–3
Rous, S. 73, 135–6, 141–5
rugby 65, 69–70, 97, 154–5
Rugby School 60
rules 28–30; disregard for 28; spirit of 62; 3 + 2 matchday squad 77
Rush Soccer 152
Russell, D. 64, 71
Russia World Cup bid 35–6, 73

sadism 28
St. John, W. 6
salary spend 9–10, 15–16nn44&45
Sally, D., and Anderson, C. 12–13, 15n44
Samuelsson, S. 219, 225
San Francisco 49ers 237
San Francisco Mercury 172
San Jose Earthquakes 237
Santos 17n84
scandals 149–50, 153
Scholte, J.A. 11
Schricker, I. 72
Schumacher Juniors of St. Louis 172, 179nn30&31
Scotland 7, 48, 61, 75, 92; club Continental tours embargo 92; and Denmark pre-war

tours (1898–1914) 83–105; and England 70–2; and FIFA 83; and first international (1872) 70; Football Association (SFA) 92; Football League 74
*Scottish Referee* 86–8, *89*, 94–5, *98*, 103n18
*Scottish Sport* and A Misanthrope 86, 93–4
Scottish-Americans soccer team 159, 163–5
scouts 222
Seattle 236–40; Food Lifeline and Operation Sack Lunch initiatives 240; Mariners (baseball) 236; Seahawks (NFL) 236; Sounders (MLS) 236, 241–3; Storm (women's basketball) 237
sectarianism 47–8
segregation 47, 50–1
self-directed learners (SDLs) 257–67; and CAC curriculum 262–3, *263*; creation through sport 260–1, *261–4*
self-organized learning (SOL) 258, 265–6
self-preservation 20
self-transcendence 34
Sen, A. 257
Serbia 7
sexism 27, 35
Seymour, H. 177n3
shamateurs 62
Shankly, W. 27
Shaw, D. 216
shipping 84–5
*Silent Spring* (Carson) 235
Sim, G. 139
*Sing Tao Daily* 144
Sirvent, M.T. 111
Six AM bucket brigade 160
Sky TV 77
slum-dwellers 6
Small, M. 110
Smart, J.T. 84
Smith, R. 203
Sobek, D. 28
soccer 1–3; aesthetics 19–24; as British export 68–80; ecstatics 21–3; elite club 9; homeless 36, 249–50; as king of sports 26; northern industrial vs. southern schoolyard representations 56–66; as opium of the people 29; role 26, 29; as social change driver 234–5; as source of hope 26; spread and standardization 8; War (Honduras–El Salvador 1969) and discourse 7, 15n22, 26–34, 37n16
Soccer Americana 168–76, *see also* American soccer
*Soccer War, The* (Kapuściński) 31
*Soccernomics* (Kuper and Szymanski) 10
social capital theory 110
social change 2, 28–35; control and mobility 32–3
socialism 31, 202

sociocultural development 56–66; cues and identities 63–4; and significance 57
Sócrates (Brazilian player) 33
soft power 33, 38n54
Solar Reflectance Index 241
SOLE food farm 240
solidarity 33, 155
Sorek, T. 34
South Africa 6, 33, 36, 85, 88, 200; and World Cups 149, 186, 247
South America 86
*South China Morning Post* 142
South Korea 13, 134, 200
Southampton 85
sovereignty 9, 246
Spain 7, 12–13, 16n45, 72, 199, 213; Alves and the banana 35; Athletic de Bilbao 44, 48–9, 216; Castile 7, 49; Catalonia 7; Civil War (1936–9) 48; Constitution (1978) 49; *La Liga* 14, 42, 48, 68
*Spalding's Soccer Guide* 165
Spartak Moscow 74
spectators 22
spirit, team (of sport) 22–4, 62
sponsorships 77–8
spontaneity 22
*Sport and the British* 62
sport for development (SFD) 256–7, 263, 266
sport psychology 215
sport studies 86
Sporting Kansas City 241
*Sporting Spirit, The* (Orwell) 28
sports space 189, 193–5, *194*, 199
Spring-Rice, Sir C. 96, 104n50
Stade Reims 74
stadiums 32, 220, 224–5; BBVA Compass (Houston) 238–9; BC Place (Vancouver) 238–42; community outreach 240; dual usage 31–2; energy efficiency and Building Management Systems 237–41; food initiatives and local business support 239–40; Gillette 239–41; green grounds and facilities management 236–9; Kingdome and CenturyLink Field and Event Center (Seattle) 238–42; LEED certification and construction 237–9; Marlins Park (Miami) 236; Nationals Park (Washington DC) 236–7; Providence Park (Portland) 236–41; Soldier Field (Chicago) 236; StubHub Center 238–41; sustainability and community initiatives 234–43; Toyota Park (Chicago) 240; travel and parking 242; waste management, water conservation and reuse 238–42; websites 237, 242
Stalin, J. 202
Starbucks 10
Stark, Archie 163–5
Stark, Tommy 163–5

state apparatus, ideological/repressive 27, 30, 37n16
statecraft 27
Stavljanin, V. 222
stereotypes 88, 187
Stockholm 84, 91, 96–7
Stoke FC 76
Stone, R. 240
Storm, R. 213
strategic alliances 214–15
struggle 21–2, 30
styles 2, 12, 62, 70; foreign inferior perception 68; Nordic 86
Suarez, L. 24
Suazo, D. 33
sublimity 21–2
sugar daddies, patrons 213
suicide 26
Sunderland 9
Surock, L.C. 172, 179n30
Suskiewicz, B., and Gates, J. 3, 256–68
sustainability 234–43; and benchmarking 236; LEED certification and construction 237–8; methodology and results 237–42; and MLS WORKS movement 240; modern movement 235–6; stadiums and soccer study 234–43
Sutcliffe, C. 73–4, 77
Sweden 2, 92, 96–7, 200; AIK Fotboll AB and networking 217–25; Djurgårdens IF (DIF) and trusts 217–25; Elite Soccer (SEF) 217–18; Gefle (Elite club) 222; innovation research project 216–26; Kalmar FF (KFF) 217; Malmö FF (MFF) 217–55; Östers IF (ÖIF) 217–55; revenues **218**; Soccer Association (SvFF) 217–18; stock exchange 219; Syrianska FC 218; and Welfare State 217; and World Cups 14, 151
Swedish International Development Cooperation Agency (SIDA) 206–8
Switzerland 70, 153, 200
Szymanski, S. 59; and Kuper, S. 10, 35

Taco Bell 12
tactics 61–2
Taiwan *see* Republic of China (ROC)
Tavria (Simferopol USSR) 125
Taylor, M. 58, 76, 86, 169; and Lanfranchi, P. 70, 75–8
teaching 2; German nationalism and study tour 248–50; history of soccer 247–8; and lessons learned 254; political economy of globalization (1863–2014) 247–8; in prisons 245–6, 250–3; soccer classes and motivations 246–54, 255nn5&6
television broadcasts 213–14; and viewing figures 11
terror era 31–2
Thailand Football Association 136

Thijssen, F. 77
Thomas, H. 33
Thorpe, J. 168
Thrassou, A., *et al.* 216
Three DeMarco Sisters 158
Thuram, L. 35, 151–3, 255n6
Tigana, J. 151
*tika-tika* possession 12
Tintle, G. 165
Tjärnström, D. 220
Tocqueville, A. de 108–9, 189, 200, 203
Togo 6
Tongun, L. 253
Torpedo (Kutaisi) 125
Torre, L. de la 116
Torsakdi, Gen. 136
Total Football 12
Tottenham Hotspur 75
Touré, Y. 36
tourism 83–5, 98–102; Danish holiday villages
    101
Traba, F. 115
trade links 84–5
trainers 89, 127
training 61–2, 126–8
transformations 2; working class and cultural
    56–66
transnationalism 6, 51–2
transport 84–5
transportation 114
Treaty of Rome 77
Trésor, M. 151
tribalism 27, 33, 45
*Tribune* 28
Trinidad 6
Trucco, R. 113–14
Tuathail, G.Ó. 26–7
Tuncel, Y. 2, 19–25
Turkey 32

UEFA Cup (2012) 49, 125
Uganda 3, 250–3
Ukraine 34, 125, 155, 172–3, 177; Dynamo
    Kiev 125; National Association 173;
    Shakhter 125
Ultra (Al Ahly supporters) 7–8
underdevelopment 11
unemployment 154
uniformity 13
Union of Europe Football Associations (UEFA)
    74, 77; and EEC Gentleman's Agreement 77
Union of Soviet Socialist Republics (USSR) 2,
    124; Admiralteets 125; Avtomobilist
    (volleyball) 125; Committee and Board
    (GOMZ named OGPU) 126, 129; competitions
    and masters teams 125–6, 132; and CPSU 126,
    129; Dynamo Leningrad 125, 131; Federation
    guidelines 129; football championship 124–5;

Lokomotiv 125; quarantine 130–1; republics
    and teams 125; scores-goals-trophies prism
    124; SKA Hockey Team 125; Spartak (football/
    basketball) 125; training schedule and
    discipline 129–30; and Voluntary Sports
    Societies 124–31, 132n4; and Zenit Soccer
    Club (Leningrad/St. Petersburg) 124–32
unions 114; Council of Sport 128; LOMO
    126–7; trade and Komosols 126–9
United Kingdom (UK) 83–105, 199–200; and
    Scandinavia relationship (1898–1914)
    83–105; separate competitions and teams 93;
    unique privileges 92–3
United Nations (UN) 5, 29, 35, 51; Conference
    on the Human Environment 235; Millennium
    Development and Sustainability Goals
    235–6, 256–7; and UNICEF 206–8
United States of America (USA) 8, 12, 29, 43–5,
    73; Air Force 8; Antiquities Act (1906) 235;
    Army 164–5, 173; Democrats 190, 197–8;
    Football Association (USFA) 165, 170, 173,
    179n38; Green Building Council (USGBC)
    236–7; Green Sports Alliance (GSA) 236–7;
    and Ivy Leagues 190; National Football
    League (NFL) 234–6; National Resources
    Defence Council 237; Republicans 190,
    197–8; September 11th attacks and incursions
    (2001) 187; and World Cups 26, 73; Youth
    Soccer Association (USYSA) membership
    and records 172, 175, 179n27, 180n62, 188,
    *see also* American soccer
unity 6, 28–30, 33; of people 35–6; worker 31
universalism 20, 34
*Upside-Down* (Galeano) 12
Upton Park FC 70
urbanity 195, 200
Uriburu, V.T. 114
Uruguay 6, 24, 46, 74, 200; and World Cups 33,
    36, 72
*US News and World Report* 192
*USA Today* 29, 193–7
Uzbekistan 125; Pakhtakor 125

values 5, 24, 32
Vamplew, W. 58
Van Gogh, V. 21
Van Uden, J. 215
Van Winkle, D. 162
Vancouver Canucks 237
Vancouver Whitecaps 238–43
Vedia y Mitre, M. de 115
Venglos, J. 78
Vergara, J. 49
victory 61
Viera, P. 151
Villoro, J. 27
Vincent, J., and Waquet, A. 97
Vinnai, G. 31

violence 7, 24, 28–9, 46, 250; biting 24; head butting 24
voluntarism 217–19, 225–6

Waalkes, S. 2, 4–18
Waddington, I., and Roderick, M. 193
Wakefield, A. 245–7
Wal-Mart 236
Wall, F. 71
Walter, F. 248
Waquet, A., and Vincent, J. 97
Washington Nationals 238
Weinstock, D. 45
Weir, T. 29
*Wen Wei Pao* 138, 142
Wenger, A. 78
Wesström, B. 222
West Bromwich Albion 57
West Hudson soccer team 159, 162–4
Wheeler, P. 2, 68–82
white non-Hispanics (WNH) 195
*Why Soccer Matters* (Pelé) 36
Williams, J. 214
win at all costs 24, 35
Wolverhampton Wanderers 74
women 6, 188, 192, 217, 248–9
Woo Po Sing 141
World Commission on Environment and Development (WCED) 235; *Our Common Future* 235

World Cups 1, 4–11, 26, 30, 150–3, 193, 197, 203, 247–50; audiences 26; British absence 68, 72–3; excessive spending 32; Homeless (2012) 36; qualification matches 7, 27; women's 248–9
*World Through Soccer* (Bar-On) 32
World War I (1914–18) 71
World War II (1939–45) 73–4

xenophobia 29, 46, 154, 203, 247–50
Xenos, N. 45

Yack, B. 45
YouGov 199
Young Kearny Cedars 161
youth 154
Yushchenko, V. 34

Zarya (Voroshilovgrad USSR) 125
Zenit Soccer Club 124–32; Committee and Board 126; funding 126; and LOMO 126–7, 132; organizational features 125–8, **128**; player dismissals 129; player education and behavior 128–30; and political news 128–9; social status 131; team annual report (1962) 127–31; team chief and head coach 126–7
Zhal'giris (Vilnius-Lithuania) 125
Zidane, Z. 30, 151–3; and headbutt (2006) 150
Zuma, J. 33

Printed in Great Britain
by Amazon